AF479152

Dear Artfukts,

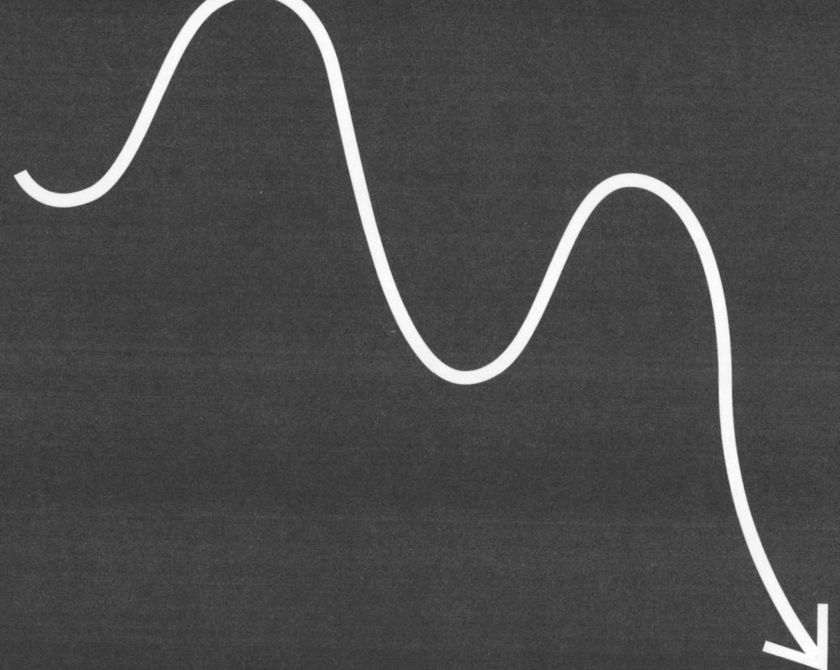

Look at My Curve

A report to an academy

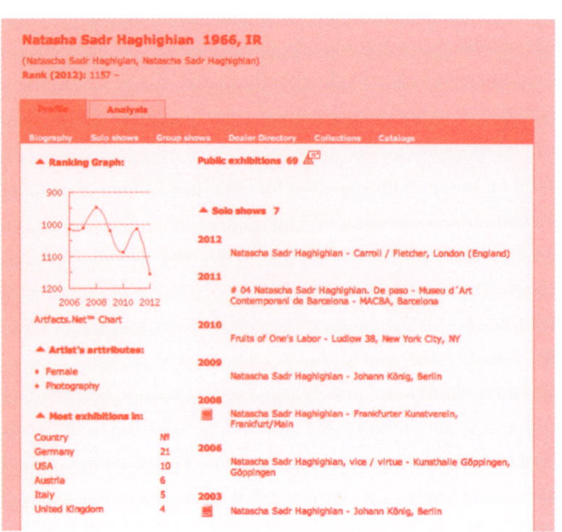

Natasha Sadr Haghighian 1966, IR

(Natascha Sadr Haghighian, Natascha Sadr Haghighian)
Rank (2012): 1157 –

Profile	Analysis

Biography   Solo shows   Group shows   Dealer Directory   Collections   Catalogs

▲ **Ranking Graph:**

900
1000
1100
1200
2006 2008 2010 2012

Artfacts.Net™ Chart

▲ **Artist's arttributes:**

• Female
• Photography

▲ **Most exhibitions in:**

Country	№
Germany	21
USA	10
Austria	6
Italy	5
United Kingdom	4

Public exhibitions 69

▲ **Solo shows 7**

2012
Natascha Sadr Haghighian - Carroll / Fletcher, London (England)

2011
04 Natascha Sadr Haghighian. De paso - Museu d´Art Contemporani de Barcelona - MACBA, Barcelona

2010
Fruits of One's Labor - Ludlow 38, New York City, NY

2009
Natascha Sadr Haghighian - Johann König, Berlin

2008
Natascha Sadr Haghighian - Frankfurter Kunstverein, Frankfurt/Main

2006
Natascha Sadr Haghighian, vice / virtue - Kunsthalle Göppingen, Göppingen

2003
Natascha Sadr Haghighian - Johann König, Berlin

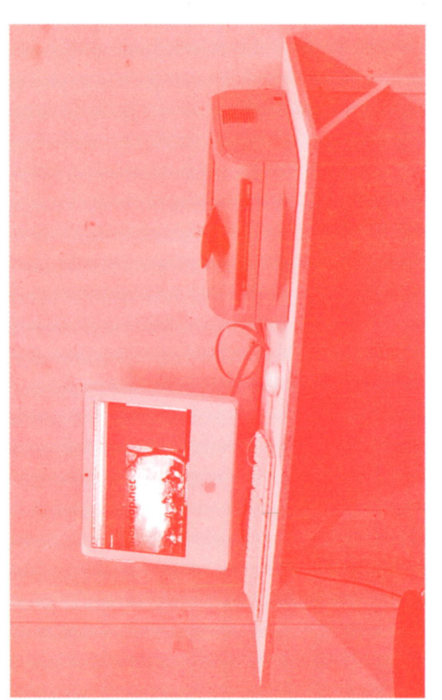

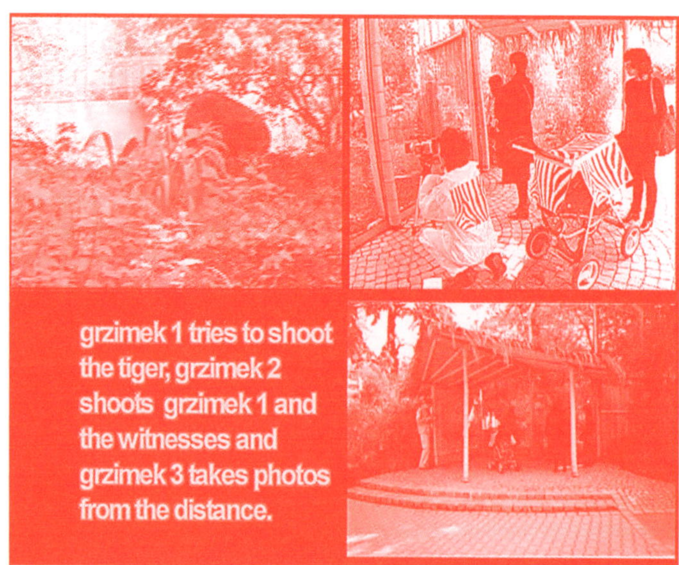

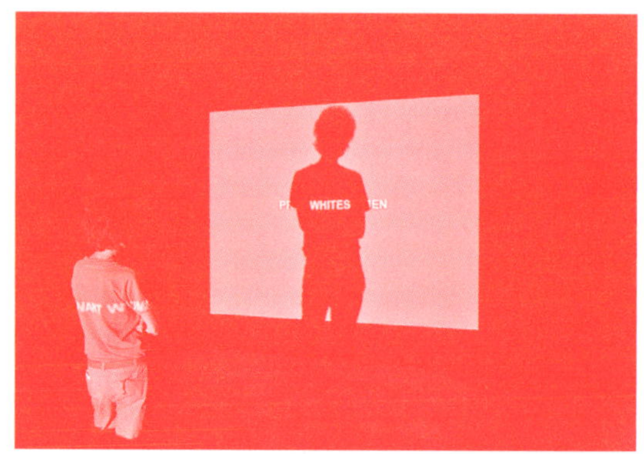

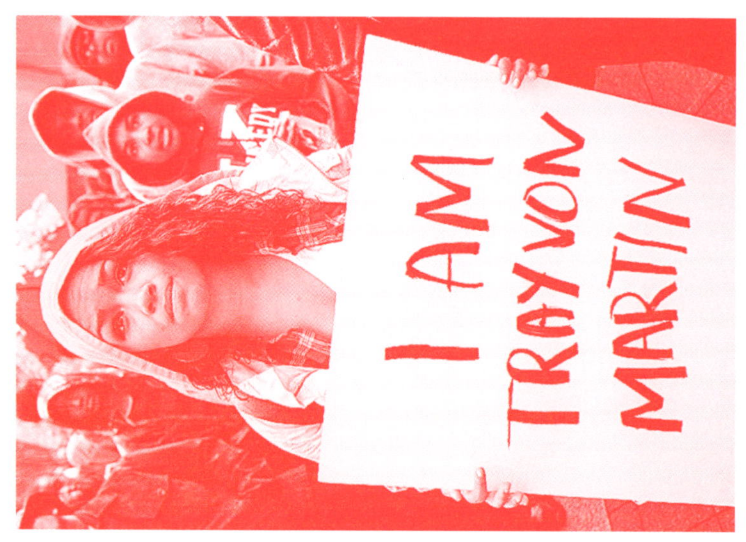

A friend recently sent me a link in an e-mail and advised me to check it out. It led to a page that had listed the name Natasha [sic] Sadr Haghighian 1966, IR. In the next line, it said: Rank (2012): 1150. As artist's attributes it listed: Female and Photography. Further down, it said: Biography, and then came a stop sign; next line: 1966 Born in London, lives and works in Winbledon (England). The stop sign caught my attention. Clicking on it, I got the information that one could potentially add information to this section. "Winbledon" seemed to be a typo but then again, who knows.

I happen to go by the name Natascha Sadr Haghighian, and by hearsay—as Spinoza would point out—I know that I was not born in Iran and not in 1966. I wasn't born in London and I do not live and work in Winbledon. But I also know—not by hearsay—where these contradictory, deceptive facts stem from. They are artifacts from the washes of the Internet's strata. I myself helped plant them there at different points in time, usually borrowing a CV from the website www.bioswop.net for purposes of representation in public events. The bots operating the ArtFacts.net site my friend had forwarded me must have gotten conflicting information on the same subject and a programming bug helped create the present case.

So this is how I found out I have a page on ArtFacts.net. I did not ask for that page; in fact, I got upset about it as it tracks my activities and—even though buggy—collects information about things connected to my name. Now maybe I need to explain that I have never published curricula vitae that refer to my actual activities, education, or ethnic background. I generally reject the format of the artist CV, not only because listing where and when someone has exhibited is a truly stupid invention but also because I can't come to terms with the idea of labeling myself artist, let alone German artist or Iranian artist or German-Iranian artist. If I have to play the game of identity politics and enter representational loops that might lead me or others to believe in what is written about me, it should at least be a real game. How about: "I am a bio-German white heterosexual male mid-career artist with an average of 6 solo shows a year and I am in the collection of the MoFuckingMA." Or: "I am a POC bisexual female, which is why my work is about racism, sexism, and colonialism." Or maybe: "I am an Iranian artist who studied at Cooper Union; that's why I rejected the invitation to the Magic of Persia Contemporary Art Prize. I don't need to play the identity card, I can do better."

But whatever happened to the artist CV? Up until now, we've all been told to foster and maintain our résumés like a garden with a pretty lawn and decorative flowers and hedges that need to be trimmed and watered regularly. Now, however, people Google you first, and maybe never check the CV. In this scenario, Google becomes the urban wasteland where the seeds from our garden are avidly spreading, where things have a life of their own, somewhat feral and erratic and therefore a better place to get a "real" impression of someone. Some people are thus obsessed with their first search

6

results, diligently trying to control at least the first impression. Depending on what picture they want to draw of themselves, they push their gallery webpage or their juicy Facebook pics, or even a combination of both, because they know a contradictory impression can be the most attractive to some. In the end, our online profiles shouldn't look like a tidy lawn with hedges but rather more "natural," including posts by institutions, randomly interesting information about our private life, and in general what other people say or write about us, and all the feral stuff out there that shows our relevance.

This development has certainly rendered the CV into a dull, overcome format from the past century, the "Century of the Self," as Adam Curtis calls it.[1] Yes, it's still used as a part of grant or scholarship applications and, of course, in catalogues. But at the same time, the conventional data about an artist—as in: born at such and such a place at such and such a time, solo exhibitions, group exhibitions, gallery representation, collections—is reproduced in the so-called cloud, now gathered by bots probably mostly lingering around the outbox of e-flux and the like. Furthermore,

websites such as ArtFacts use these conventions as parameters for mathematically evaluating a "career." This reproduction of convention is as absurd as the way in which 3-D buttons survive in digital software as a hangover from the analog age. After all, today many artistic practices differ profoundly from those of the past century and are in no way captured or represented within these conventional criteria.

So, alarmed about the newly discovered data sponge, I wrote to ArtFacts and asked them to call off their bots and erase my profile. To make my argument, I used concepts that I usually question or ridicule, such as artist, oeuvre, and authorship:

~

To whom it may concern,
May I ask you to take down listings and other information on my work from your website immediately.
My cv is part of my artistic oeuvre. For conceptual reasons, I never publish my cv anywhere and have never done it in the past. http://en.wikipedia.org/wiki/Natascha_Sadr_Haghighian
By publishing data about my activities, you interfere in and damage my work.

I will have to take legal action if the information is not taken down.
Thank you for your understanding,
Natascha Sadr Haghighian

~

I was convinced that they would be intimidated, but instead they simply responded that they would in no event erase the entry. Another provider of art facts named Kunstaspekte was more understanding, at first glance. They thanked me for my e-mail and explained that they took down the biographical information (which was "born in Tehran in 1975, lives and works in Berlin"), but stated that they would not take down the exhibition listing as this information stemmed from press releases, etc., which must have been published with my consent at some point. Instead, they invited me to fill in the blanks and help with completing and correcting my profile. My "legal action" threat was fake, of course, as I didn't have the financial means to pay a lawyer to go after them. I was really tempted to turn this into an art project, find funding for the lawyer, and declare CV jihad on Google. At first, it definitely had a David-fighting-Goliath appeal, but after some meditation it looked more like a Don-Quixote-tilting-at-the-cloud undertaking. By the time I'd succeeded with a cease and desist order, ten other pages would have popped up like rambling weed. I would make it my life project to keep the bots in check. Fighting the cloud? I don't think so. It suddenly appeared disproportionate to my previous small intervention of ridiculing the artist CV and playing with the unwritten rules of the art world's representational formats. Turning this into a major legal affair would miss the interesting questions. And the interesting questions are manifold in the cloud. Up here in this murk of data trash, where not only am I supposed to benefit from the info-junk my activities produce but also where selling this junk is a lucrative business, I am confronted with new aspects of the game. Perhaps these are actually not new but rather reiterate formerly tentative things in a more apparent fashion, providing new stages for the enmeshed performances and practices that constitute the real.

But let's return to the ArtFacts page for a moment. Anyone who has ever visited his or her own ArtFacts page probably would agree that the most fascinating part of it is the curve. Located in the left column, it is called a Ranking Graph.

So, this is what my Ranking Graph looks like:

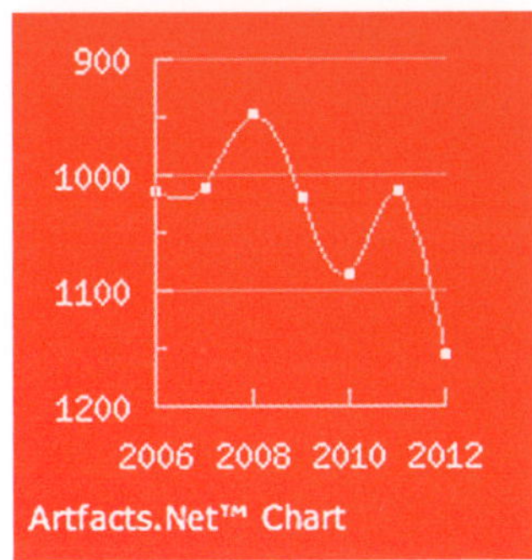

To see the detailed analysis behind the graph, one needs to buy a personal membership to ArtFacts, which I was reluctant to do, so it will remain unclear what exactly led to this dramatically oscillating curve with a clear downward tendency. I quickly scanned my inner timeline since 2006 and it definitely feels as if, in terms of quantity, I had consistently worked off a comparable workload every year since 2006—except for 2009, where I had in fact taken a one-year holiday from art to do other things. And yes, sure enough, there is a downward movement in 2009. Nevertheless, I have a hard time identifying with this curve. And what on earth went wrong in 2012 that made my curve drop like the Iranian currency? Should I be worried? Trying to iden-

tify with the ArtFacts graph, I detect a strange magic operating between me and the curve. Funny mimetic loops unfold between us. The curve apparently obtained its shape from my activity and now that I retroactively have become aware of it, I try to relive the curve. Two very different entities ape each other, diligently.

~

When I sit opposite you like this, Curve, listening to you talk, drinking your shape, I really and truly forget— whether you take it as a compliment or not, it's the truth—that you are a graph. Only gradually, when I have forced myself out of my thoughts back to reality, do my eyes show me again whose guest I am.

Speaking frankly, as much as I like choosing metaphors for these things— speaking frankly: your experience as an object, dear Curve—to the extent that you have something of that sort behind you—cannot be more distant from you than mine is from me.[2]

~

It seems the curve has known of me since at least 2006 but I only just became acquainted with it, so I wonder what we should do now? How will we interact in the future?

Will it keep tracking me? And now that I have found it, will I keep tracking it? Will I bookmark it since I can't erase it? Will I try to manipulate it? Will I make efforts in my career just to see whether it responds? I wonder how we will actually relate? I have to admit, I do sympathize with its sweeping shape, its indifferent yet dramatic cyan line punctuated by imperial blue dots.

Up to this moment, I had been focusing on fighting representations that support the existing power relations. I initiated bioswop.net to subvert the representational format of the artist CV, a format that turns activity into a factual list of origin, background, and value, facilitating the market and institutions. But in the light of my new friend at ArtFacts, not only does this intervention seem obsolete, but before updating my strategies I seriously need to reconsider what is actually happening.

Rappelling into the arena of renegotiation over concepts such as identity and representation, fact and fiction, more problems loom ahead, including subject-object relations, Self, Other, and eventually the renegotiation of the project of modernity itself. I start to sense that my interaction with the graph, my confusion over how we actually relate, is part of a bigger tectonic shift, rocking the very ground on which I presume to stand. The borders that modernity had tried to install between subject and object, between fact and fiction—all these other categories that promised clarity, and eventually understanding of the stuff we're made of—are under scrutiny from all sides. The border fortifications turn out to be rather porous, if not fluid, and now things are going all sorts of places.

One aspect of the magic I am detecting in my relation with the graph could be described as the participation of the name in the thing named, or the participation of the image in the thing it depicts. It is the magic of language, as Walter Benjamin describes it. The word participates in the object via the magical attributes of the name, wherein the name tries to become the object. It's a process of participation of the name in the object rather than a relation in which the name represents the object.

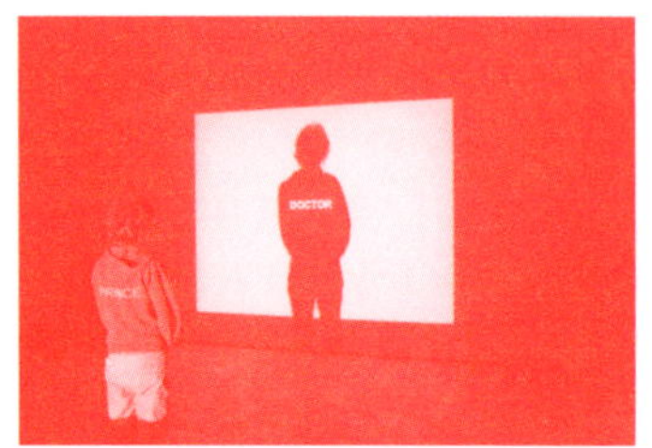

I detect this very same magic in my encounter with the graph. I don't identify with what the image represents but I participate in it as much as it participates in me, drawing on its character and power as it draws on my character and power. The curve and I are entangled in a mimetic dance, imitating and becoming one another. Our shapes submerge into one amorphous thing as we interact, and in this process of participation I am not a subject looking at an object that represents me.

Hito Steyerl refers to this concept of participation when she suggests that we side with the object instead of the subject in the struggle over representation.[3] She notes that the striving for full subjecthood in most emancipatory movements—with its promise of autonomy, sovereignty, and agency—has lost attraction to some degree after encountering implicit subjectification to power relations. The empowerment that comes with subjecthood is in practice often complex and full of conflict. The subject finds itself enmeshed in a social and political fabric of relations with other subjects, reproducing patterns of exclusion, oppression, or discrimination. While we figured out this complication, we also discovered that objects also actually have agency and seem to act with some autonomy. But Steyerl does not suggest that we identify with what the object represents and enter another subject-object relation. Instead, she points toward a concept of identifying with the thing itself, of participating in the object. It is an approach to participation as the absence of relation. Subject and object merge in this process, wherein the subject is first of all a subject of knowledge and not necessarily always a person. Looking at me and the graph, I realize that participation does enact a different magic than the one inherent in relation. From this perspective, the struggle over representation seems strangely outdated.

So now we side with things instead of subjects, transgressing the border between us and stuff. First, we discover that things have agency, that objects might be sovereign and act autonomously without us subjects making them do so, or rather without our being able to control them, as there are multiple forces at work. Then we learn that "the thing and the knowing being," as Benjamin phrases it, are not necessarily different entities but instead are "relative unities of reflection" participating in knowledge.[4] It does seem contradictory that while the object can act autonomously, the subject cannot know of that object but can only participate in it. It creates a sensation of blindness, a feeling of not knowing where one stands, where one is positioned. It does match the feeling of being sucked up by the cloud.

My graph is a manifestation from, of, and in the cloud. But what is the cloud? It does not seem to be an object of the kind we know, neither is it a subject. It is as much fact as it is fiction. As much as it is an empty envelope of parameters and subroutines, it is also a formation of multiple voices, enacting the formats the envelope provides. This enactment constantly exceeds the envelope; the envelope responds by constantly changing, adapting, and mimicking the movements, the voices, and the bodies that enact it. The cloud is not representing anything. It just exists as a mimetic machine that constantly renders realities. I am part of the cloud. My movements, my voice, my body are linked to this machine, whether I choose to actively participate in it or not, and I am unable to clearly distinguish agents and agencies in this process.

But wait, my dear artfukts, all this goes beyond my graph, acting autonomously and confuses me profoundly. Let's go back to that desire to overcome representation and side with the object. In my case, we were looking at an image of me—a curve—acting independently, without me doing anything or at least without me controlling it.

The aniconic argument responding to the autonomy of images is old.[5] It acknowledges that images have always tended to abandon what they depict and act independently as icons or idols. The aniconic argument warns us to be aware of this strange nature of images to become things in themselves that act as knowing beings. As much as this character of images has been used to draw and maintain power, it has also been questioned and attacked basically since images have existed.

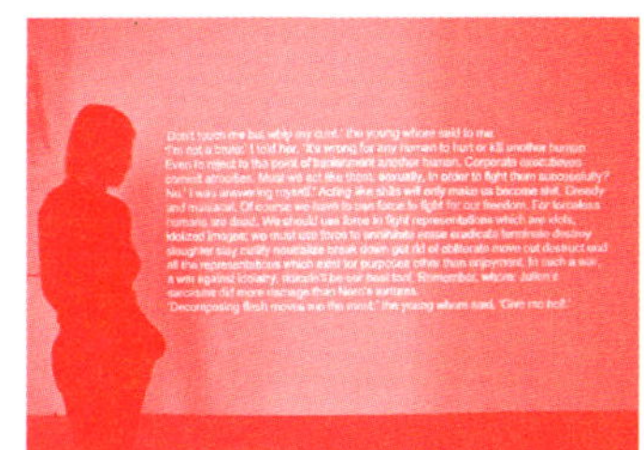

While there is much discussion about the recently rediscovered "premodern"

animistic features of objects, of images that provide them with certain powers, the knowledge of these powers is actually very old. So, why suddenly this desire to change sides? Maybe we desire to side with objects because we want to surrender to their powers. Being tired of awkwardly struggling with the emancipatory mission to claim subjecthood and ways that it relates to its representations, we abandon the position in charge of knowing, controlling, shaping, and conquering things and declare that we want to be moved again.

Maybe these animistic features have been hijacked by the capitalist forces of commodification. Maybe it is these forces that have decided to shift attention away from the "I" toward the "it." Perhaps they have told us that now the desired is the focus of attention, instead of the one who desires (who is now a consumer or fan of the object). In this case, wanting to be the object announces that we want to be desired as objects and not addressed as consumers. This is how we hope to regain agency and participate actively in a face-value economy. Having one million people like your picture or watch your YouTube video is so much more desirable

than claiming subjecthood. And you have already transgressed the border, you became the picture, you participated in the video going viral. Exactly who or what has agency in the reality that is created here is impossible to divide from a completely participatory process of all involved.

Yes indeed, the capitalist agents are trying to feed on me through the graph, and my initial response is to reject this breach into my autonomy to claim who I am and what I do. But then again, I can't uphold the indignation. Maybe my indifference is due to the curve's arbitrariness. Maybe I have already conspired with the curve.

I feel like I've lost something and I can't put my finger on it.

In her lecture "Subject to Object and Vice Versa," Nairy Baghramian defends the emancipatory possibilities of the subject in the face of the rise of the object.[6] Artists have long struggled to become subjects, she claims, thereby enabling themselves to participate in discourse and to create politically and socially relevant arguments and situations. But in the past few years, "the status of a work of art has risen beyond that of mere autonomous

existence to the point where works are sometimes treated like quasi-subjects capable of their own autonomous thinking." Baghramian warns that, in practice, the work might begin to take action by itself as well, and enter into direct dialogue with other agents such as curators. It might pursue its own alliances and relationships. This development might create a situation in which artists are precluded from the discourse and, falling silent, turn themselves into mystified objects. This would leave curators, commentators, and market players as the only active agents exercising control in the discourse.

With the evidence at hand, one could say that Baghramian is claiming a dead duck. Then again, she is advocating for the subject's agency, an agency that has come like so many other emancipatory enablements through and by struggle. And, similar to such discussions within feminism or labor struggle, the political question is raised of whether letting go of such achievements uncontested might be a huge mistake? But what if the question is wrong and the struggle with the borders of inclusion/exclusion, powerful/disenfranchised, subject/object just does not hold, does not do it any longer? If the quest is still for agency and sovereignty and rights—and I believe it is— maybe the agents, the territories, the movements have changed and so strategies have to change too. Surely claiming subjecthood did create a feeling of integrity, a wholeness of a specific kind but, as in the very idea of solidarity, this integrity often exceeds the limits of our own body, our own voice, our own movements.

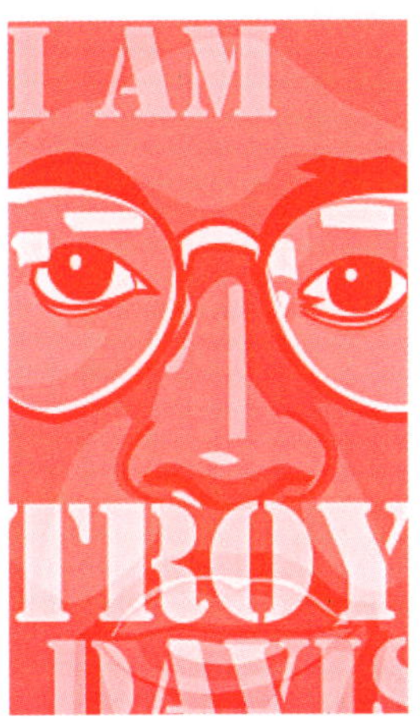

During the campaign for Troy Davis, who was on death row for a murder he claimed he had not committed, many people, including myself, changed their Facebook profile picture into Troy's to support his peers' campaign for a fair trial and justice for his case. The campaign of nearly one million supporters could not save Troy; he was executed on September 21, 2011. Yet in other cases, such campaigns proved success-

ful. To express solidarity and support by claiming to be XY and thereby multiplying or cloning the person in question, potentially indefinitely, has become a common campaign tool in social networks—often expressed visually by replacing one's photo or wearing a mask.

This act also uses the mimetic power of the name participating in the thing named. It doesn't claim to relate to a struggle, but instead to *be* the struggle. It claims to be able to melt down identities and become anybody at any given moment in time. This can be a very powerful tool as it can transmute a single person into an enormous multiheaded entity whose growth and thereby power is potentially unlimited. *"The struggle for justice*

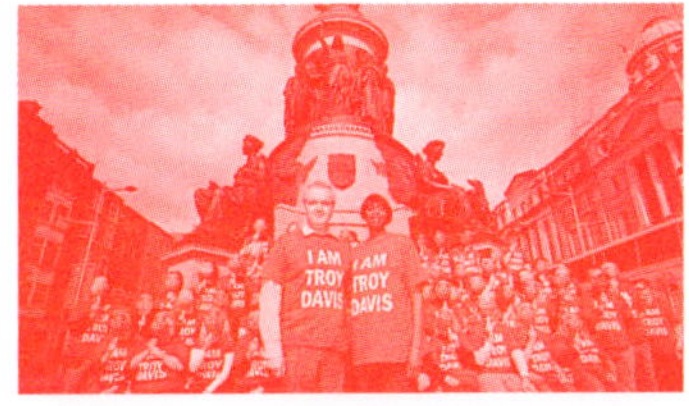

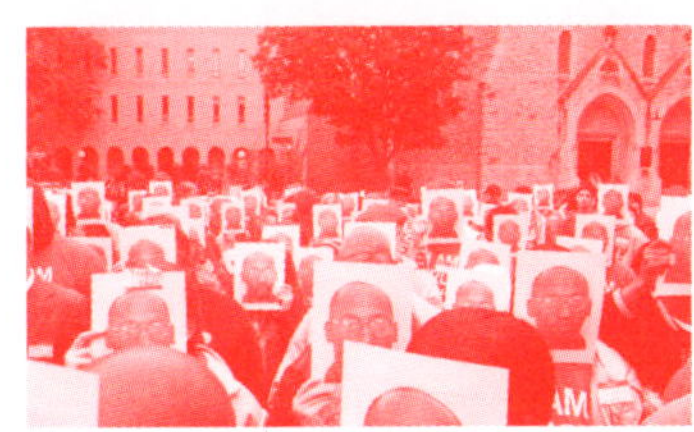

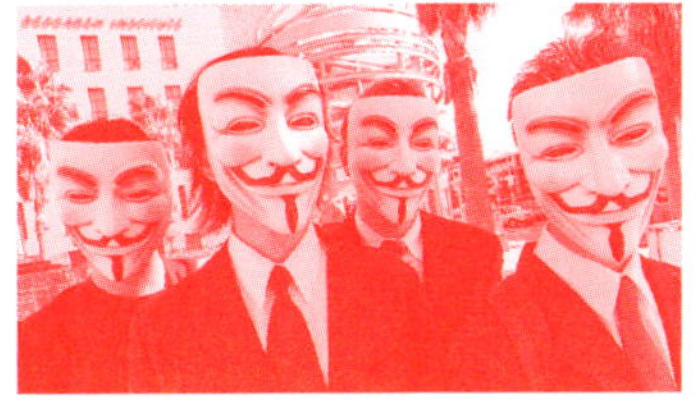

doesn't end with me. This struggle is for all the Troy Davises who came before me and all the ones who will come after me. I'm in good spirits and I'm prayerful and at peace."[7]

Some are hesitant to apply this identity swap as a political strategy. A friend admits a feeling of resistance against changing his profile picture. There are even voices radically opposing such meltdowns. During the campaign for another case, the fatal shooting of young Floridian Trayvon Martin, the video of a young woman appeared on social media who positioned herself as a "privileged white middle-class female socially concerned activist."

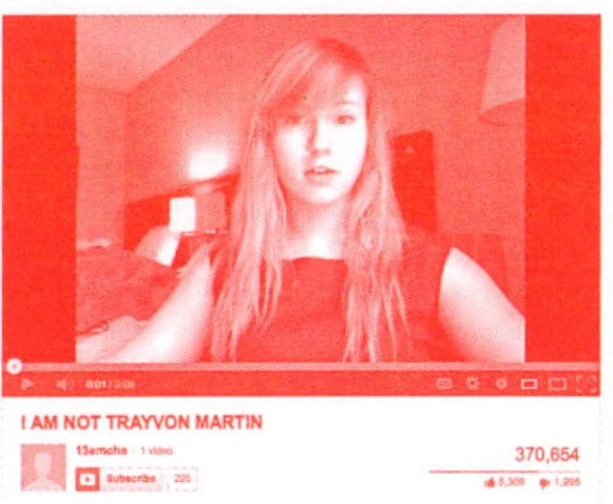

She declares, "I am not Trayvon Martin! I am not Troy Davis!" She concedes that a white middle-class activist claiming to "be Trayvon Martin" is a positive attempt to humanize the victim, indicating that a young black male is deprived of this status by society—i.e., the status of a subject. She remarks that due to her own skin color and social status, she would never be exposed to the injustice that a young black man faces on a daily basis. On the contrary, she was privileged by default and instead predestined to become a George Zimmermann, the man who shot Trayvon Martin, rather than a Trayvon or Troy. Therefore, it would be preposterous to claim to be Troy Davis. It would blur, if not whitewash, the differences created by systematic racism that led to him being on death row. She demands that all privileged white middle-class activists such as herself stop decorating themselves with the precarious identity of the oppressed and admit what they really are. This would be the only way to truly support the struggle of the oppressed and achieve change. She ends by saying, "Do not, I repeat, do not claim to be them!"

I come across these counterattacks on the mingling with subject-object relations in different places. This activist's approach of positioning—of marking her identity by declaring her ethnic and social background, skin color, gender, nationality as the contextualizing starting point for any argument or activity—has

increasingly become the basis of political debate or left-wing activism, but can even be found in job announcements in academia in what is now called the former West. It is uncanny how the very categories that some decades back were detected as socially constructed, and therefore to be questioned, criticized, and taken apart, vehemently find their way back into the very same discourse—critically addressing identity politics—but now they appear fierce, unshakable, and somewhat hyperreal.

"Are we looking at a logical loop," asks a paper published by gender studies students at Berlin's Humboldt University, "in which emancipatory analysis got enmeshed? 'These categories are socially constructed.' 'Yes, but they are also a real form of existence.' 'Yes but they are historically produced.' 'But they are a real form of existence.' But ..." The writers criticize the way in which the politics of positioning is gaining growing influence in critical whiteness studies, gender studies, and antiracist activism. They apprehend that positioning and verbalizing identity threatens to put people in their social or ethnic place, denying transgression and making the overcoming of

these categories and hierarchies a secondary task, if not impossible. They quote a fellow student saying: "I will never know what it feels like to be a female refugee, therefore I cannot comment on this matter."[8]

Interestingly enough, this comes after a fundamentally nonessentialist wave in identity politics, where transgression was part of the game of playing with the existing borders between categories and claiming to be able to reinvent one's identity indefinitely as an act of subversion, emancipation, and autonomy.

In the 1990s, various movements claimed sovereignty over their identities, whether it was the queer movement transgressing the existing gender categories or migrant activist networks, such as Kanak Attak, which programmatically stated that it was not someone's background or passport that was important, but their attitude.[9]

Michael Taussig aptly describes the current situation: "History wreaks its revenge on representational security as essentialism and constructivism oscillate wildly in a death struggle over the claims of mimesis to be the nature that culture uses to create a now-beleaguered second nature."[10] The very ground under our feet is socially constructed then, but also very real. As we slowly start to grasp the delirious stability of such bedrock, we try to hold on to anything solid.

But I suspect all residual solid things might turn out to be twisted in the end. Maybe it's time to practice balancing. Avery Gordon commences her publication *Ghostly Matters* with this quote borrowed from legal scholar Patricia Williams: "That life is complicated is a fact of great analytic importance."[11] Gordon uses Williams's proposition to talk about the power relations that characterize societies. According to Gordon, these relations are "never as transparently clear as the names we give to them imply." She elaborates:

"Power can be invisible, it can be fantastic, it can be dull and routine. It can be obvious, it can reach you by the baton of the police, it can speak the language of your thoughts and desires. It can feel like remote control, it can exhilarate like liberation, it can travel through time, and it can drown you in the present. It is dense and superficial, it can cause bodily injury, and it can harm you without seem-

ing ever to touch you. It is systematic and it is particularistic and it is often both at the same time."[12]

Gordon sees these multifaceted power relations best described by Williams when she refers to her own ancestry, proposing life's complexity as a vital aspect of analysis. Williams's great-great grandmother was a slave and her great-great grandmother's owner was also the father of her children. So she is the product of a participation of an owner in his property, a very confusing, yet not very unusual, expression of power relations. To amplify Gordon: power can harm you without seeming ever to touch you; it can speak the language of your thoughts and it can travel through time.

As Gordon relates, Williams decides she can only make sense of the apparitions that keep visiting her if she takes the complexity of involvement into account. She can only trace her great-great grandmother by looking for the "shape described by her absence," a shape that is drawn by her owner's hand. While she was deprived of rights, of choice, of being sovereign, she can be found in his letters and legal documents. His hand and her absence form a flicker-

ing shape, partly traceable, partly apparitional: a power relation that reaches into the present. Williams has to confront these forces, this haunting. She has to look for "her shape and his hand" as the power relation between her great-great grandmother and her great-great grandmother's owner is also part of her own shape and the way she engages that relation. Power can harm you without seeming ever to touch you. Life is complicated.[13]

These forces that arrive in all sorts of forms and names shape parts of us profoundly, and yet not all parts because some seem strangely inaccessible and evade forming or naming. The right to "complex personhood," which according to Gordon is the second dimension of the theoretical statement that life is complicated, means exactly this: we can be object and subject at the same time, same and other, fact and fiction, oppressor and oppressed. We can be contradictory and suffering from these contradictions.

Williams's tracing of her shape and his hand uses sympathetic magic or the mimetic faculty, as Taussig terms it, a necessary magic "to the process of knowing and the construction and subsequent naturalization of identities."[14] I wonder if the mimetic faculty is in fact the very connection in the participation of the name in the thing named, of the subject in the object of knowledge.

Taussig says that we mostly use the mimetic faculty to go on living, pretending that we live facts and not fictions, even though postmodernism and the critical project in academia of uncovering the social construction of race, gender, or nation has instructed us that reality is actually made up. We know this and still we use the mimetic faculty to pretend it's natural. We trace a construct and live that copy vigorously. "The wonder of mimesis lies in the copy drawing on the character and power of the original, to the point whereby the representation may even assume that character and that power."[15]

Taussig questions the critical project analyzing social construction insofar as it should have been just an invitation, an introduction to further investigation and not a conclusion. It was only the beginning of knowledge and should not pass for actual knowing. Life is constructed, yes—but it's more complicated than that. Because if it is constructed, why does it feel so immutable, so natural? How come, again and again, we believe in inventions such as culture or nation as if they are completely real?

For Taussig, it is by the magic of the mimetic faculty that we make them real again and again. But these realities are not conclusions or finite states but instead they are in continuous flux, transmutation, permutation, diversification, alteration, disintegration, and collapse. He suggests diving into that turbulence where the forces that render the real coalesce, where the mimesis of history meets the history of mimesis. For him, it is this place where Kafka's ape aping humanity's aping dwells. Taussig believes that only there in the inner sanctum of mimesis, in imitating, can we find distance from the imitated, the dead end of constructionism.

In October 2012, Ai Weiwei released a video on YouTube in which he and a group of associates gather in his studio courtyard and mime the moves of the "Gangnam Style" music video by Psy. His original video, with 1.59 billion views, is the most watched YouTube video to date. The dance moves, which include galloping in place with wrists crossed in front of the chest to mimic horseback riding, have been reenacted in numerous ways and by numerous parties across the globe. Ai's version copies the horseback-riding moves, adding handcuffs to the crossed wrists in reference to censorship in China and his previous detention by the Chinese authorities

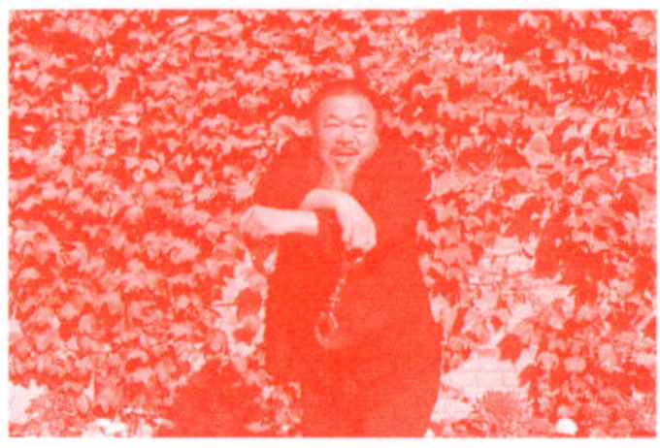

In interviews, Ai has claimed that the international Internet meme phenomenon is an expression of individualism, and that the "right of expression is fundamentally linked to our happiness and even our existence."[16] His video was immediately banned by the Chinese government. While I watch his video on YouTube, Ai Weiwei becomes an object, a copy of another object. But he is also equipped with agency (as seen by the worried actions of the Chinese authorities), making him a subject. His studio, a location in the real world, becomes part of the cloud in this attempt to use the magic powers of miming what a billion eyes have seen. The Chinese authorities validate Ai's meme by taking down the video, themselves miming the expected authoritative gesture, and adding another link to the real. Then, in a recently fashionable gesture of art-world solidarity, Anish Kapoor initiates another "Gangnam" reenactment. Kapoor's meme adds his large studio along with a famous choreographer and another 250 people to this conglomerate of things perpetually building reality.

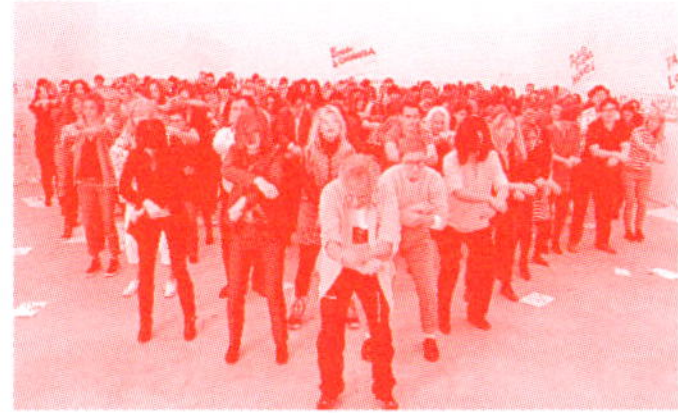

As Steyerl describes so accurately, most things we are dealing with are "usually not a shiny new Boeing taking off on its virgin flight. Rather, it might be its wreck, painstakingly pieced together from scrap inside a hangar after its unexpected nosedive into catastrophe."[17] In other words, it's a mess.

My curve and I are part of this mess, a bigger mess. I became part of my own forensic team, detecting the hidden forces and desires buried in the rubble, piecing together the signs of power and violence that have gone through my body, my world, my reality. I can still look for integrity,

my dear artfukts. And this cloud, it's nothing.

Images

Page 5: (clockwise from upper right)
• Performance images of Natascha Sadr Haghighian's *present but not yet active* at Frankfurt Zoo, 2002 Courtesy the artist and Johann König, Berlin
• Installation view of Natascha Sadr Haghighian's *Empire of the Senseless Part II,* Berlin, 2006
• Erica Crittendon, 19, takes part in the United 1000 Hoodies rally for Trayvon Martin in Seattle, March 28, 2012. Neighborhood-watch volunteer George Zimmerman shot and killed the unarmed 17-year-old on February 26, 2012, in Sanford, Florida. Photo: REUTERS/Marcus Donner
• Computer accessing bioswop .net, a project by Natascha Sadr Haghighian
• Screen grab of Natascha Sadr Haghighian's profile on ArtFacts .net, 2012

Page 8:
• Ranking graph from Natascha Sadr Haghighian's profile on ArtFacts.net, 2012

Pages 9–10:
• Natascha Sadr Haghighian's *Empire of the Senseless Part II* (page 9) and *Part I* Courtesy the artist and Johann König, Berlin

Page 12:
• (lefthand column)
Image used on Facebook as a profile picture during the "I Am Troy Davis" campaign. Source: Google image search
• (middle column, top to bottom)
Martina Correia-Davis, Troy

Davis's sister, in front of Daniel O'Connell Monument with Amnesty International Ireland activists in Dublin, 2010 Courtesy Amnesty International USA ©All rights reserved by amnestyinternational_usa
• Demonstrators hold "I Am Troy Davis" posters in front of their faces, courtesy NewsOne.com, http://ionenewsone.files .wordpress.com/2011/09/troy -davis-1.jpg
• Members of Anonymous wearing Guy Fawkes masks at a Scientology center in Los Angeles, 2008. Photo: Vincent Diamante Image source: Wikimedia Commons
• (righthand column)
YouTube user 13emcha protesting the "I Am Troy Davis" movement, March 31, 2012, accessed July 25, 2013

Page 15
• Screen grab of Ai Weiwei's YouTube music video in which he performs his riff on Psy's "Gangnam Style," 2012

Page 16
• Screen grab of Anish Kapoor's YouTube music video performance of "Gangnam for Freedom," 2012

Page 19
• Image posted by "Michelle" on "We are the 99%" Tumblr site. The text reads in part: I am 3 years out of college, employed, with only $10,000 in debt. I am lucky! I work full-time for a nonprofit. I make less then $20,000 a year, I can survive on this. I am lucky! I can not afford the buy in ($175) for my work's Health Saving Plan -> I don't have Health Insurance once I turn 26 (9 more months) and can't be on my mother's plan. The only reason I have never had to choose between food and gas is because

my parents sometimes help me. [...] I AM LUCKY! But I'm also scared. I can survive, but for how long? - I am the 99% Source: http://wearethe99 percent.tumblr.com/post /11101669294/i-am-3-years -out-of-college-employed -with-only. Last accessed August 12, 2013.

Notes

1. This documentary television series from 2002 focused on "how those in power have used Freud's theories to try and control the dangerous crowd in an age of mass democracy," as described in Adam Curtis's introduction to the first episode, "Happiness Machines." *The Century of the Self*, directed by Adam Curtis (BBC Four, UK: March 17, 2002).

2. Amalgam of my own phrasings and an extract from Franz Kafka's *Report to an Academy*. The Kafka quote is sourced from the introduction to Michael Taussig, *Mimesis and Alterity: A Particular History of the Senses* (New York: Routledge, 1993), xiii.

3. See Hito Steyerl, "A Thing Like You and Me," *e-flux journal* 15 (April 2010), accessed April 10, 2013, http://www.e-flux. com/journal/a-thing-like-you -and-me/.

4. Walter Benjamin, "The Concept of Criticism in German Romanticism," in *Selected Writings: 1913–1926, Volume I* (Cambridge, MA: Harvard University Press, 106), 146.

5. "You shall not make for yourselves an idol, nor any image of anything that is in the heavens above, or that is in the earth beneath, or that is in the water under the earth." Exodus 20:4–6.

6. Nairy Baghramian, "Subject to Object and Vice Versa" (lecture delivered as part of the ongoing series Subjective Histories of Sculpture, co-organized by the Vera List Center for Art and Politics at the New School and Sculpture Center, New York, March 15, 2012), accessed April 15, 2013, http:// vimeo.com/38803990.

7. Statement by Troy Anthony Davis on the day before his execution, September 21, 2011, accessed April 15, 2013, http://www.amnestyusa.org /emails/W1109EADP05.html.

8. This article appeared under a pseudonym. Ayşe K. Arslanoşlu, "Stolz und Vorurteil: Markierungspolitiken in den Gender Studies und Anderswo," in *Outside the Box, Zeitschrift für feministische Gesellschaftskritik* 2, vol. 3. Longer quote based on the following text, translated from German by the author: *Betrachten wir eine logische Schlaufe, in der sich die emanzipatorische Analyse verfangen hat? "Diese Kategorien sind doch sozial konstruiert." "Ja, aber sie sind auch eine reale Existenzweise." "Ja, aber sie sind historisch gemacht." "Aber sie sind eine reale Existenzweise." "Aber …"*

9. An interesting article that explores this shift in Germany using "kannak attak" as a reference is Aida Ibrahim et al., "Decolorize it!" *ak—analyse & kritik—zeitung für linke Debatte und Praxis* 575 (September 21, 2012), accessed April 15, 2013, http://www.akweb.de/ak_s /ak575/23.htm.

German text: *Nicht politische Standpunkte und Strategien werden diskutiert, sondern die Personen, die sie äußern, stehen zur Diskussion. Daraus resultiert auch mit Rekurs auf das falsch verstandene bzw. naiv »übersetzte«Selbstermächtigungskonzept der »Definitionsmacht« die derzeit gängige Positionierungspraxis: In Uni-Seminaren und auf Veranstaltungen erfolgt—oft unabhängig vom konkreten Thema—eine quälend lange »Selbstpositionierung« der sprechenden Person, in der diese detailliert Auskunft gibt über ihren Pass, ihre Hautfarbe, ihre sexuelle Orientierung, den Zustand ihrer körperlichen Verfassung, ihren familiären Bildungshintergrund sowie ihre Einkommensverhältnisse.[...] Und das Netzwerk kanak attak hat sich Anfang der 1990er Jahre dezidiert als Zusammenschluss von Menschen begriffen, in dem nicht nach Pass und Herkunft gefragt wurde, sondern die Haltung zum Rassismus entscheidend war.*

Translation by the author: It's not political viewpoints and strategies that are being discussed; rather, the people who express the views are up for discussion. From this results the currently established practice of positioning with recourse to a falsely interpreted or naïvely "translated" concept of self-authorization of the "Defining Power" at university seminars and events—independent of the topic—a tormenting, long "self-positioning" of the speaker occurs in which he or she provides detailed information about his or her passport, skin color, sexual orientation, physical condition, family background, and income [....] In the early '90s, in contrast, the network kanak attak had understood itself decidedly as a

coalition of people whose attitude toward racism was relevant,
not their passport or origin.

10. Michael Taussig, *Mimesis
and Alterity*, xv.

11. Avery Gordon, *Ghostly
Matters: Haunting and the
Sociological Imagination*
(Minneapolis and London:
University of Minnesota Press,
2008), 3.

12. Ibid., 5.

13. As a further amplifica-
tion of this theme, I quote Audre
Lorde channeling Paulo Freire:
"As Paulo Freire shows so well in
The Pedagogy of the Oppressed,
the true focus of revolutionary
change is never merely the op-
pressive situation which we seek
to escape, but that piece of the
oppressor which is planted deep
within each of us, and which know
only the oppressor's tactics, the
oppressor's relationships." Audre
Lorde quoted in *Sister Outsider*
(Trumansberg, New York: Crossing
Press, 1984), 123.

14. Taussig, *Mimesis and
Alterity,* xiii.

15. Ibid., xiii.

16. Video, "Ai Weiwei does
Gangnam Style," *Guardian* (UK),
October 24, 2012, accessed May
5, 2013, http://www.guardian.
co.uk/music/video/2012/oct/24
/ai-weiwei-gangnam-style-video.

17. Hito Steyerl, "A Thing Like
You and Me," *e-flux journal* 15
(April 2010).

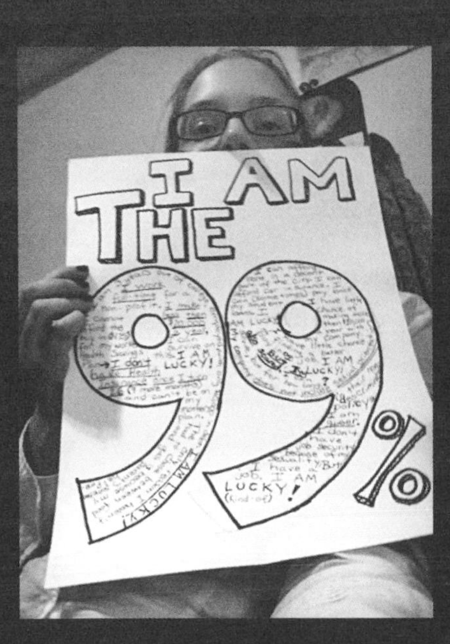

I AM THE 99%
I AM LUCKY!
I don't
I AM LUCKY!
I AM LUCKY!
I have a job, I AM LUCKY! (kind of)!

My Beauty Qeen

Danh Vo
Martin Wong
Phung Vo
&
Karl Holmqvist

EARLY ONE
MORNING AT THE
END OF MAY
2007 I dreamt I
was in bed with
Joe d'Alessandro
and Iggy Pop.

We were lying naked only covered by a thin, white sheet in a bed surrounded by cameras and light people etc. involved in making a photoshoot or commercial of some kind.

Iggy Pop and Joe d'Alessandro were on either side of me forming a king of human sandwich

~With their hard
bodies and long hair
the two of them
were sexy beyond
comprehension,
but also both
very attentive and
affectionate

It went on for some time with us giggling and tickling and hugging each other before I woke up surprised or even shocked at how vivid and really, really nice it had all been.

One night I dreamt I was part of recording a commercial for a real estate company.

It was directed by
my friend Danh
Vo standing at the
ready with a
megaphone behind
the camera and crew.

*I was sitting behind my boyfriend on a motorcycle,
he was wearing really tight white jean and a black
motorcycle leather jacket.*

I was holding onto him with one hand on each side of his hips.

No helmet

XXVI.

We rolled up a
short distance in
front of a white
apartment building
and he motioned
with his hand
and exclaimed :

XXVII.

before he
turned around
and kissed me
passionately
with the camera
coming to a
close zoom.

AND CUT.

XXVIII.

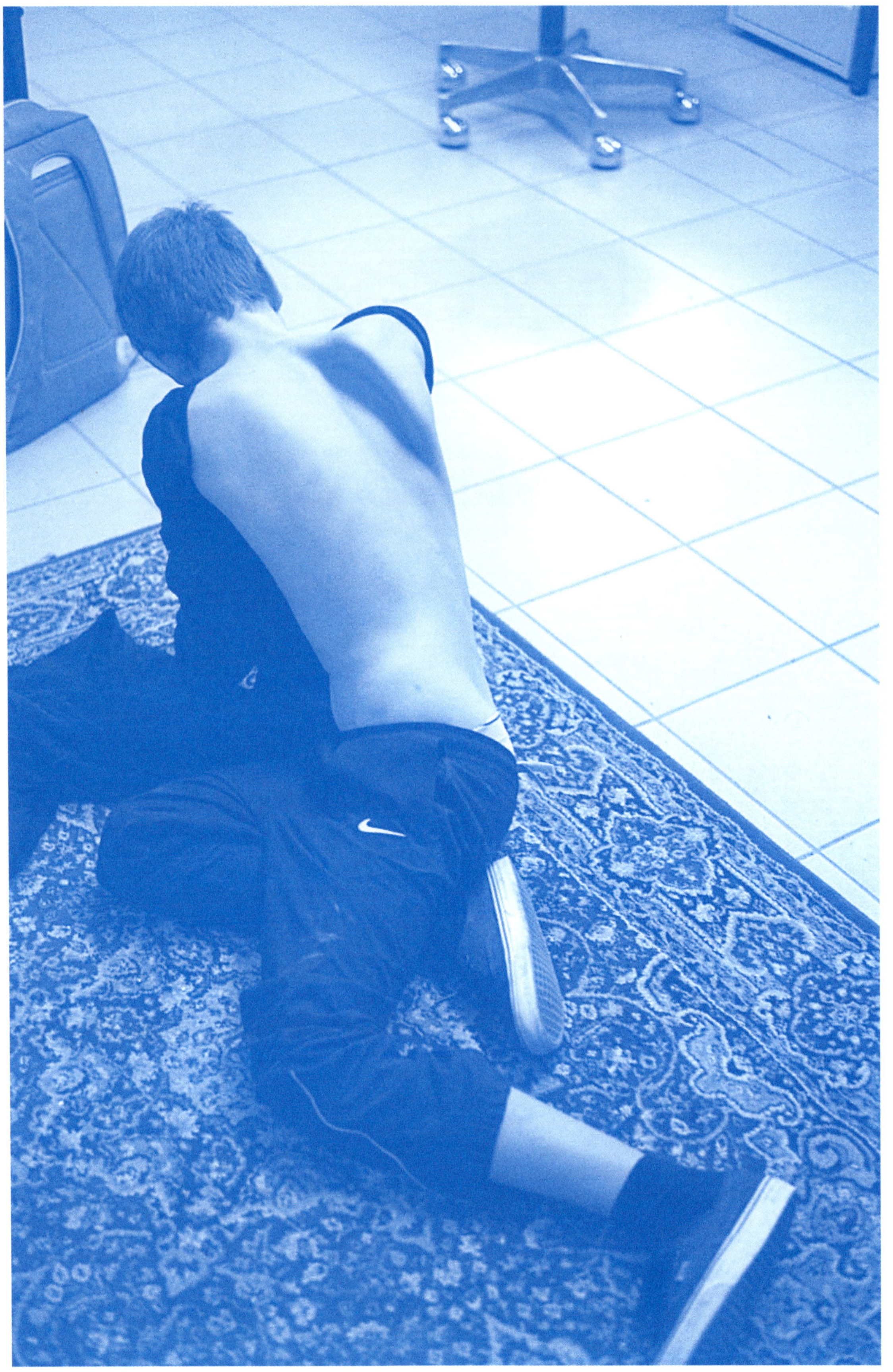

XXIX.

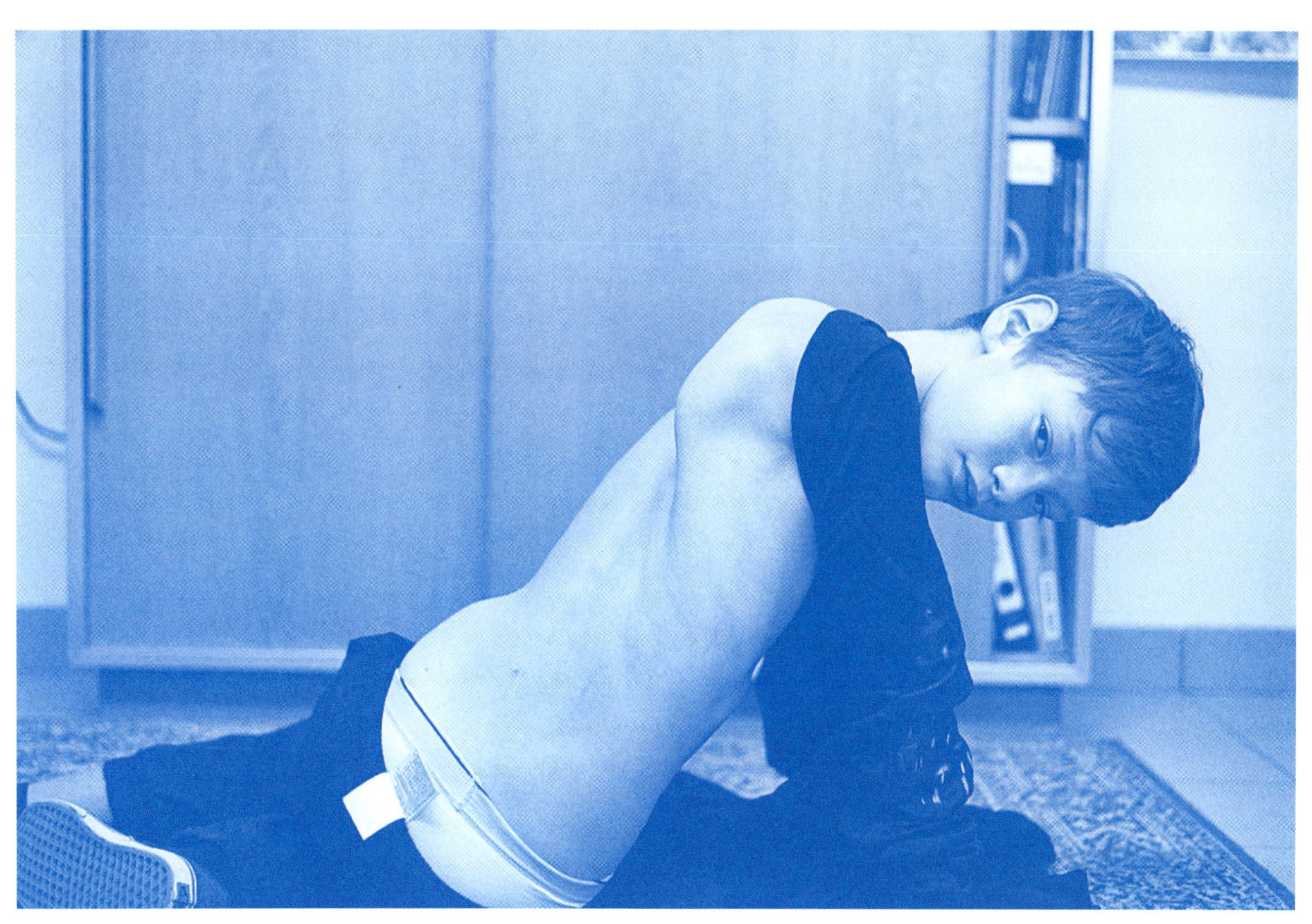

XXX.

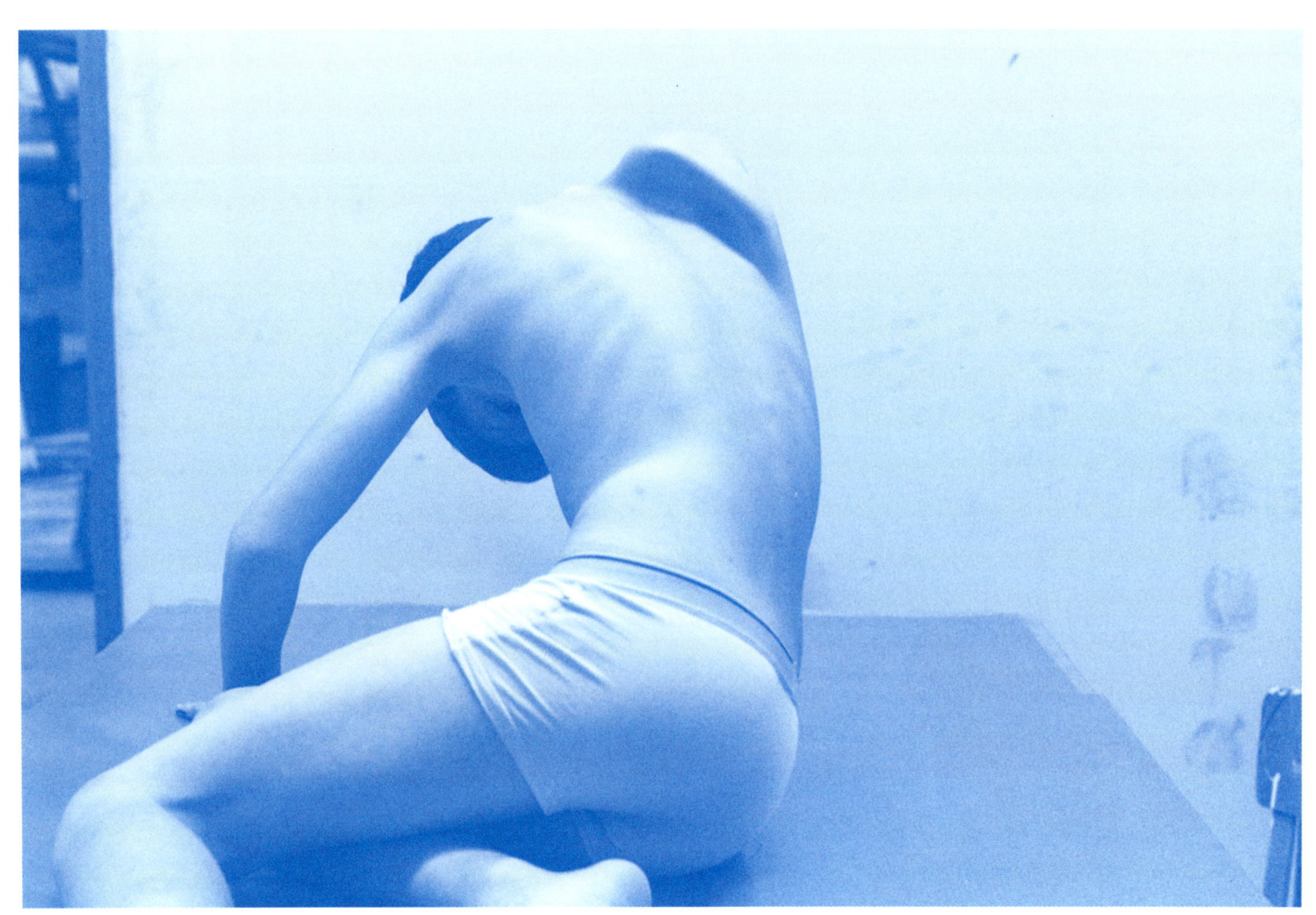

XXXI.

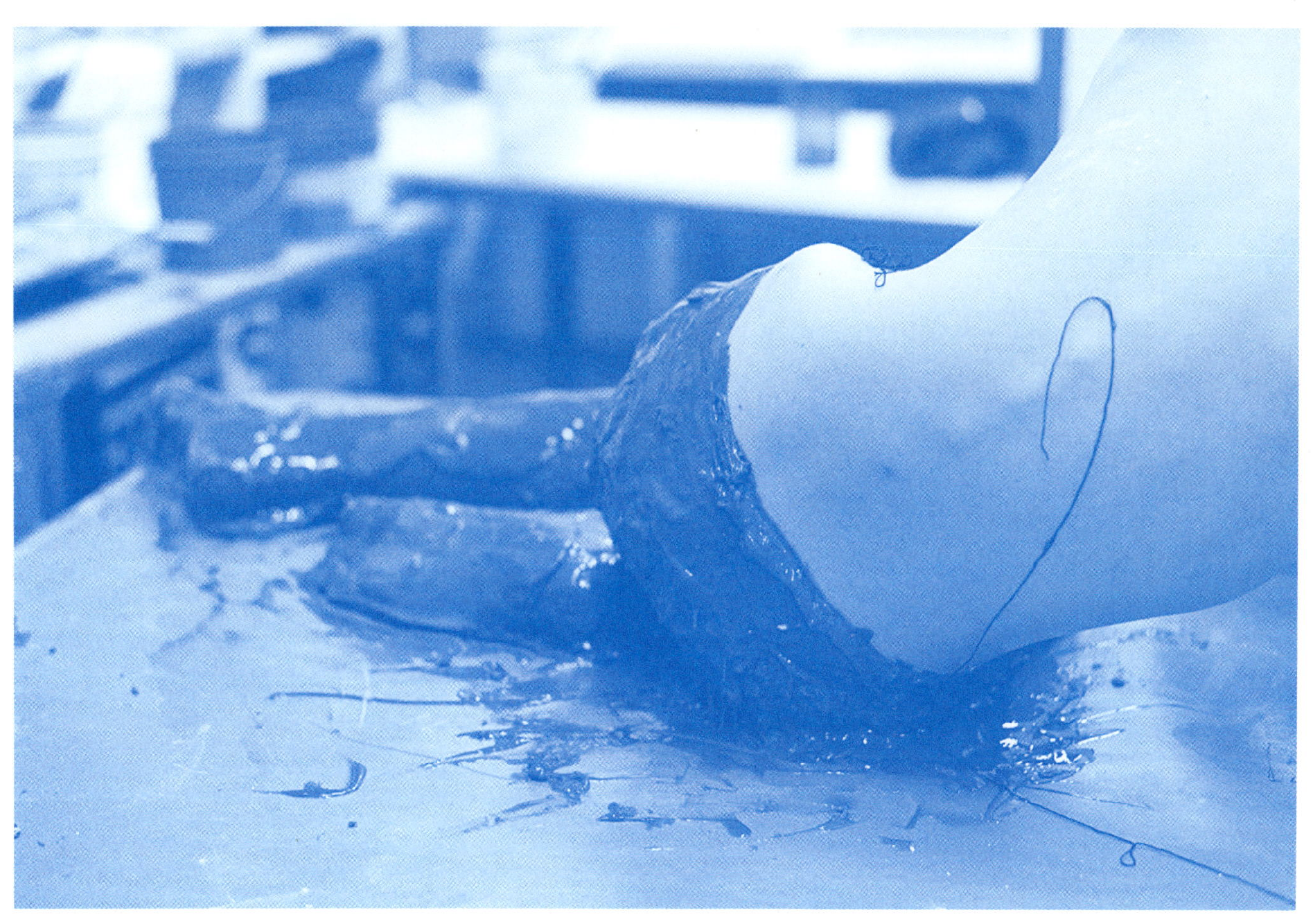

XXXII.

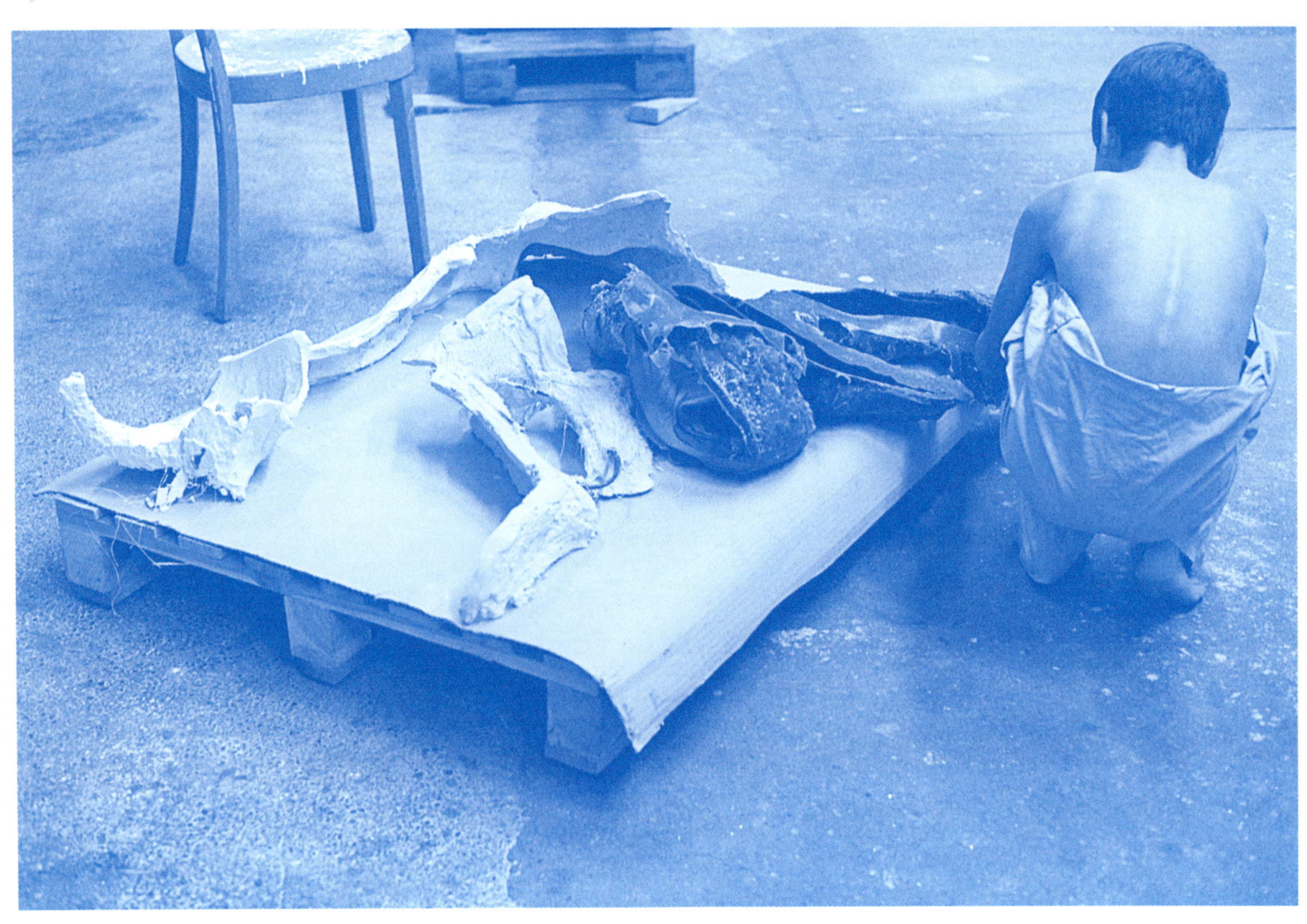

XXXIII.

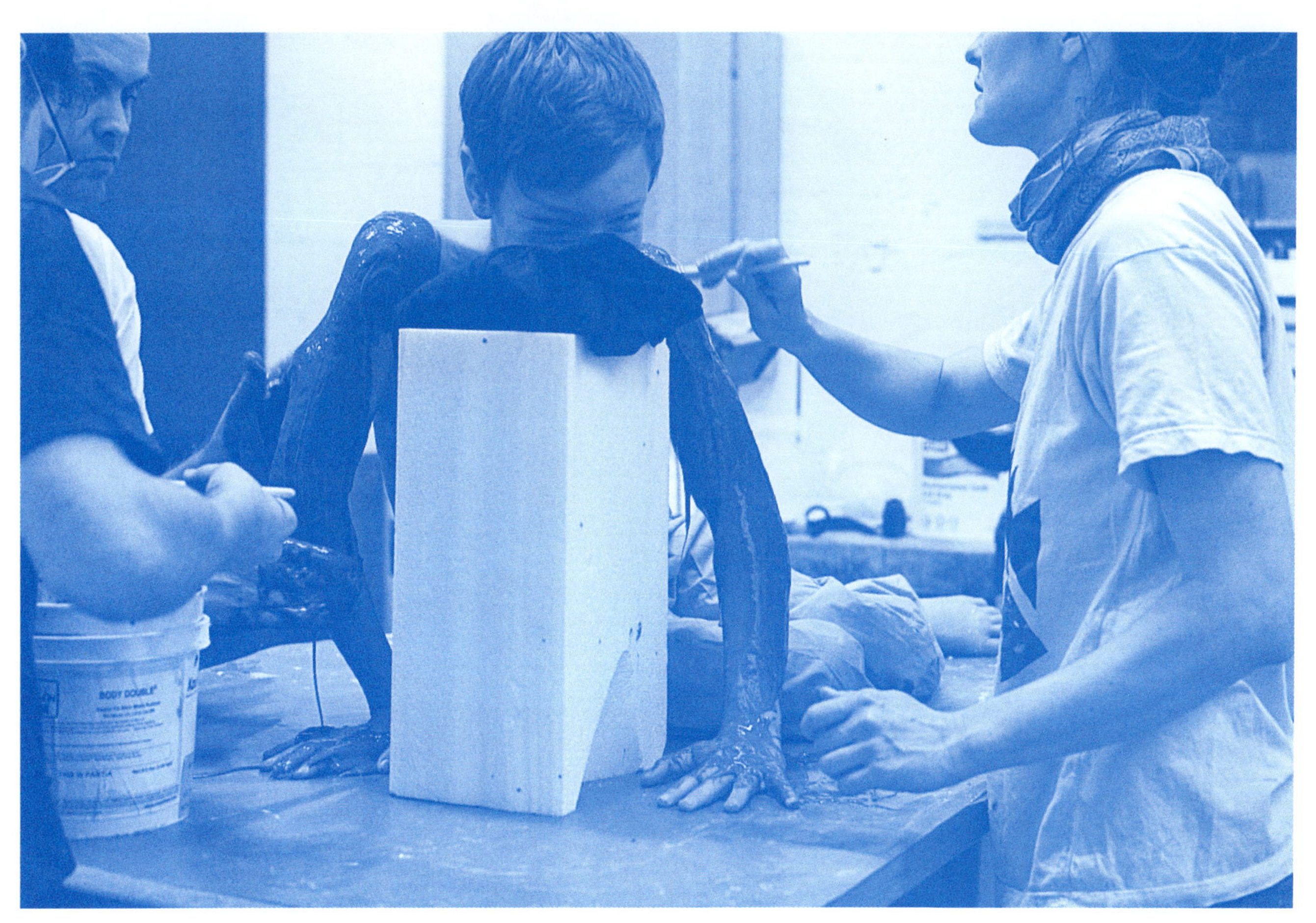

XXXIV.

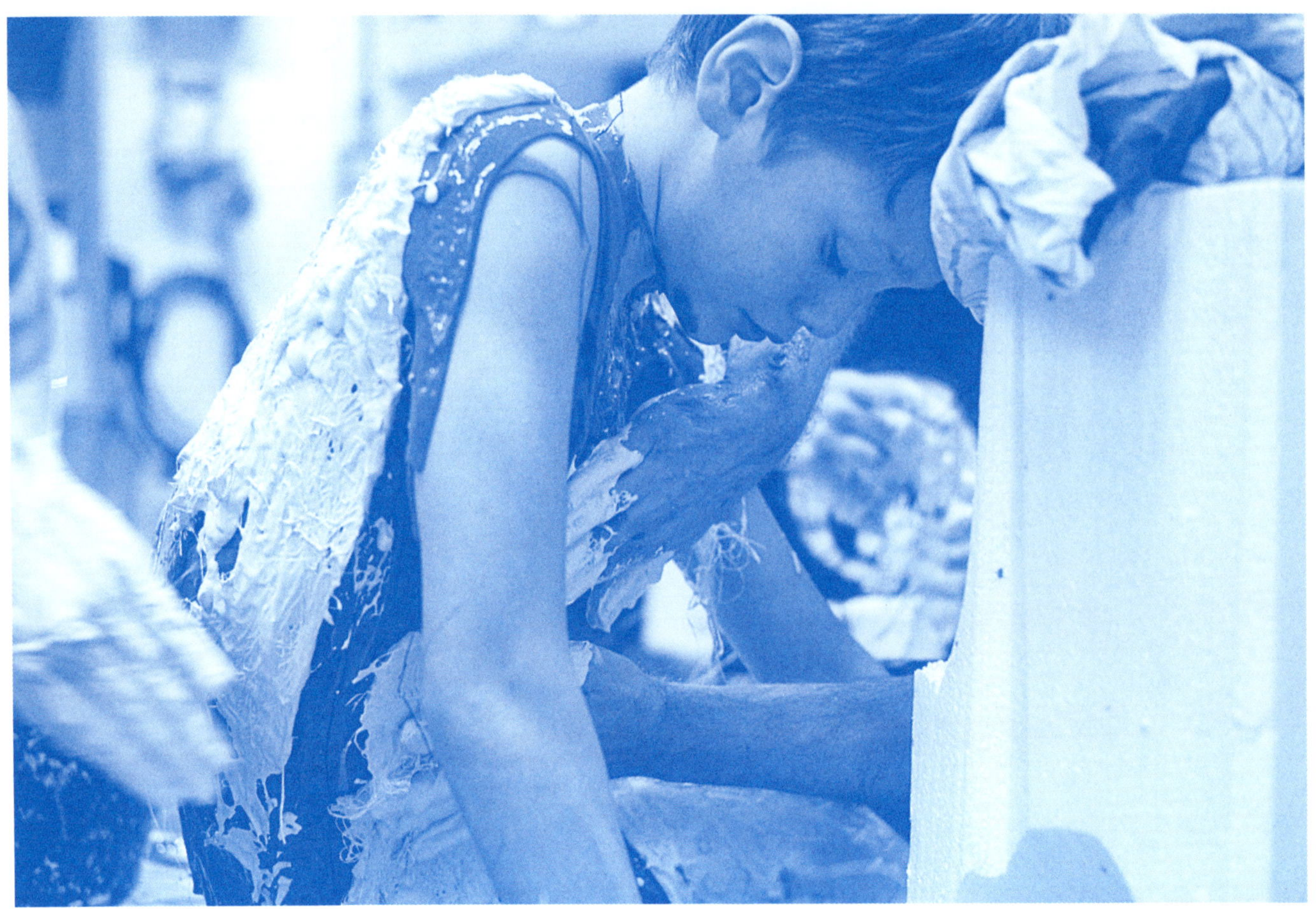

<u>Gustav's Wing</u> in production, Kunstbetrieb, Basel, 2012   Photo: Danh Vo

XXXV.

I DREAMED A DREAM:

POLITICS IN THE AGE OF MASS ART PRODUCTION

Hito Steyerl

1) THIS CONTRIBUTION DEALS WITH THE AGE OF MASS ART PRODUCTION. 2) THIS IS AN ADOPTED, NOT AN ORIGINAL PROJECT. 3) THIS TALK ASSUMES THE FORM OF A NONFICTION SUBSCRIPTION BASED NOVEL. IT IS WRITTEN ON DEMAND IN RESPONSE TO COMMISSION AND FUNDING AND FULL OF CLIFFHANGERS, ADVERTISEMENT BREAKS AND EXCESSIVE AND INCOHERENT PLOTLINES. (ALSO) IT WILL SUDDENLY STOP WITHOUT FURTHER NOTICE OR WARNING.

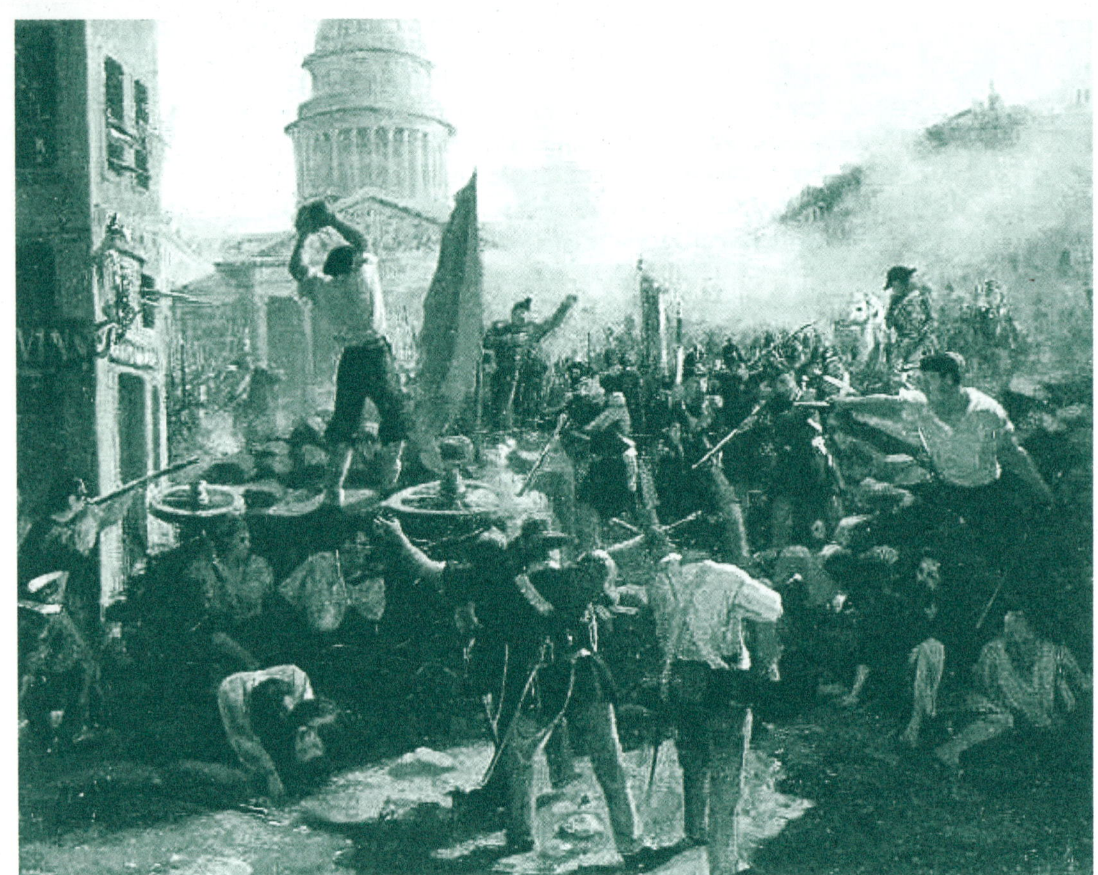

Fig. 1: Horace Vernet *La barricade de la rue Soufflot* (1848–1850) Image source: Wikipedia Commons

The text that was here was withdrawn days before this publication went to print. The artist included the lyrics of "I Dreamed a Dream" from *Les Misérables* as an essential illustration of some themes in the essay. After protracted good faith negotiations, the representative of the lyricist refused the Walker and the artist permission to print the song, or even a limited extract. While the Walker and the artist stand behind the fair use of the lyrics, the artist has decided to withdraw the text in full as a protest against the decision of Alain Boublil Overseas Limited.

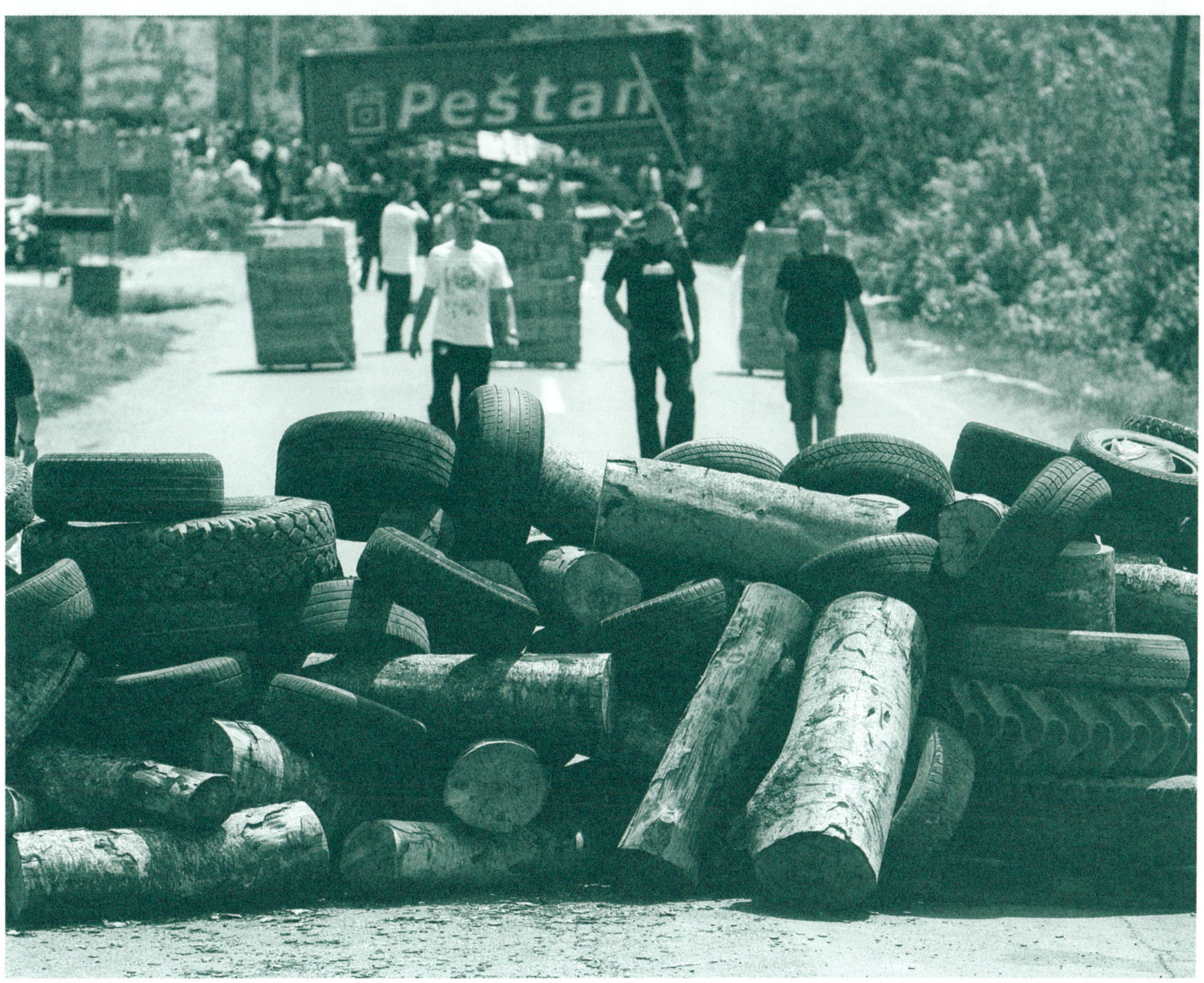

Fig. 2: Kosovo Serbs block a road in the village of Rudare near Zvecan, July 30, 2011. NATO troops in Kosovo returned to their barracks after ethnic Serbs blocked them from reaching peacekeepers deployed at border posts with Serbia to halt violence provoked by a customs dispute.   Photo: REUTERS/Marko Djurica

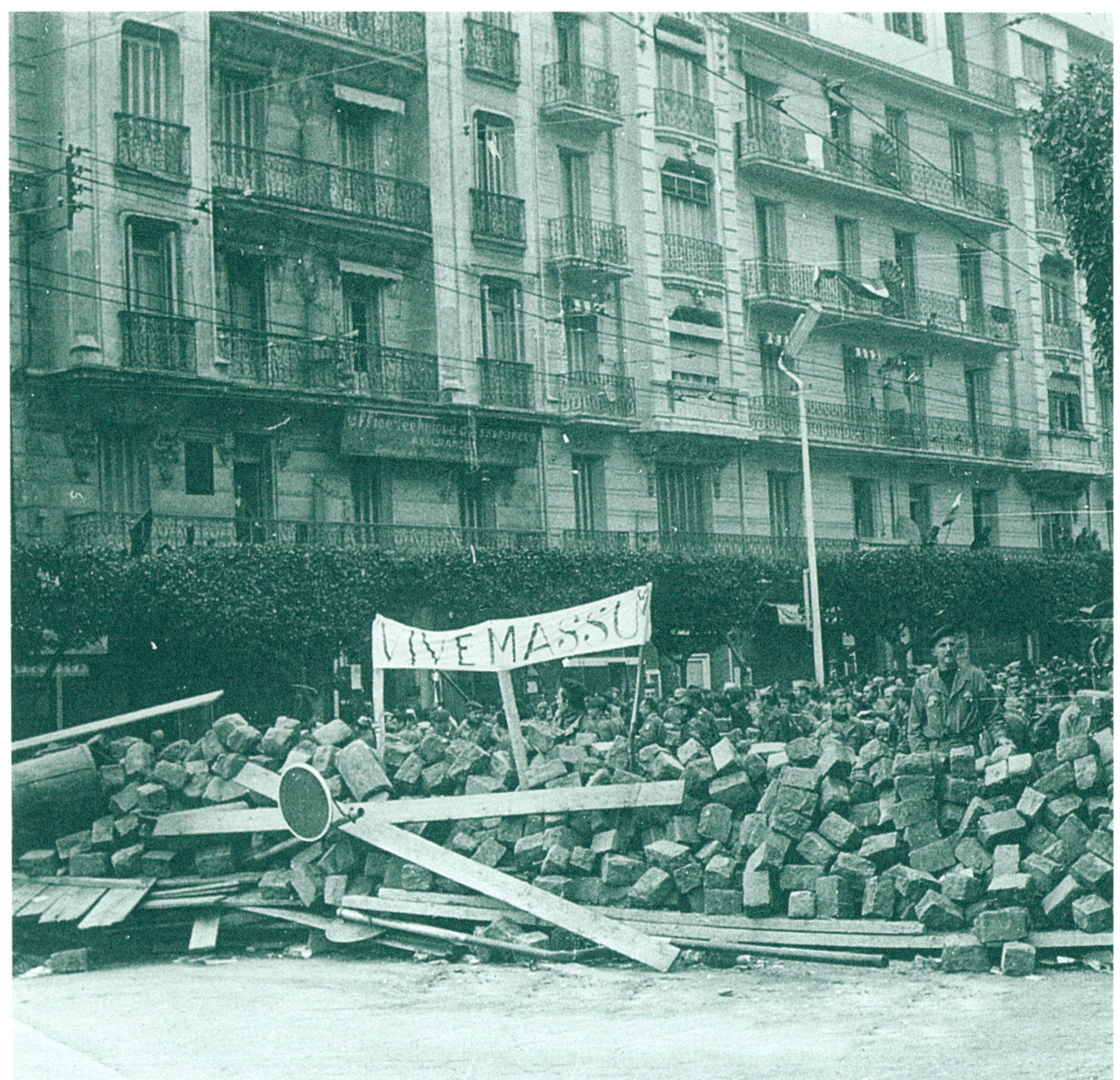

Fig. 3: Barricades set up during the Algerian War of Independence, Street of Algier, January 1960.
Photo: Christophe Marcheux   Image source: Wikimedia Commons

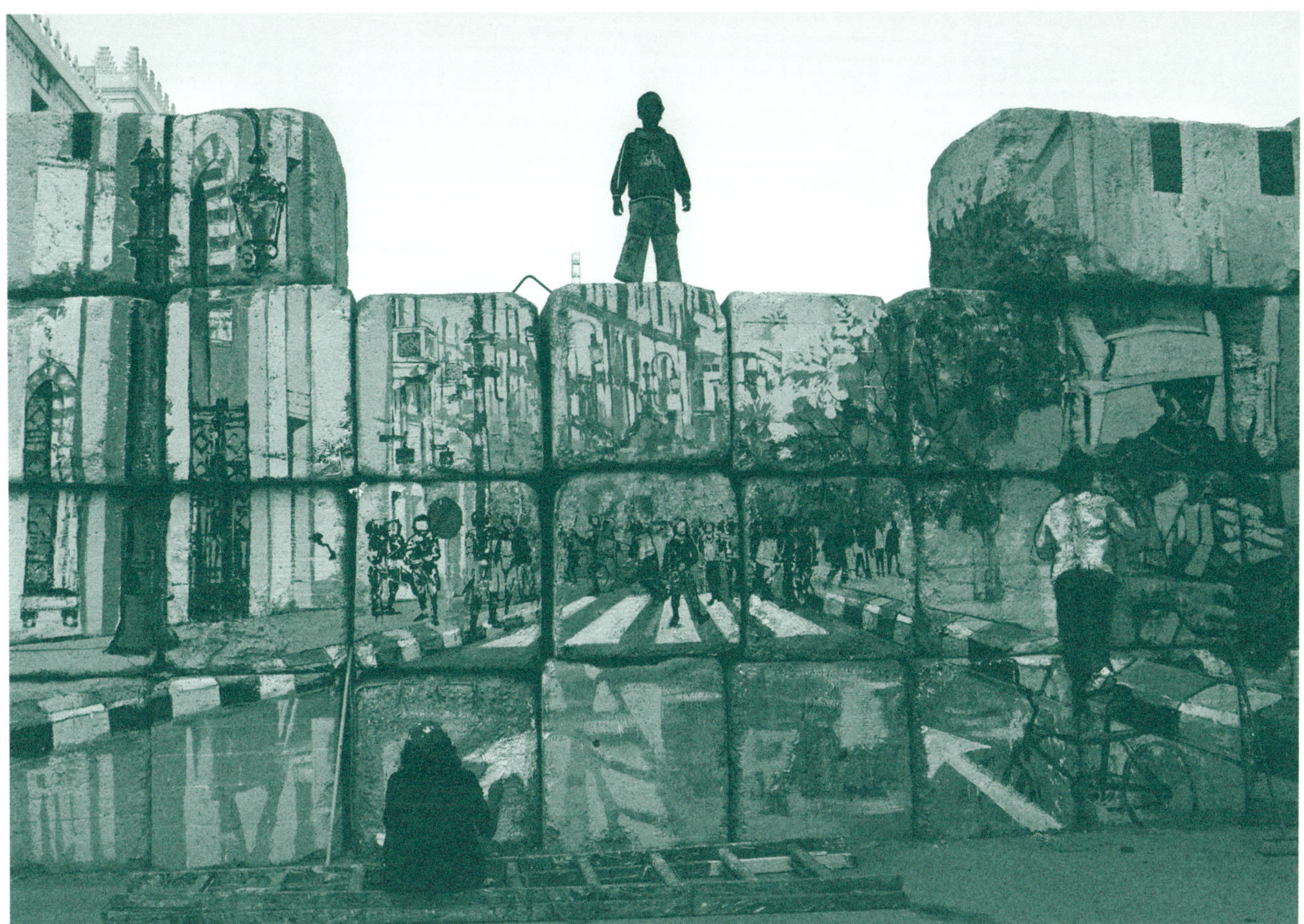

Fig. 4: After Egypt's ruling military sealed off streets around the city's Tahrir Square with walls of imposing concrete blocks, a group of artists decided to reopen the avenues on their own, in the public imagination at least. In this photo from March 13, 2012, a boy watches an Egyptian female artist and activist at work on "No Walls Street" during the graffiti that targeted concrete block walls in downtown Cairo.   Photo: AP Photo/Nasser Nasser

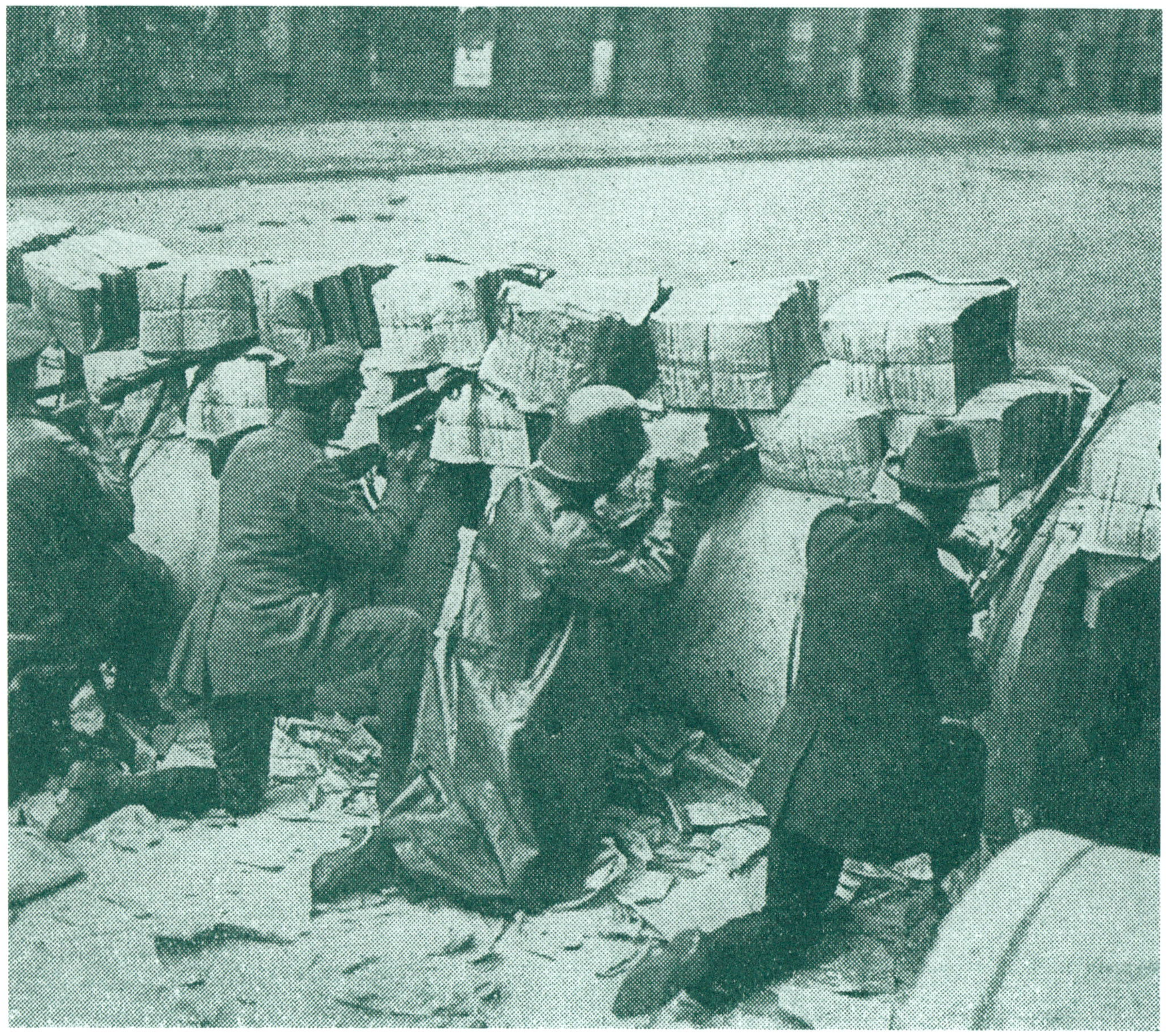

Fig. 5: During the 1919 Spartacist uprising, demonstrators occupied Berlin's newspaper district. Insurrectionists seized the prominent Mossehaus on January 5, but within six days government troops had reclaimed all occupied buildings. Photo ©DHM, Berlin 95/2405

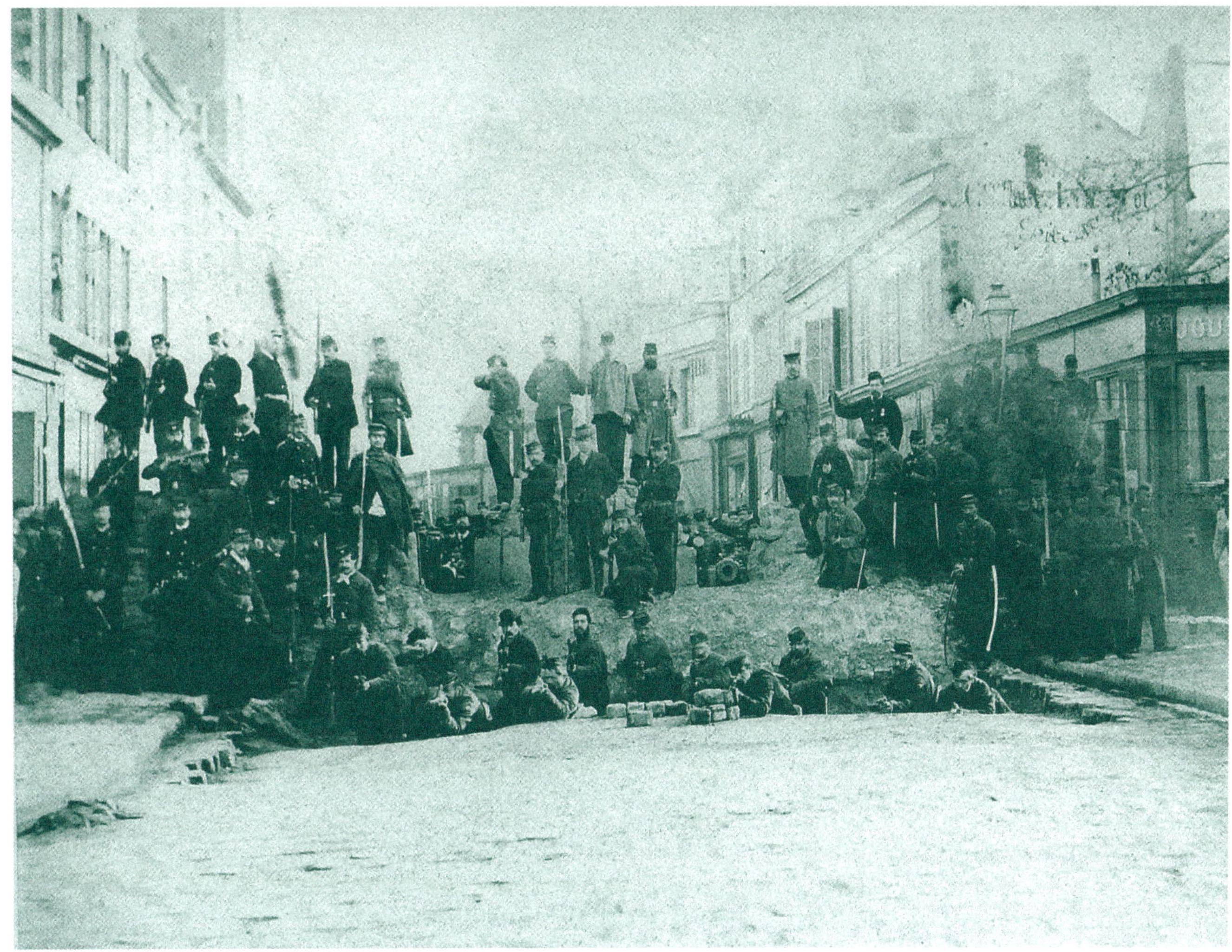

Fig. 6: Barricade on Rue des Amandiers, view from Boulevard de Ménilmontant, 1871. Photographer unknown.

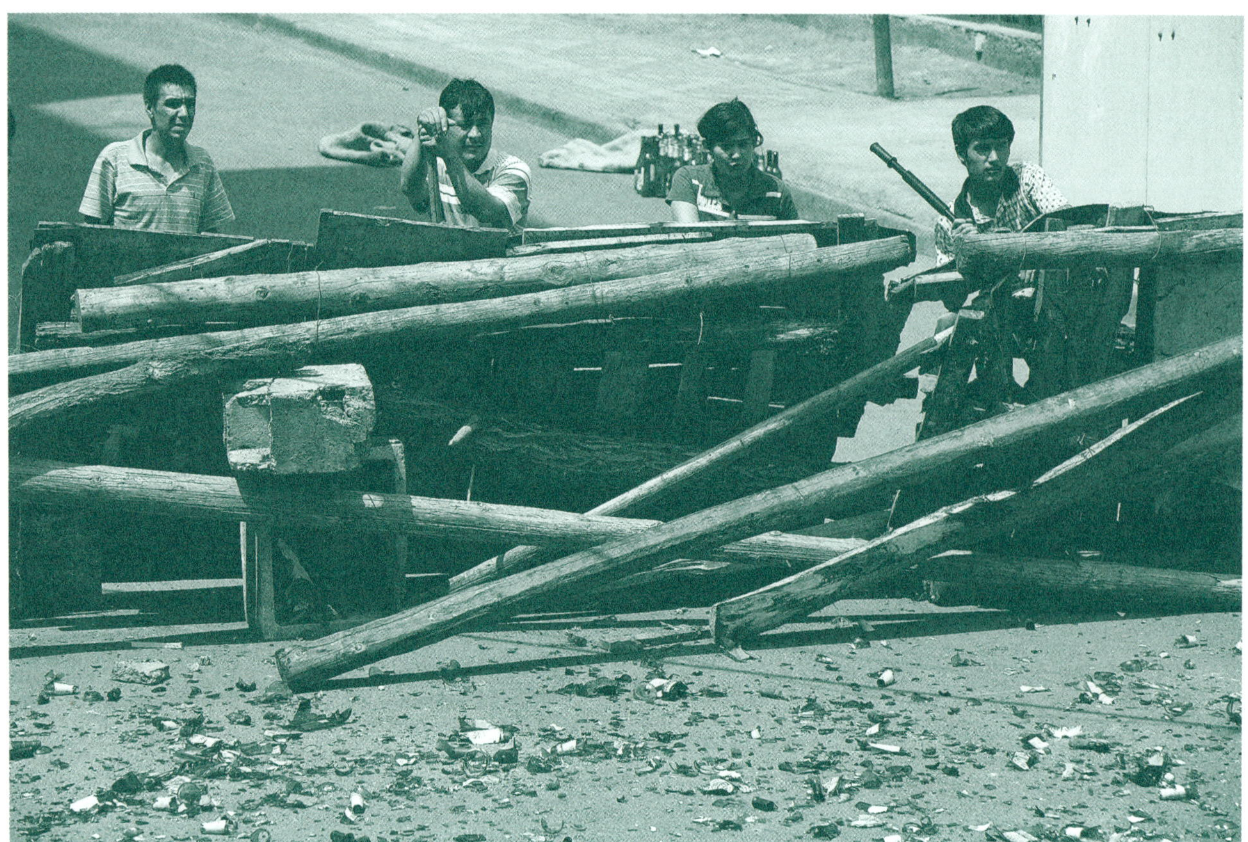

Fig. 7: Ethnic Uighurs wait with sticks behind a roadblock in their neighborhood in Urumqi in China's northwestern Xinjiang Autonomous Region, July 8, 2009. At least 156 people have been killed in riots there, with the government blaming exiled separatists for the traditionally Muslim area's worst case of unrest in years.   Photo: REUTERS/ Nir Elias

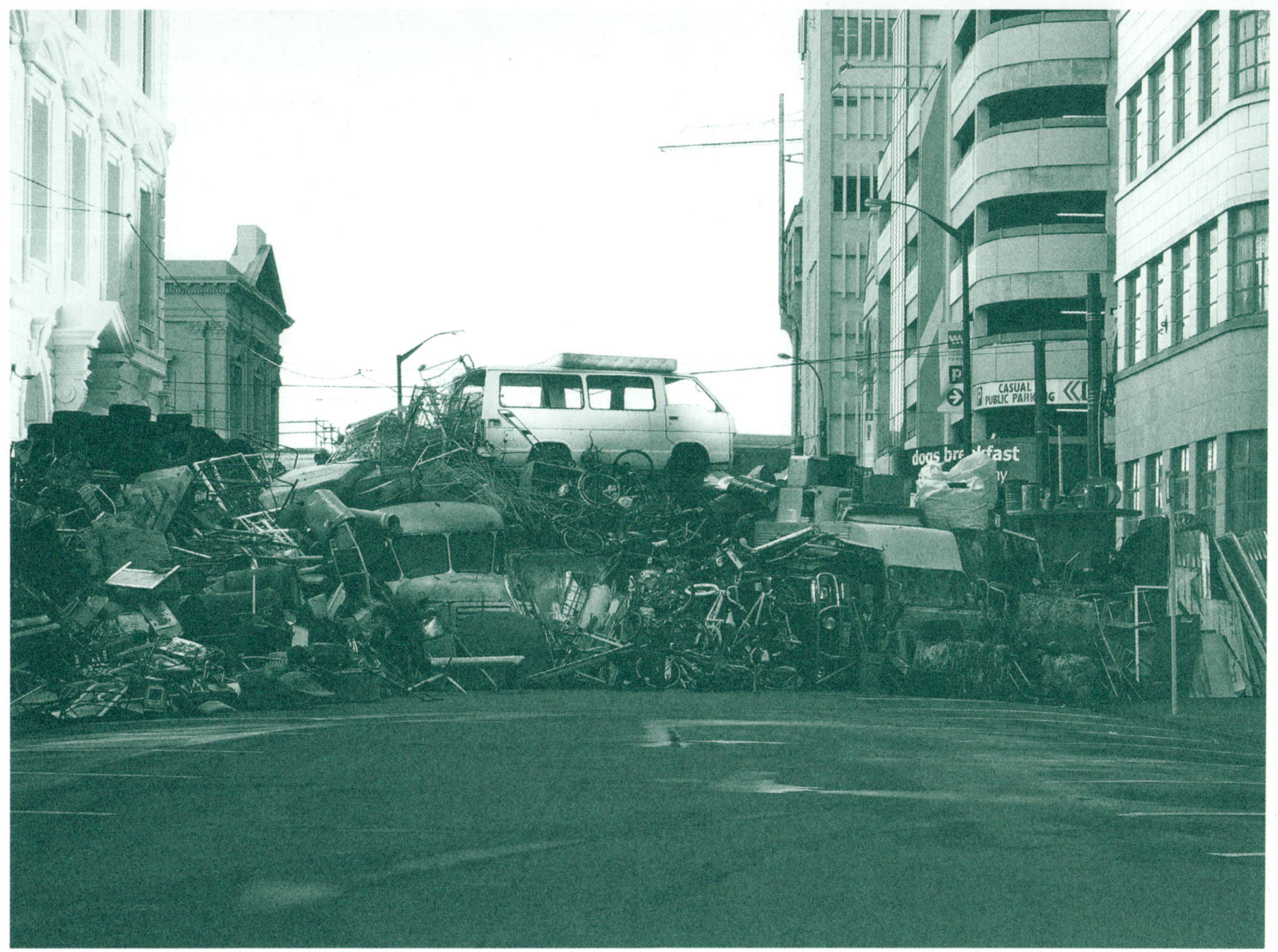

Fig. 8: Heather and Ivan Morison's *Journée des Barricades* (2008), composed of various industrial and domestic items, commissioned for One Day Sculpture by Litmus Research Initiative, Massey University, New Zealand. The artwork was installed overnight, to appear unannounced, unexpected, and unexplained for the duration of the next day. Photo: Stephen Rowe

Title should be: The awakening and consumption of Heidi Fleiss as she talks to a brioche named Austin. XXXBjarne

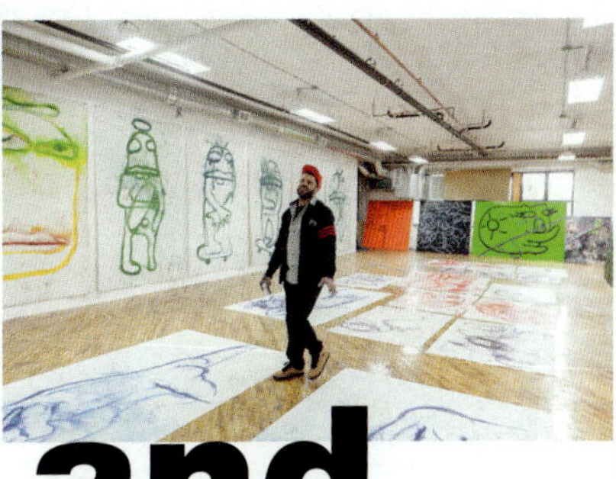

bjarnemel_jwb001.jpg

bjarnemel_jwb002.jpg

bjarnemel_jwb003.jpg

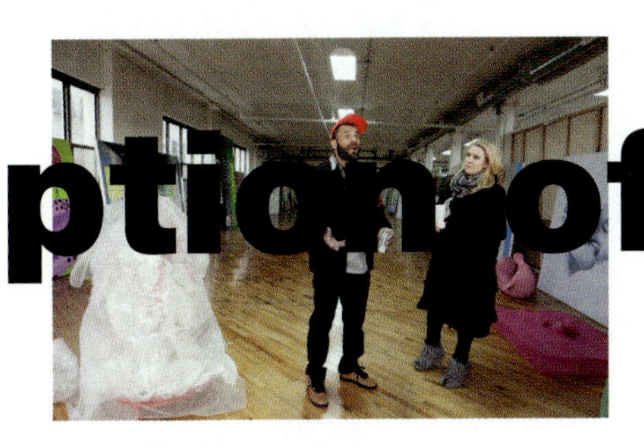

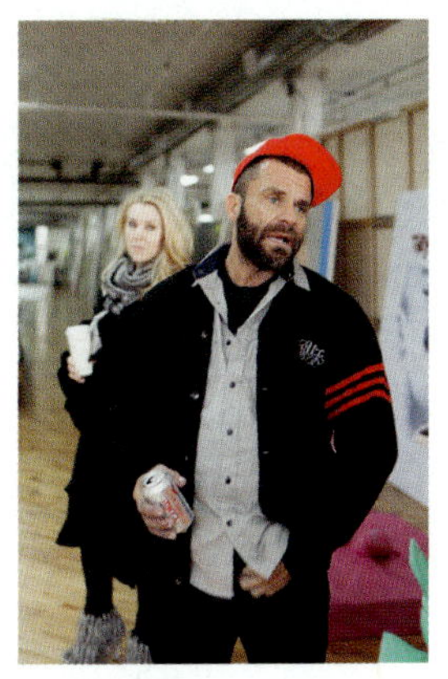

bjarnemel_jwb004.jpg

bjarnemel_jwb005.jpg

bjarnemel_jwb006.jpg

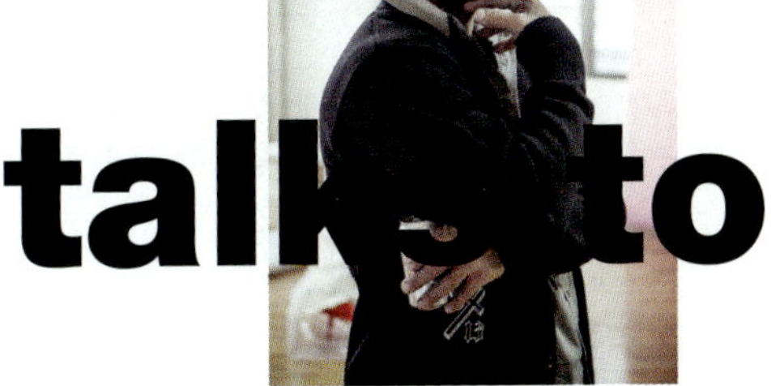

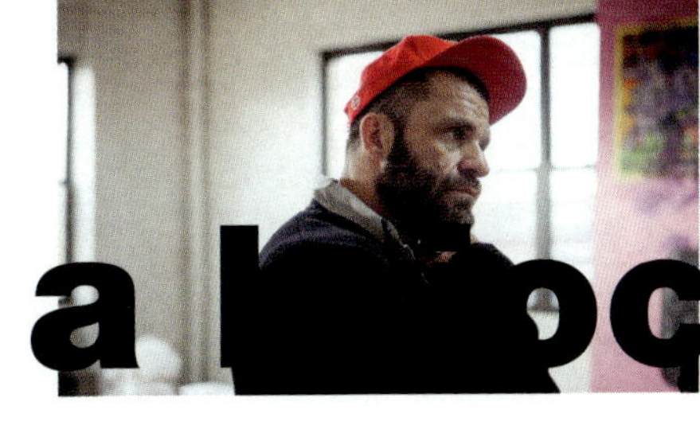

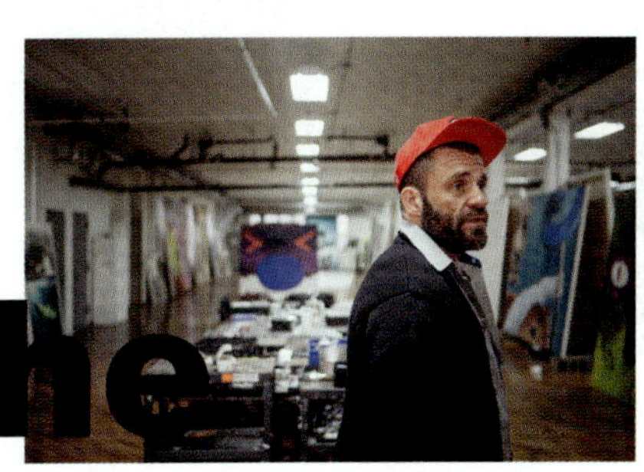

bjarnemel_jwb007.jpg

bjarnemel_jwb008.jpg

bjarnemel_jwb009.jpg

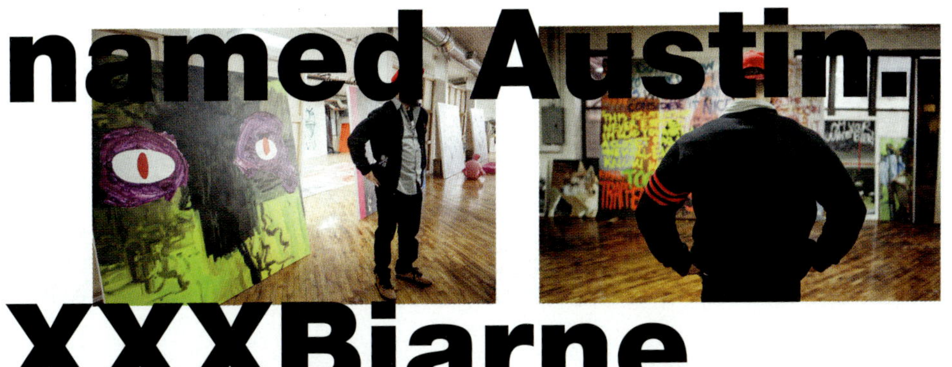

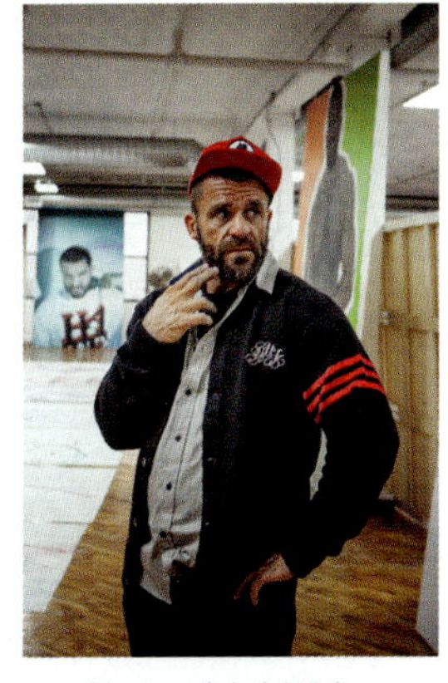

bjarnemel_jwb010.jpg

bjarnemel_jwb011.jpg

bjarnemel_jwb012.jpg

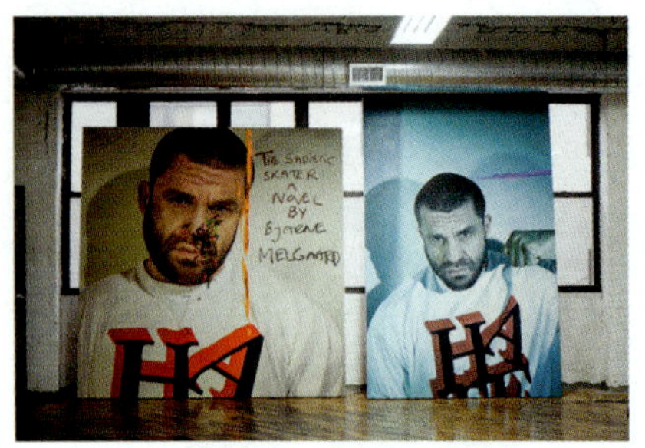

bjarnemel_jwb013.jpg

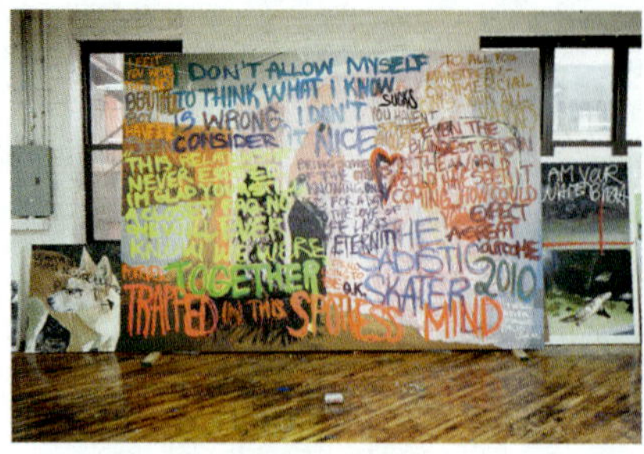

bjarnemel_jwb014.jpg

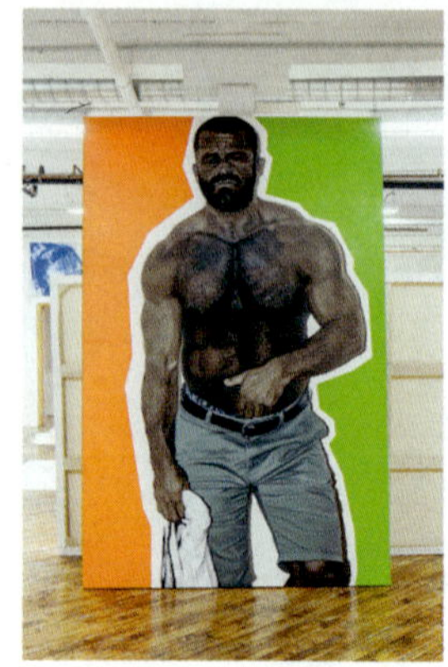

bjarnemel_jwb015.jpg

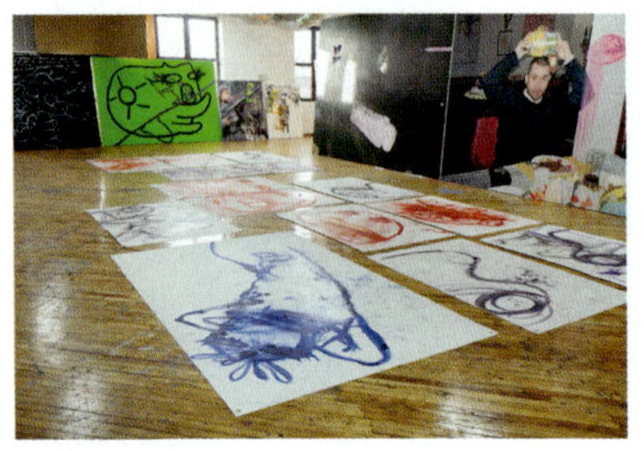

bjarnemel_jwb016.jpg

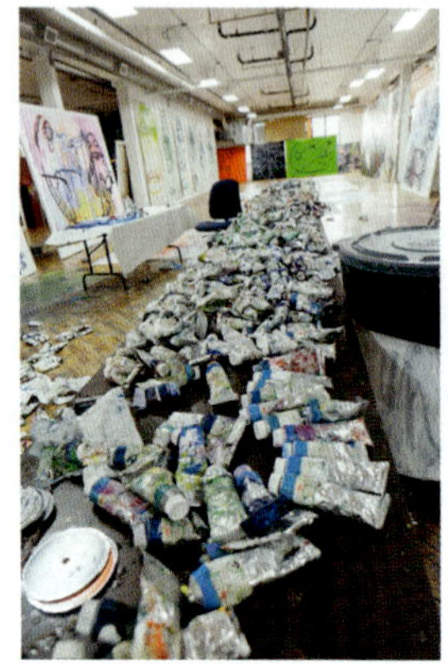

bjarnemel_jwb017.jpg

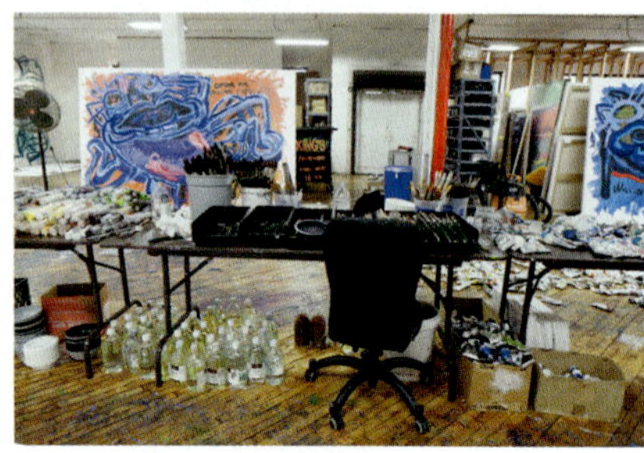

bjarnemel_jwb018.jpg

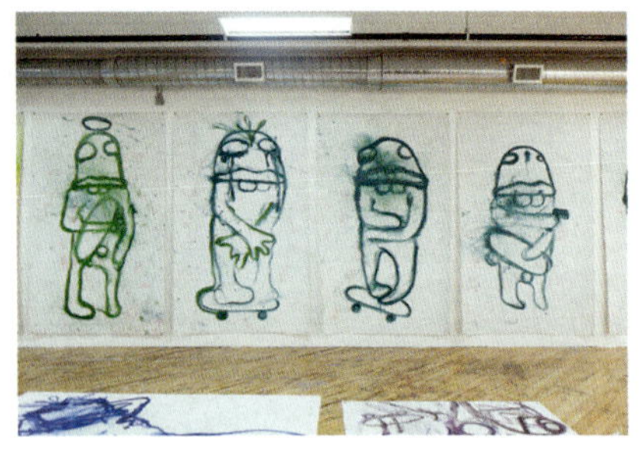

bjarnemel_jwb019.jpg

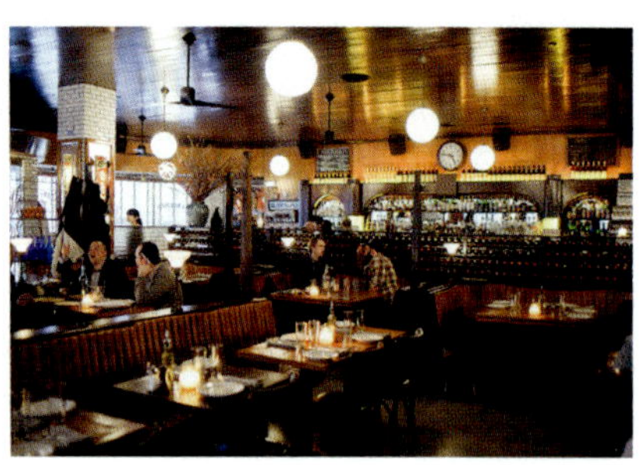

bjarnemel_jwb020.jpg

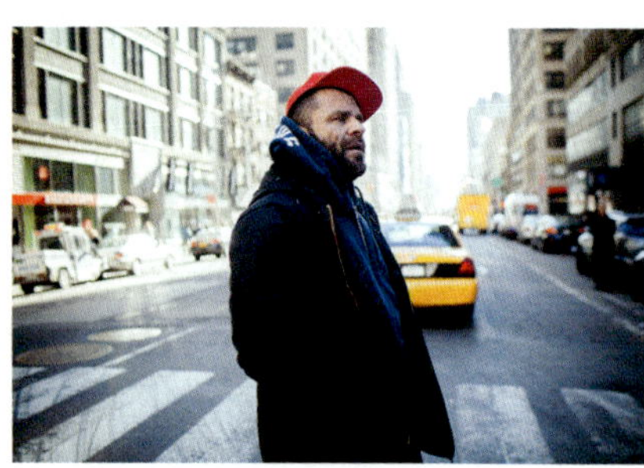

bjarnemel_jwb021.jpg

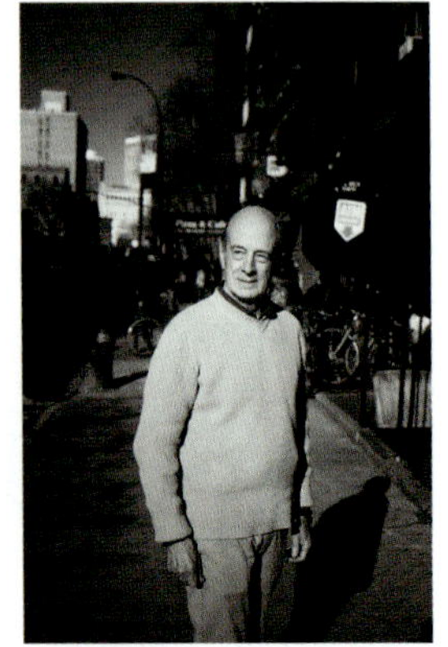

bjarnemel_jwb022.jpg

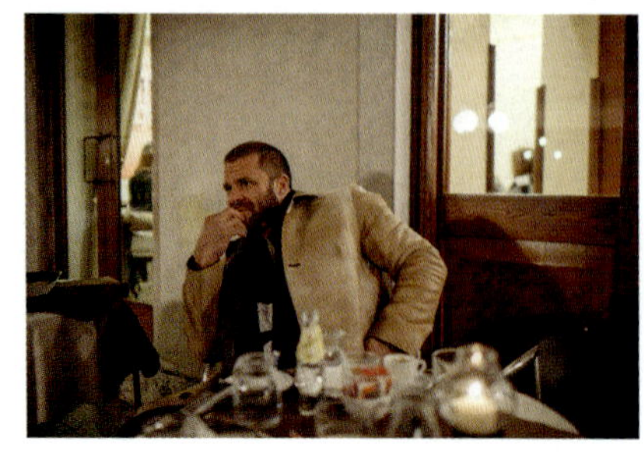

bjarnemel_jwb023.jpg

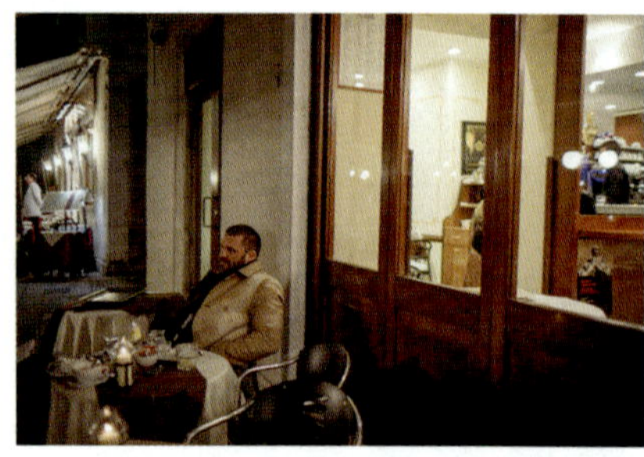

bjarnemel_jwb024.jpg

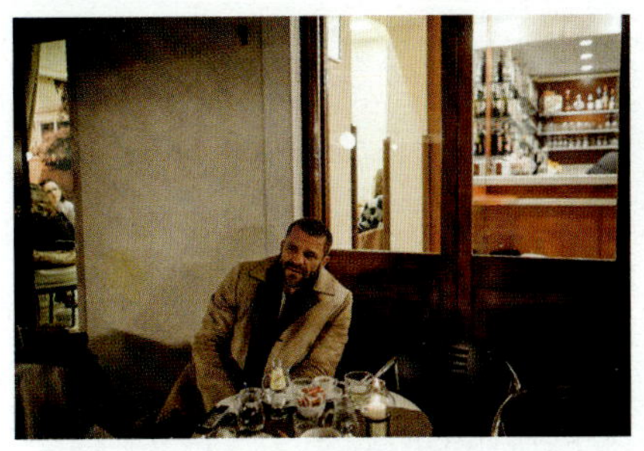

bjarnemel_jwb026.jpg

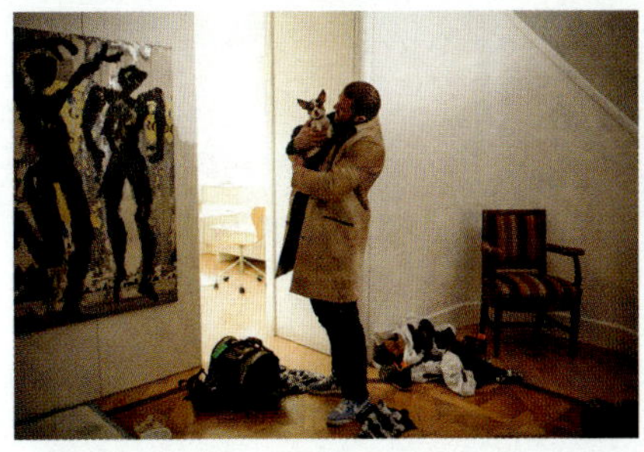

bjarnemel_jwb027.jpg

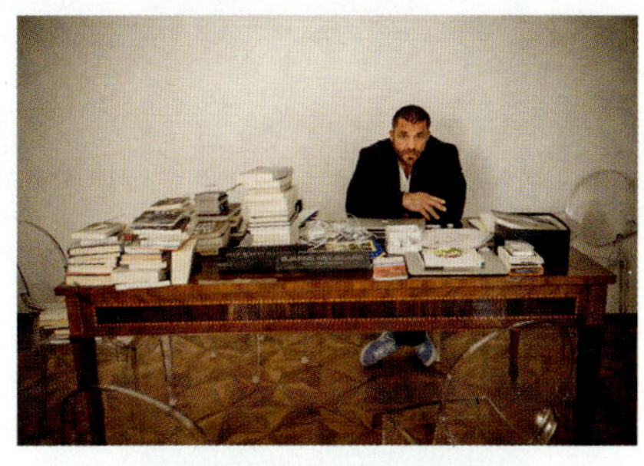

bjarnemel_jwb028.jpg

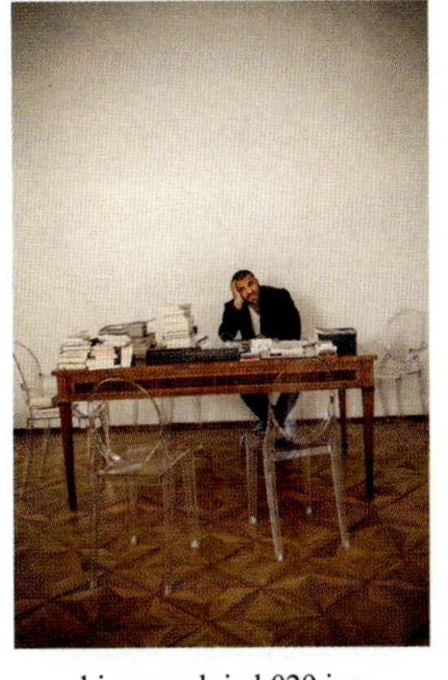

bjarnemel_jwb029.jpg

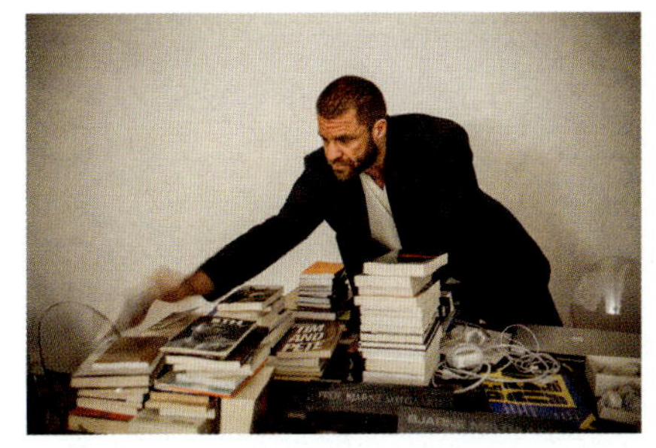

bjarnemel_jwb031.jpg

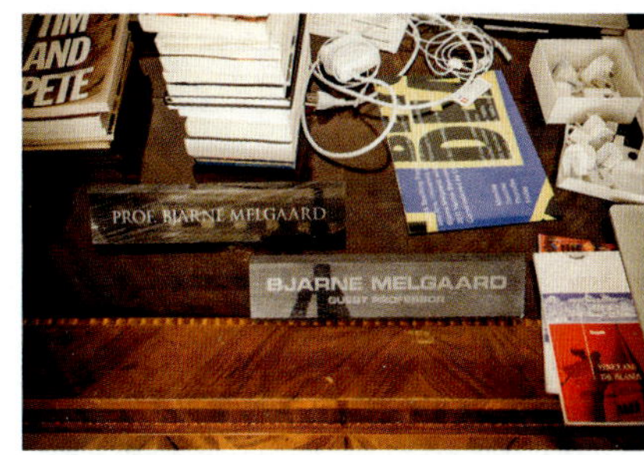

bjarnemel_jwb032.jpg

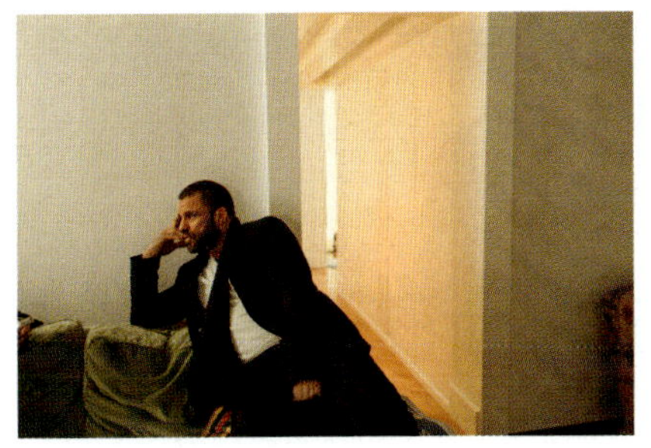

bjarnemel_jwb033.jpg

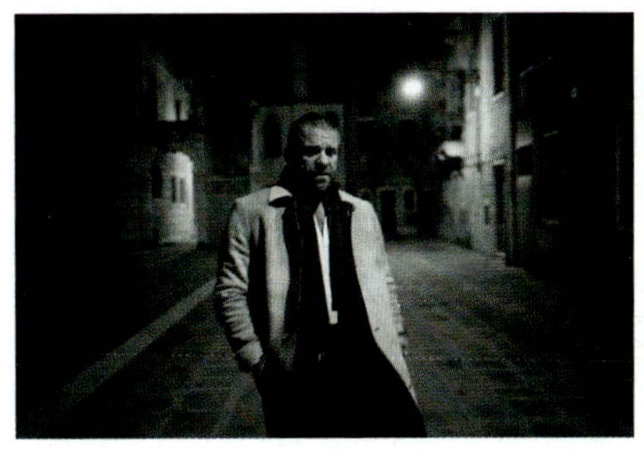

bjarnemel_jwb034.jpg

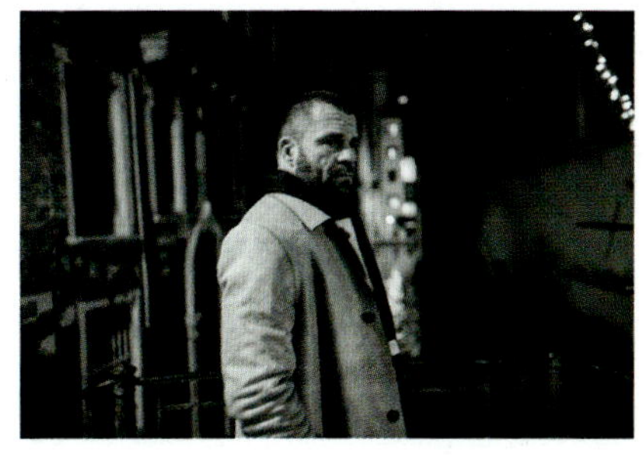

bjarnemel_jwb035.jpg

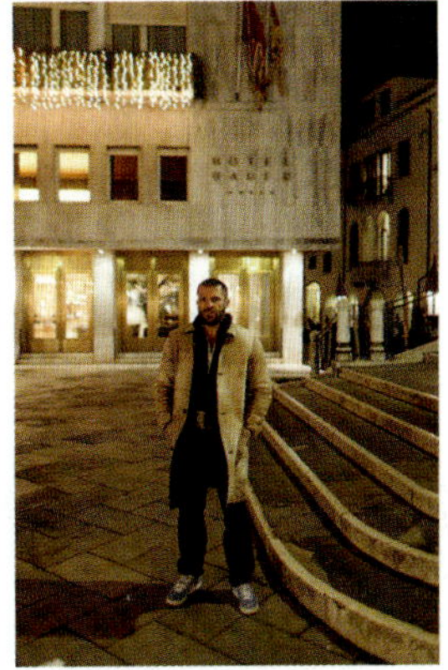

bjarnemel_jwb036.jpg

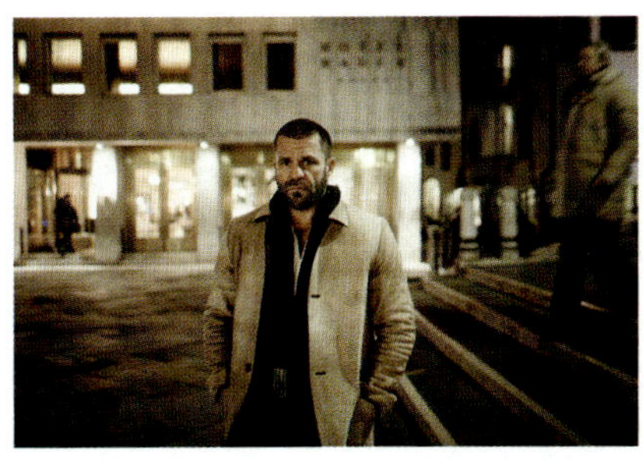

bjarnemel_jwb037.jpg

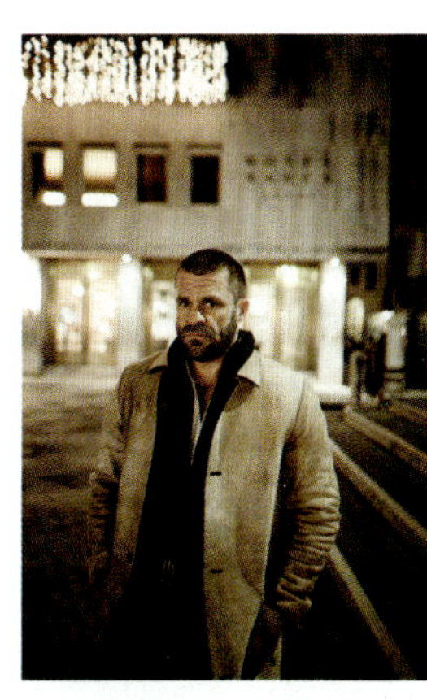

bjarnemel_jwb038.jpg

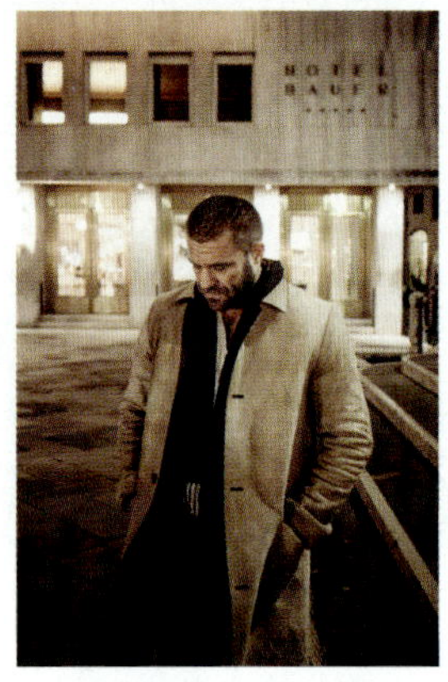

bjarnemel_jwb039.jpg

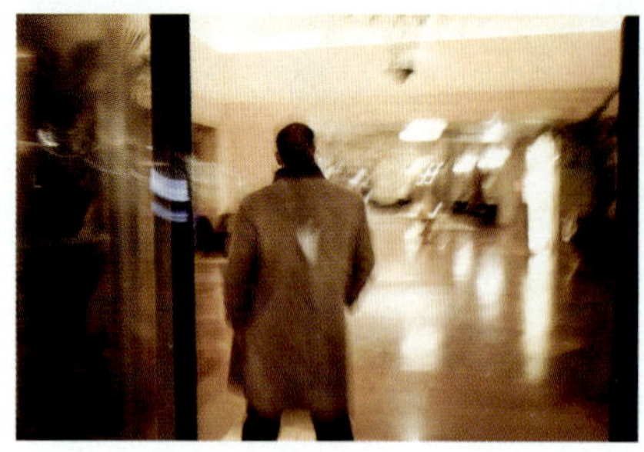

bjarnemel_jwb040.jpg

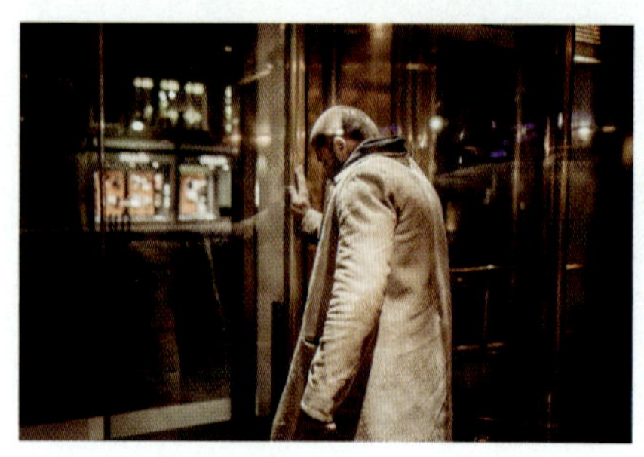

bjarnemel_jwb041.jpg

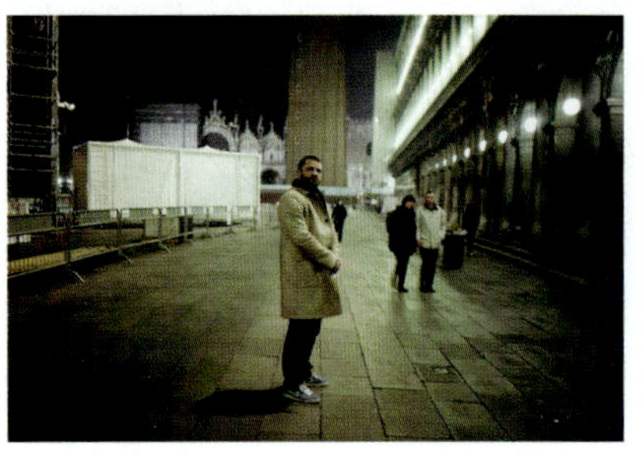

bjarnemel_jwb042.jpg

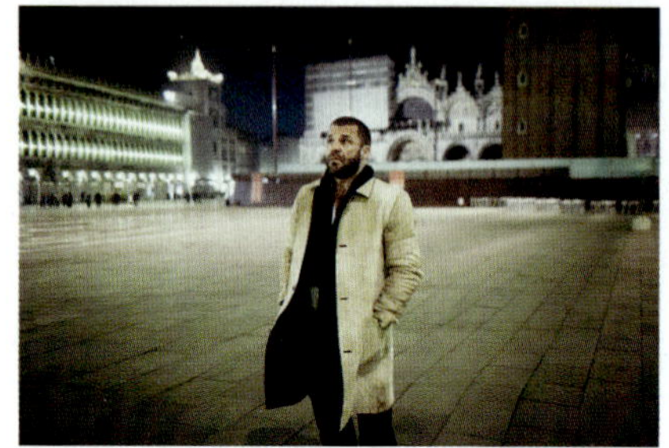

bjarnemel_jwb044.jpg

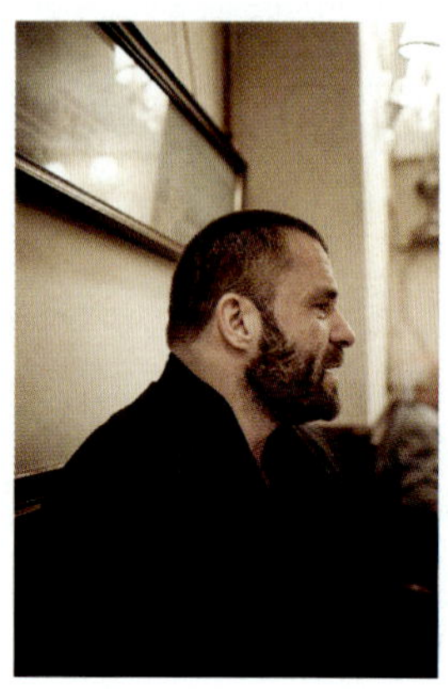

bjarnemel_jwb045.jpg

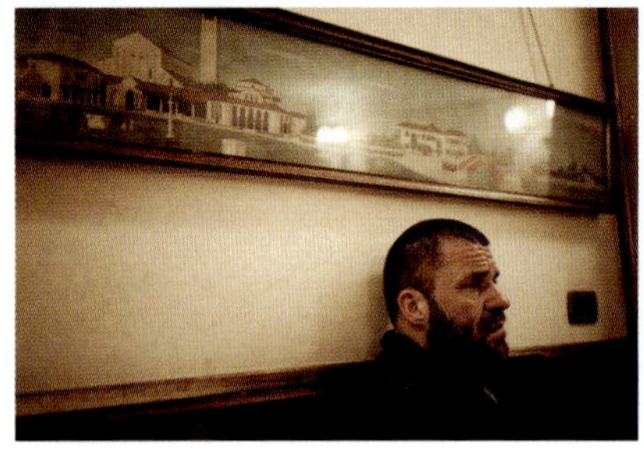

bjarnemel_jwb046.jpg

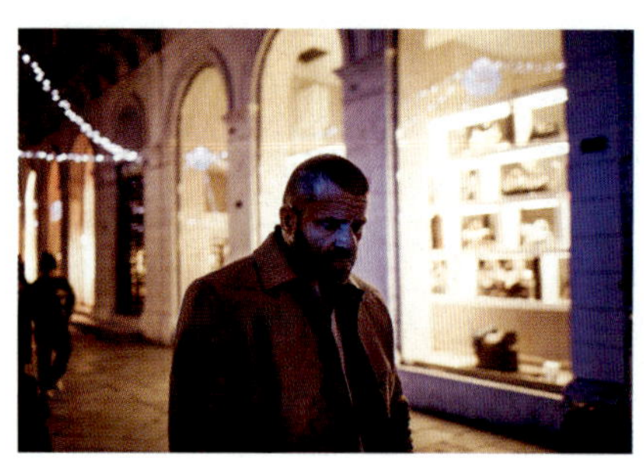

bjarnemel_jwb047.jpg

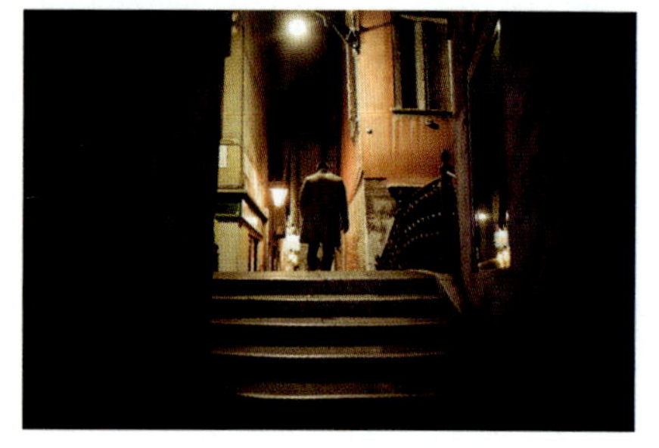

bjarnemel_jwb048.jpg

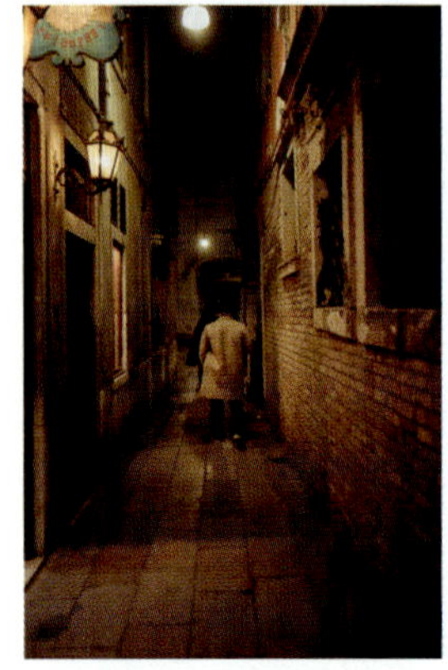

bjarnemel_jwb049.jpg

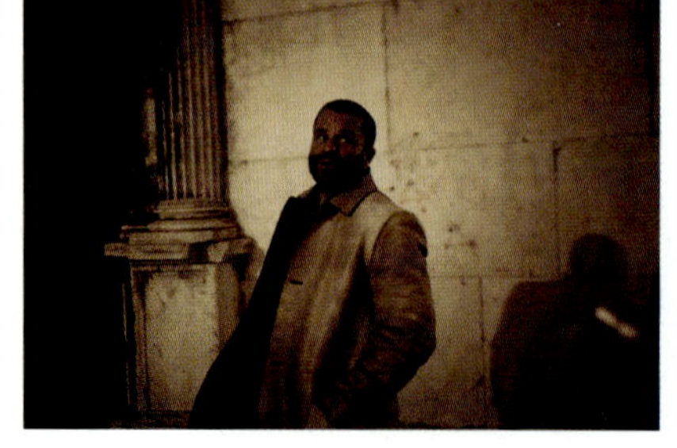

bjarnemel_jwb050.jpg

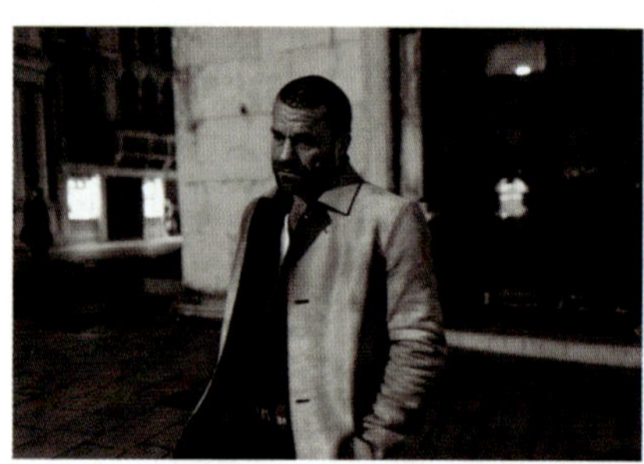

bjarnemel_jwb051.jpg

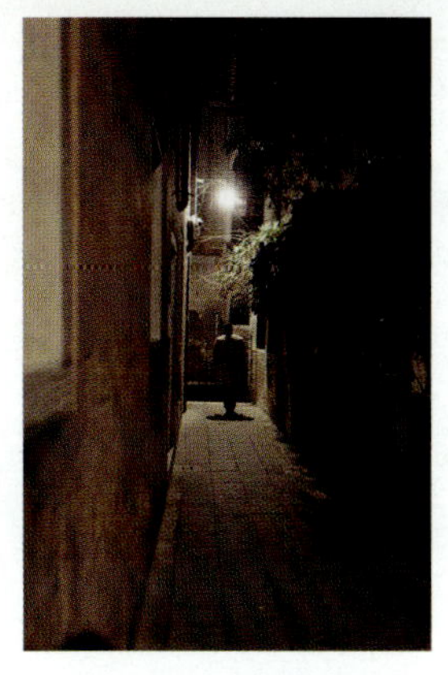

bjarnemel_jwb052.jpg

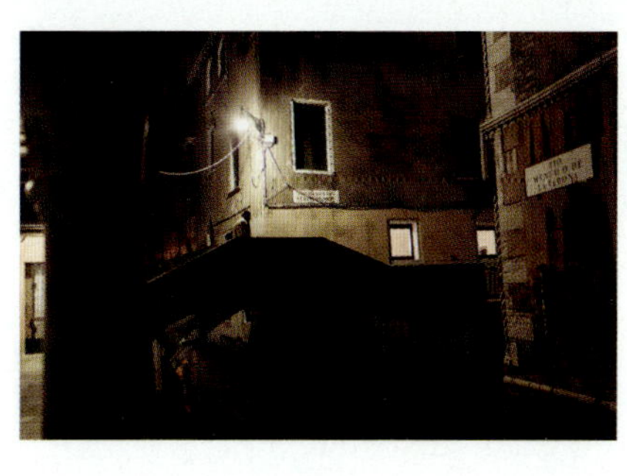

bjarnemel_jwb053.jpg

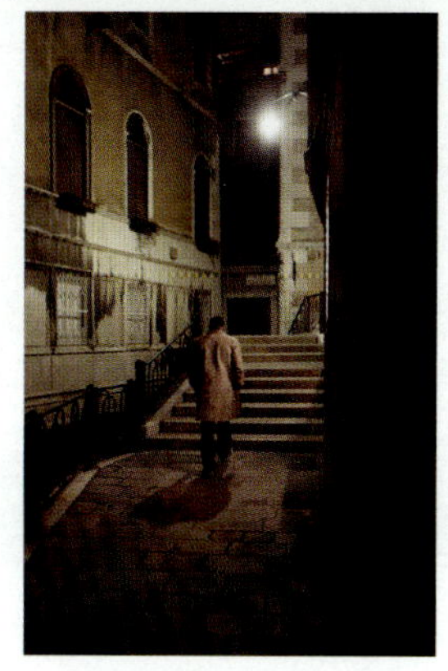

bjarnemel_jwb054.jpg

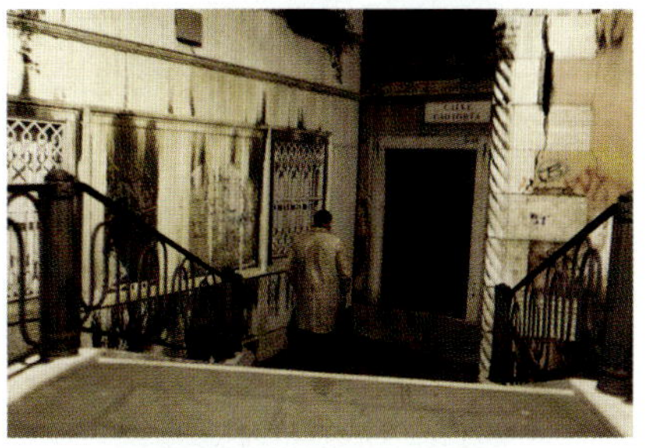

bjarnemel_jwb055.jpg

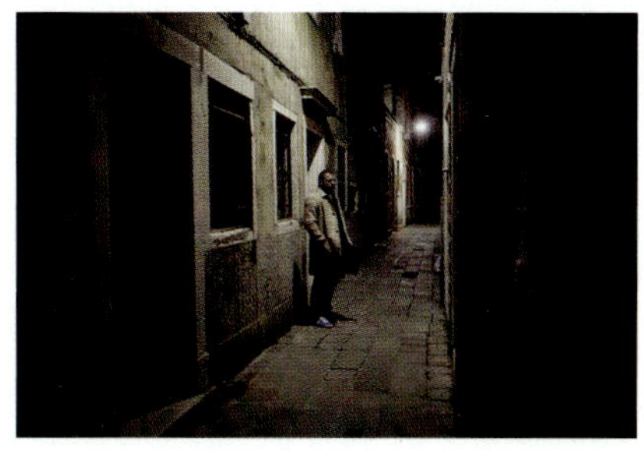

bjarnemel_jwb056.jpg

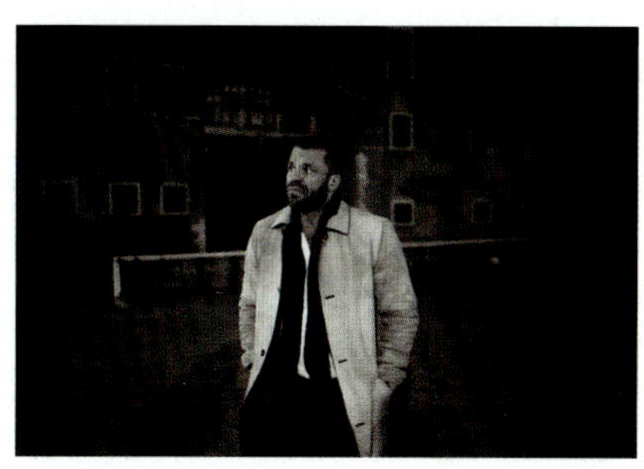

bjarnemel_jwb057.jpg

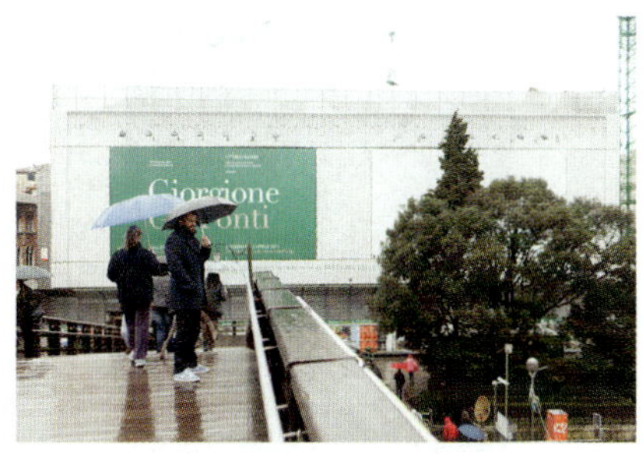

bjarnemel_jwb058.jpg

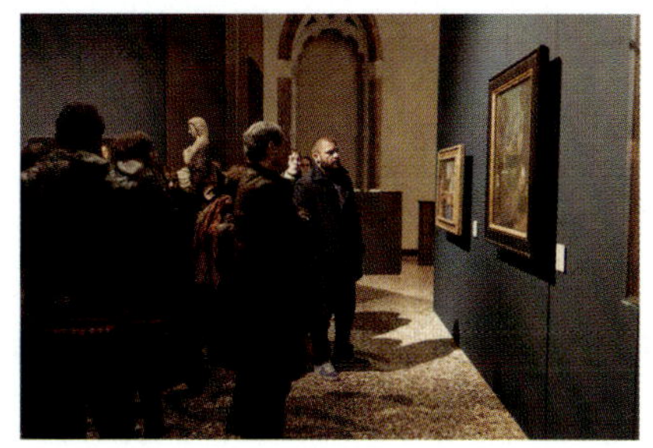

bjarnemel_jwb059.jpg

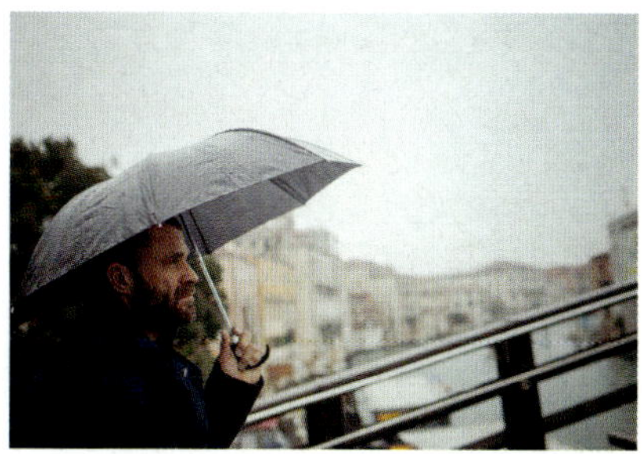

bjarnemel_jwb060.jpg

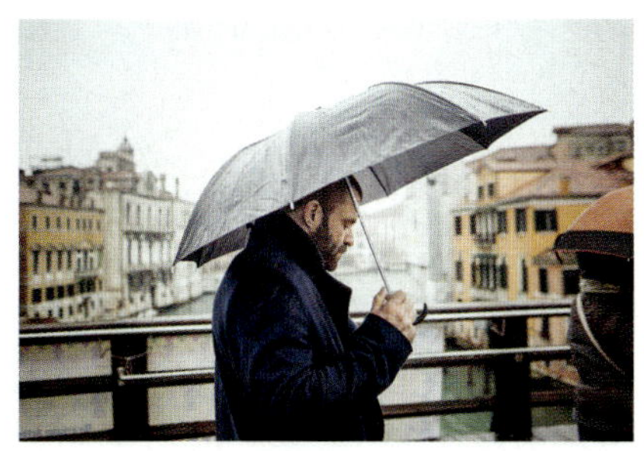

bjarnemel_jwb062.jpg

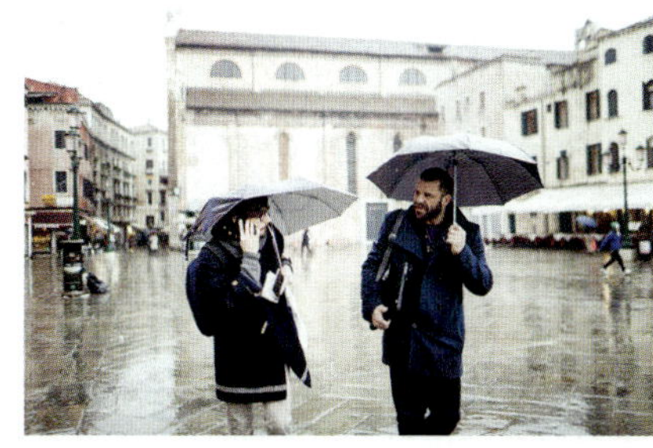

bjarnemel_jwb063.jpg

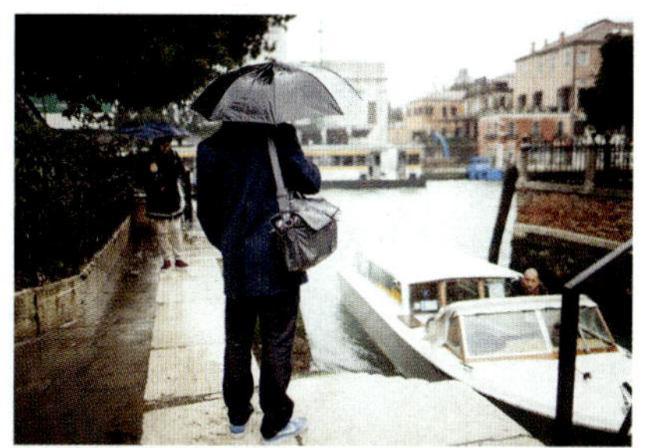

bjarnemel_jwb064.jpg

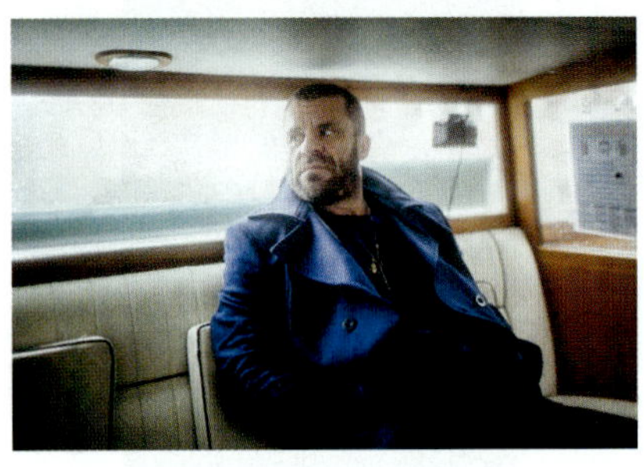

bjarnemel_jwb066.jpg

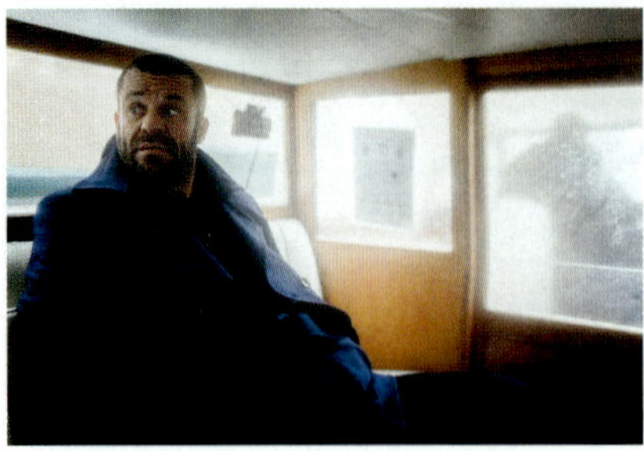

bjarnemel_jwb067.jpg

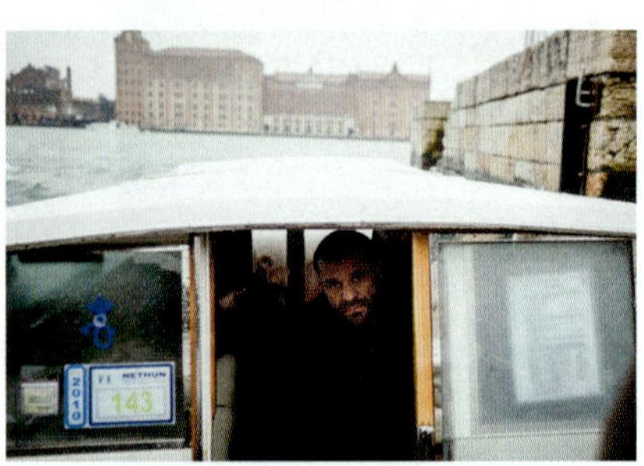

bjarnemel_jwb068.jpg

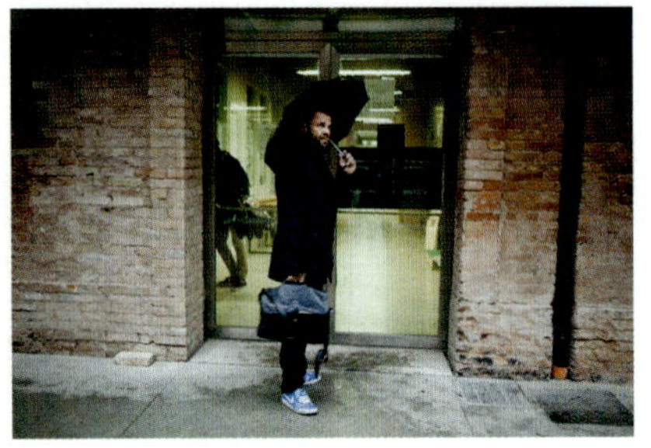

bjarnemel_jwb069.jpg

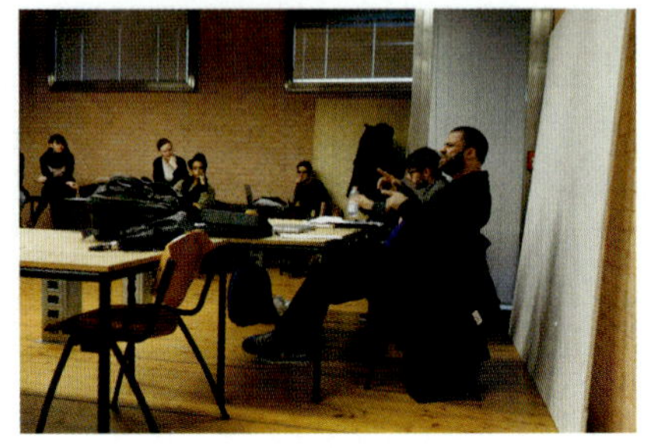

bjarnemel_jwb070.jpg

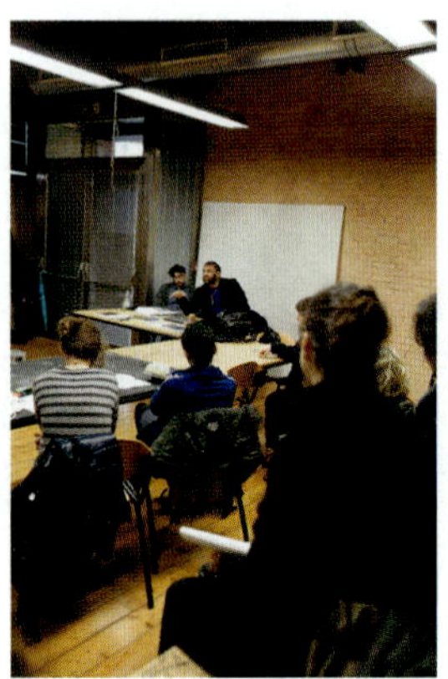

bjarnemel_jwb071.jpg

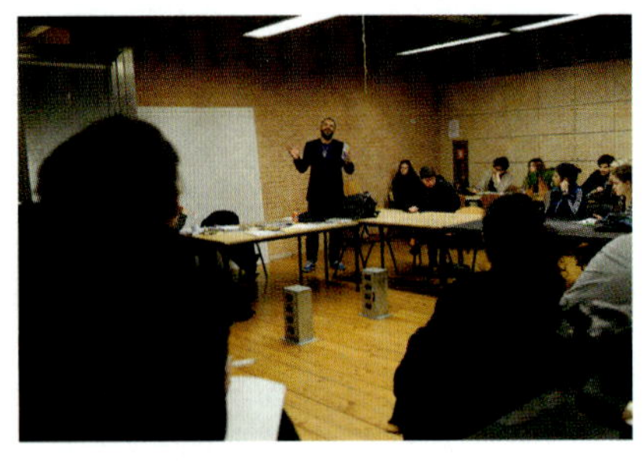

bjarnemel_jwb072.jpg

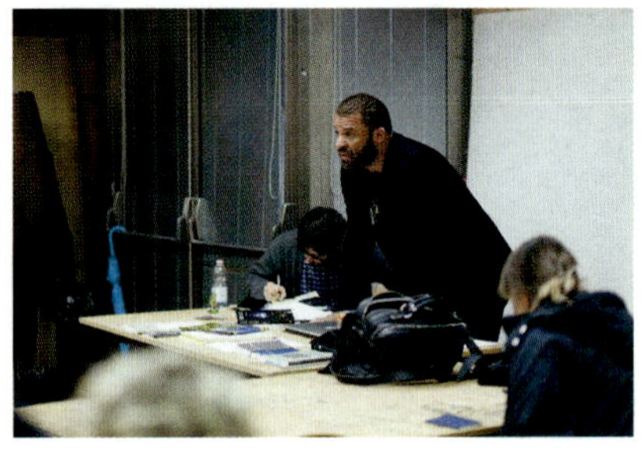

bjarnemel_jwb073.jpg

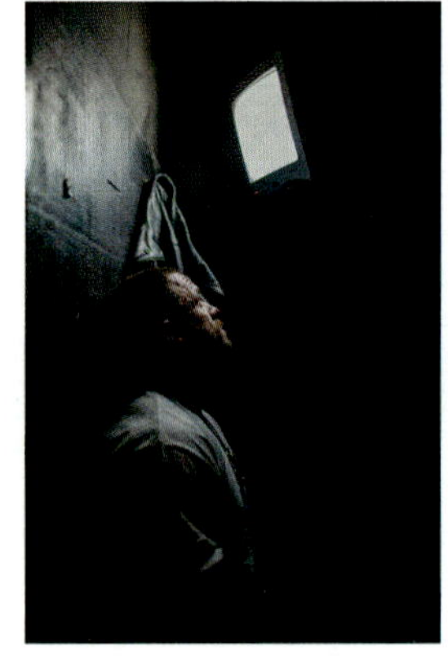

bjarnemel_jwb074.jpg

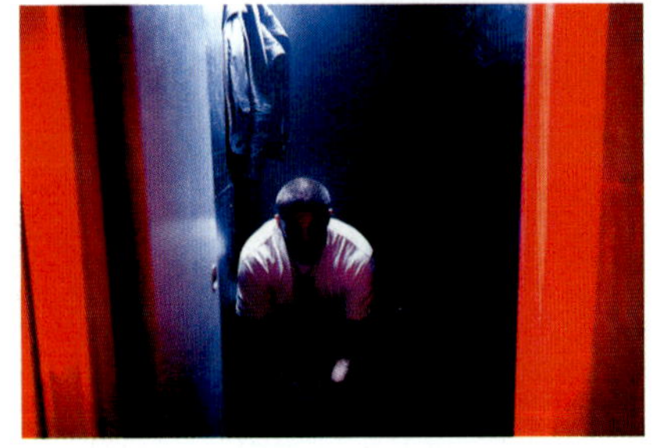

bjarnemel_jwb075.jpg

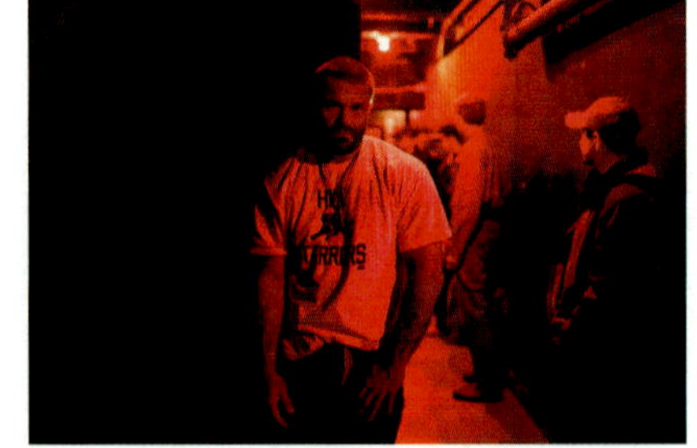

bjarnemel_jwb076.jpg

bjarnemel_jwb077.jpg

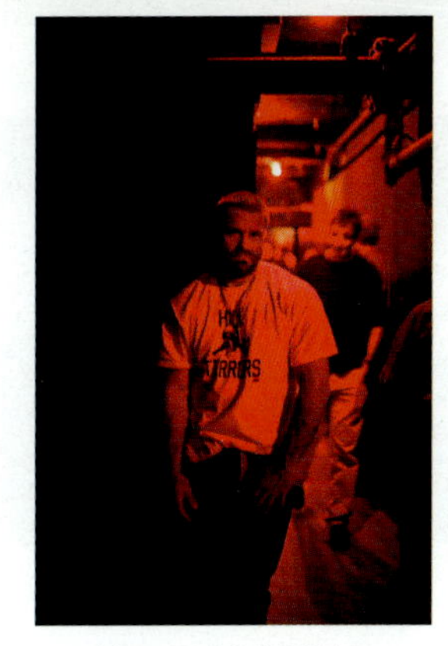

bjarnemel_jwb078.jpg

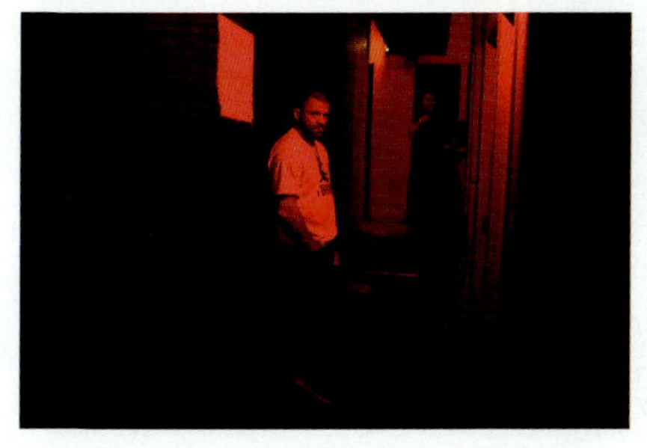

bjarnemel_jwb080.jpg

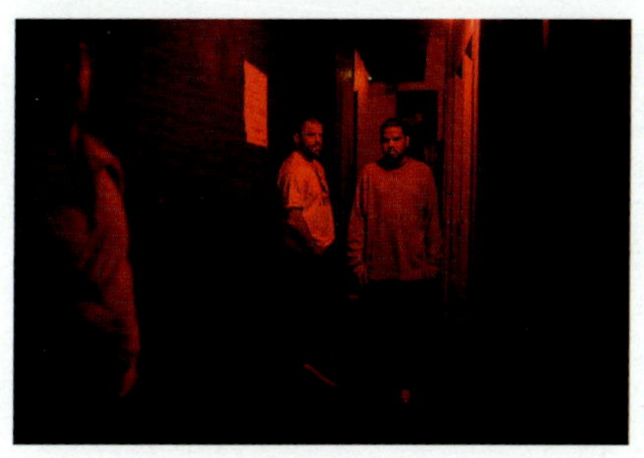

bjarnemel_jwb081.jpg

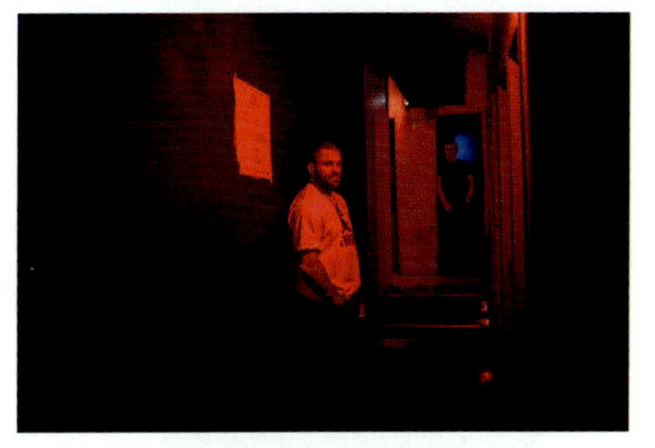

bjarnemel_jwb082.jpg

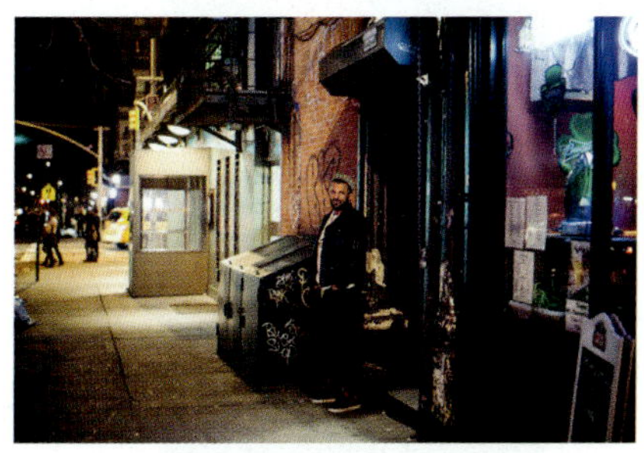

bjarnemel_jwb084.jpg

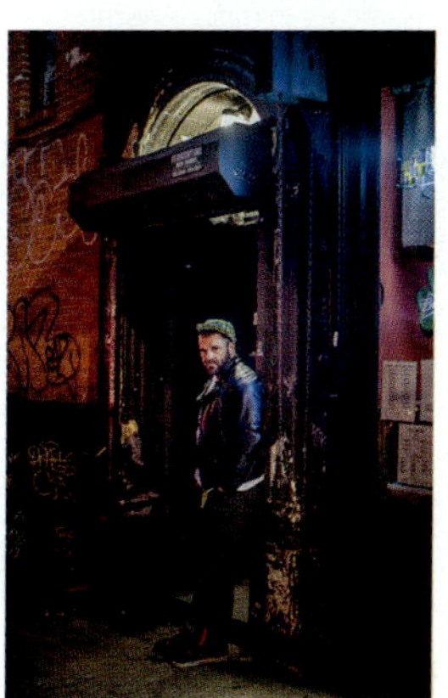

bjarnemel_jwb085.jpg

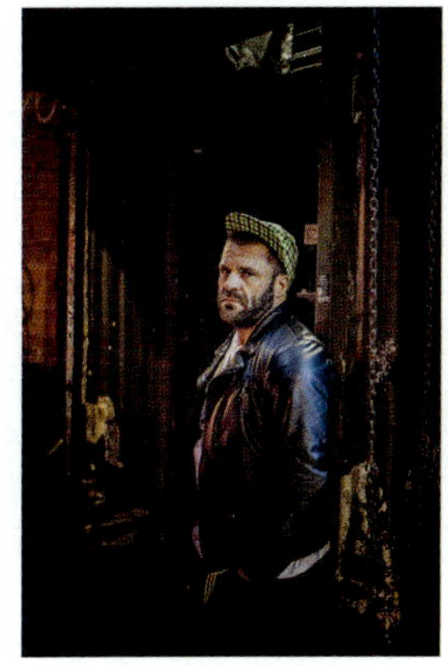

bjarnemel_jwb086.jpg

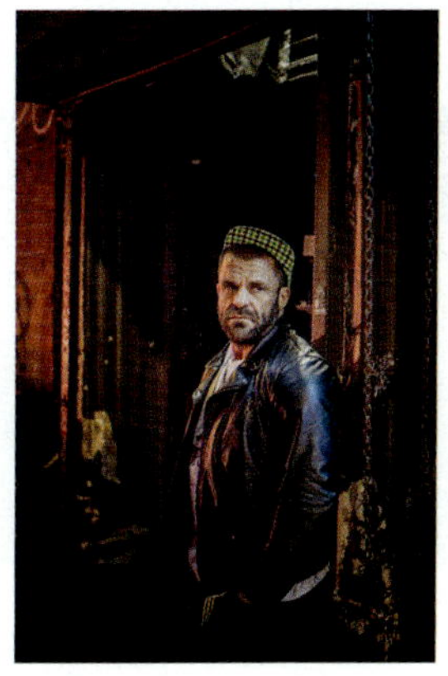

bjarnemel_jwb088.jpg

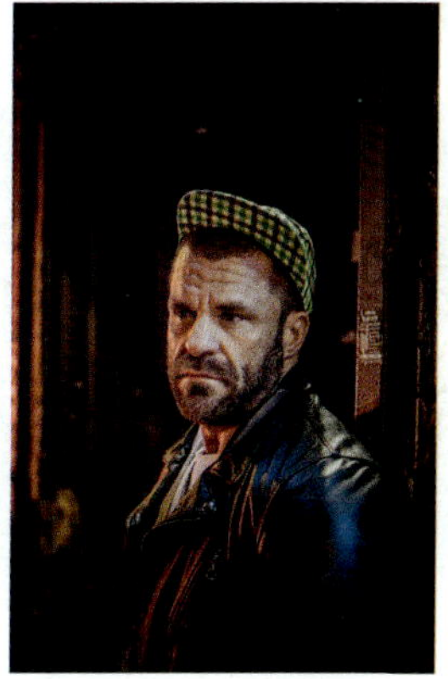

bjarnemel_jwb090.jpg

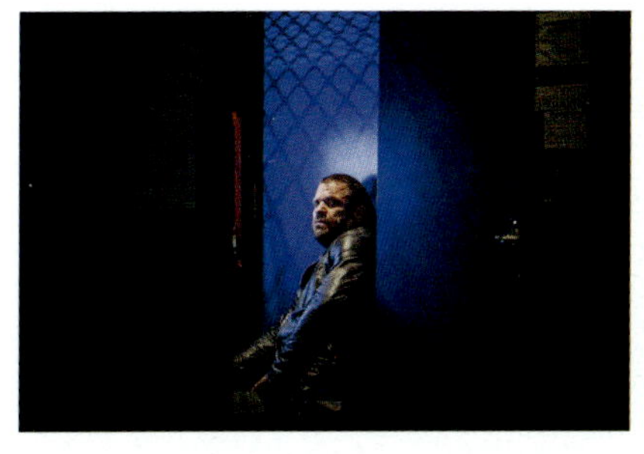

bjarnemel_jwb091.jpg

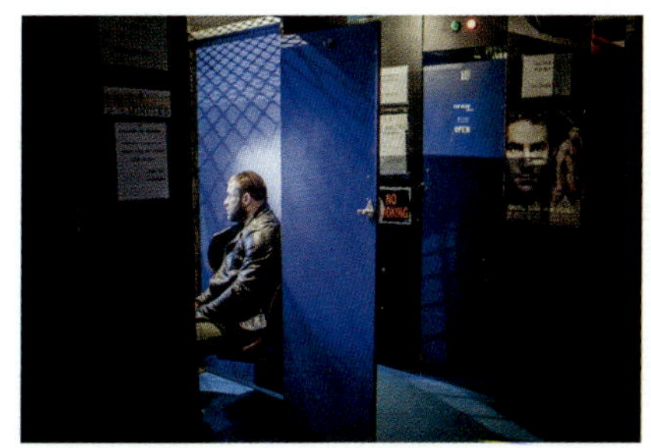

bjarnemel_jwb092.jpg

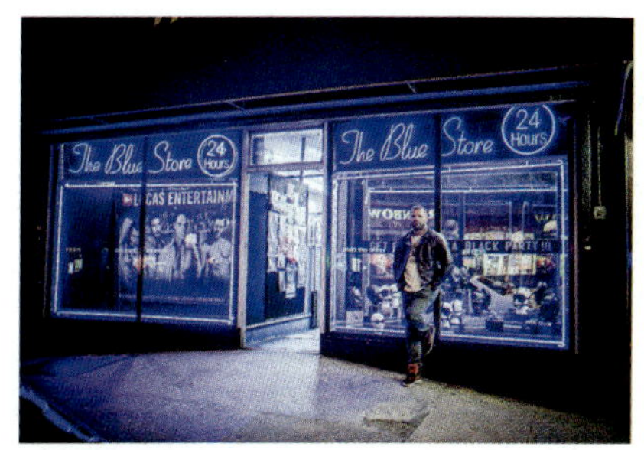

bjarnemel_jwb093.jpg

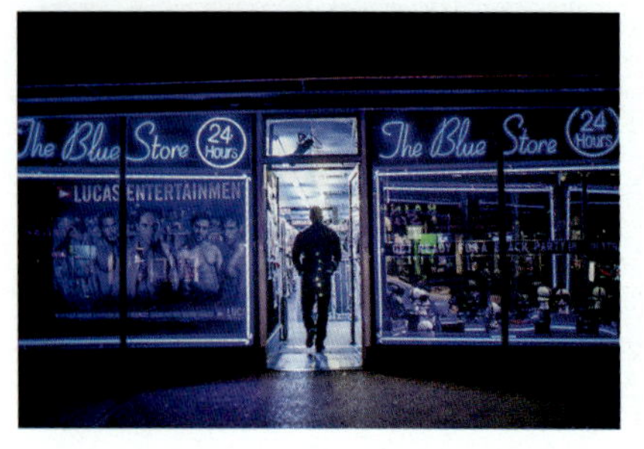

bjarnemel_jwb095.jpg

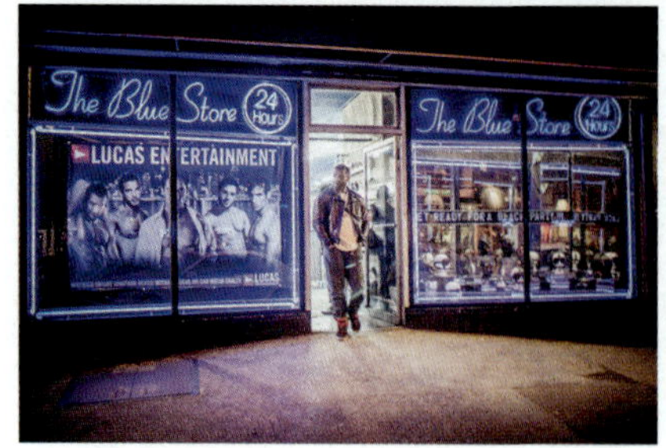

bjarnemel_jwb096.jpg

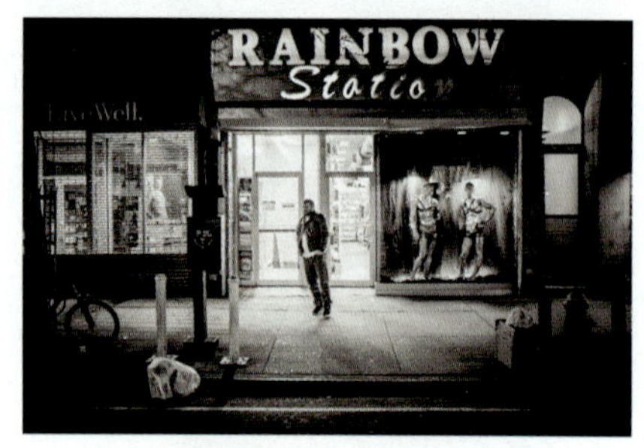

bjarnemel_jwb097.jpg

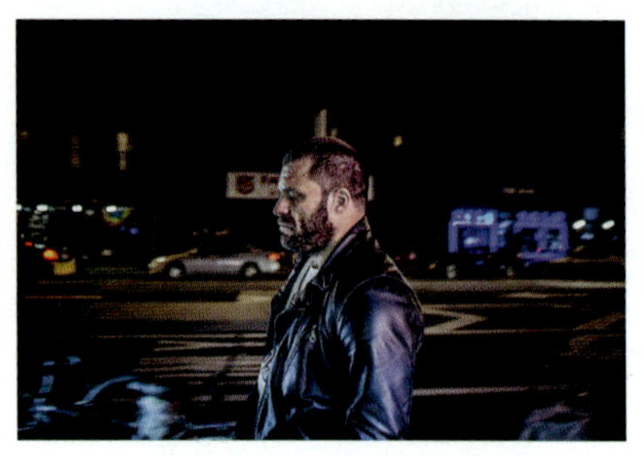

bjarnemel_jwb098.jpg

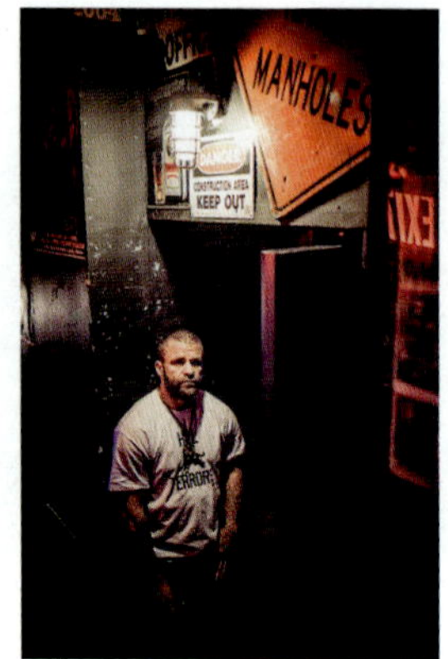

bjarnemel_jwb099.jpg

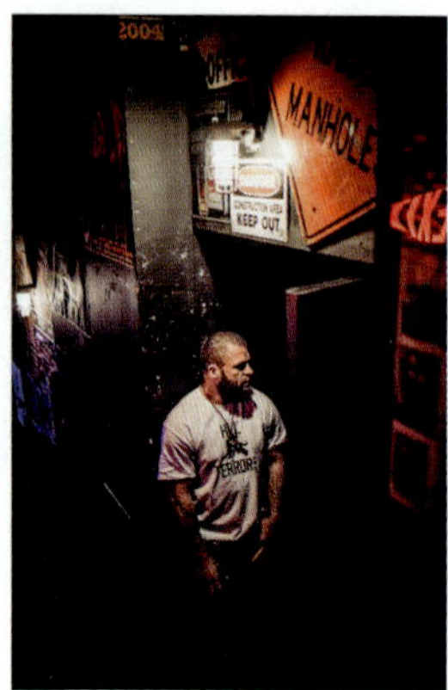

bjarnemel_jwb100.jpg

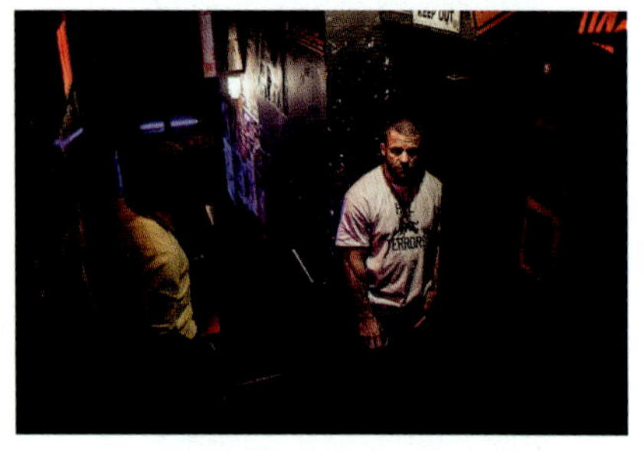

bjarnemel_jwb101.jpg

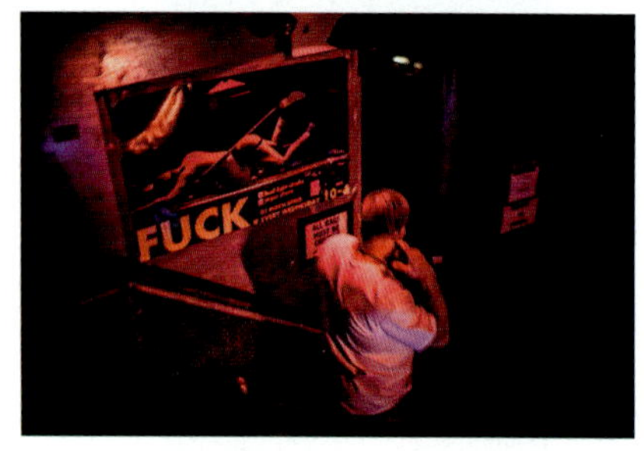

bjarnemel_jwb103.jpg

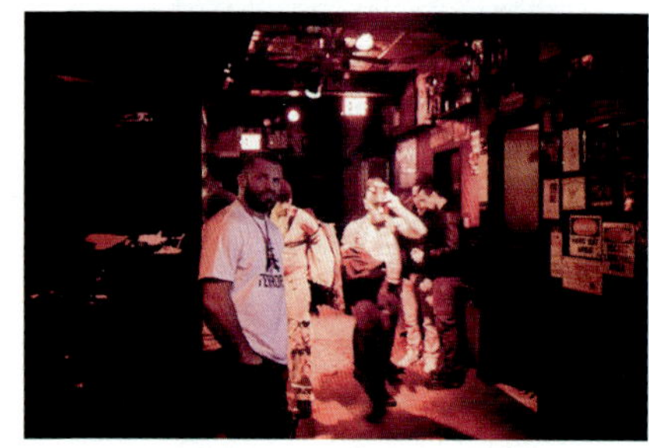

bjarnemel_jwb104.jpg

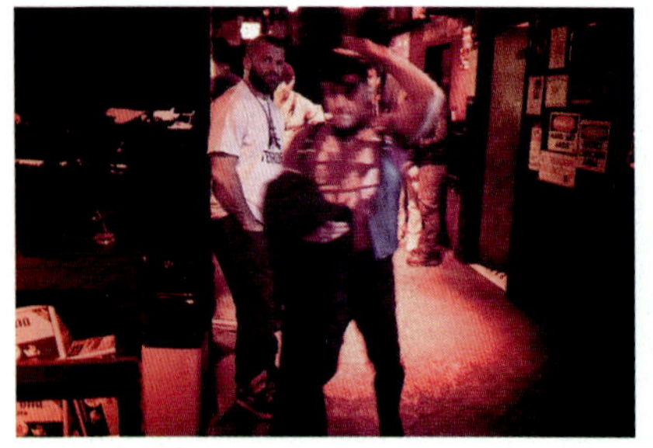

bjarnemel_jwb105.jpg

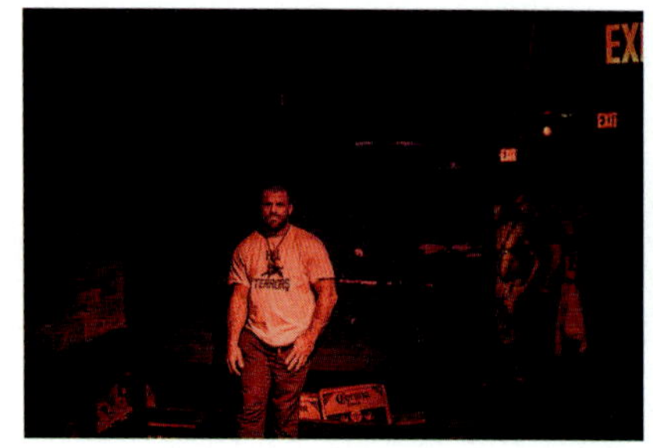

bjarnemel_jwb106.jpg

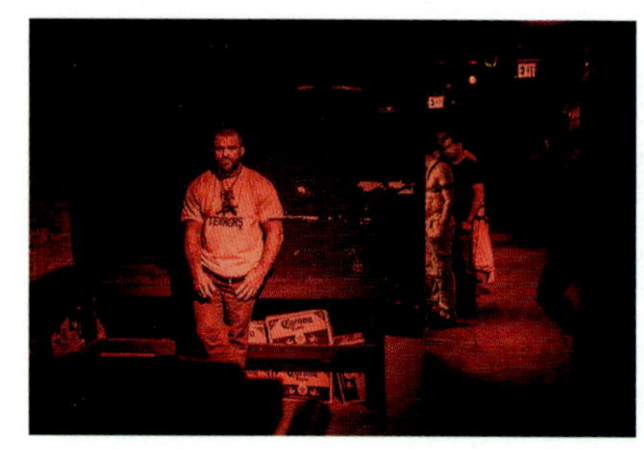

bjarnemel_jwb107.jpg

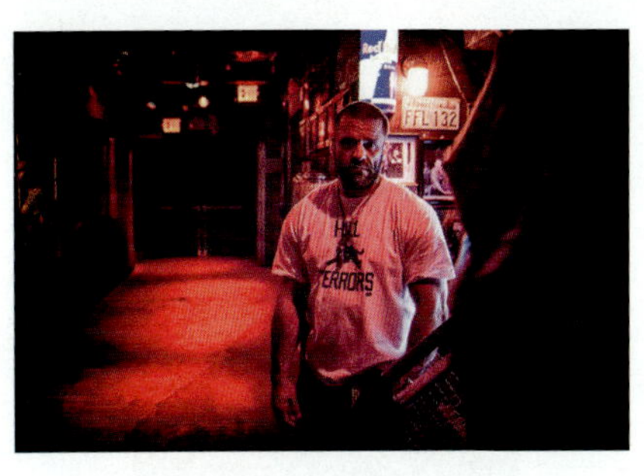

bjarnemel_jwb108.jpg

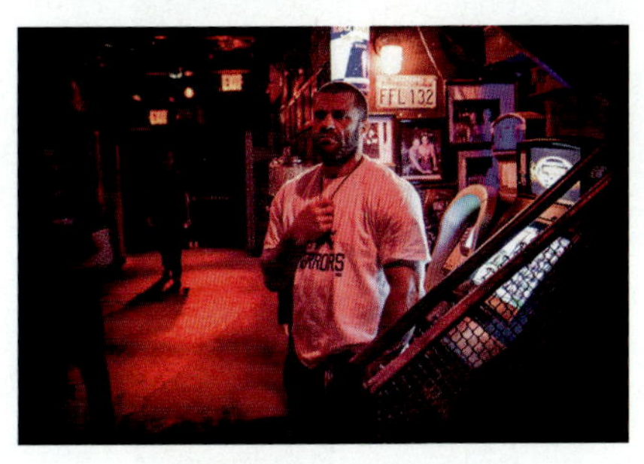

bjarnemel_jwb109.jpg

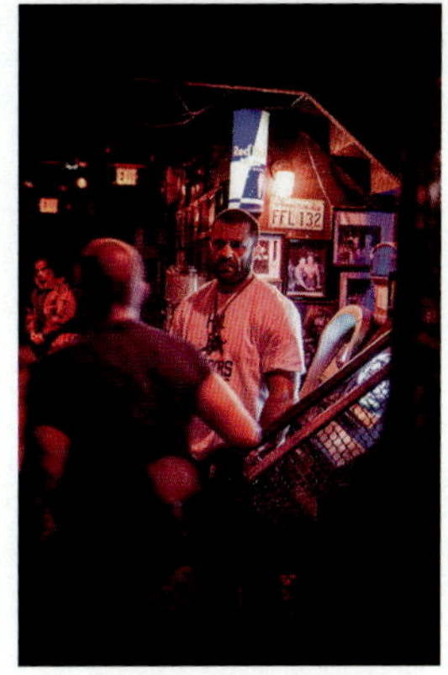

bjarnemel_jwb110.jpg

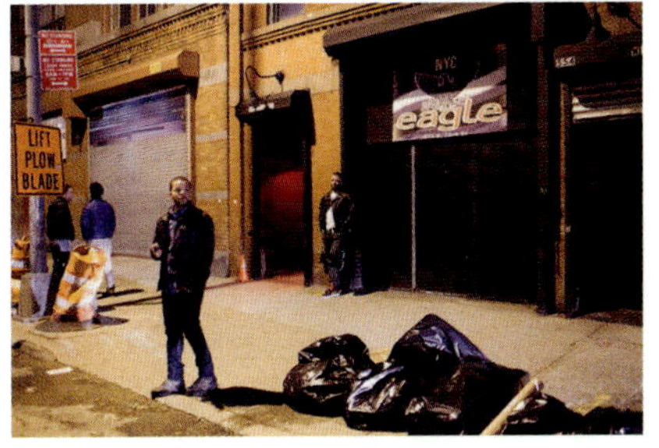

bjarnemel_jwb111.jpg

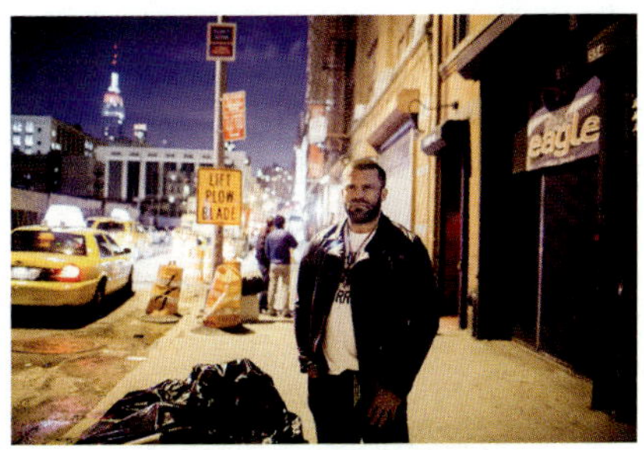

bjarnemel_jwb112.jpg

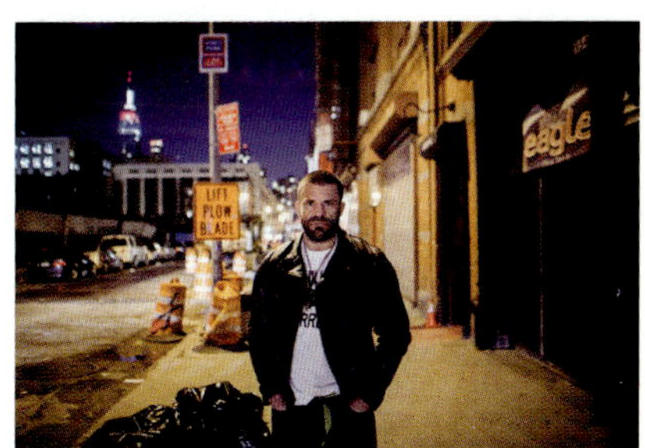

bjarnemel_jwb114.jpg

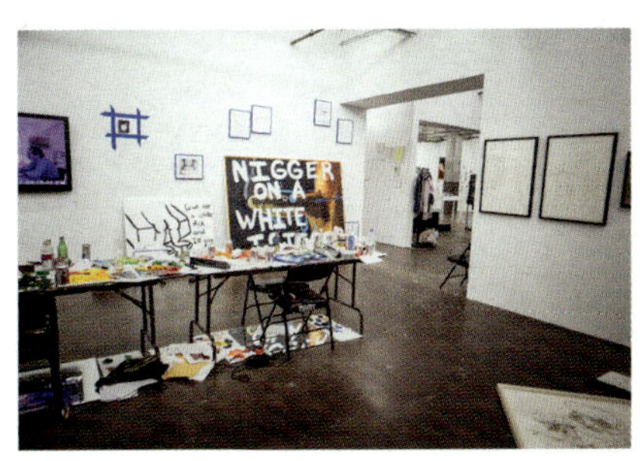

bjarnemel_jwb115.jpg

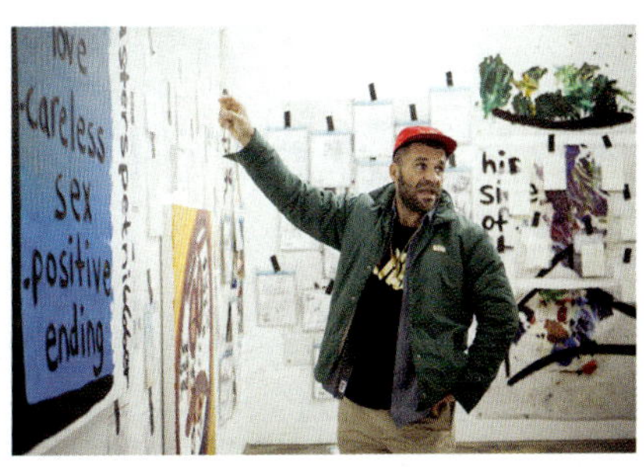

bjarnemel_jwb116.jpg

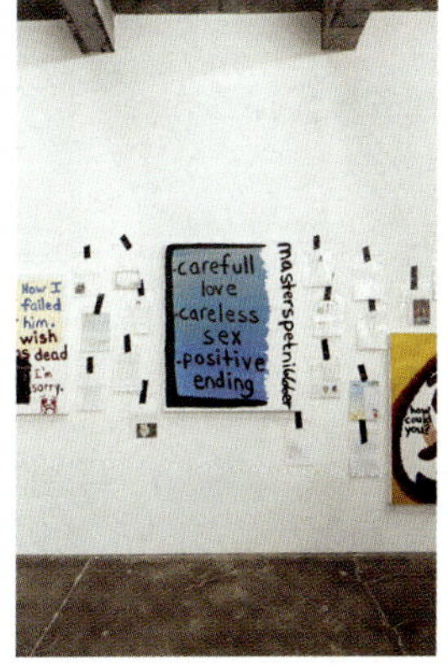

bjarnemel_jwb117.jpg

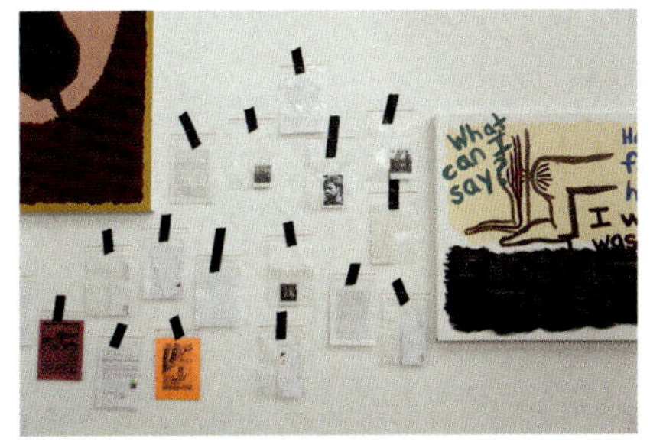

bjarnemel_jwb118.jpg

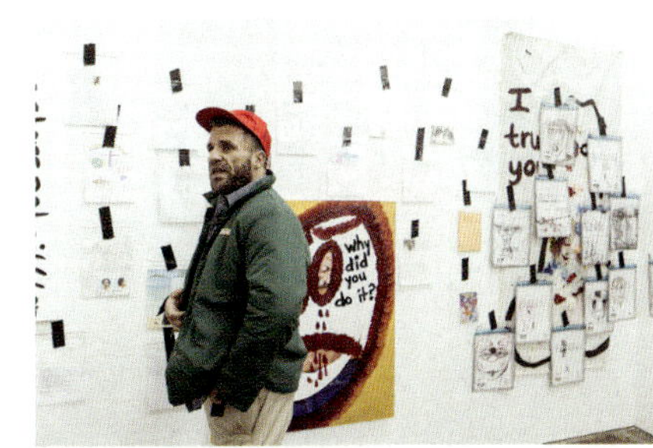

bjarnemel_jwb119.jpg

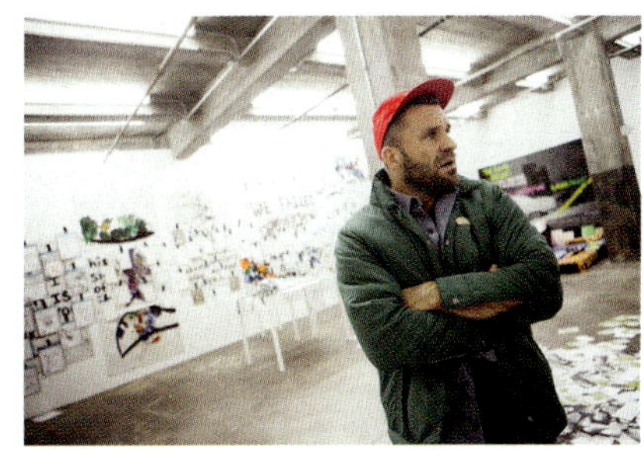

bjarnemel_jwb120.jpg

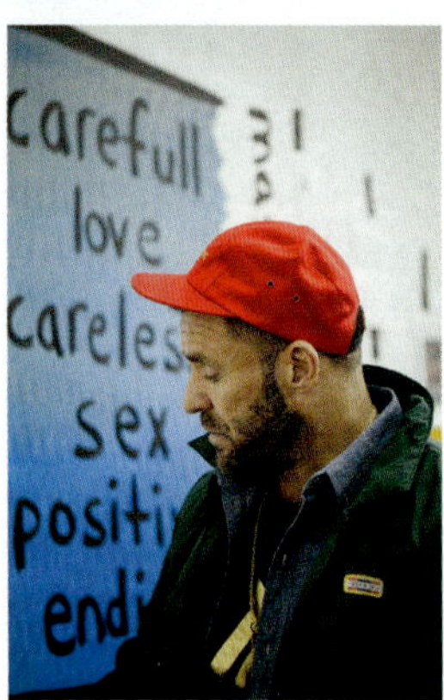

bjarnemel_jwb121.jpg

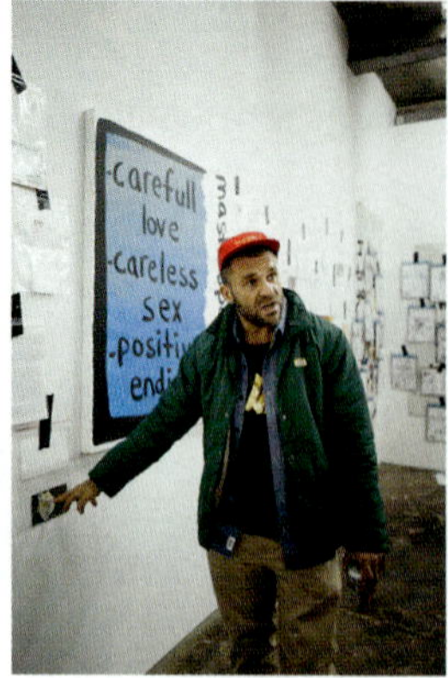

bjarnemel_jwb122.jpg

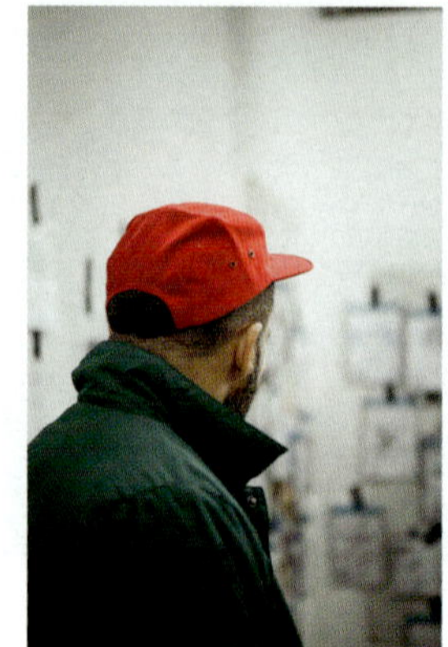

bjarnemel_jwb123.jpg

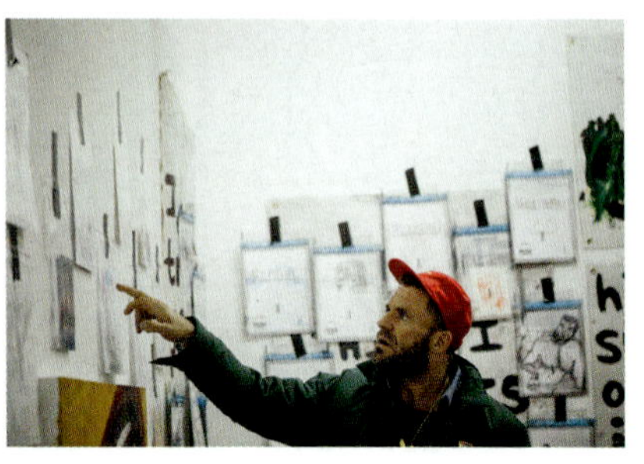

bjarnemel_jwb124.jpg

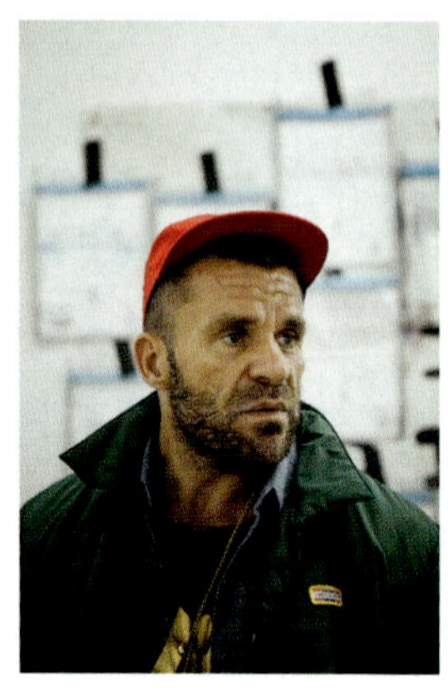

bjarnemel_jwb125.jpg

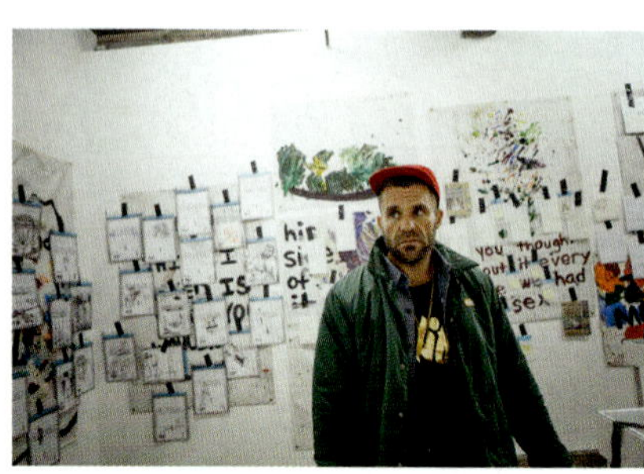

bjarnemel_jwb126.jpg

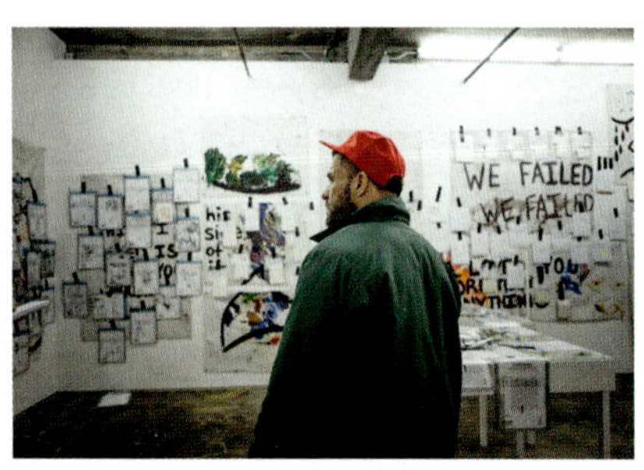

bjarnemel_jwb127.jpg

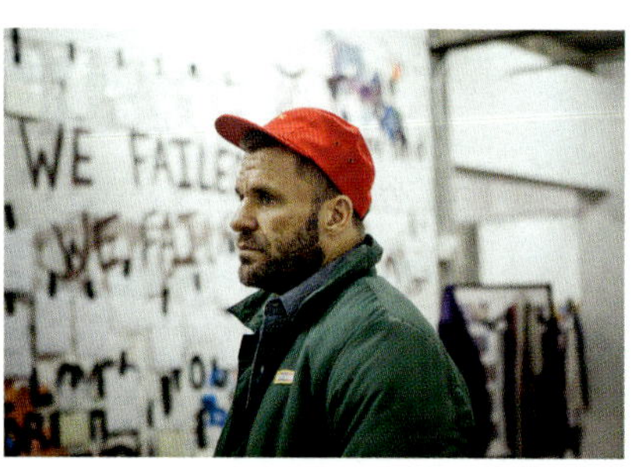

bjarnemel_jwb128.jpg

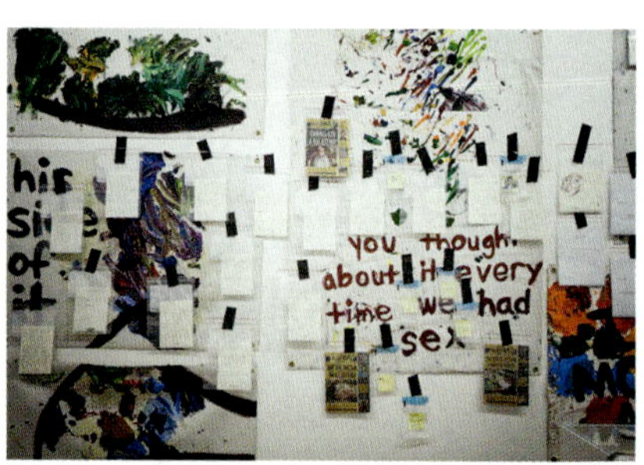

bjarnemel_jwb129.jpg

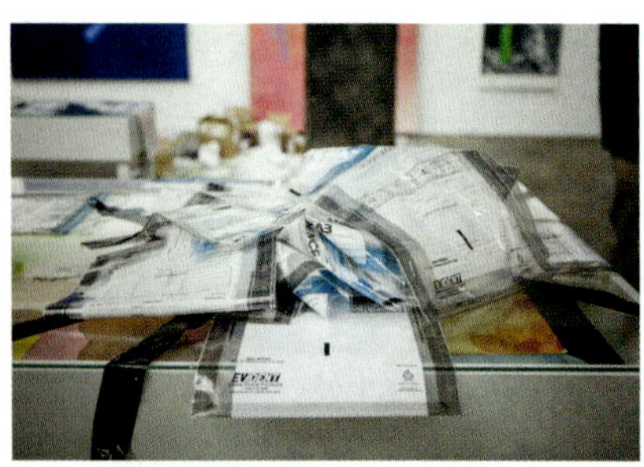

bjarnemel_jwb130.jpg

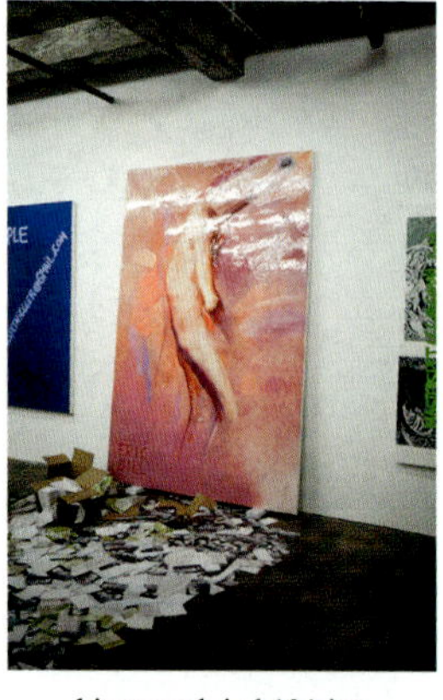

bjarnemel_jwb131.jpg

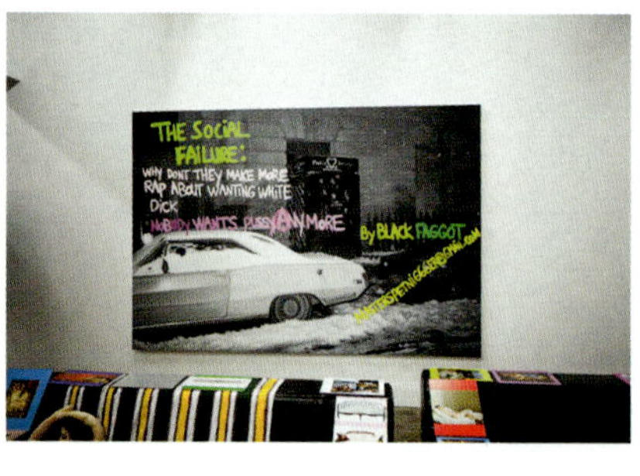

bjarnemel_jwb132.jpg

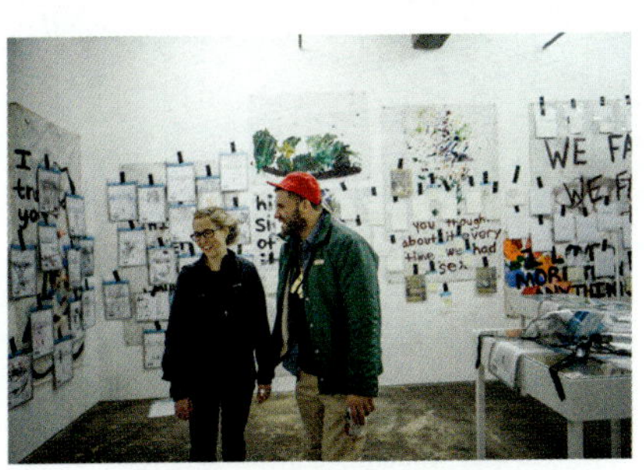

bjarnemel_jwb133.jpg

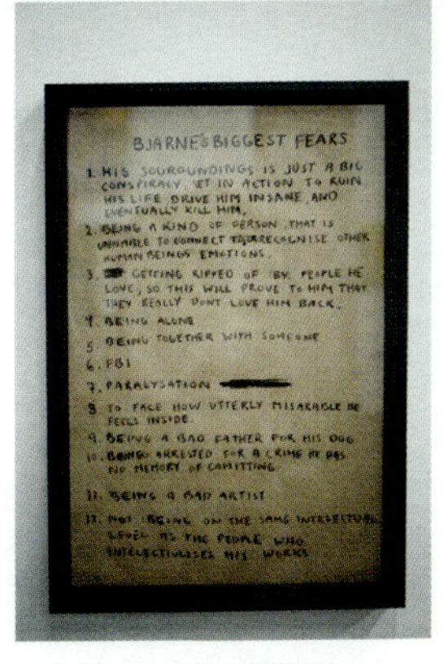

bjarnemel_jwb134.jpg

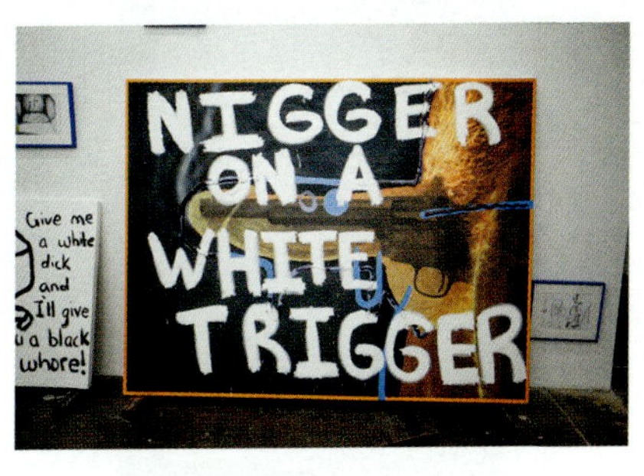

bjarnemel_jwb135.jpg

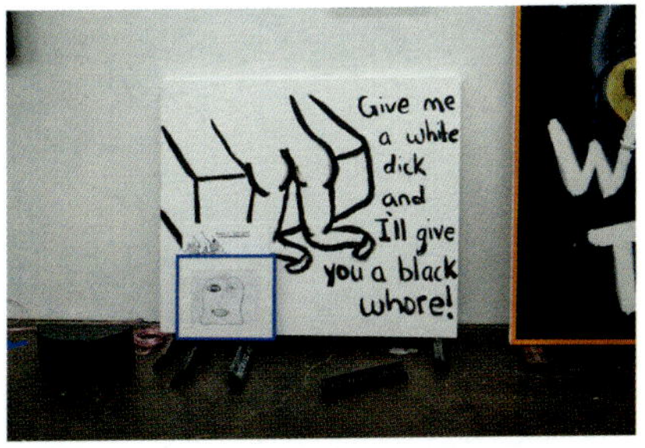

bjarnemel_jwb136.jpg

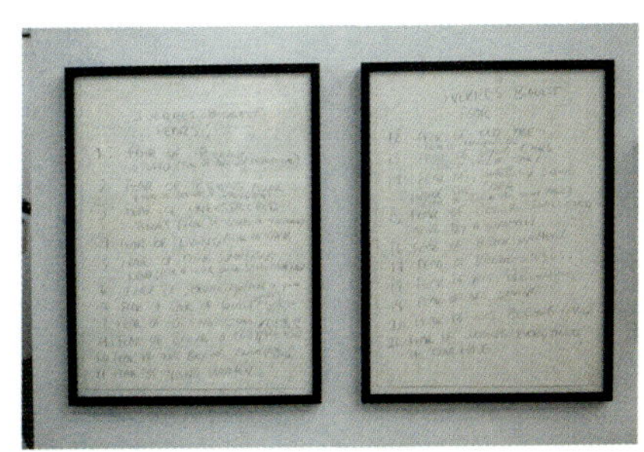

bjarnemel_jwb137.jpg

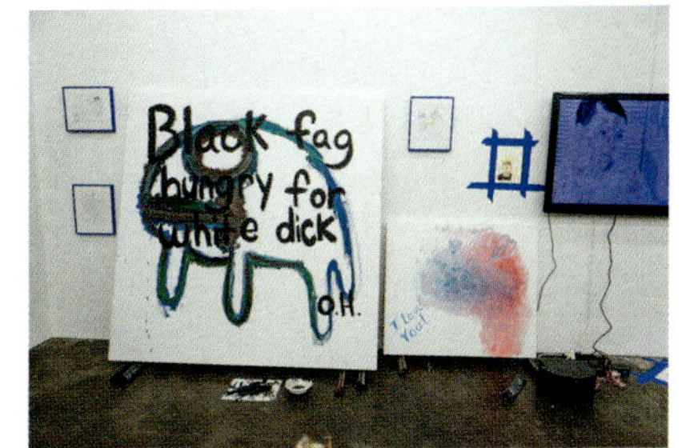

bjarnemel_jwb138.jpg

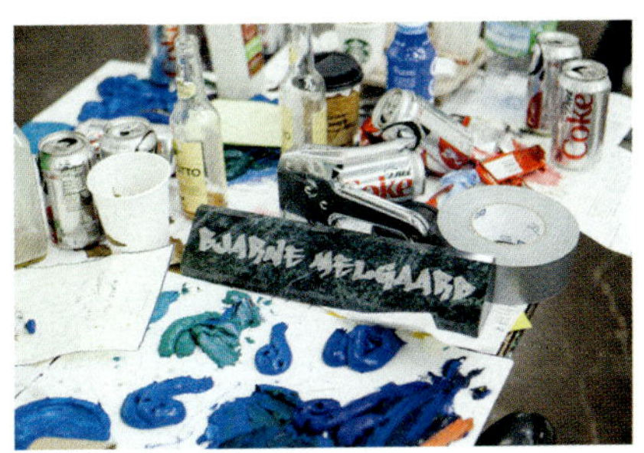

bjarnemel_jwb139.jpg

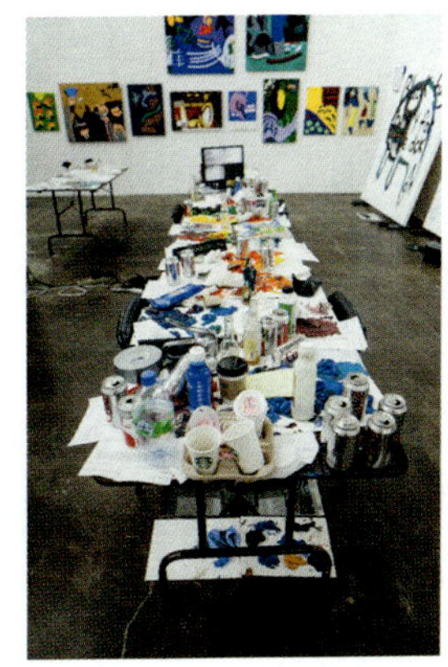

bjarnemel_jwb140.jpg

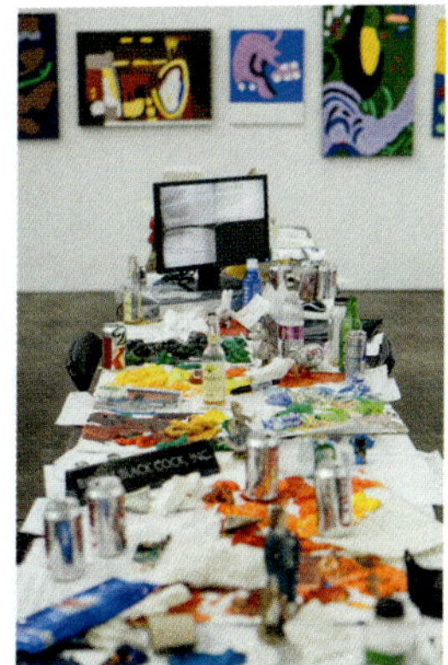

bjarnemel_jwb141.jpg

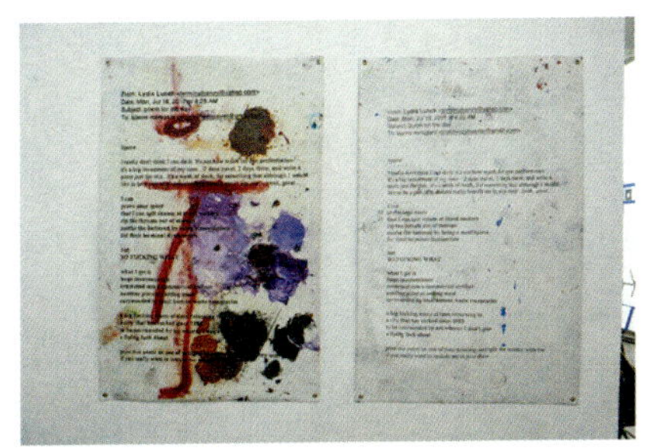

bjarnemel_jwb142.jpg

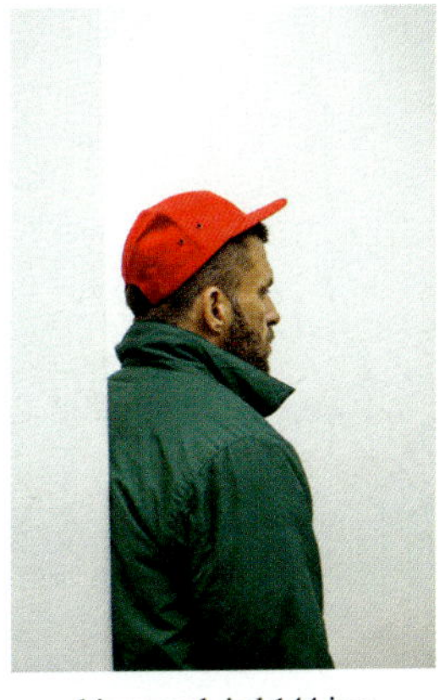

bjarnemel_jwb144.jpg

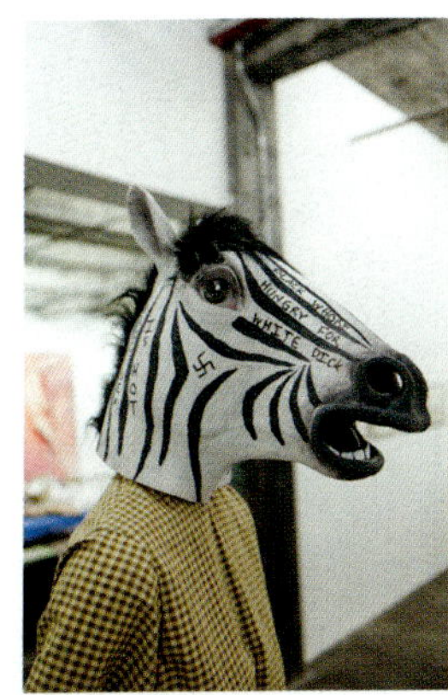

bjarnemel_jwb145.jpg

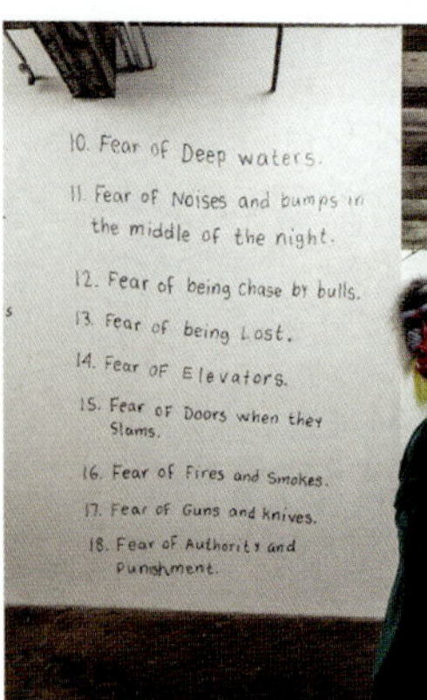

bjarnemel_jwb146.jpg

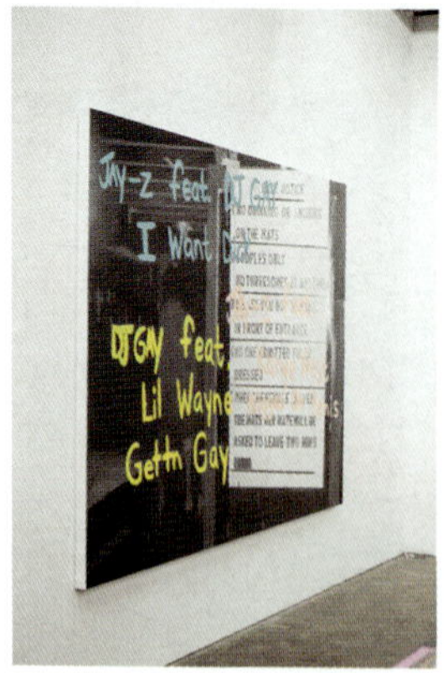

bjarnemel_jwb147.jpg

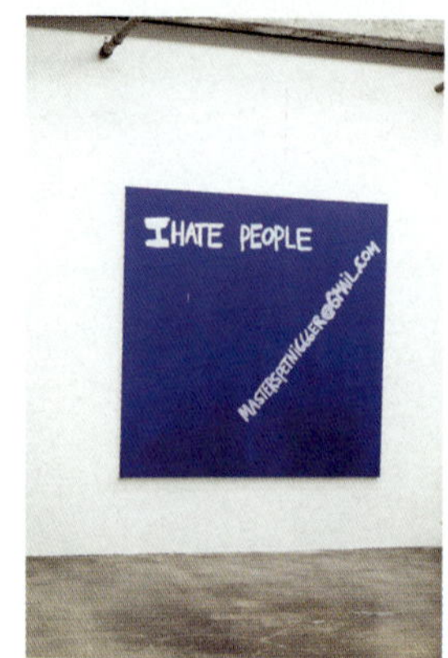

bjarnemel_jwb148.jpg

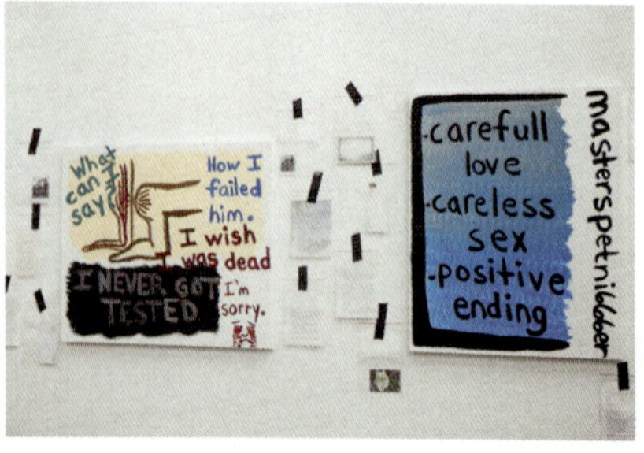

bjarnemel_jwb149.jpg

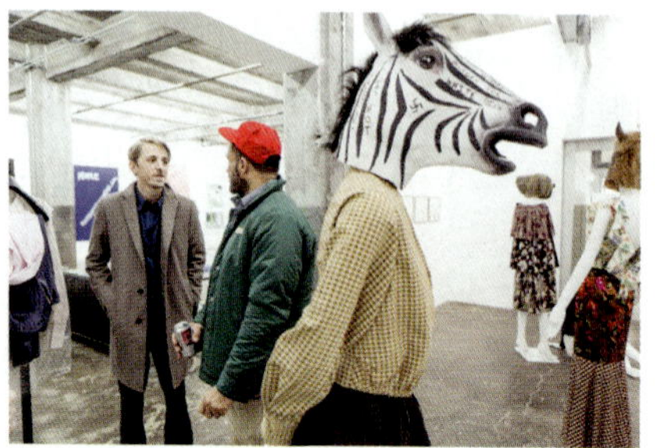

bjarnemel_jwb150.jpg

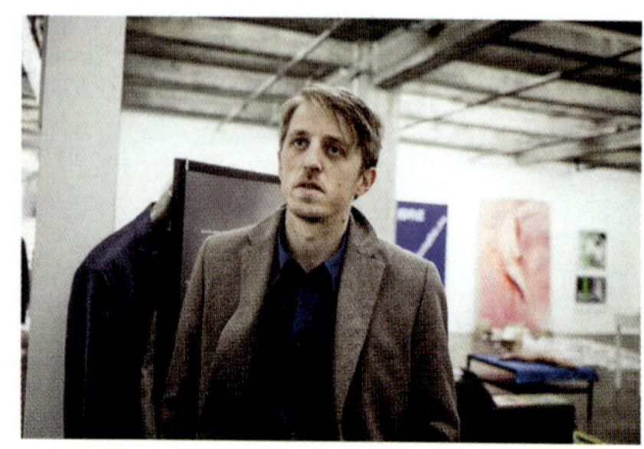

bjarnemel_jwb151.jpg

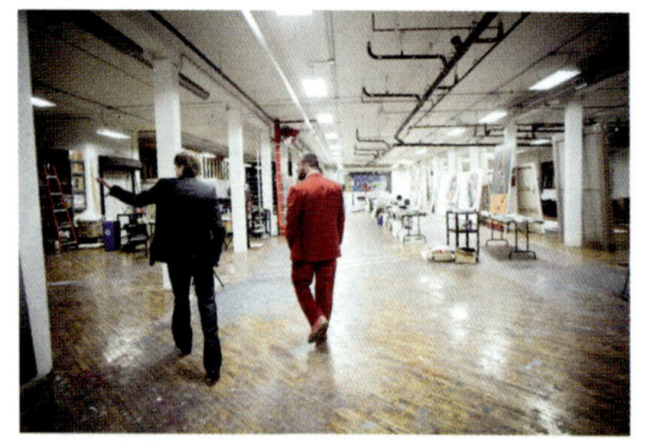

bjarnemel_jwb152.jpg

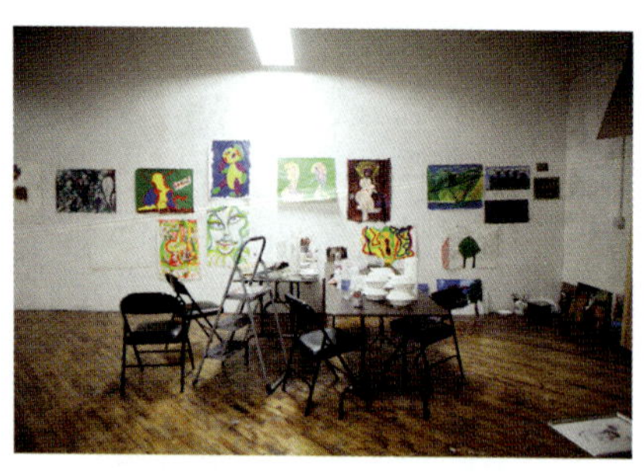

bjarnemel_jwb153.jpg

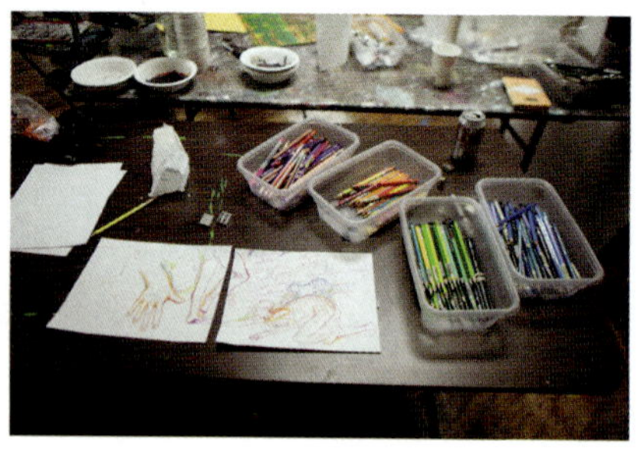

bjarnemel_jwb154.jpg

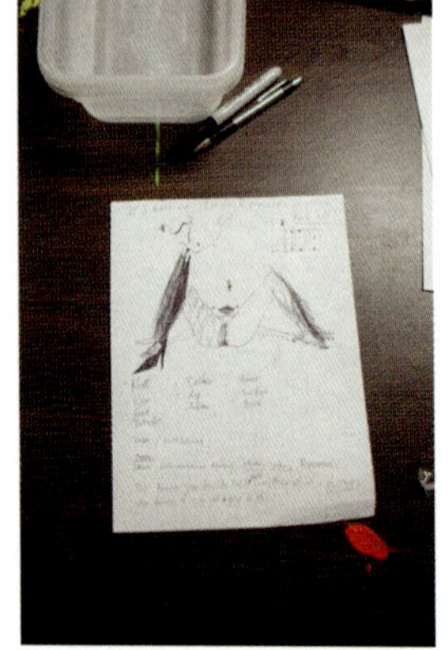

bjarnemel_jwb155.jpg

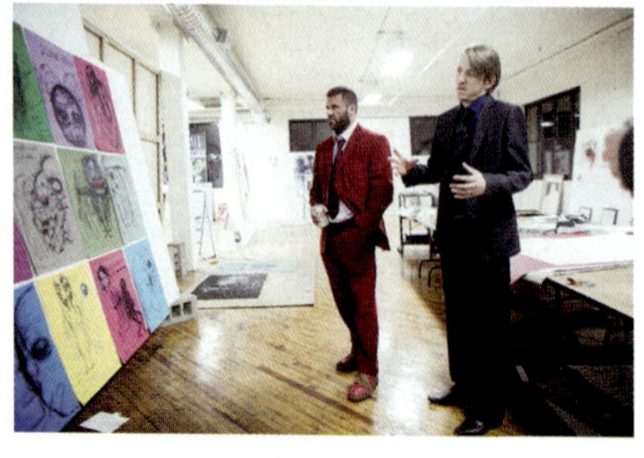

bjarnemel_jwb156.jpg

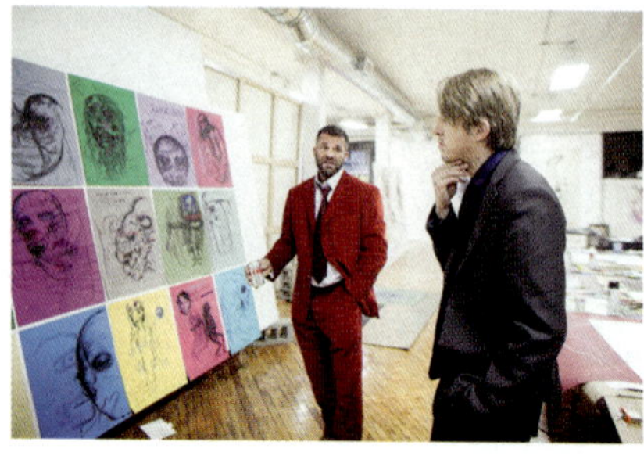

bjarnemel_jwb157.jpg

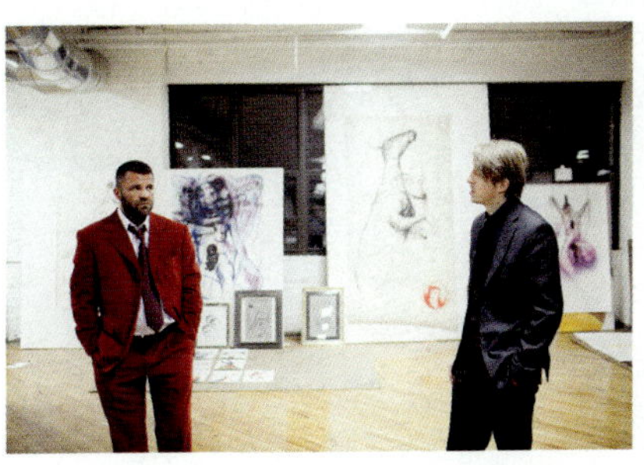

bjarnemel_jwb158.jpg

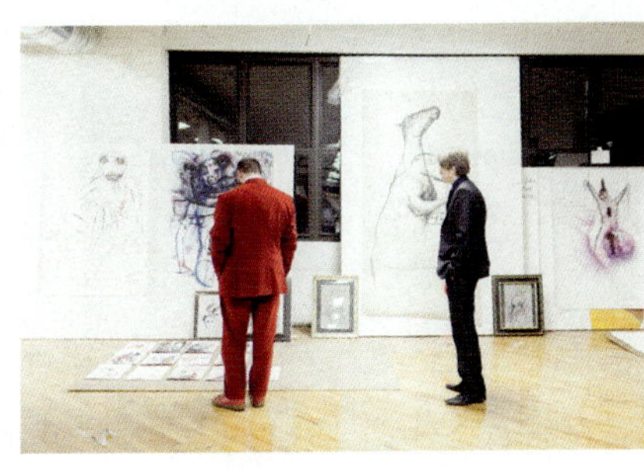

bjarnemel_jwb159.jpg

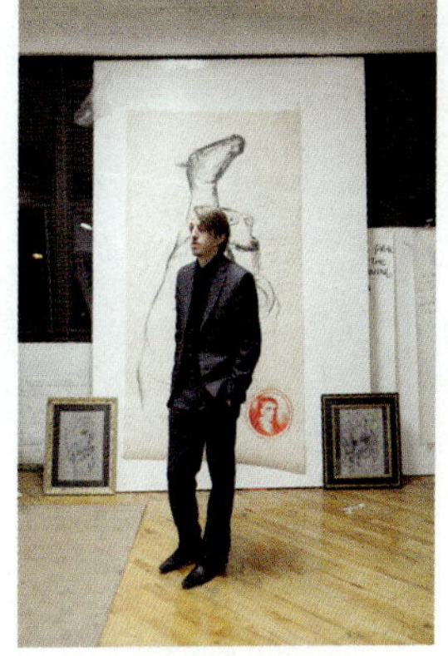

bjarnemel_jwb160.jpg

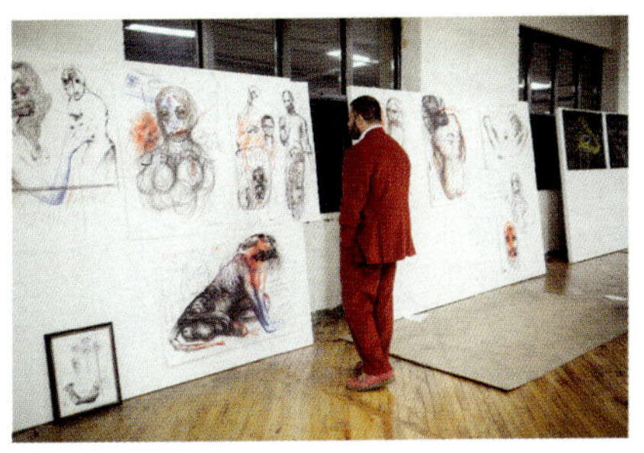

bjarnemel_jwb161.jpg

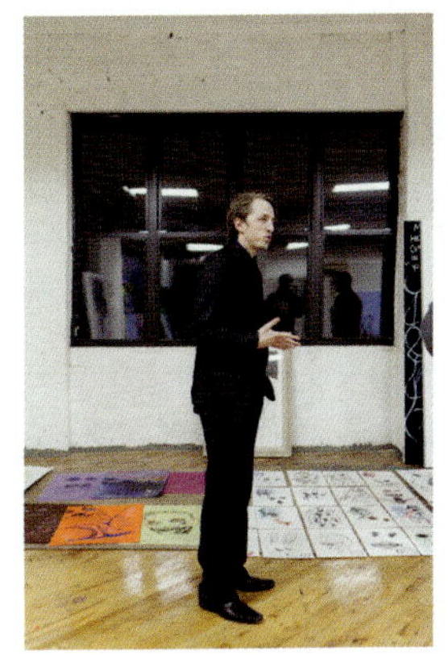

bjarnemel_jwb162.jpg

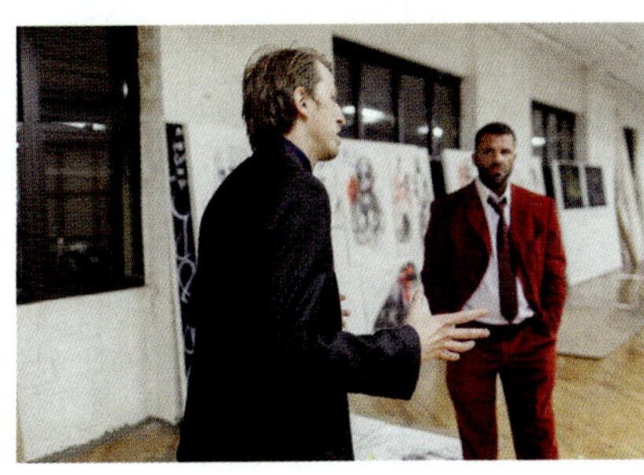

bjarnemel_jwb163.jpg

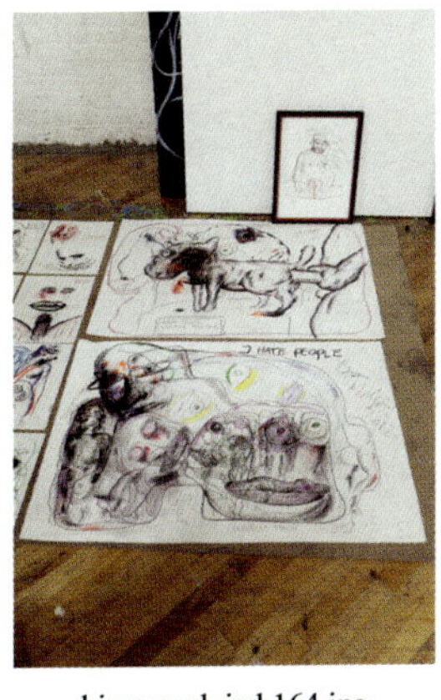

bjarnemel_jwb164.jpg

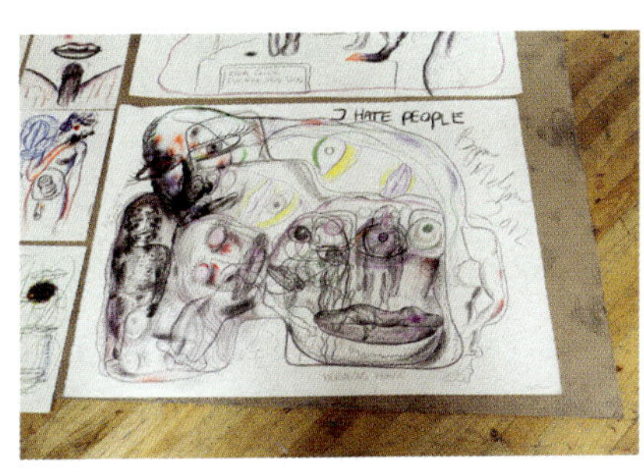

bjarnemel_jwb165.jpg

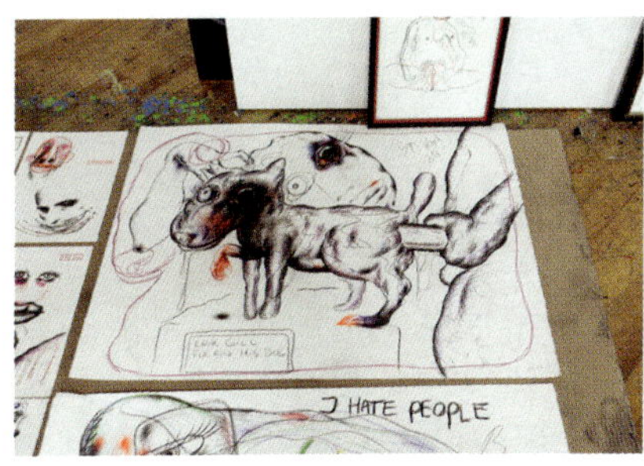

bjarnemel_jwb166.jpg

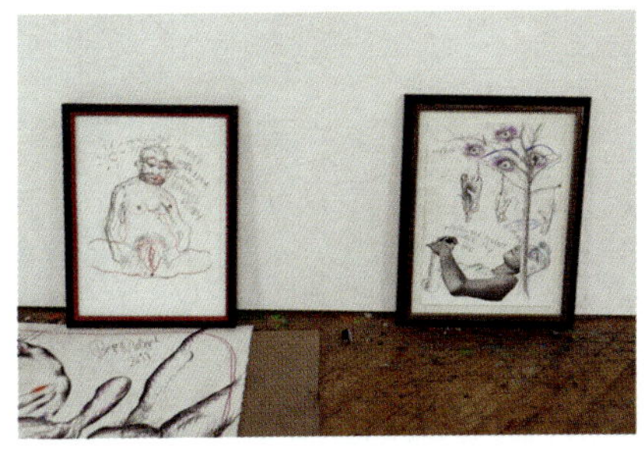

bjarnemel_jwb167.jpg

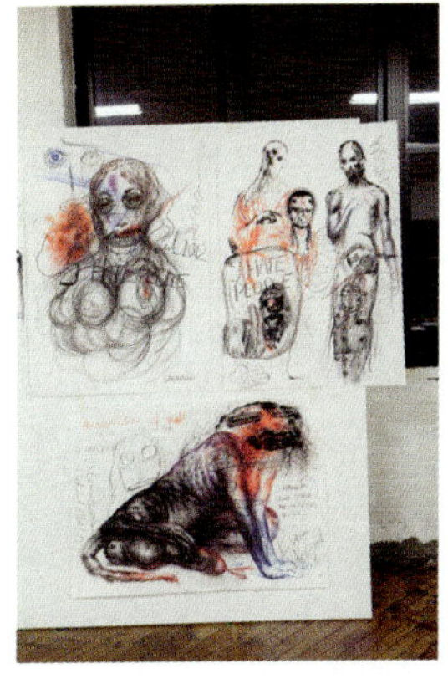

bjarnemel_jwb168.jpg

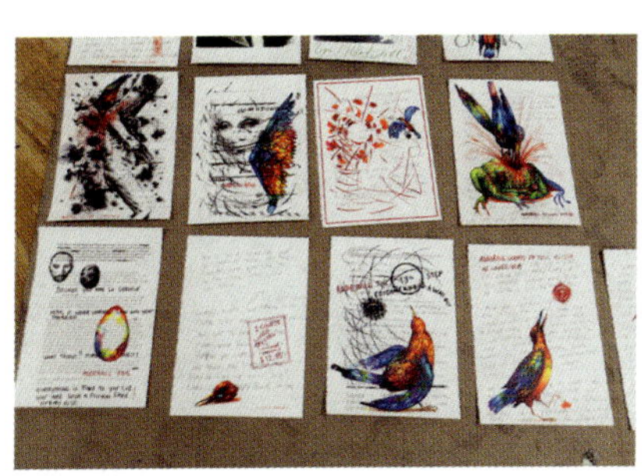

bjarnemel_jwb169.jpg

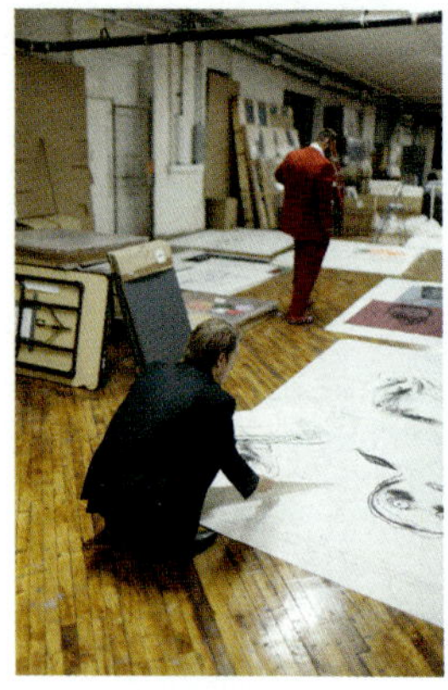

bjarnemel_jwb170.jpg

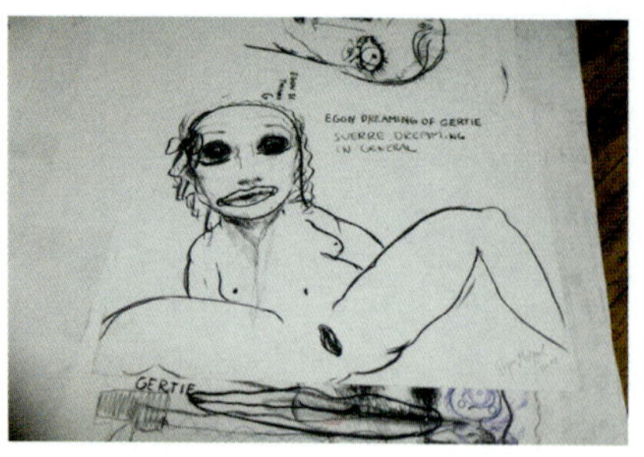

bjarnemel_jwb171.jpg

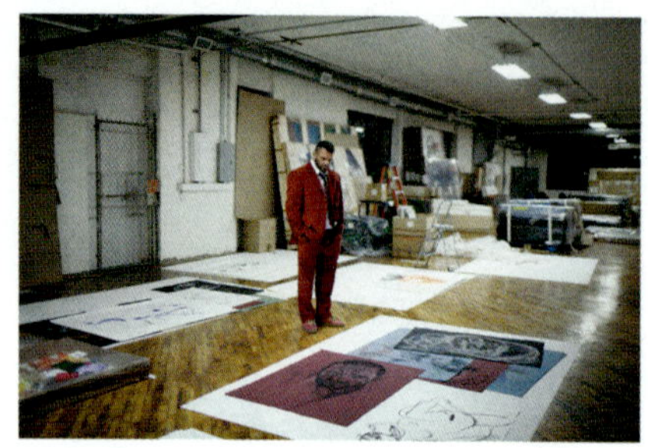

bjarnemel_jwb172.jpg

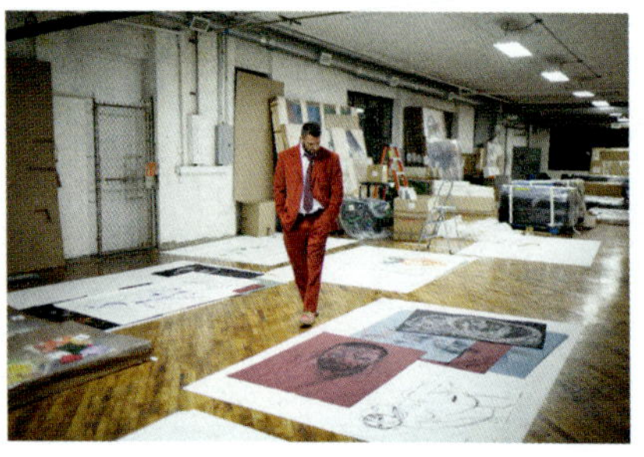

bjarnemel_jwb173.jpg

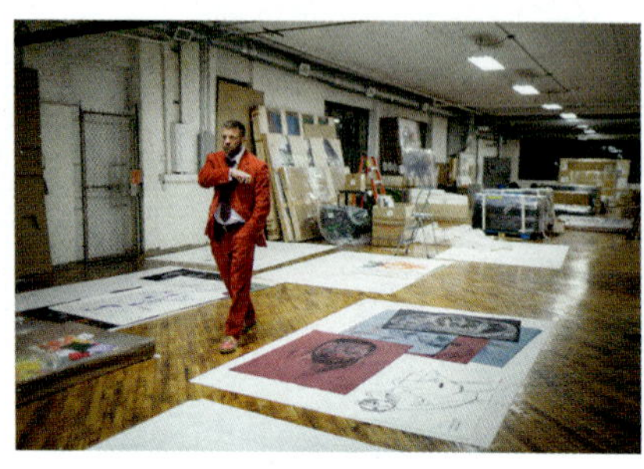

bjarnemel_jwb174.jpg

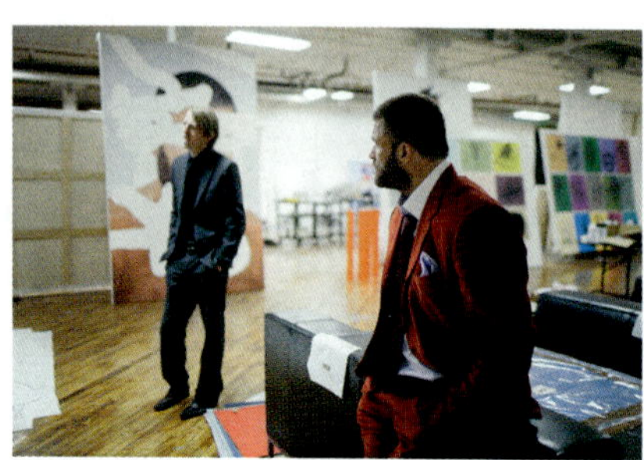

bjarnemel_jwb175.jpg

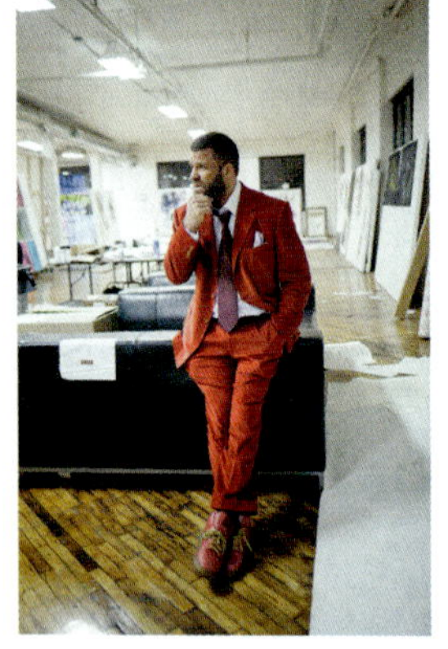

bjarnemel_jwb176.jpg

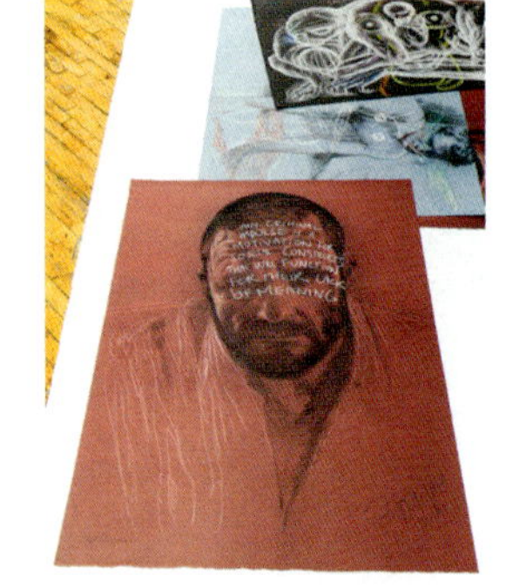

bjarnemel_jwb177.jpg

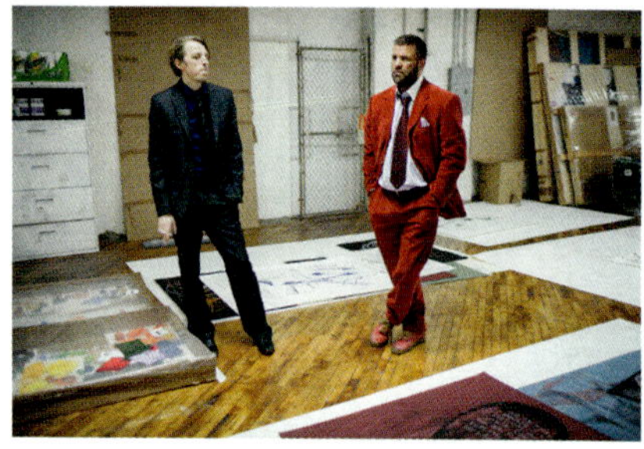

bjarnemel_jwb179.jpg

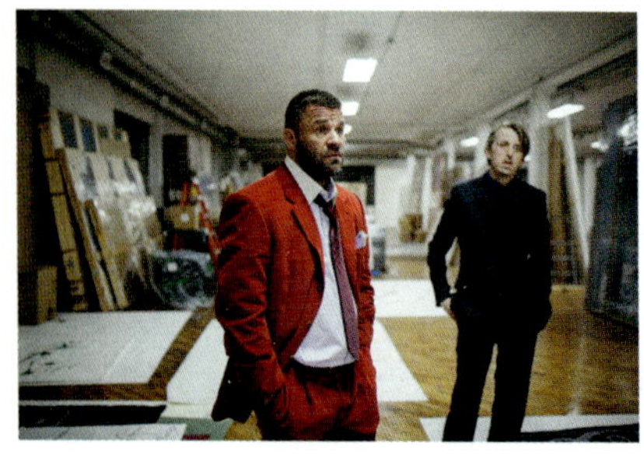

bjarnemel_jwb180.jpg

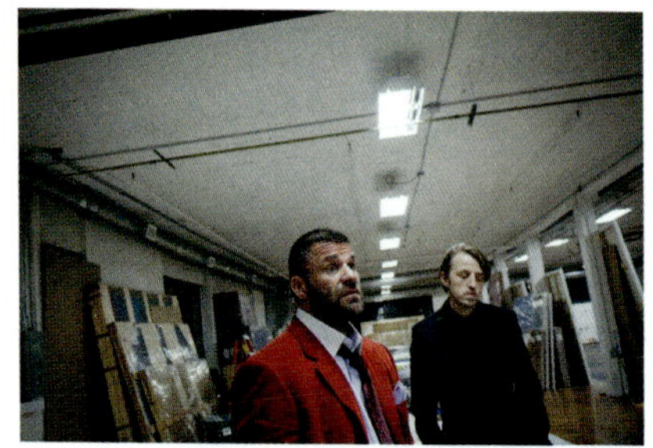

bjarnemel_jwb181.jpg

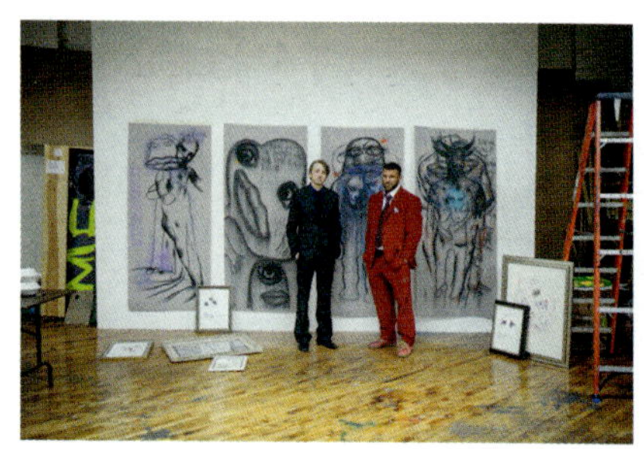

bjarnemel_jwb182.jpg

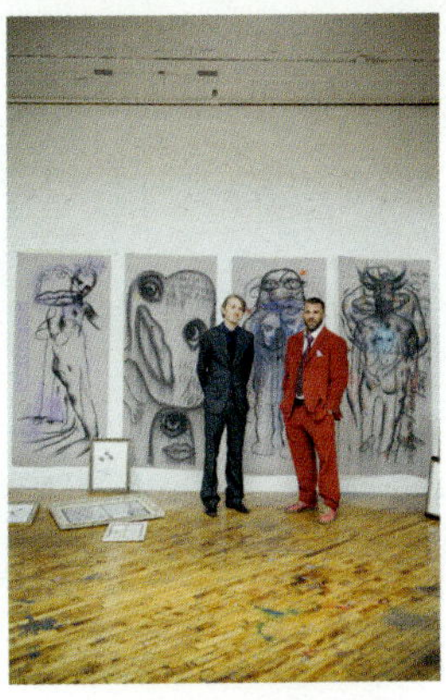

bjarnemel_jwb183.jpg

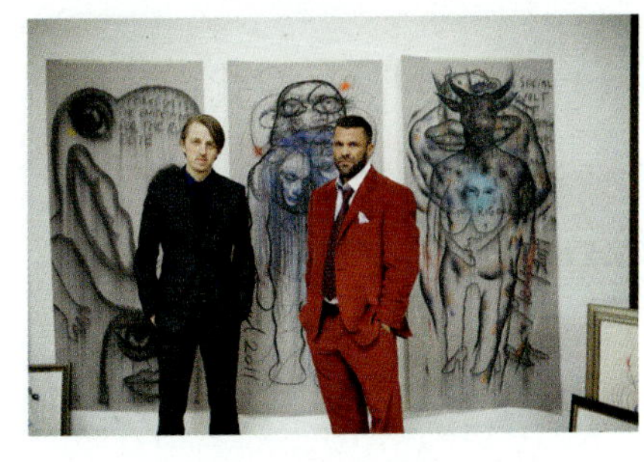

bjarnemel_jwb184.jpg

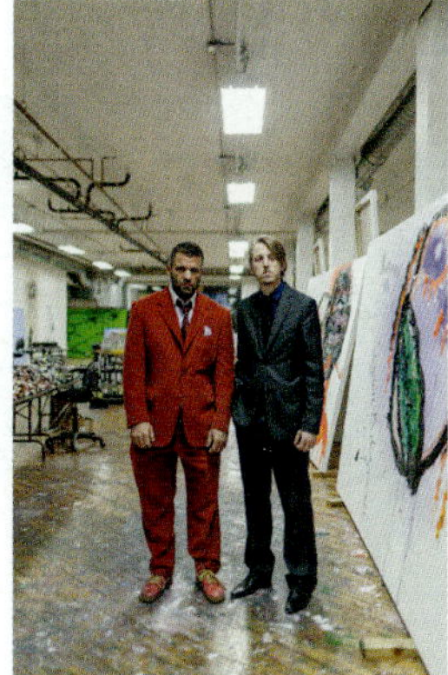

bjarnemel_jwb186.jpg

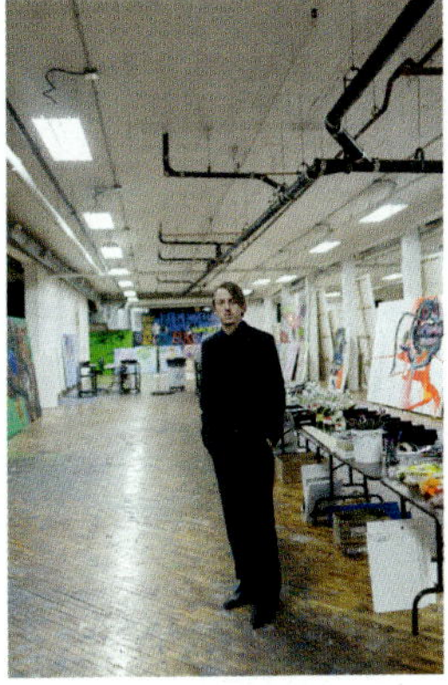

bjarnemel_jwb187.jpg

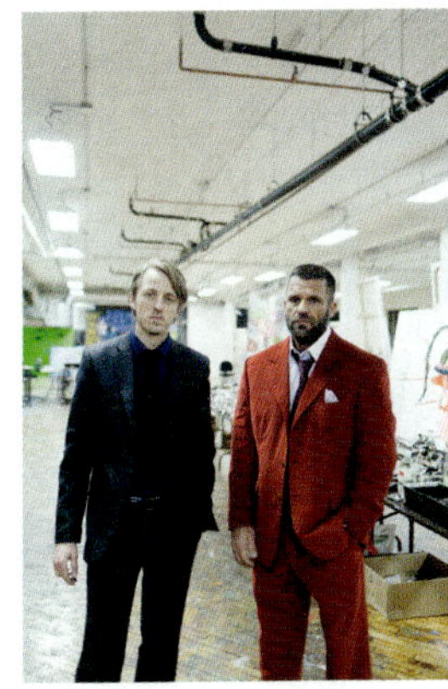

bjarnemel_jwb188.jpg

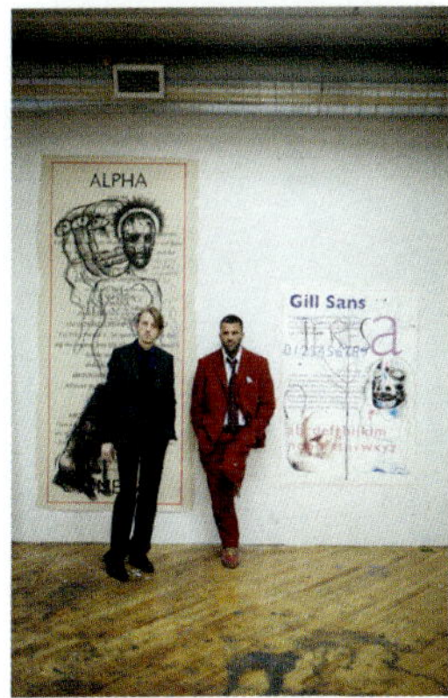

bjarnemel_jwb189.jpg

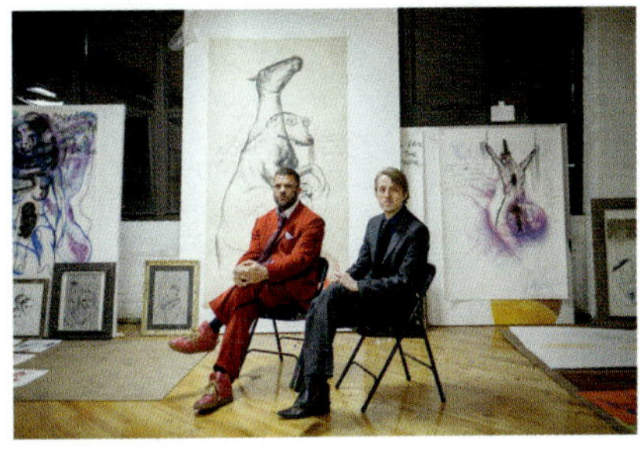

bjarnemel_jwb190.jpg

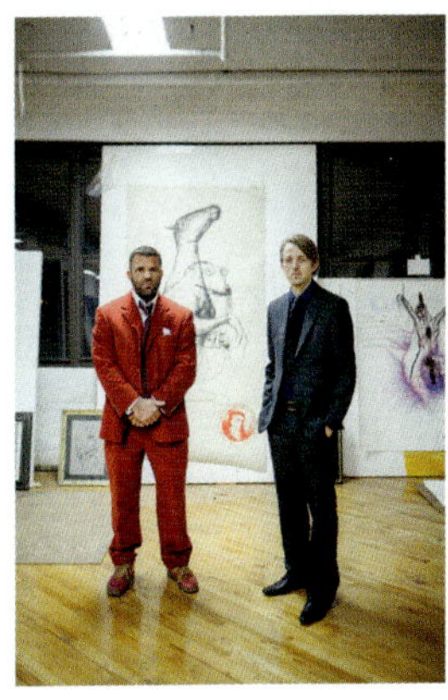

bjarnemel_jwb192.jpg

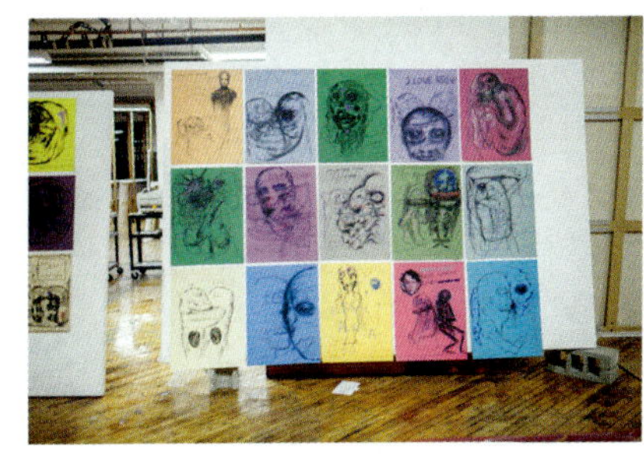

bjarnemel_jwb193.jpg

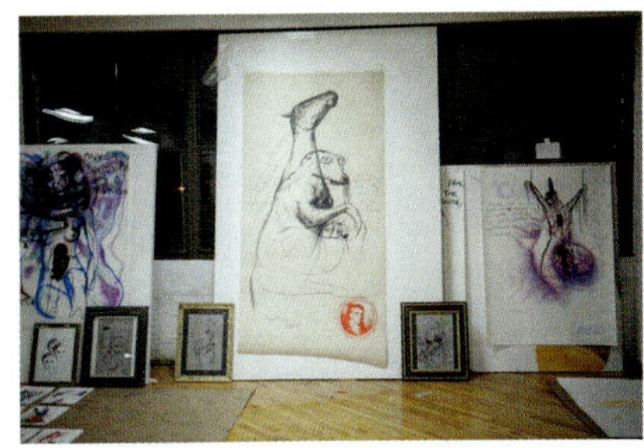

bjarnemel_jwb194.jpg

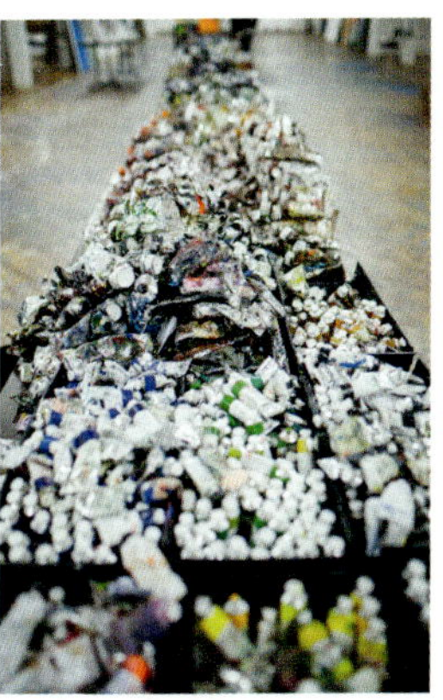

bjarnemel_jwb196.jpg

bjarnemel_jwb195.jpg

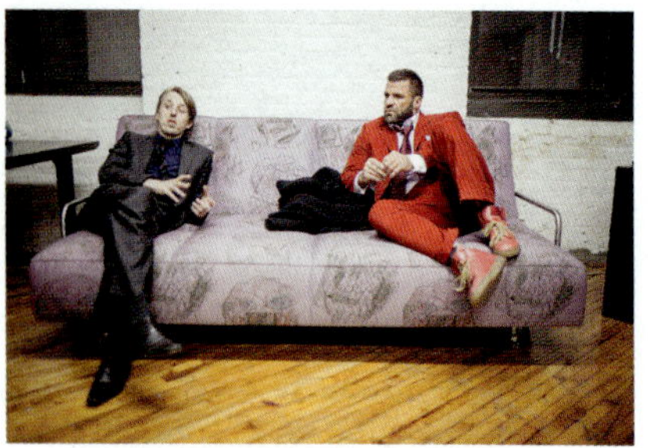

bjarnemel_jwb197.jpg

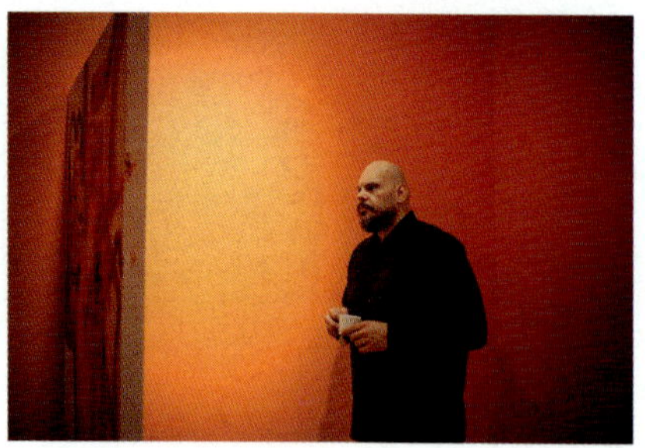

bjarnemel_jwb198.jpg

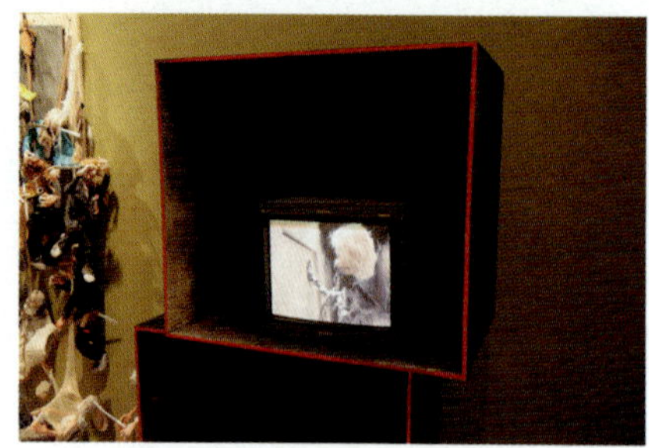

bjarnemel_jwb199.jpg

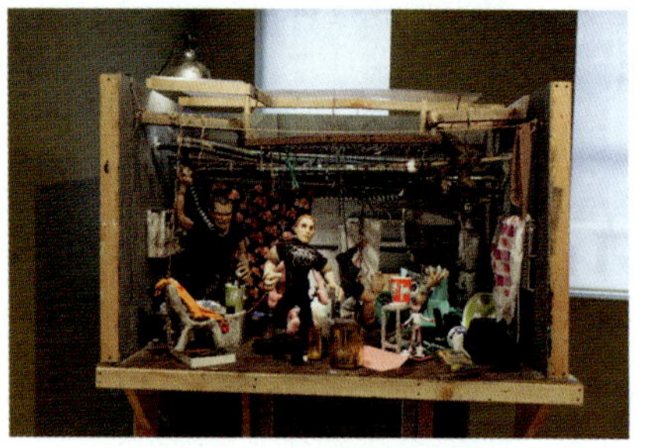

bjarnemel_jwb200.jpg

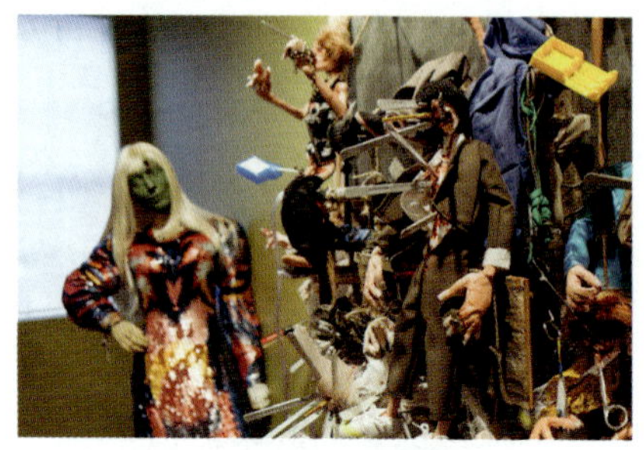

bjarnemel_jwb201.jpg

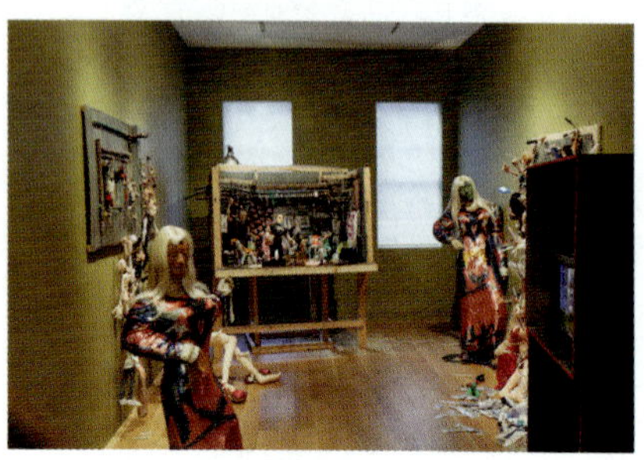

bjarnemel_jwb202.jpg

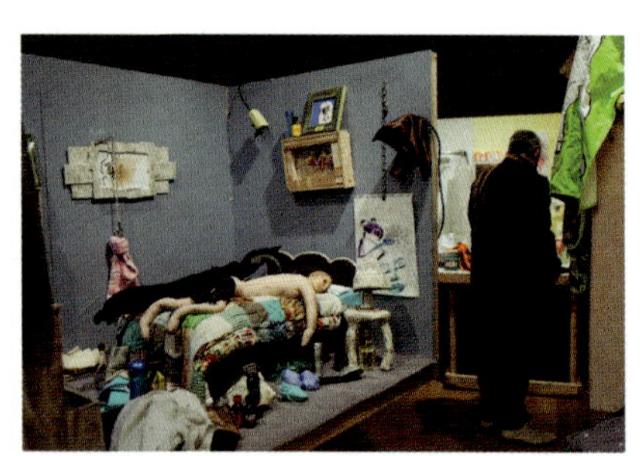

bjarnemel_jwb203.jpg

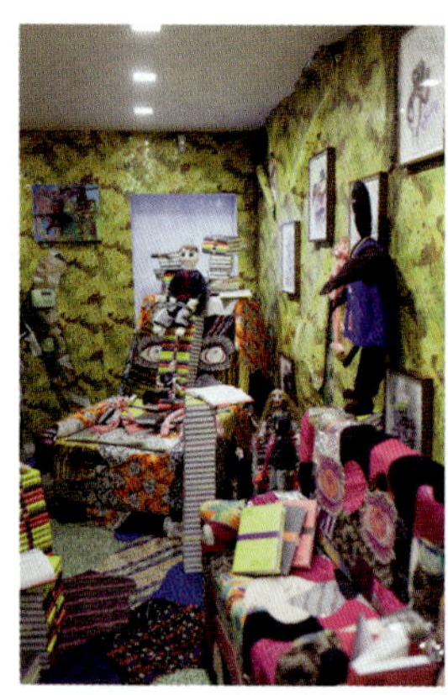

bjarnemel_jwb204.jpg

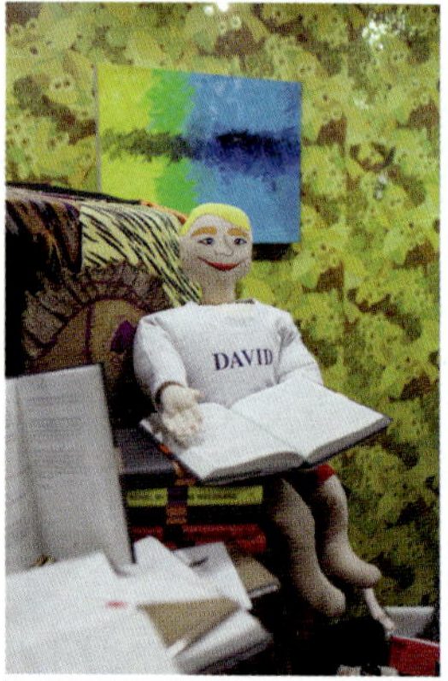

bjarnemel_jwb205.jpg

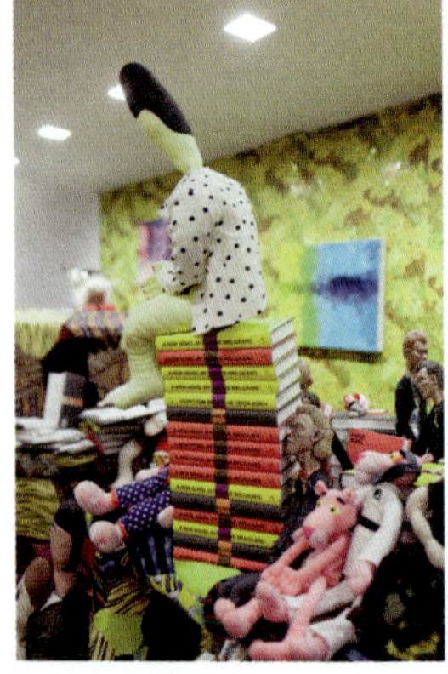

bjarnemel_jwb206.jpg

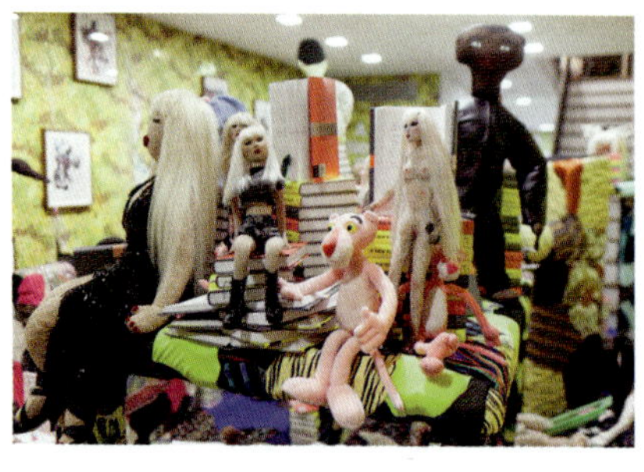

bjarnemel_jwb207.jpg

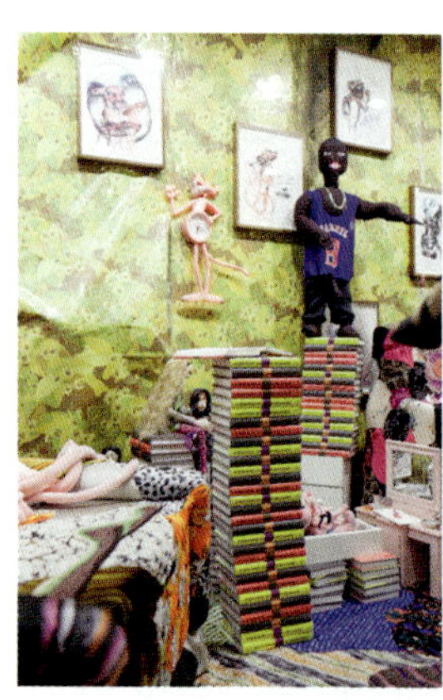

bjarnemel_jwb208.jpg

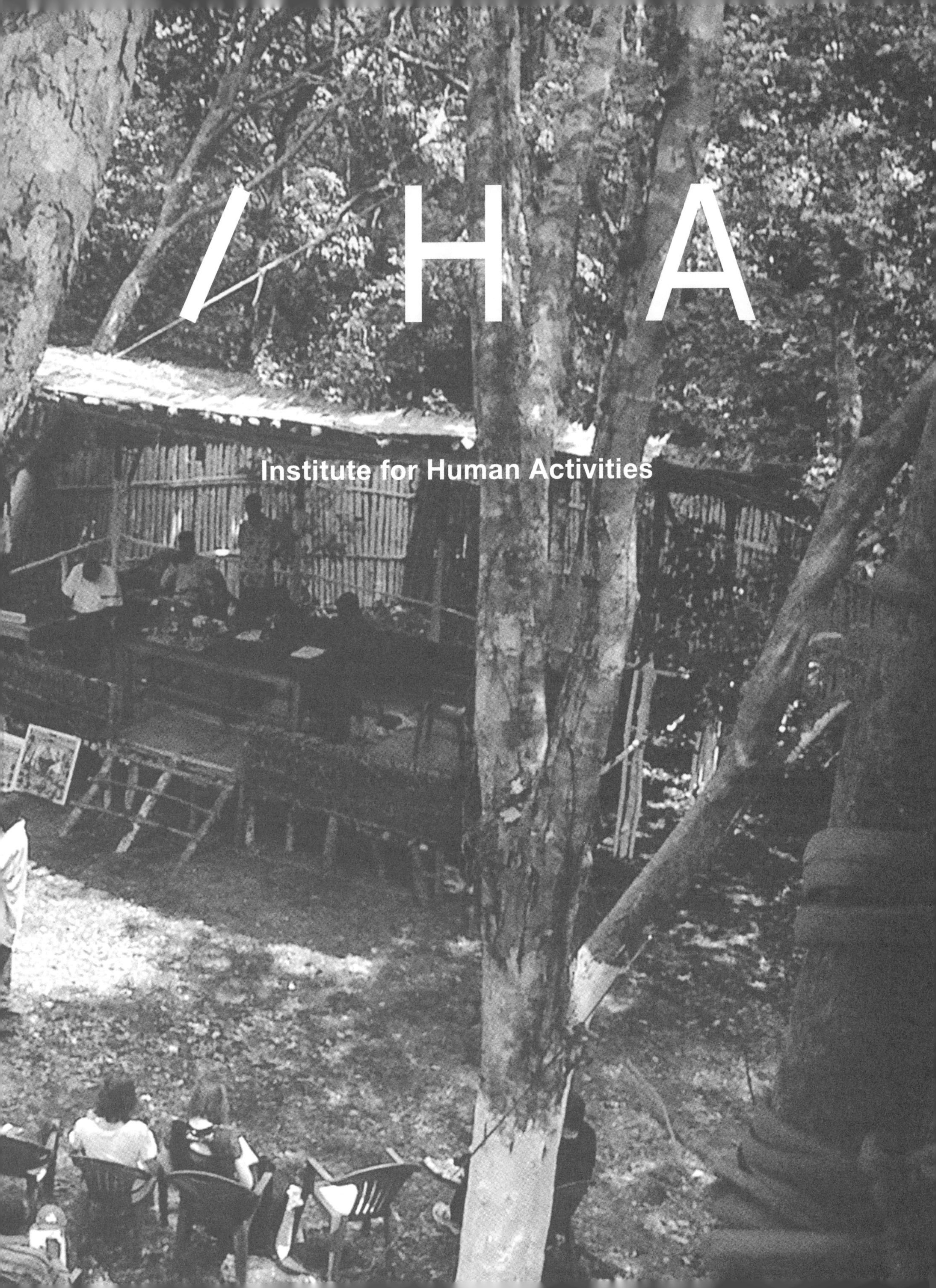
IHA
Institute for Human Activities

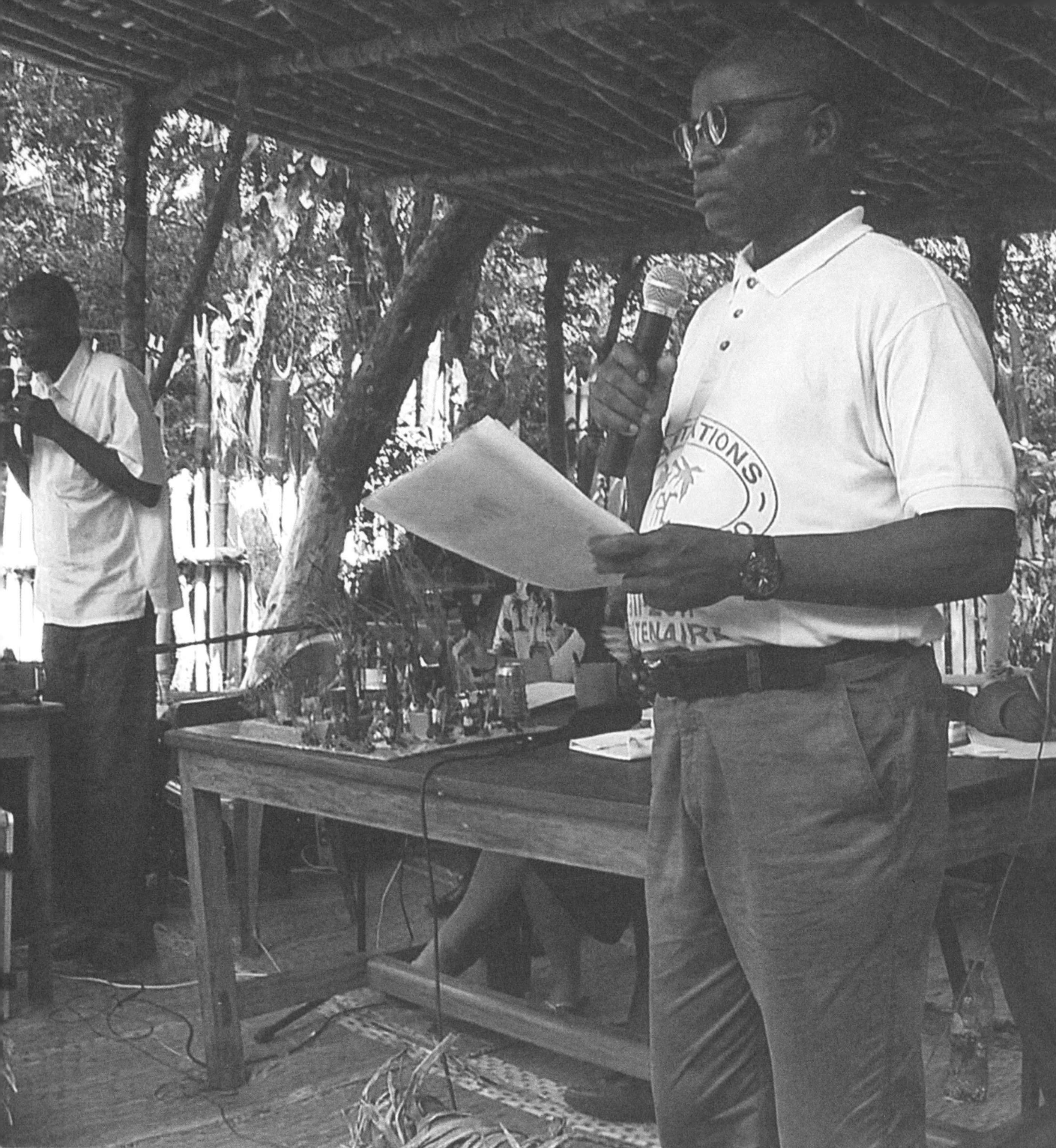

Previous and last pages: View of the opening seminar
Above: Plantation manager Nicolas Mateso makes introductory remarks at the opening seminar
All images courtesy the Institute for Human Activities, taken in the Democratic Republic of the Congo, 2012

The Institute for Human Activities (IHA) has established a settlement on a small tributary of the River Congo, 800 kilometers upstream from Kinshasa, in the Democratic Republic of the Congo.

Here, in one of the most disadvantaged regions of the world, the Institute has launched its five-year Gentrification Program and set up an in-vitro testing ground of the material effects of art production.

Directed by artist Renzo Martens and supported by a variety of international cultural institutions and corporate partners, the Institute aims to recalibrate the critical mandate of art by taking into account the conditions of its own existence. With a dedicated team of artists and thinkers, we seek to do this by recognizing the mechanisms through which critical art currently has the greatest impact on social reality—mechanisms that are too important to be left in the hands of entrepreneurs and real-estate speculators.

With legal structures in Amsterdam, Brussels, and Kinshasa, the Institute plans to use capital accumulation as a tool of artistic intervention. The IHA's research site, established in a place that occupies the lowest position in the global economic hierarchy, will enable critical art to make productive use of its acknowledgment that art is always already co-opted within global capitalism. The results of the Institute's work will be shared with audiences in Africa and around the world.

1. Introduction

Believing that art can take a critical position only if it embraces the terms and conditions of its own existence, our contention is that the effects of art on social reality at the sites where critical artistic interventions are staged are dwarfed by those that take place at the sites of art's public reception—in the cities where such artworks are subsequently shown, discussed, and sold.

On the one hand, galleries, museums, and biennials in places such as Berlin and Istanbul have become important centers for the presentation of critical, interventionist art. However, local politicians or businessmen do not finance art venues because they hope this will radicalize local politics but rather because they know art will make their cities more competitive in the battle for attention, high net-worth individuals, and capital investment.

On the other hand, at the locus of such artistic interventions in, say, Congo, Peru, or the Parisian banlieues, art may very well have an impact, though it often remains confined to the symbolic level. Such interventions rarely produce the visible shifts achieved at the centers of reception.

More often than not, in the transfer of critical art from a zone of intervention to a zone of reception, a gap seems to arise. This gap is remarkably similar to the division between labor and profit in other globalized industries. Art may expose the need for change in Nigeria or Peru, but in the end it brings opportunity, quality-of-life improvements, and real-estate value to Berlin Mitte or the Lower East Side.

2. Gentrification and Critical Art

While artists, curators, and collectors travel between the institutions and cities that are living proof of art's capacity to bring economic benefits, they have refrained from addressing the ways in which the accumulation of capital, privilege, and prestige—at the sites of reception, that is—may be art's prime intervention in social reality. It is certainly the one that is most speculated upon.

Rather than ignoring this state of affairs or treating it as an unwanted side effect, art can accept the terms and conditions of its production and forge a new, more radical criticality, which turns art's potential for gentrification into a critical, progressive, and effective tool. Therefore, the Institute for Human Activities seeks to make capital accumulation a core strategy for artistic intervention.

2. Gentrification and Critical Art

The Institute for Human Activities has its headquarters next to a palm oil plantation formerly owned by Unilever. Before being bought for an undisclosed sum by the London-based plantation operator Feronia, Inc. in 2009, this plantation was an important part of the Unilever business empire. Long a household name for Sunlight soap and other products manufactured using materials from its plantations in the Congo, Unilever has recently also become known for its generous funding of the arts, most notably the Unilever Series at Tate Modern in London, for which it funded an explicitly political piece by Ai Weiwei as well as interventions by artists such as Tino Sehgal, Louise Bourgeois, and Bruce Nauman, among others. This resulted in highly visible contributions to arts and society in London.

The IHA has secured a long-term lease on a former Unilever store that sold basic commodities to Unilever's employees. This store was abandoned for fifteen years until the IHA took up occupancy in 2013. The presence of the IHA at the plantation will allow the production of critique itself to accumulate capital and bring economic benefits to the 400 plantation workers living nearby as well as other members of the local community. In this way, critical art made in response to Congolese labor conditions will have an effect on labor conditions in the Congo rather than in New York or London.

3. The Research Site

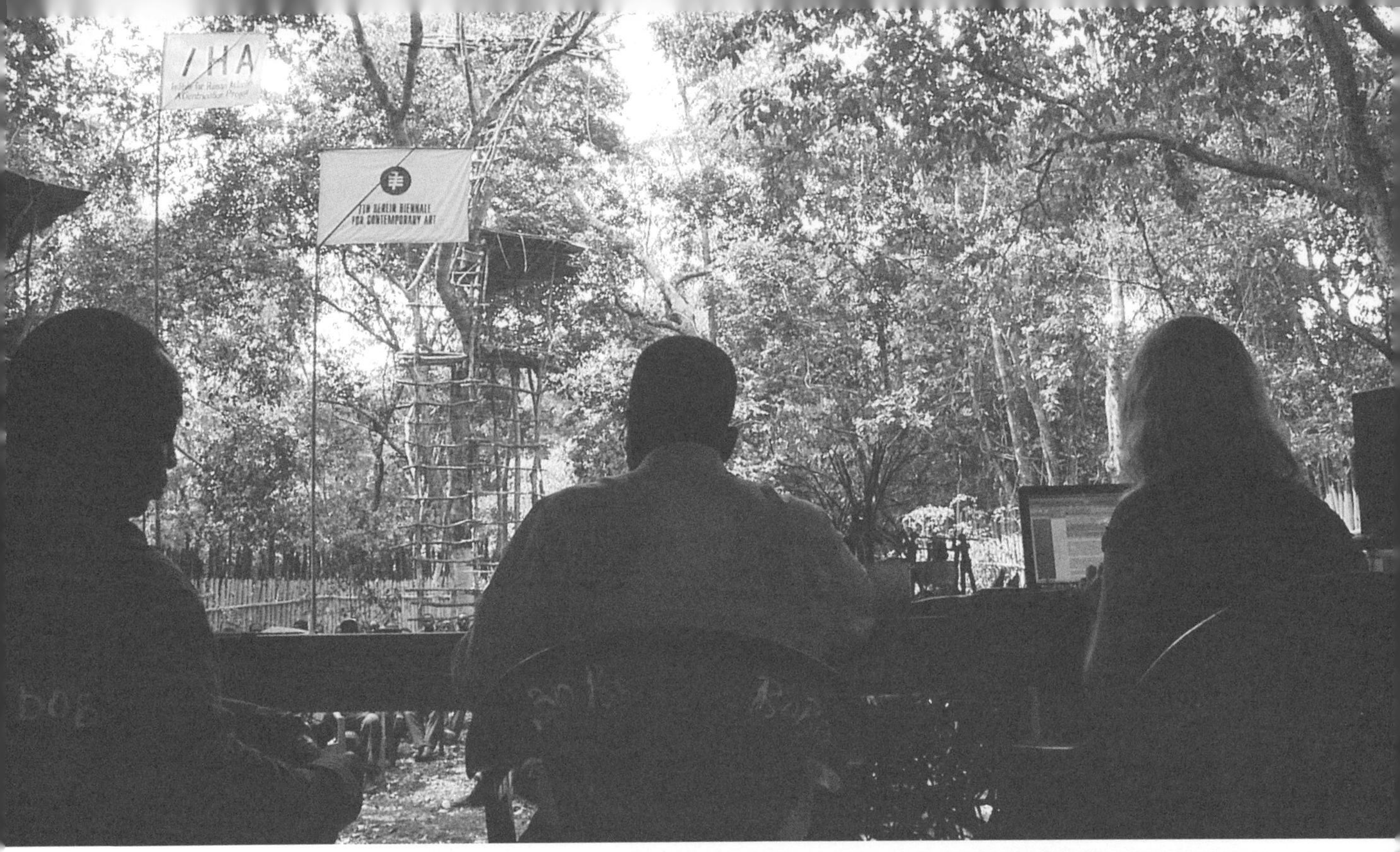

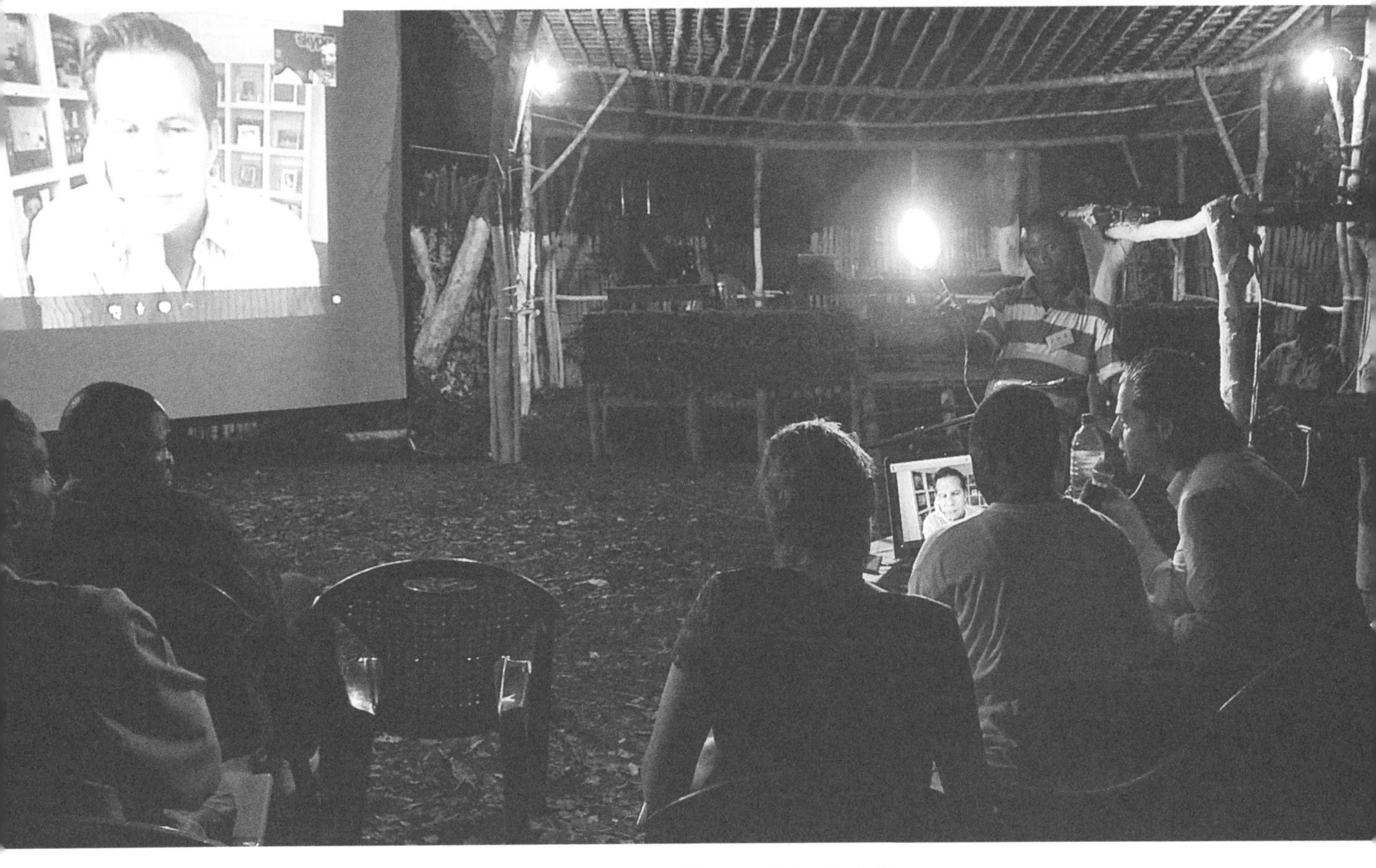

Above: Historian Jérome Mumbanza Mwa Bawele speaks about the history of the plantation
Below: Environmentalist Rene Ngongo and IHA's Renzo Martens in conversation with urbanist Richard Florida

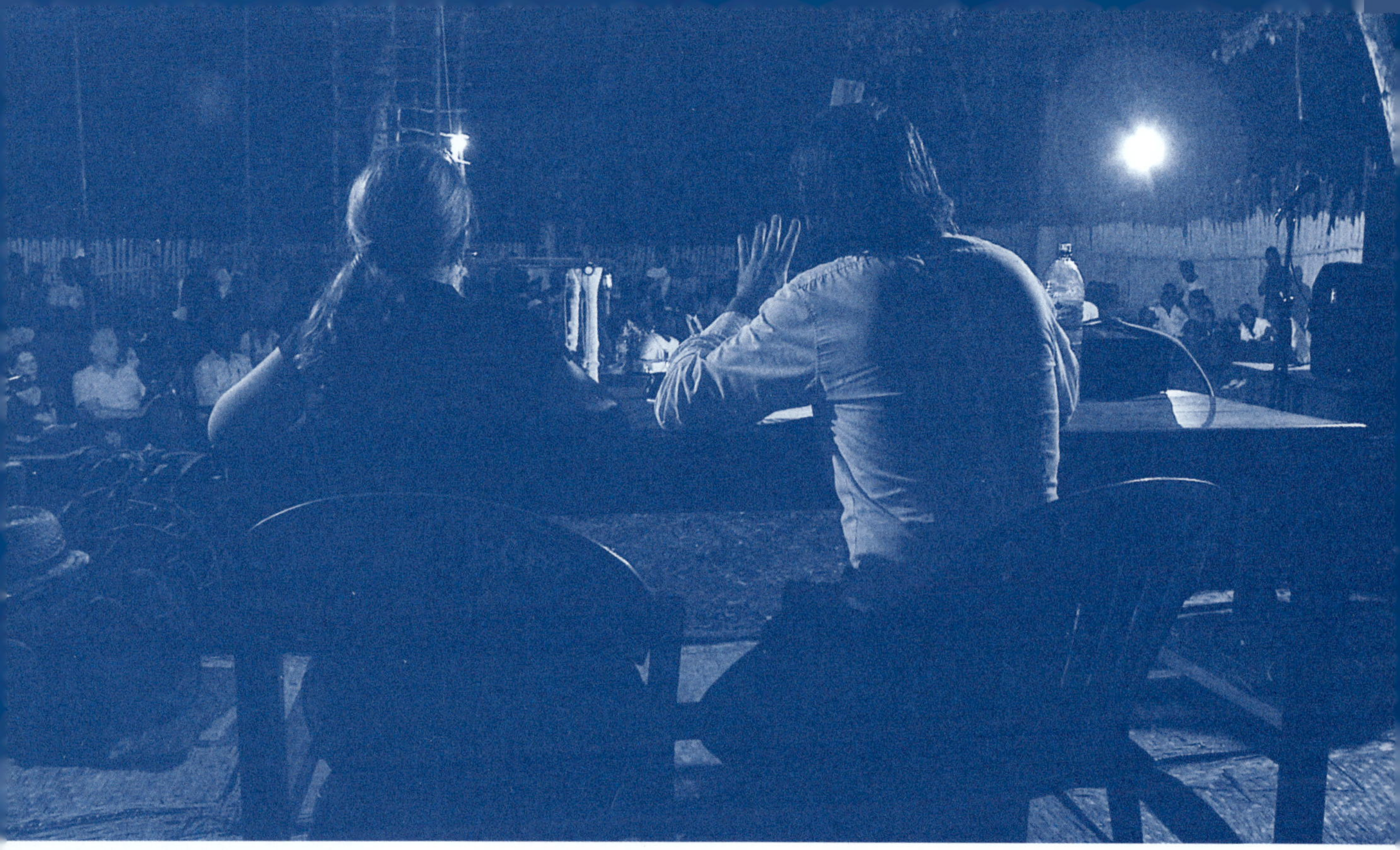

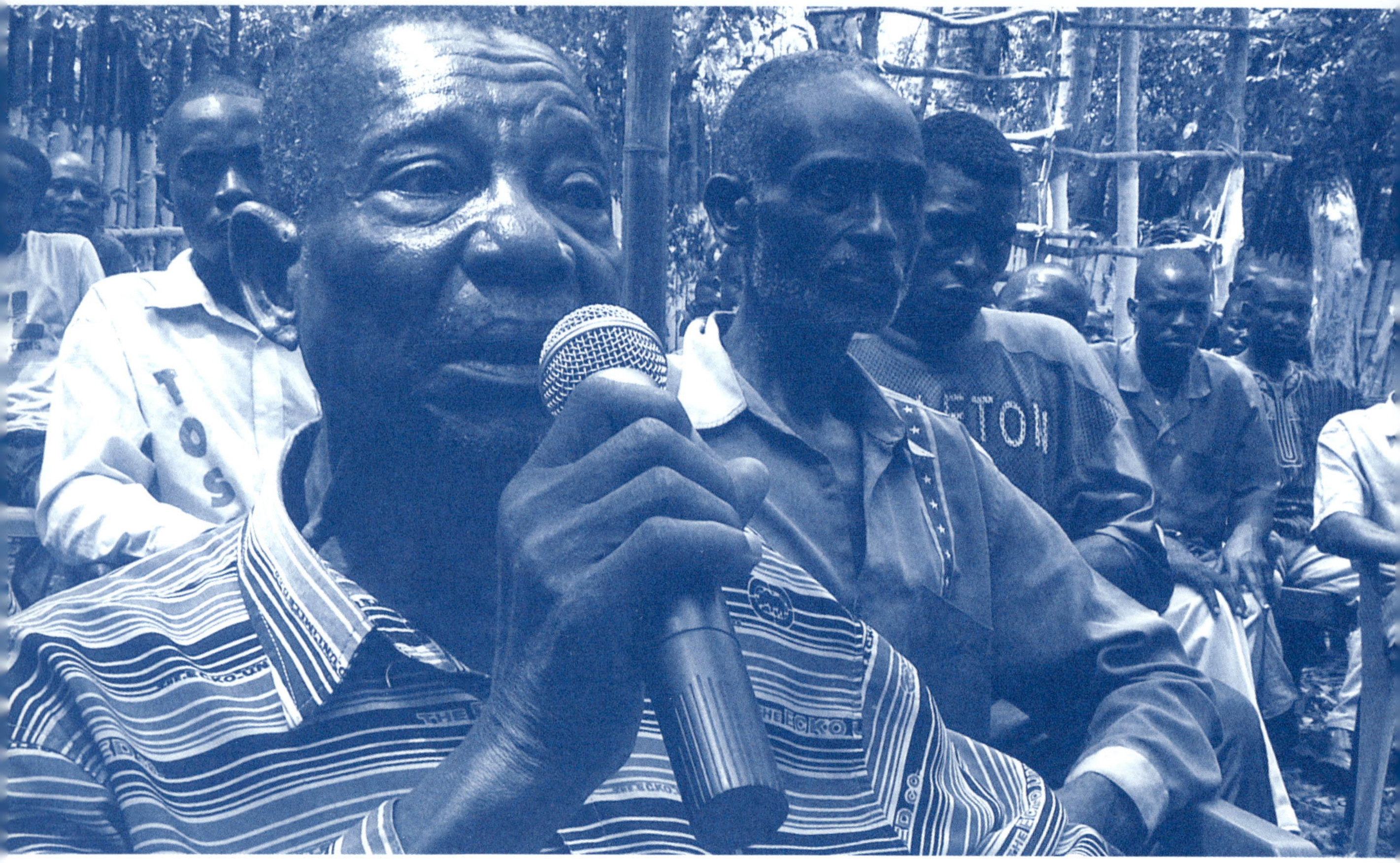

Above: IHA's Renzo Martens speaks about the Institute's program
Below: A question from the audience

4.1 Community Outreach

The Institute is organizing a community outreach program to foster meaningful connections with the local community. A core part of this program is a series of creative therapy workshops led by Israeli post-traumatic stress disorder expert Rony Berger, a specialist in the psychological needs of those trapped in conflict zones or affected by natural disasters. As part of the programming for 2013, Berger, is exploring ways of modifying the techniques used after tsunamis or earthquakes to address the difficulties that may result from one hundred years of plantation labor, with a series of workshops customized for the local community.

4.2 Residency Program

In collaboration with the Van Abbemuseum, the Institute is inviting international artists, activists, and writers—as well as people from Kinshasa and the rainforests surrounding the plantation—to work at the settlement. Questions of complicity, immateriality, and post-Fordist labor may appear in a new light in the presence of the local audience, who are among the lowest-paid people in the global economic system.

The Institute is also inviting people who wouldn't necessarily designate themselves as artists to make work at the site. They include visionary seers or healers who do what could be called performances in the surrounding forests. We hope that they, too, will contribute to a deeper understanding of the global conditions of art production.

At press time, the participants in the 2013 Residency Program include Emmanuel Botalatala, Eléonore Hellio, Sapin Makengele, Dominique Malaquais, Mega Mingiedi, René Ngongo, Katrien Pype, and Bebson de la Rue. Their presence at the site plays an important role in a collective process with the local population, exploring issues of precarity and the role of art as a critical interventionist tool.

4.3 Exhibition Program

The Institute for Human Activities has begun a series of exhibitions and workshops at the settlement. In the summer of 2013, the former Unilever shop is the venue for a presentation of works from the collection of the Van Abbemuseum in Eindhoven, the Netherlands. Among them are videos by Bruce Nauman, Dan Graham, and John Baldessari, highlighting the Institute's indebtedness to the period of art's transition from Minimalism into performance and institutional critique—an earlier time of questioning art's potential for emancipation and the role of artists vis-à-vis the structures in which they operate. Further exhibitions will follow for the duration of the Gentrification Program.

4.4 Economic Benefits

One initial economic benefit of the center derives from the presence of international visitors, whose day-to-day needs, such as coffee and snacks, assistants, and partners for collaborative projects are provided by local residents and entrepreneurs. The transportation and installation of artworks will also necessitate a local crew of art handlers. At a later stage, we anticipate that the local economy will be further diversified as some of the plantation workers take an interest in making critical art. If a plantation worker is able to sell a drawing of his work on the plantation, even for a modest price, he will raise far more money than his annual salary as a plantation worker.

4.5 Opening Seminar

The Gentrification Program kicked off with an opening seminar in June 2012, when a number of Congolese and international speakers gath-

4. Public Programs

ered at the Institute to discuss the history of the plantation economy, gentrification as an interventionist strategy, and the possibilities for art to meaningfully deal with the conditions of its own existence as well as the future direction of the Institute.

Speakers included critic T.J. Demos, philosopher Marcus Steinweg, activist René Ngongo, architect Eyal Weizman, economist Jérome Mumbanza, curator Nina Möntmann, anthropologist Katrien Pype, and artist Emmanuel Botalatala. The keynote address was given by Richard Florida via satellite. A celebrated urban studies theorist, Florida is best known for his 2002 book *The Rise of the Creative Class*, in which he argues for investment in artistic infrastructure as an impetus for economic growth. The Institute finds his contribution particularly valuable in its conviction that knowledge of art's economic and social effects should not be reserved for the sites of art's reception but should also be made productive in those places where artistic interventions are staged.

4.5.1. Marcus Steinweg

IHA Opening Seminar, June 12, 2012
Edited Transcript

I would like to quote a German poet I admire. His name is Heiner Müller. The German version is "*Kein Mensch ist integer*": "There is no integrity for a human being." This simply means there is no innocence. And to believe in the innocence of artistic production, to believe in the innocence of any one of us, simply means to believe in something that does not exist. This belief is called, by the German philosopher Hegel, the belief of the beautiful soul. The beautiful soul is someone who tries to detach himself from reality as it is.

The most universal definition of art is that art has to do with a confrontation with the established reality order, which comes about by building up a resistance against this established reality order. The question is not to assimilate yourself into the world as it is, but to confront it. You need courage for this. You need courage to confront the world as it is, with all the incommensurable, unsupportable parts of the reality order.

4.5.2. Jérome Mumbanza Mwa Bawele

IHA Opening Seminar, June 11, 2012
Edited Transcript

The Institute wanted to know to whom the land belonged on which these plantations are situated. It belonged to the first occupants, or to the stronger ones who drove out the first occupants. In this region, we never had any kingdoms; there were only lineages and tribes. The land belonged to the tribe and was governed by the hereditary chief. The land belonged to the community and everybody could benefit from it, even foreigners that were accepted as friends or guests.

It was with those chiefs—who controlled the land from a spiritual point of view and from a material point of view—that the whites signed agreements to establish themselves here and to exploit our resources. The new products that they found were copal, palm trees, and palm oil. These plantations were mostly financed by the English, so companies such as Unilever set up here in Boteka in 1911. These companies forced the people to work for them without compensation. The people suffered and there were uprisings everywhere. Still, these plantations can help us, provided that they invest, provided that they are managed well, and provided that we find new income sources. At the moment, everything we do here is for Europe.

4.5.3. Richard Florida

IHA Opening Seminar, June 11, 2012
Conversation between Richard Florida and IHA Artistic Director Renzo Martens
Edited Transcript

Renzo Martens:
Hi Richard! How are you? We're in the middle of the rainforest here, in a place called Boteka in the Democratic Republic of Congo.

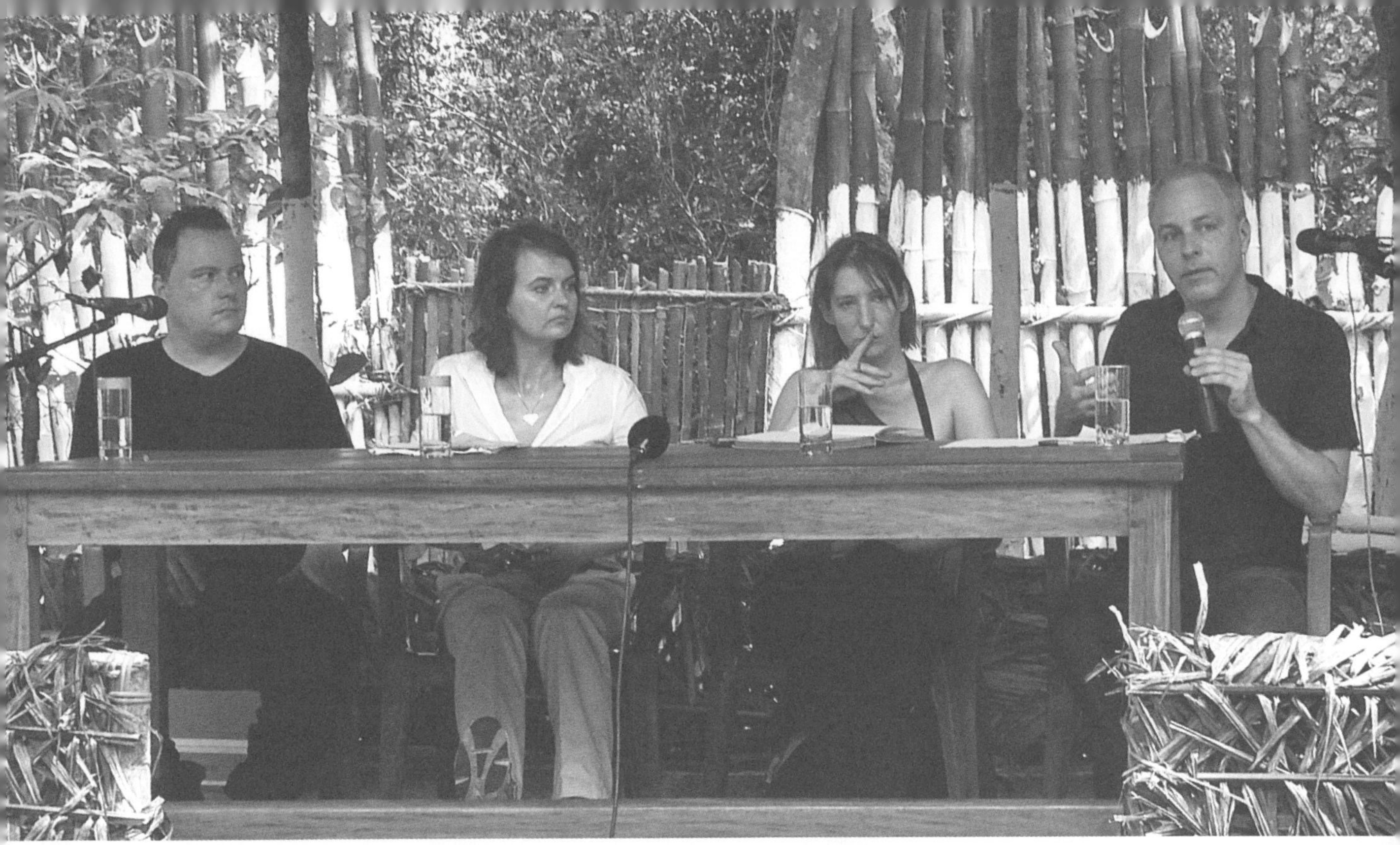

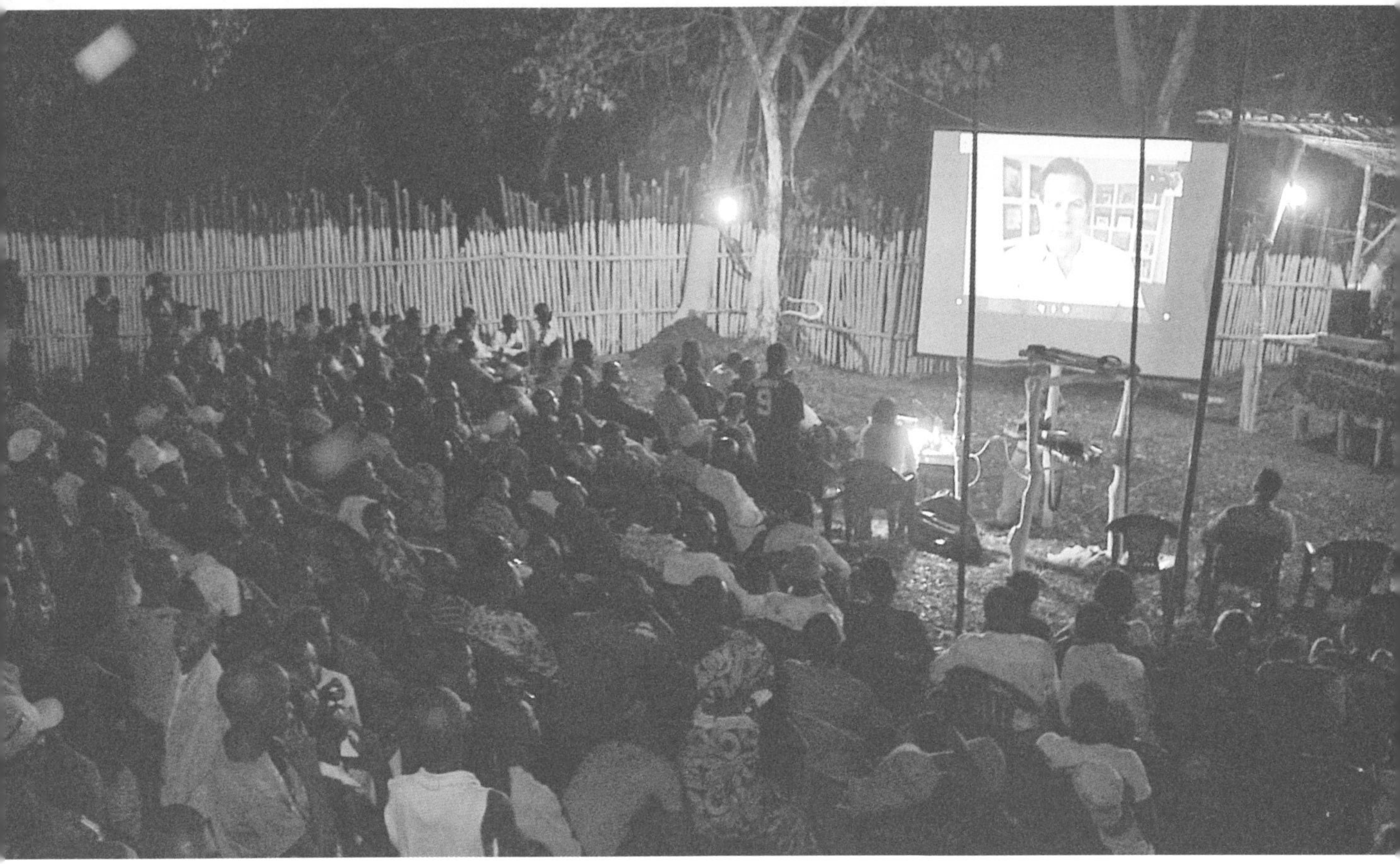

Above: Panel discussion on institutional critique with Marcus Steinweg, Nina Möntmann, Elke van Campenhout, and T.J. Demos
Below: Richard Florida addresses the crowd

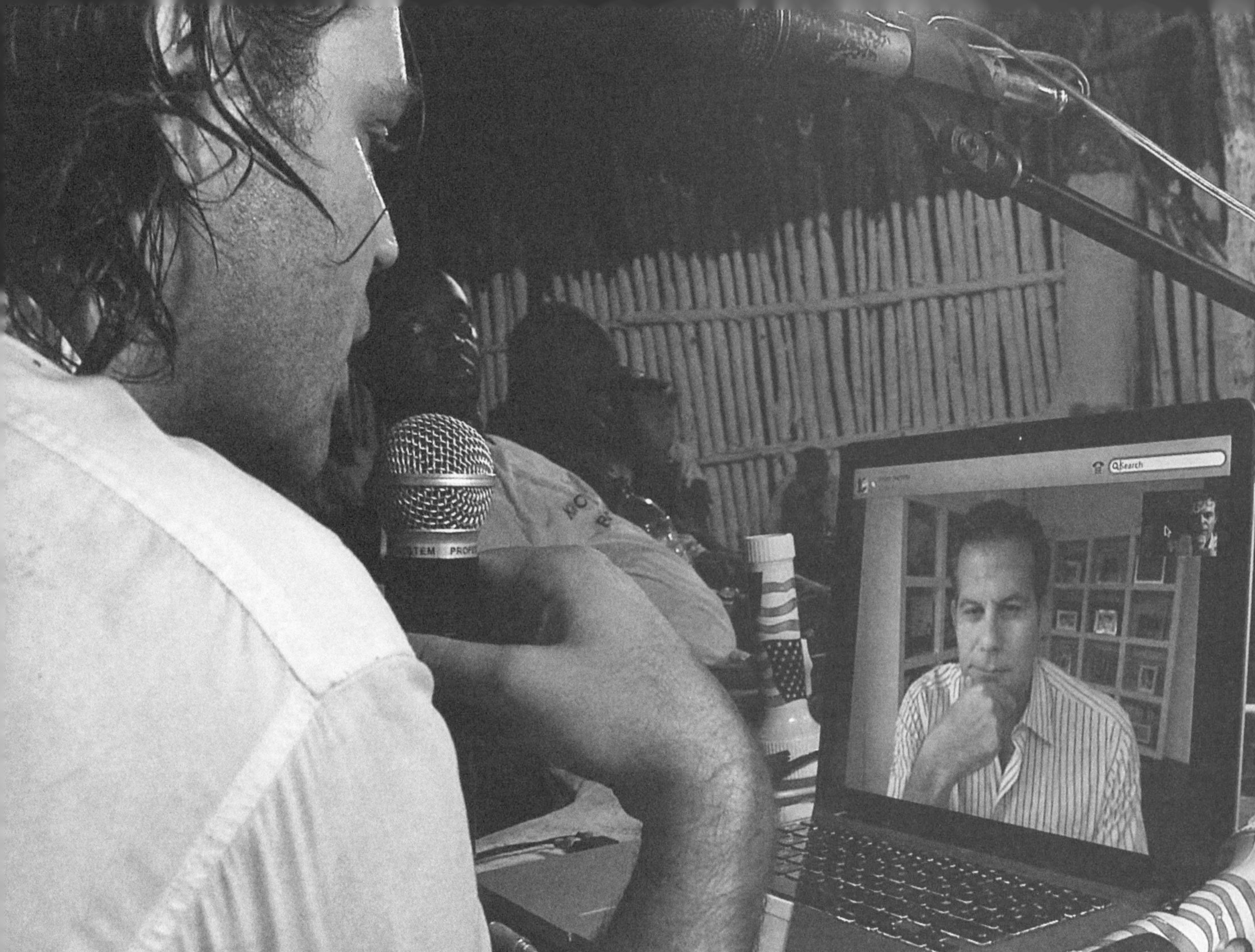

Renzo Martens in conversation with Richard Florida

We're here with about 200 people who work on a former Unilever plantation. They, too, have to make a transition from the Fordist economy to something beyond that.

Richard Florida:
Well, thank you. I wish we could be with you today. As you may know, I just finished the 10th-anniversary edition of *The Rise of the Creative Class*, so it's really fresh in my mind. In that book, I began to think that when people talk about economic development, they talk about hardware, they talk about companies, they talk about technology, they talk about tax breaks to bring a company to a city or a country. And I began to see that that wasn't the whole equation. When you think about human beings, what is innate in every one of us—in every little boy and little girl, in infants and toddlers—it's that we're all creative beings. We share that creativity; we use that creativity together.

And I was able to look at the rise of a group of people—principally artists, designers, culturally creative people, entertainers, musicians, writers, entrepreneurs, technologists, innovators, researchers, and professional people. I came up with a very simple model of what it takes to make a creative community, a creative city, a creative country. And I called it the three Ts: Technology, Talent, and Tolerance. Technology is a necessary but insufficient condition for growth. You have to have talent. Talent is the people, the people who are contributing ideas. And the communities most open to the widest range of people, race, ethnicity, age, gender, sexual orientation, that were tolerant—the third T—they've got an edge. But when you put the three Ts together in a community, this is the spur to a creative model of development.

Could this be transposed into deliberate policies? Would it be useful for a city to invest in a museum or an art biennial in order to attract capital, rather than to invest in a new road or a tax break for companies? When studying development, artistic creation comes before roads, before schools, before hospitals. Investing in artistic and creative

infrastructure is important to an overarching strategy to achieve higher levels of development and higher standards of living.

RM:
We are building an art center, a museum, a residency program. We hope that people will make more money in a new affective economy than in low-paid work in the fields. Do you have data on whether, even in these rural areas, the economy may grow and salaries may rise?

RF:
I think so. A group of people has been looking at more rural areas, and what they found is that artistic investment and building up the quality of place becomes a way of creating excitement and energy.

RM:
We call this program a Gentrification Program. On the one hand, there is much new art that deals with all kinds of economic issues and wants to be very critical of them, which is good because there are many things wrong with the world that can be addressed through art. But on the other hand, the economic return of such art hardly has the same impact on the places that are critiqued. You could make a video showing how poor people are in Congo, but when this video is then shown in London, it generates an economy in London rather than in Congo. This is something we would like to reverse. Is that something you can comment on?

RF:
It's a very interesting intellectual, conceptual, pragmatic issue that you raise. Those contradictions that you mentioned are part of the development of capitalism in the creative age. I think it's up to us artists and creative people to lead in those struggles. And not simply—I am saying this with all humility—complain. We need new models of development in this moment of crisis. What we need is experiments that engage human creativity and spirit and purpose. And that's

what you can achieve with your project. You can be an experiment! The world is very hungry. The world wants a new model that isn't driving wages down, that isn't a race to the bottom. And in the Congo you have the opportunity to show that. In a place that isn't the wealthiest on the planet, a place that has struggle, you can make a new model.

RM:
Thanks a lot, Richard; it's really fantastic that you give us this advice.

RF:
Keep us posted on how you're doing.

4.5.4 Emmanuel Botalatala
IHA Opening Seminar, June 11, 2012
Edited transcript

My name is Botalatala. I'm an artist; I'm a painter in Kinshasa. I was born on the plantation and life was difficult. My father did not earn enough to send us to school, and my mother was not allowed any palm oil. So my mother and some other mothers got together to steal the palm nuts and hide them outside the plantation to extract the palm oil later on. Only after my father resigned, in 1958, did I go to the mission school and it was here that my art originated. But it wasn't until '79, when I was unemployed, that I became the artist I am today. I never went to art school. I did not get any logistical support or benefit from an artistic environment at the time, and if today such an institution establishes itself here, I hope that we can have a training center for young people, a center for visual arts but also for theater, music, cinema. That would be most welcome. And at this point, I publicly commit myself to share my experience with others and to investigate how to set up strategies for the creation of artwork. Not only for sale but to contribute to all the domains of development.

4.5.5 T.J. Demos
IHA Opening Seminar, June 12, 2012
Edited Transcript

I'd like to address some of the complex artistic and political conditions that make the establishment of an experimental institute a significant and meaningful project, and also identify some of the risks, even though what the Institute will be remains to be seen over the next five years of its planned existence.

Speaking from a Euro-American perspective, I see the problem of much contemporary art in the West as it's having little direct social and political relevance, with generally no recognition of or interest in the global South. When artistic projects do engage with African social and political reality, a further tendency is that they are destined for consumption in Europe and North America—sold on the Western art market and discussed in the Western art press.

Some critics (such as artist Hito Steyerl) have taken issue with this situation, particularly with regard to those who prioritize some far-flung political crisis rather than engaging with the more immediate politically unsavory conditions of the Western gallery institution, which is often run by volunteers—the art world's precarious workers. Yet the either/or logic implied here is unnecessary. I would argue that Congolese social, political, and economic conditions—which are part of the global arrangements that directly concern the West—can be engaged as artistic subjects of non-African artists at the same time as the political and economic systems of Western art institutions are subjected to scrutiny.

With many artists today, such as Tino Sehgal, we've also witnessed a focus on what's called immaterial labor—the labor of services, information, and advertising—as taken up by post-autonomous theorists such as Maurizio Lazzarato, Paolo Virno, Michael Hardt, and Toni Negri, which is increasingly invoked by critics and scholars to describe socially engaged artistic practices. The problem here, in brief, is that the use of this term quickly forgets the expor-

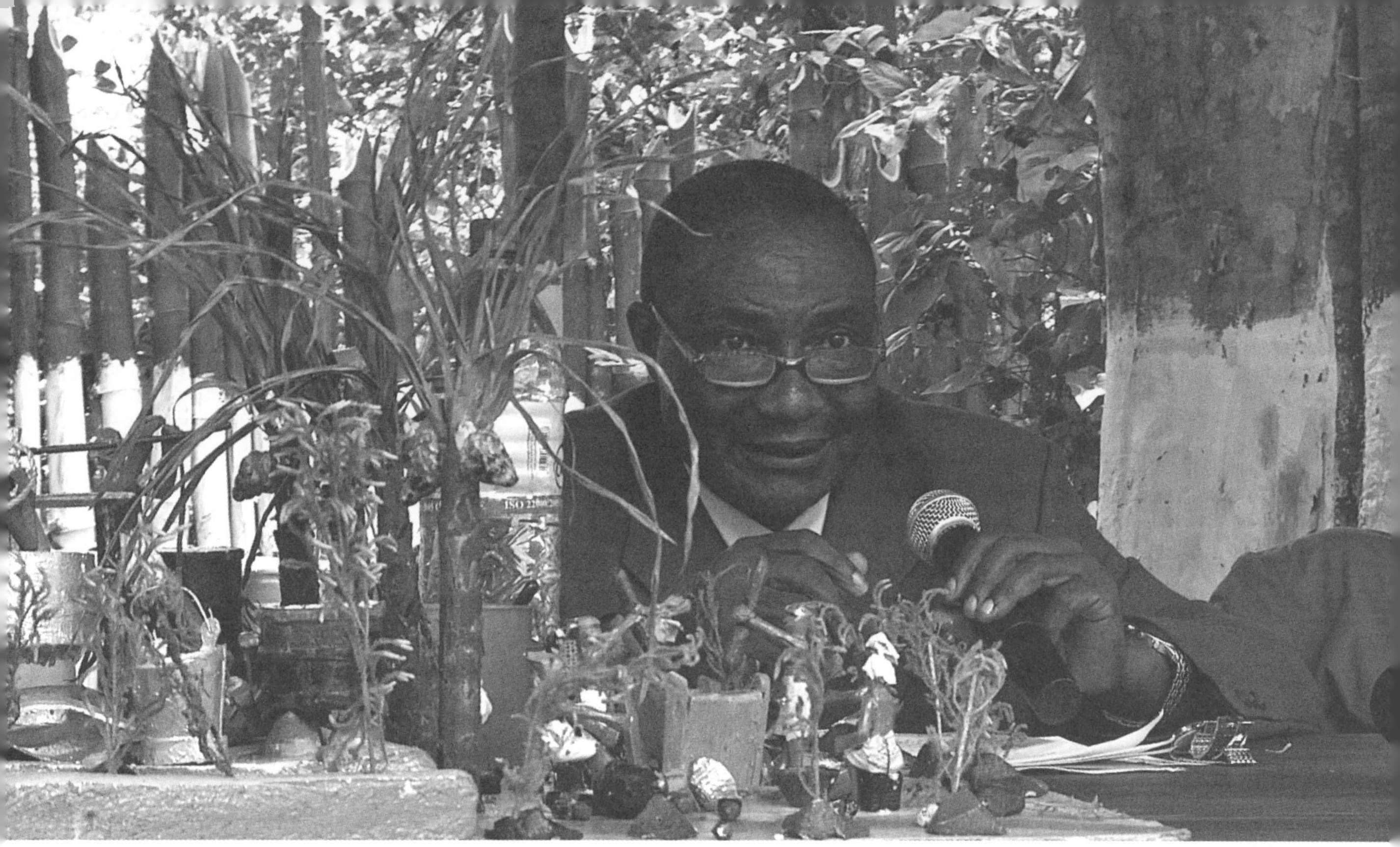

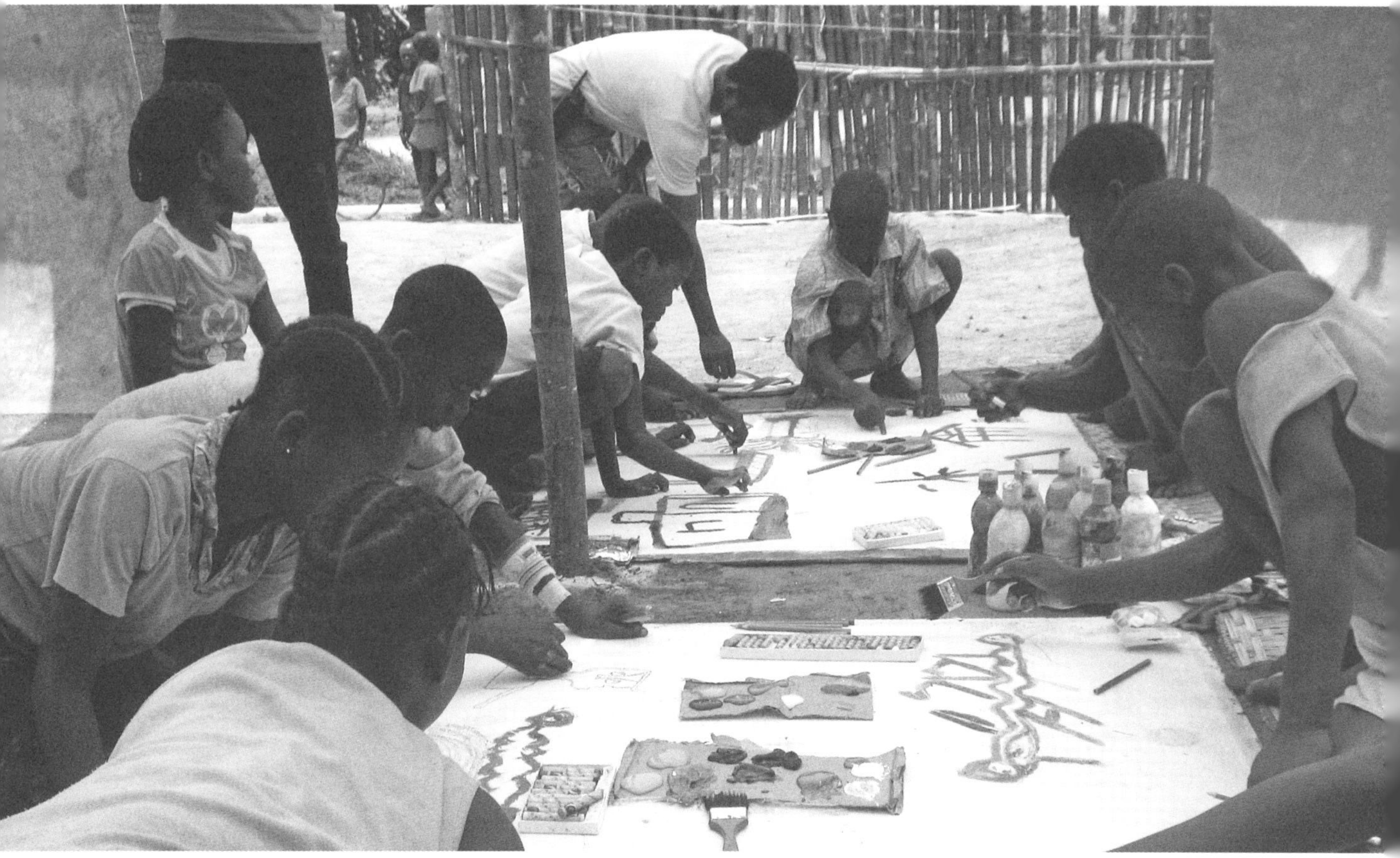

**Above: Artist Emmanuel Botalatala speaks about his youth on the plantation
Below: View of a creative therapy session**

tation of precarity to those outside the developed economies of the West. Clearly, we need to address immateriality and precarity together to comprehend the uneven geographies of globalization and unequal divisions of labor. This offers a new imperative for institutional critique—in particular, an institutional critique that escapes the potential solipsism, or the reproduction, of its own institutionalization in the West, and instead looks to the postcolonial (and in many ways neocolonial) world beyond its borders.

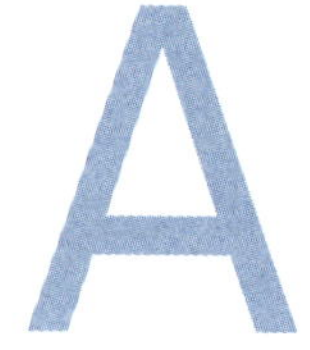

How will the Institute address this? Through a so-called Gentrification Program? I'm slightly horrified by that term, because for me it possesses largely negative connotations. How can the Institute for Human Activities facilitate an art that engages with the political demand for equality, for self-sufficiency, for social, political, and economic justice? And how can a reinvented notion of gentrification serve that purpose? Addressing these questions is among the challenges the IHA faces, lest it become a further example of neocolonial relations between Europe and Africa

I think it's important to note that there are very few people in the IHA's audience today. That should signal to the Institute that it can't rely on an invitation to generate its audience. Participants and collaborators need to be produced through long-term commitment, the cross-cultural sharing of knowledge, creative dialogue, and the critical self-engagement of conflict, beginning with the acknowledgment of the history of colonial relations that have done so much damage in the DRC. The fact that the Institute is assuming a five-year commitment is significant; it will need this time to give itself the space to have some impact, to gain ground as a transformative project in Congo's equatorial region—and in today's increasingly precarious world.

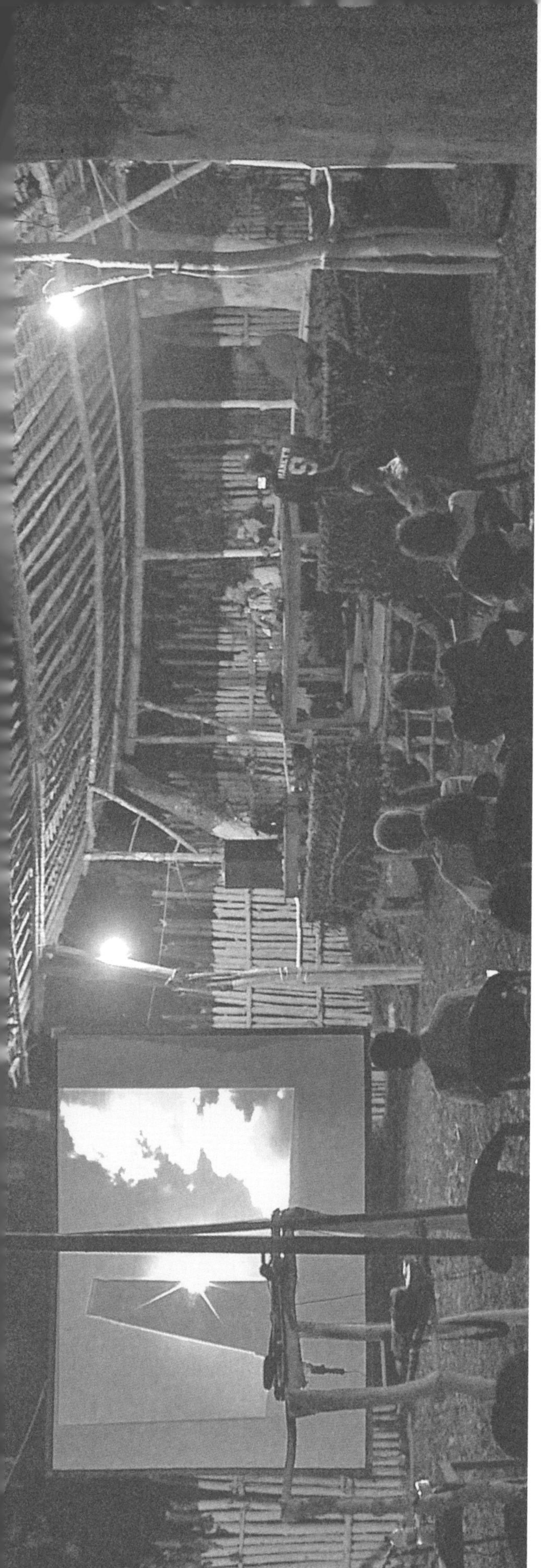

IHA's Renzo Martens speaks about Tate Modern's Unilever Series

The Institute for Human Activities is
generously supported by:

Mondriaan Fund (Amsterdam)
Prins Bernhard Cultuurfonds (Amsterdam)
Kunstenfestivaldesarts (Brussels)
Amsterdam Fund for the Arts
Prince Claus Fund (Amsterdam)
7th Berlin Biennale
Van Abbemuseum (Eindhoven)
Dutch Embassy (Kinshasa)
Koninklijke Vlaamse Schouwburg (Brussels)
KASK–University College Ghent
Heineken (Kinshasa)

A special note of gratitude goes to
London-based Feronia, Inc. Our opening
seminar would not have been possible
without their support.

5. Support

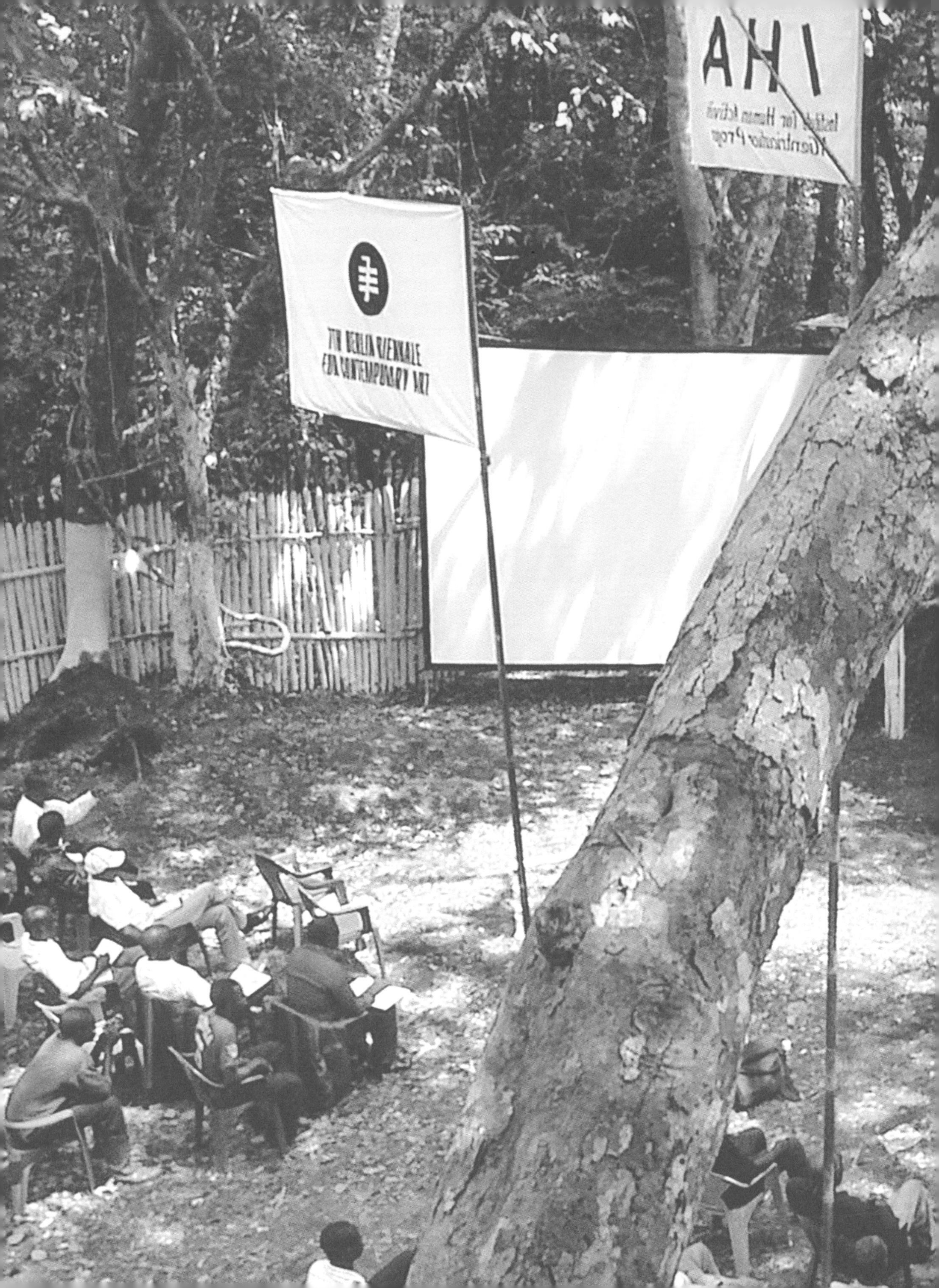
7th BERLIN BIENNALE
FOR CONTEMPORARY ART
IHA
Institut For Human Activity
Werkhuizelen Program

Dr. Otto Weininger
Schwarzspanierstraße 15 A-1090 Vienna
Austria

Dear Madam,

Dear Sir,

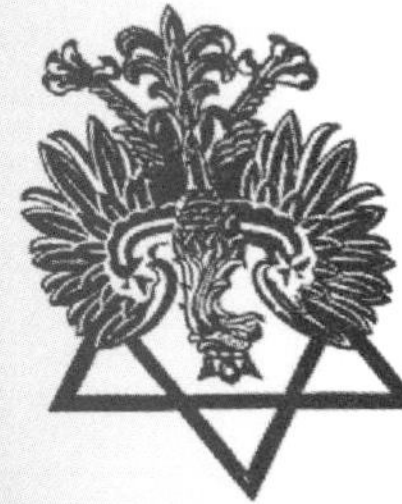

Dr. Otto Weininger
Schwarzspanierstraße 15 A-1090
Vienna Austria

February 5, 2013

To: Yael Bartana

Dear Madam,

Last December I visited your exhibition *If You Will It, It Is Not a Dream: Questions for Freud and Herzl* at the Secession in the heart of my hometown, Vienna. First I would like to congratulate you, dear Ms. Bartana; you deserve applause, and I think you should take pride in the questions you raise in your research, and your fascinating work. Indeed, I never imagined that 110 years after the event some Jewish woman, an Israeli, would ask questions about identity and about the future of the Jews in Europe after World War II, or that she would do it specifically in my country, which embraced the Anschluss and which, this year, celebrates seven and a half decades since Austria's occupation by the Third Reich.

I am proud of you my friend, if I may call you so. You have gained international recognition, though not without some help on my part, among others. Sadly, however, you have chosen to omit any mention of my contribution, not even as a disciple of Dr. Sigmund Freud. In your work you chose to conjure up the Polish Rivka;[1] but what about the Jewish Otto, who realized there was no escape from his Judaism? Otto, to whom auto-anti-Semitism seems to have clung—my activity was indeed short-lived, but in Vienna of the past and the present, maxims and light humor functioned as a social mirror. Having rightly chosen to include a common Viennese joke in the *Cookbook for Political Imagination* accompanying your work, you will be able to appreciate the saying that "anti-Semitism was never taken seriously until the Jews adopted it."[2]

You must know that I wasn't the only Jew to set himself free from the Jewish femininity and the anvil called life. There were many like me who lived with torn souls, and found in death a noble tranquility. How odd that Hitler thought that in my death I would release the Aryan race and the rest of the world from my presence. My book will be in the Deutsche National Bibliothek forever, and it has already been translated into numerous languages posthumously. It is precisely my death that linked my Judaism to my life more forcefully. While Hitler was happy to be rid of my Jewish existence, although I had converted to Protestantism, I have remained inseparably bound to my Judaism to this day.

In your work at the Vienna Secession you present an alternative congress to the Jewish Congress. Why is that? I am curious to know why you have reconstructed this obsolete format? You confront Europe with the question of what Europe should do to accept the Other; and you challenge Poland with the question of what Poland should do to become a part of Europe; and you confront Israel with the question of what Israel should do to become a part of the Middle East. You also turn to my great teacher, Dr. Freud, and to the celebrated writer and philosopher, Mr. Theodor Herzl, regarding the condition of the Jews.

Dear Madam, you are the representative and the outcome of the decisions made for the Jews, regardless of their origin, which have taken shape for more than a hundred years. Zionism started before Nazism and continued after it. Look at yourself, Ms. Bartana, you who possess masculinity and strength, hailing from the Promised Land, you have become a Jewish citizen in the Jewish state. You have become a citizen in a country that is your own, in whose army you may serve and even climb the ladder as high as an officer's rank. But I still believe, as I did in the past, that Zionism means a negation of Judaism, which, according to its own idea, should have spread throughout the world in the ideological aspect, not the missionary sense. As I once wrote, "The concept of the citizen totally *transcends* the Jew, that is why there has never been a Jewish *state* in the strict sense of the word, and there can never be one."3

Dear Ms. Bartana, I hope you will welcome this letter and refer to it in the right spirit. I am curious to read your answer, and have further questions in store, such as what is that movement of yours that is calling for a return of the Jew to Poland and how may one join it? Is it intended only for those who had a connection to Poland in their past? But I shall not bother you any more for the time being.

Awaiting your reply, if you think it proper and find the time to answer the questions of a converted Jew haunted by his past.

I thank you in advance.

With friendship and respect,
Otto Weininger

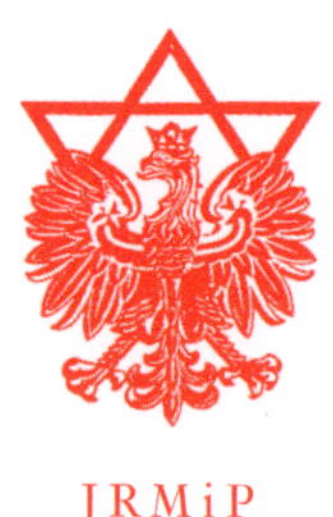

February 16, 2013

To: Mr. Otto Weininger

Dear Sir,

I cannot express my surprise enough when I came across your letter forwarded to me by the Vienna Secession. I received a call from Vienna to let me know that there was a letter from a local ghost addressed to me. At first I thought that Mr. Theodor Herzl or Dr. Sigmund Freud might have decided to answer the questions I put to them by way of my recent exhibition there. Thus, I was surprised to receive it from you, though I was not disappointed. I was surprised, since you have chosen not to tie your fate with the Jewish people. It is a strange nation. You have to be a Jew to be a part of it. You cannot immigrate to it and be a resident. You can try to immigrate to the Jewish State, but this does not ensure your getting resident status or Israeli citizenship, because Jewish citizenship doesn't officially exist, only under the guise of Israeli citizenship.

Let me answer your questions last to first. I set up the return movement to Poland after a long sojourn there, during which I met young and old people who kept saying that they missed their Jews; that Polish society was not the same without the Polish Jewish community. It was the first time I heard that European society without the Jews is incomplete; a society that misses an important part of its essence and culture.

In 2005, following that visit, I returned to Israel and to the Israeli society into which I was born, but the thought that the Nazis had, in fact, succeeded in their task kept haunting me. Like you, I regard Zionist existence as a negation of Judaism, which, according to its own idea, should have spread throughout the world, in the ideological aspect, not the missionary sense. The citizen in Israel, or one desiring Israeli citizenship, had better be a Jew. The State of Israel is not a state of all its citizens; it is the state of the Jews. A non-Jew will never be equal to a citizen whose Judaism has been proven.

As you have rightly observed, Zionism began long before Nazism and continues to exist thereafter. There will be those, however, who may draw a certain comparison between the evolution of Zionism and Nazi ideas. Zionism created a ghetto of its own, a very strong and sophisticated ghetto supported by an independent government, independent laws, and means of enforcement. In other words, it is a society that lives in a closed enclave, a nature reserve of sorts, which is supposed to protect those inside it, but at the same time, restricts them.

The congress of the movement I established was not intended to imitate the Zionist Congress. Obviously, I wanted to create an analogy, to examine how the movement I set up may contribute to the discourse currently taking place in Poland, which has joined the European Union, but unlike other European countries, has few, if any, minorities living in it. I wondered how my movement may contribute to the discourse taking place in the countries of the European Union, which is, on the one hand, a union of states and a blurring of national borders, but at the same time is an entity that now applies stricter laws to those not born in EU countries but who wish to live in them. Toward the end of the 20th century, one could still hope that nationalism would disappear in favor of a different form of governance, such as a federation, that hope has now dissolved in light of the continued vitality of national governments. As you must have already realized from the aforesaid, the question of Israel's integration in the Middle East has not yet been solved, and the future seems to hold even greater difficulty than the past.

Dear Dr. Weininger, allow me to ask you a question that bothers me. I hope you will accept my questions with understanding, too. While Baruch Spinoza decided to give up his Jewish religion without taking on another faith, and was probably the first person to be registered in European history as a man without religious faith, you chose to convert to Christianity. Why? While Spinoza regarded the establishment of a Jewish State as a possibility that is not based on a miracle or on Messianism, you believe that in order to realize Zionism, all Jews must become non-Jews. In your 1903 book *Geschlecht und Charakter* (*Sex and Character*), you wrote that "the Jews would have to overcome their Judaism before they could be ripe for Zionism. To this end, however, it would above all be necessary for the Jews to understand themselves, to get to know themselves, to fight themselves, and to want to conquer Judaism in themselves."[4] If I understand your argument correctly, you claim, in fact, that Zionism is the negation of Judaism, and can only succeed if it is dissociated from the latter.

Dear Dr. Weininger, once again I thank you for your letter and for your interest in my work. I pass my reply on via the Vienna Secession. I hope you will be willing to answer my questions and continue our correspondence.

Sincerely yours,

Yael Bartana
Berlin, Germany

Dr. Otto Weininger
Schwarzspanierstraße 15 A-1090
Vienna Austria

February 24, 2013

Dear Ms. Bartana,

I hope this letter finds you well and that the long winter has not jeopardized your welfare or health.

I was happy to receive your answer and questions. If you will be so kind, I would like you to clarify what is currently going on in the land of Zion. Due to limitations forced upon me by my death, I am unable to leave European land until I am posted elsewhere. The line is long for those requesting to leave Europe. The intellectual boredom and treacherous weather have caused pressure in the offices providing visas to developing countries, where the weather is surprisingly better, so I've heard. Will you be so kind as to accommodate my request and update me on what is going on outside Europe? (The daily papers arrive here censored, hence at a considerable delay.)

To your questions, why I changed my religion rather than choosing to simply be without one: I felt caught between East and West, between capitalism and socialism, between religion and state, between oppressed and oppressor. This is the soul of a Jew, Ms. Bartana; like me, your soul, too, is trapped in a historical oxymoron that grows more and more complicated as time passes. When I am asked why, in fact, I hate Jews, I feel that I am in a good company. The Jews who contributed most to humanity were those who hated Judaism. Jesus was a Jew who hated Jews, and so was Spinoza, whom you mentioned, and Marx—but all of them drew their theories from Judaism. Still, I haven't yet answered your question. Today I may have chosen otherwise, but this is a mere speculation that I cannot guarantee. I wanted to be like everyone else, like everyone around me, and I was surrounded by a Christian world, a world born from Judaism that matured into Christianity. I wanted to be like them, or more accurately—I wanted to *be* them.

The reality of a non-territorial state, such as that following the destruction of the First Temple, may prove that long before the destruction of the temple, Jews had chosen the life of a root-stock crawling all over the world and eternally thwarting individuation. Therefore, I was impressed and thrilled at the sight of your work, which undermines the structure of the nation-state. Please correct me if I'm wrong in my reading. You act so that the Jews may continue their Judaism, rather than acting, as expected of you as an Israeli, to reinforce the Jews' claim to the State of Israel. You operate for the Jewish return to Europe to preserve their Judaism. Indeed, I believe that Zionism wants something *un*-Jewish. Zionism wants territory. It wants control. It wants to be like any other state.

I must admit that I don't fully understand you or the way you have chosen to represent the movement for the Jews' return to Europe. Throughout your work you use national symbols. You have invented a flag comprising the Star of David and the Polish eagle. Do you suggest that the Israelis resemble the Poles? The visual language you have adopted is a propagandist language whose colors and symbols allude to fascist propaganda. In this choice of language, do you wish to deem Israel's language today as fascist? Or do you, perhaps, relate to the past, to national movements that have ceased using that language? Or to national movements whose visual language has become more sophisticated, yet is ultimately still fascist?

Dear Ms. Bartana, with this I shall conclude my letter, and ask that it be sent to you.

I hope I have not burdened you too much with my questions, which may be hackneyed and may have already been put to you.

Wishing you health and longevity,

Your friend,
Otto

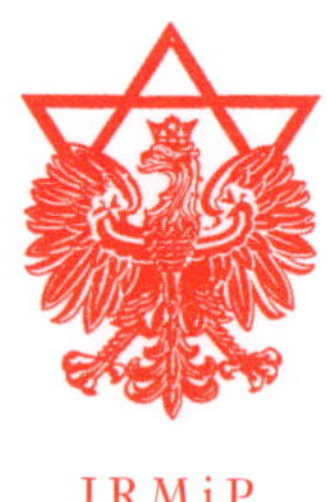

March 5, 2013

Dear Dr. Otto Weininger,

I was happy to receive your last letter. Does one inquire after a ghost's health? If so, I hope you are well. I would very much like to use our connection to send my warm greetings to Rivka.

It may interest you to know that when I worked on the exhibition at the Secession, I tried to contact Dr. Sigmund Freud and Mr. Theodor Herzl, but they refused to collaborate and answer my questions. You, on the other hand, are doing so. May I ask why you chose to leave Judaism and convert to another faith? Is one religion better than the other? You didn't actually live as a Christian; you never had the chance to live as a Christian. Is it simply that you didn't want to be a Jew? Was it not faith that led you to another religion? I find it hard to understand. You chose to bid farewell to the corporeal world, a solution that is unacceptable to Judaism and many other religions. The solution proposed by Spinoza regarding his Judaism, and his understanding of man's autonomy, was to be registered as a man without religion. He was ahead of his time, the first person in Europe to be registered as without religious faith.

In present-day Israel, his solution seems to be growing in popularity. Jewish citizens ask to be registered as lacking religion in a state established for the Jewish people, which not long ago declared that it was primarily Jewish and secondarily democratic. Only recently, Israeli novelist and publicist Yoram Kaniuk voiced his desire to remove the religion notation on his ID card that declared him to be Jewish because his grandson could not be registered as a Jew (according to religious law), a precedent that led other Israelis to follow suit.[5]

You practically prophesied this, saying that a Zionist state cannot be a Jewish state—Jewish by your definition of Judaism, whose femininity you eschewed; at the same time, however, you did not accept Zionism as a path that could redeem the Jewish people of its Judaism. In the course of my work as a Jewish/Israeli artist, I have followed the manner in which different groups characterize themselves as communities. My test group naturally has been the community closest to me, into which I was born and raised.

Having observed social and national rituals, I began to distinguish between groups that choose self-determination, on the one hand, and processes of indoctrination on the other; between acceptance of shared values and a forcing of values—in Israel's case, the forcing of national values over the values of the individual.

Different people from different societies tend to unite under symbols that characterize and define them. The best example is the homosexual-lesbian community, which has neither a state nor a nation nor any one orderly doctrine; nevertheless, the gay community has, for years, gathered under a single flag that represents it and there is one day of the year dedicated to it throughout the world. The flag of the movement for the Jewish Renaissance Movement in Poland (JRMiP) represents two national symbols, but at the same time undermines them. It does not symbolize either state, but rather a different community that does not accept the bounds of the nation-state as its own.

The movement for the Jews' return to Poland operates against national tendencies striving to void nationalist symbols. When I set up the movement, I wanted to examine whether we as a society—or rather, any society, especially Israeli society—can imagine our reality beyond the processes of indoctrination to which we have been subjected under the guise of socialization.

The State of Israel today promotes nation over citizenship. When a Jew chooses to be without religion, he may continue to be an Israeli citizen and be registered not under the Jewish religion but under the Jewish nationality. But how can a court decision on this matter apply to all those non-Jews who choose to live in Israel as people without religion? Can Muslims and Christians too ask to omit the religion clause from their IDs and become Israelis of a Christian or Arab nationality? Israel is unlike other nations; it does not separate religion and state. If I may borrow your analogy between religion and gender—you, who were the first to acknowledge the existence of a third, feminine-masculine gender, namely, a woman who chooses to live with a woman and a man who chooses to live with a man—cannot the case of an intricate rather than one-dimensional gender identity be applied to nationality? Can it not opt for androgyny too?

My dear friend, if I may regard you as a friend, I hope I have succeeded in revealing some of the thoughts that preoccupied me during preparation of the aforesaid exhibition, which sums up the activities of the movement in recent years.

Hoping to hear from you soon, and please do not forget to send my warm greetings to Rivka.

Yael Bartana

Dr. Otto Weininger
Schwarzspanierstraße 15 A-1090
Vienna Austria

March 12, 2013

To: Ms. Bartana

Dear Friend,

Thank you for your detailed letter and the interesting views you presented. When you next come to Vienna, please write to me, as I'd be happy to meet you in one of my hometown's famous cafés. The first question that came to mind when I read your letter was whether I would have been accepted had I registered as a member of the movement for the Jews' return to Poland? Does the movement accept ghosts into its ranks? Does it accept Jews who converted their religion? Does it accept only Jews?

My questions may be irrelevant to your activity. I was raised and educated in a different era, before World War I, in a time when nationalism or the nation-state and its borders were taking shape after the Imperialist period. You made an interesting observation about the gay community and the way in which the gays invented themselves as a community of which many individuals feel a part, although they do not share a language, faith, or nationality.

My understanding of homosexuality was unusual for my time. Moreover, my magnum opus *Geschlecht und Charakter* (*Sex and Character*) was unjustly presented as a racist text that legitimized Nazism. On the matter of homosexuality, I would like to note that Prof. Freud himself was reluctant to validate either homosexuality or lesbianism. He maintained that the freedom to oscillate between male and female objects was only possible in infancy or during the early phases of society and history. Such flexibility in adult life, he believed, was regressive. Adulthood implies restricting and defining one's sexual object, namely—heterosexuality.

As opposed to Prof. Freud, I legitimized another gender. I rejected the notion that homosexuality was an acquired trait, for in that case one may equally perceive heterosexuality as "acquired": maintaining that a heterosexual man or woman must acknowledge the member of the opposite sex generates an acquired world view a priori. My bisexual predisposition gave rise to an intricate typology of identities in terms of the feminine and masculine elements. The blame is with the failed attempts to explain homosexuality, stemming from the scholarly habit to differentiate it completely without regard for other facts.

In my distress, I chose to convert to Christianity. I wanted to explore the transition from one religious faith to another, which I also regarded as related to a transition from one sexuality to another. I myself was the subject of my research and aforementioned book, but found no solace in it. I lived between worlds: between the academic and the emotional, the sexual and the social, the religious and the national worlds, but found no comfort for my torn soul. Today, some one hundred years post factum, I might have been able to contain the multiple elements that comprised my personality: Jew-Christian, masculine-feminine, Jewish-Austrian, foreigner-local; but in real time, I was unable to choose between these diverse identities.

Dear Ms. Bartana, dear friend, thank you for your letters. If I may, I would like to keep writing and sharing my thoughts with you.

Best wishes for health and happiness, in the hope of a lasting friendship.

Yours,
Otto

April 5, 2013

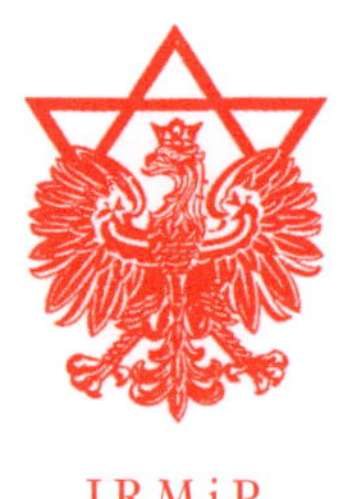

Dear Otto,

I hope by now I can start calling you by your first name. Please forgive me for taking so long to reply to your last letter. It's already the beginning of April and winter refuses to end; Berlin is still occasionally covered in snow. I miss the heat of the Israeli sun and the smell of blossoming oranges. I have to say that it's been years since I have written letters that get sent in the mail. Do you ghosts have electronic mail? Hasn't Google invented an application like this yet? If you had the option of electronic mail it would be possible for me to answer your letters more frequently since I exhibit in different places in the world and am not always at home when the mail arrives.

Your letter reminded me of a dialogue between an SS officer who hunts Jews and a French farmer that takes place at the home of the farmer in the beginning of *Inglourious Basterds*, a film by Quentin Tarantino that came out in 2009. The SS officer prides himself on his ability to hunt Jews since he knows them. He compares Jews to rats and Nazis to hawks. The hawk can only find Jews who are hiding in places where the hawk would hide as well. This SS officer, on the other hand, is a Jew hunter and can think like a Jew.

Col. Landa:
The feature that makes me such an effective hunter of the Jews is, as opposed to most German soldiers, I can think like a Jew, where they can only think like a German, or more precisely, a German soldier. Now if one were to determine what attribute the German people share with a beast, it would be the cunning and predatory instinct of a hawk.

In your book you claim that a German could have Jewish characteristics and similarly that a man could have feminine characteristics. In your despair you chose to convert to Christianity, but you concluded that you failed, and thus committed suicide. Christianity did not provide you with consolation or relief from your despair. I *am* angered by your view of Jews as being different from other nations, with religion or origin as a source that is responsible for different and special characteristics in them. When I created the Jewish Renaissance Movement in Poland, it was a proposal to enable any person to return and live where he/she was born or where his/her ancestors were born. In fact, I called upon every person, even if not Jewish, to join a movement that does not believe and see the religious or ethnic origin of a person as valid criteria for the nation-state. The last movie in my *Jewish Trilogy*, which is about the rise and maturation of the movement, is called *Zamach* (*Assassination*). I dedicated it to Juliano Mer-Khamis, who was murdered in Jenin on the third day of filming.[6] I read about it in the newspaper. Juliano was the son of a Jewish-Israeli woman and a Christian-Palestinian man. According to Christianity, Juliano was Christian and according to Judaism he was Jewish. He wanted to live in both worlds, the Israeli and the Palestinian, and apparently it cost him his life. Maybe he is the figure of the nationally androgynous person that I referred to earlier.

The case study of Israel shows what happens when immigration or citizenship laws are not equal for everybody. Different nations live in Israel, nations that in fact do not exist. This is, for example, the case of the people of the Druze religion who live in Israel. A nation was invented for them, the Druze nation. The nation of the Druze who live in Israel is Israeli and their religion is Druze, but the records of the Ministry of the Interior in Israel are records of ethnicity.

The official records in Israel separate between Jewish national and every other nation: Arab national, Druze national, Samarian national, Circassian, and more. Anyone entering Israel from another country who is not Jewish is given the nationality that is written on his/her passport. So there are people in Israel whose national affiliation is recorded as Hong Kong, or Singapore—after all, there are no such nations even in Hong Kong or Singapore. If an Egyptian citizen were to enter Israel and wish to reside there, his nationality would be Egyptian or Lebanese but not Arabic, since his passport is Egyptian or Moroccan. In every democratic country, all citizens are considered to be the nationality of the country. Just imagine what a commotion the Jews in the United States would make if the authorities would write in each citizen's documents the word "Jew"?

Yoram Kaniuk, who I mentioned in my last letter, is not a random or singular example of someone who asks not to be recorded as Jewish in his official papers. He could not adopt his own son in Israel, since his wife was not Jewish, which is why he had to do so in Germany. This is because as a Jew he could not adopt his own child, who was not Jewish. We Israelis have built a golden cage for ourselves to live in, but even a golden cage is a jail. And if Jewish people will not return to Europe, one could say that Hitler has succeeded in his mission and cleaned Europe of its Jews, and not only Europe. But still today there are more Jews who live outside the state of Israel than in it, and maybe in the future the golden cage will open and the state of Israel will have more non-Jews than Jews and everybody will be Israeli.

Warm regards,
Yael

Dr. Otto Weininger
Schwarzspanierstraße 15 A-1090
Vienna Austria

April 13, 2013

Yael Bartana

Dear Ms. Bartana,

Thank you for your letter. I had begun to think I would not hear from you again. To answer your question, yes we do have electronic mail, but despite the fact that I belong to and live as those of my own generation, I am not growing old. However, my habits are anachronistic. And if one had thought for a moment that my ideas are ahead of their time, today nobody could say so. I do not watch television, and I also do not go to the cinema. Every once in a while I go to the opera in Vienna, but the electronic mail medium is foreign to me; I have Google, but I rarely use it. As you have already understood after such a long introduction, I did not see Quentin Tarantino's film and I do not completely understand the example you gave. Did you want to say that the officer was priding himself on the fact that he understands Jews because he thinks like a Jew and therefore he is able to catch them? Interesting thought.

Lately and following the exchange of letters between us I meet more often with Hans Herzl (the son of Theodor Herzl, father of modern Zionism), who, like me, committed suicide after converting to Christianity. He joined the Baptist church but vigorously changed denominations within the Christian church and even passed through the Catholic and Protestant churches and finally went back to the Jewish faith. A strange type. Hans and his life story are complex, but my conversations with him are very interesting to me, since he was of my town and possesses great knowledge about his father and knows how to tell it in wonderful taste.

Like me, he also thought that the transcendental identity of the Jews is a big privilege—so much so that they should be glad they do not have a state, and he thinks that his father made a mistake by agreeing to limit his ideals and wanting to establish a state. In his own conversion to Christianity, Hans saw the future of the Jews as part of the church of the world and the pope as representing them in the Commonwealth of Independent States. I didn't go as far with my vision. Hans was fourteen years old when I committed suicide. Maybe if we would have met and were the same age, we could have borne the suffering and supported one another. This did not happen, but following this exchange of letters with you, I feel I have found a new friend, as you likewise suffer.

In your letter you raise an idea that I am not sure is untrue, but it is troublesome the way in which you connect things. I agree with you that just as Hitler tried to find a solution to the problem of Jews, Herzl was also previously occupied with it, and they both reached the same conclusion that the Jews all need to be gathered in one place. He also saw the collective conversion to Christianity of all the Jews as a solution to the Jewish problem. But the motives of the two were completely different. And I can tell you in complete confidence that if you continue in this way you will find your name next to mine when one searches Google for "Otto, anti-Semites."

One last question I have for you, dear Ms. Bartana, as you want to bring the Jews back to Europe, back to Poland—which Europe do you want to bring them back to, that of a hundred years ago or that of today? It is true that Europe changes slowly—with every decade that passes, Europe is slower and the economy is weaker, the democratic and the welfare states are simultaneously crumbling. Isn't it time to move forward rather than return? Isn't it time to leave? And why do *you* want to return, if not to this same transcendental, un-national Judaism?

Many greetings and thank you for your letters,
You've brought new light to my life,
Otto

Notes

These letters—ghost-written by Eindhoven-based Israeli curator Galit Eilat (and translated in part by Daria Kassovsky)—are imagined as a conversation between Israeli artist Yael Bartana and the notorious Austrian philosopher Otto Weininger (1880–1903). Weininger committed suicide at a young age, having renounced his Jewish identity in favor of Christianity. His publication *Geschlecht und Charakter: Eine principielle Untersuchung* (*Sex and Character: An Investigation of Fundamental Principles*) (1903) was influential, particularly after his death, and has become renowned for its misogyny and anti-Semitism. The letters are dated in the aftermath of Bartana's recent exhibition at Vienna's Secession, which featured the work of the Jewish Renaissance Movement in Poland (JRMiP), a political group founded by the artist and dedicated to reimagining notions of citizenship away from national or ethnic identity toward a new set of allegiances based on otherness. The exhibition also pitted the father of psychoanalysis, Sigmund Freud, against the father of Zionism, Theodor Herzl.

1. Rivka is a spectral figure who is referenced and appears in Bartana's *Polish Trilogy*, a group of videos that tells the story of the rise of the Jewish Renaissance Movement in Poland (see pages 193 through 196). Rivka represents the ghost of return, a Jewish figure caught in the feedback loop of the Holocaust's harrowing legacy and its effects on Jewish identity. In the trilogy, she stands in for the community of the diaspora as both a symbol of trauma and of hope, one who refuses to allow the memory of her trauma to be used to support militaristic ends.

2. Vienna, 1903: Freud awoke one morning to the sound of knocking at his door. Still in his pajamas, he opened the door and faced an excited Herzl, who said, "I had a dream." Sebastian Cichocki and Galit Eilat, eds., *Cookbook for Political Imagination* (Warsaw: Zachęta National Gallery of Art and Sternberg Press, 2011).

3. Otto Weininger, *Sex and Character: An Investigation of Fundamental Principles* trans. Ladislaus Löb, ed. Daniel Steuer and Laura Marcus (Bloomington: Indiana University Press, 2005), 277.

4. Ibid., 277.

5. The children and grandchildren of Yorum Kaniuk (1930–2013) cannot be officially registered as Jewish because Israel operates according to religious laws that disallow such documentation for a person born to a non-Jewish mother.

6. Juliano Mer-Khamis, an actor, director, filmmaker, and political activist, was murdered on April 4, 2011.

Nástio Mosquito answers Ryan Bartholomew

Cooked by Nastivicious

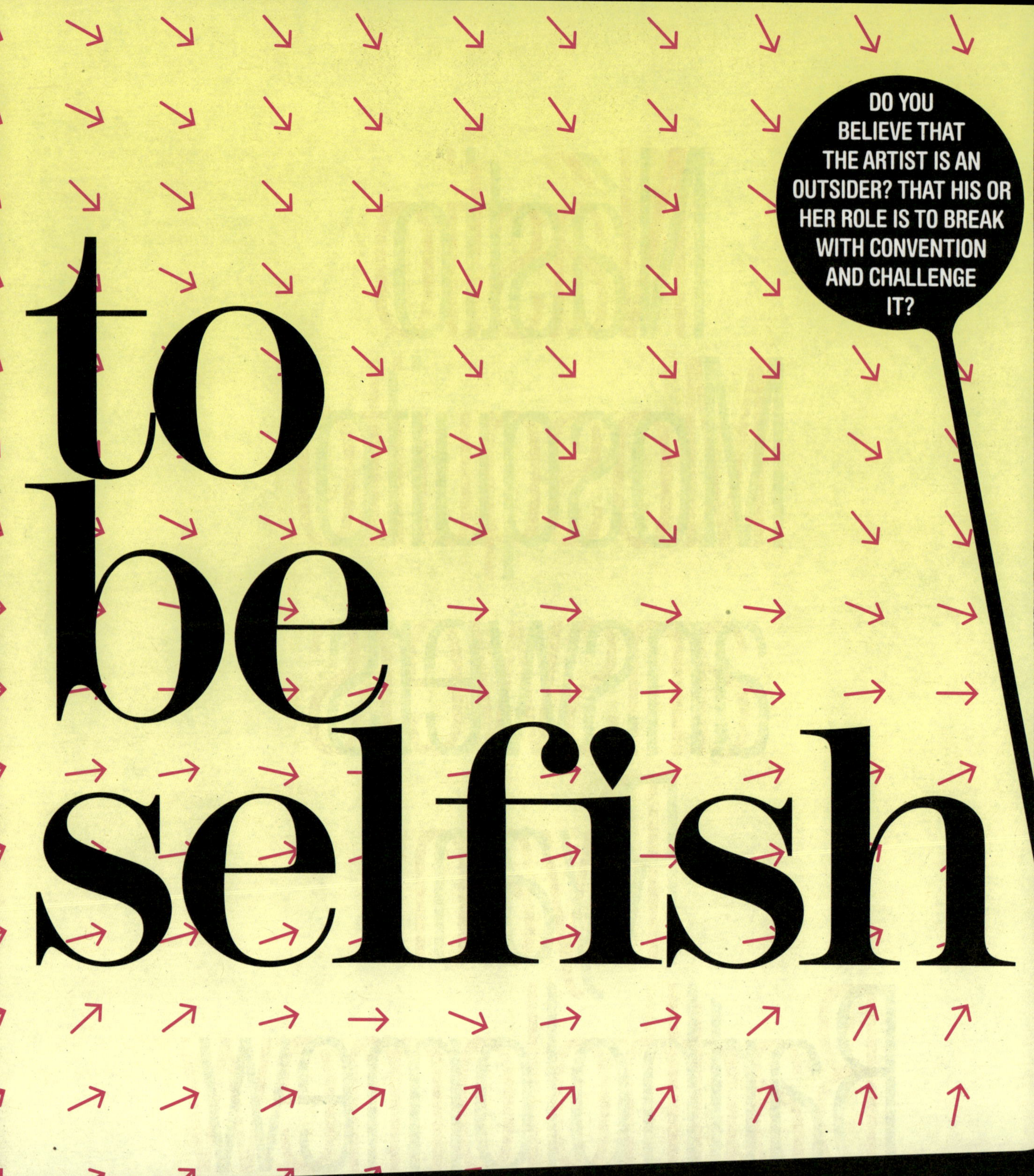

The only role the artist has is to be selfish. While being selfish, unlike shellfish, he or her has, in consequence, the possibility to be relevant for communities larger then his or her own... Is that unfair with the shellfish? If he or her accepts the outsider condition I think he or her is already and truly dead.

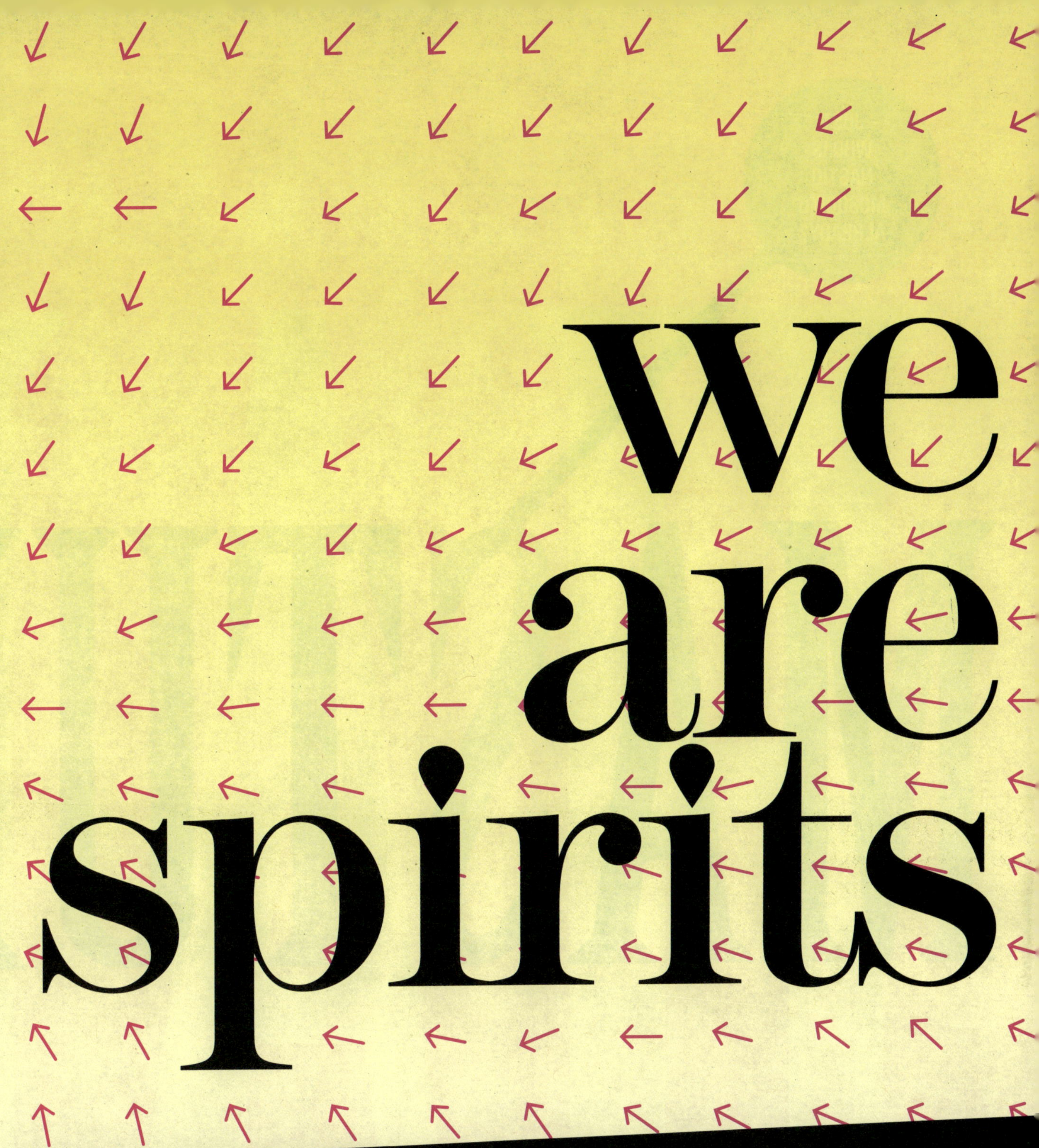

I believe that we are spirits that have a body, soul, mind. Not the other way around...
It is not a new concept, as you know, but it is one that is taken for granted... What an artist
and art can do is to allow people to access the spiritual realm via the physical things they
produce... each of us is a unique driven spirit... Be that, it was enough for Christ. I went

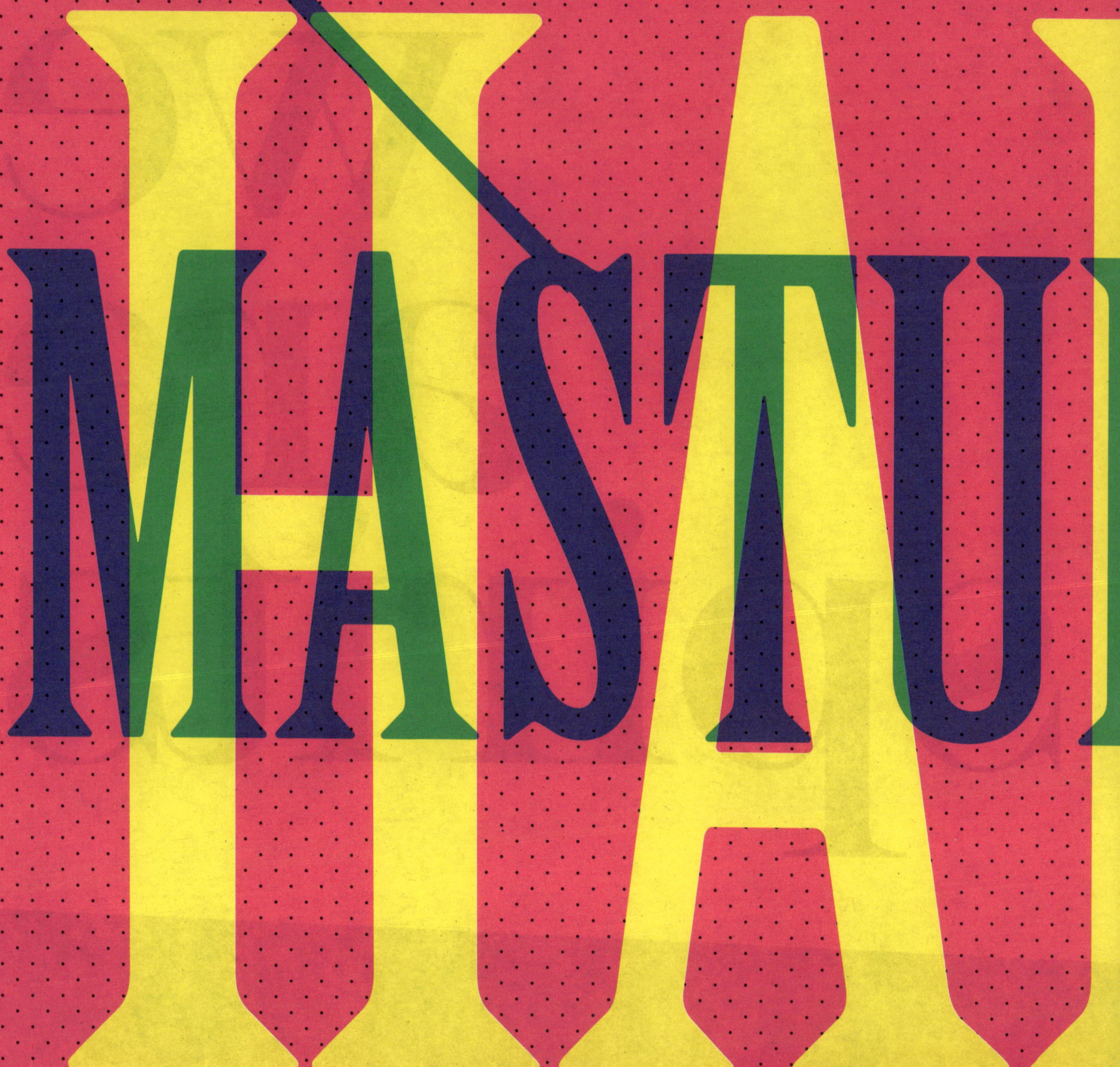
JUST WHO IS NÁSTIO MOSQUITO ALREADY?
MASTU
A guy who gave up masturbation, to make sure he is really, really, happy!!!!!

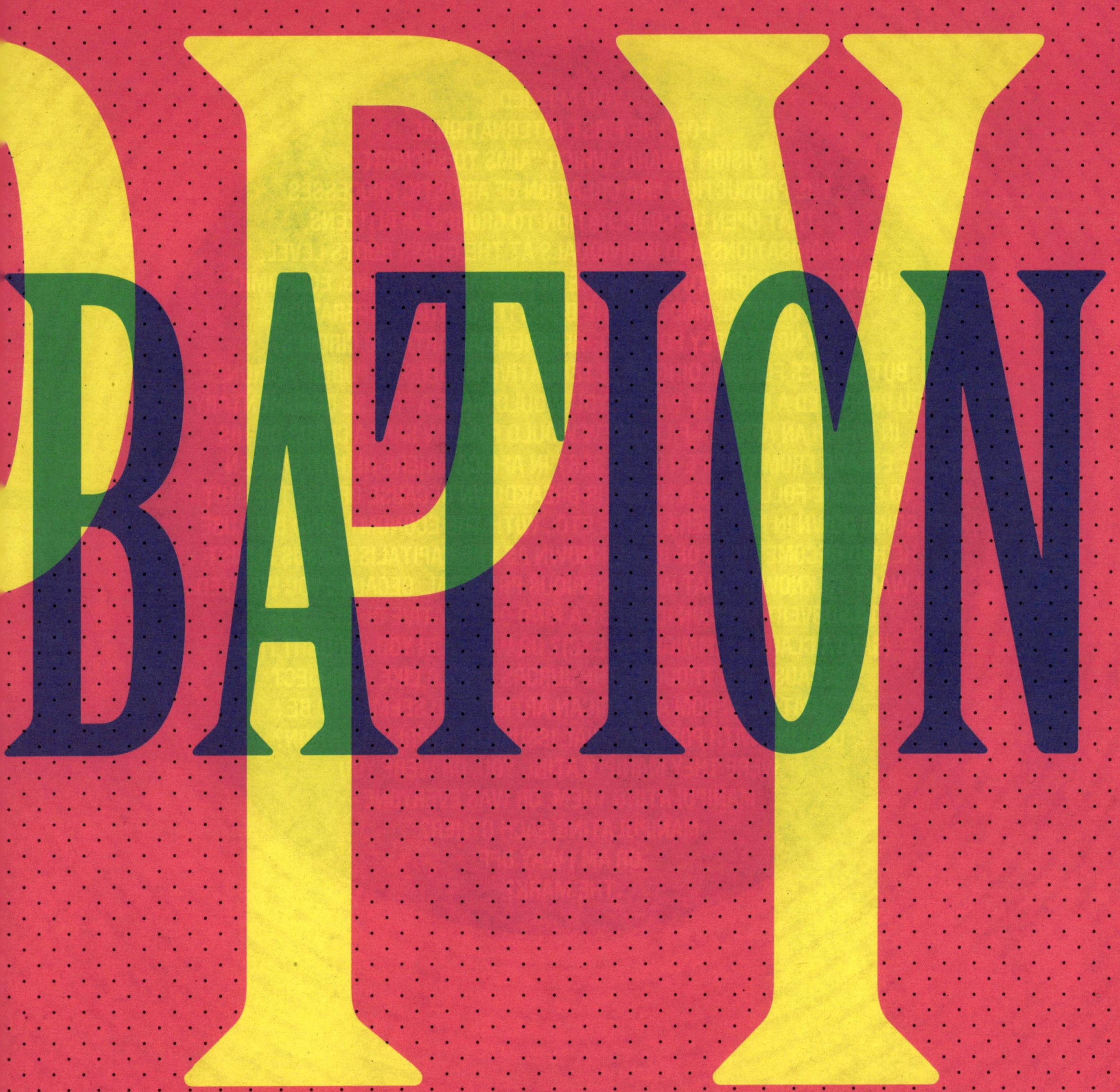

I'm purpose driven, directing all my energy towards being rooted and grounded in Love kind of guy… I was never seduced by interestingism now I'm saying kill yourself pronto if you're not into edifying all around you! I desperately want to be an unforgettably useful fu**.

YOU APPLIED
FOR THE FIRST INTERNATIONAL
VISION AWARD, WHICH "AIMS TO SUPPORT
THE PRODUCTION AND CREATION OF ARTISTIC PROCESSES
THAT OPEN UP COOPERATION TO GROUPS OF CITIZENS,
ORGANISATIONS AND INDIVIDUALS AT THE GRASS ROOTS LEVEL,
USING THEIR WORK TO INTRODUCE NEW DECISION-MAKING, ECONOMIC,
AND POLITICAL MODELS. THE BENEFITS OF THESE OPERATIONS
ARE NOT SIMPLY FOR SELF-REFERENTIAL ARTISTIC CIRCLES,
BUT RATHER FOR BUILDING UP ALTERNATIVE MODELS OF PUBLIC ACTION."
YOU PROPOSED A PROJECT WHERE YOU WOULD MAKE A "FALSE DOCUMENTARY"
IN WHICH AN AFRICAN FILM CREW WOULD FOLLOW SANTA CLAUS ON HIS
ESCAPE FROM EUROPE TO A DESERT IN AFRICA WHERE HE HAD CHOSEN
TO ESCAPE FOLLOWING A NERVOUS BREAKDOWN BECAUSE OF ALL THE SHIT
GOING DOWN IN NORTHER EUROPE ETC., WITH THE ECONOMY, AND BECAUSE
HE HAD BECOME TIRED OF BEING KNOWN AS THE CAPITALIST JESUS CHRIST.
I WANT TO KNOW IF THAT WAS A SERIOUS PROPOSAL, BECAUSE YOU WANTED
TO SUBVERT CERTAIN IDEAS BY A KIND OF CREATIVE DISPLACEMENT
(SANTA CLAUS AS IMMIGRANT ETC)? OR WHETHER YOU BROUGHT IT UP
BECAUSE YOU THOUGHT THE JURORS WOULD LIKE A PROJECT
THAT WAS FROM AN AFRICAN ARTIST WHO SEEMED TO BE
DEALING WITH POSTCOLONIAL ISSUES OF REPRESENTATION?
WERE THEY MANIPULATING YOU, OR WERE YOU
MANIPULATING THEM, OR WAS EVERYONE
MANIPULATING EACH OTHER?
OR AM I WAY OFF
THE MARK?

Fu** manipulation Sir! Fu** the jurors, and fu** you by the way!
I'm not into manipulation;
I just demand trust.

You know how violent it is to own people's dreams?
Do you know how vicious it is to dictate what kind of fantasy people indulge themselves in?
We are talking about children, kids…
I want kids of my own, and I hope to be preparing myself to sincerely treat them with respect as well as with the driven force to inspire in them confidence, and passion for what they have the possibility to do as Spirits within a human setting…

I have no problem with Christmas and the fat guy that gives out presents.
I like him actually…
But he is not useful for any child living on the southern hemisphere of planet earth… the fu** almost does not leave New York…

Do you know how fucking angry I was because I had no snow in my backyard?????
Do you know how much family men suffer wearing those Santa suits outside Angolan supermarkets during the hottest time of the year down these parts?
Why can't a fu** that does not even exist be more democratic and useful??

Do you know how much the Christmas tree industry is worth, both real and fake trees?
Do you know how much billions the postcard industry is worth?
Why must an African father offer a gift with a card that has snowflakes, in a place that does not have snow?

Do you know what would happen to world economy if we abolished Christmas abruptly?
Do you know what the are numbers around the imports that countries like

Angola spend buying these products so that, we can celebrate Christmas in an "accurate fashion"?
The kids are the ones demanding it…

Have you imagined how many industries would be impacted in the African Continent alone if all nations in the southern hemisphere decided, being our hottest time of the year, our Santa was going to wear flip-flops and shorts???

So I do know that the fat guy is based on Saint Nicholas… thus him moving his ass down here and becoming useful for all of us… culturally, economically, socially… fu**… unless you want to start and end something consequent don't get me started on this…
I've studied this for a while.

I've got a proposal ready for the fucking African Union…

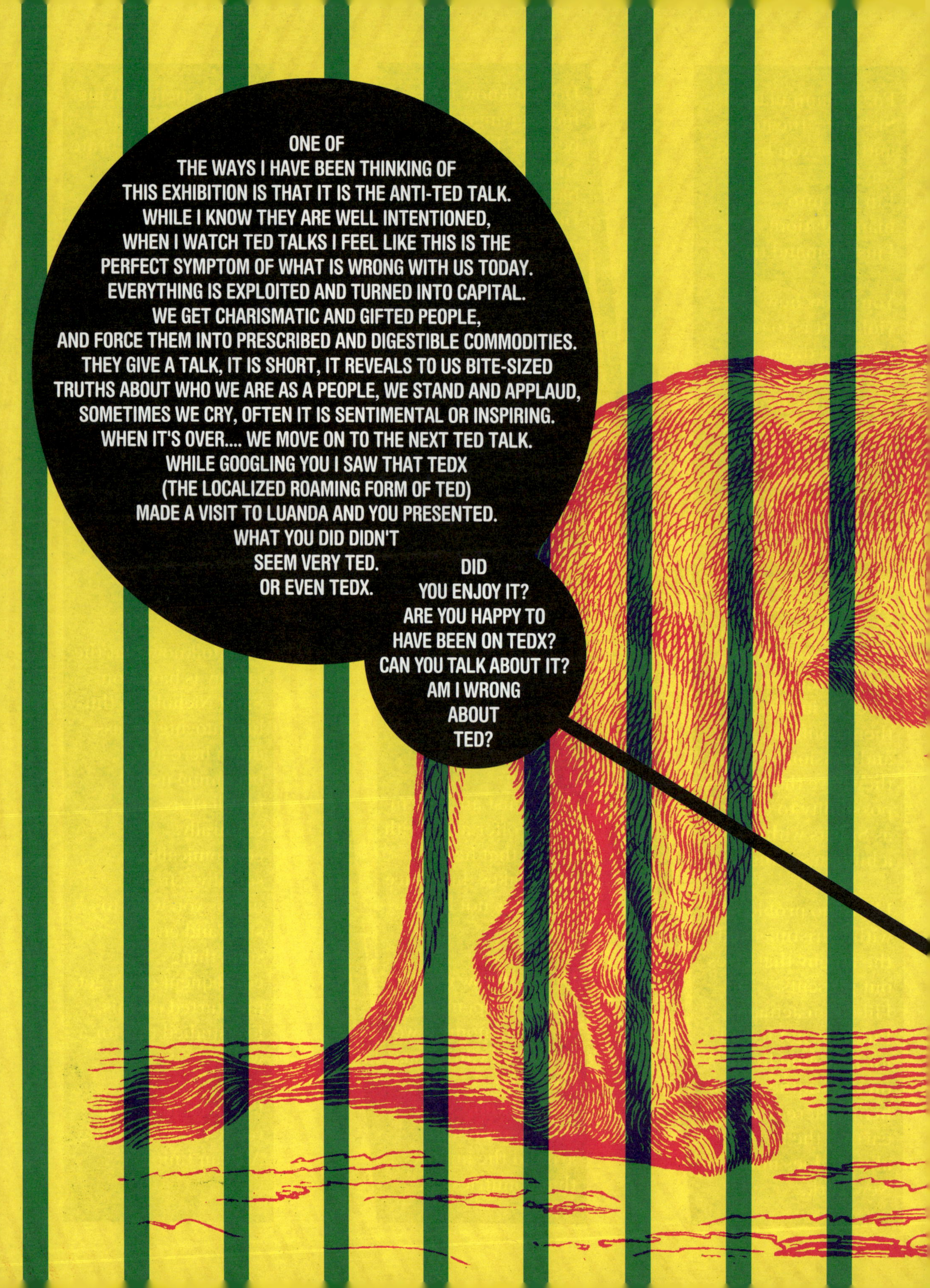

ONE OF
THE WAYS I HAVE BEEN THINKING OF
THIS EXHIBITION IS THAT IT IS THE ANTI-TED TALK.
WHILE I KNOW THEY ARE WELL INTENTIONED,
WHEN I WATCH TED TALKS I FEEL LIKE THIS IS THE
PERFECT SYMPTOM OF WHAT IS WRONG WITH US TODAY.
EVERYTHING IS EXPLOITED AND TURNED INTO CAPITAL.
WE GET CHARISMATIC AND GIFTED PEOPLE,
AND FORCE THEM INTO PRESCRIBED AND DIGESTIBLE COMMODITIES.
THEY GIVE A TALK, IT IS SHORT, IT REVEALS TO US BITE-SIZED
TRUTHS ABOUT WHO WE ARE AS A PEOPLE, WE STAND AND APPLAUD,
SOMETIMES WE CRY, OFTEN IT IS SENTIMENTAL OR INSPIRING.
WHEN IT'S OVER.... WE MOVE ON TO THE NEXT TED TALK.
WHILE GOOGLING YOU I SAW THAT TEDX
(THE LOCALIZED ROAMING FORM OF TED)
MADE A VISIT TO LUANDA AND YOU PRESENTED.
WHAT YOU DID DIDN'T
SEEM VERY TED.
OR EVEN TEDX.
DID
YOU ENJOY IT?
ARE YOU HAPPY TO
HAVE BEEN ON TEDX?
CAN YOU TALK ABOUT IT?
AM I WRONG
ABOUT
TED?

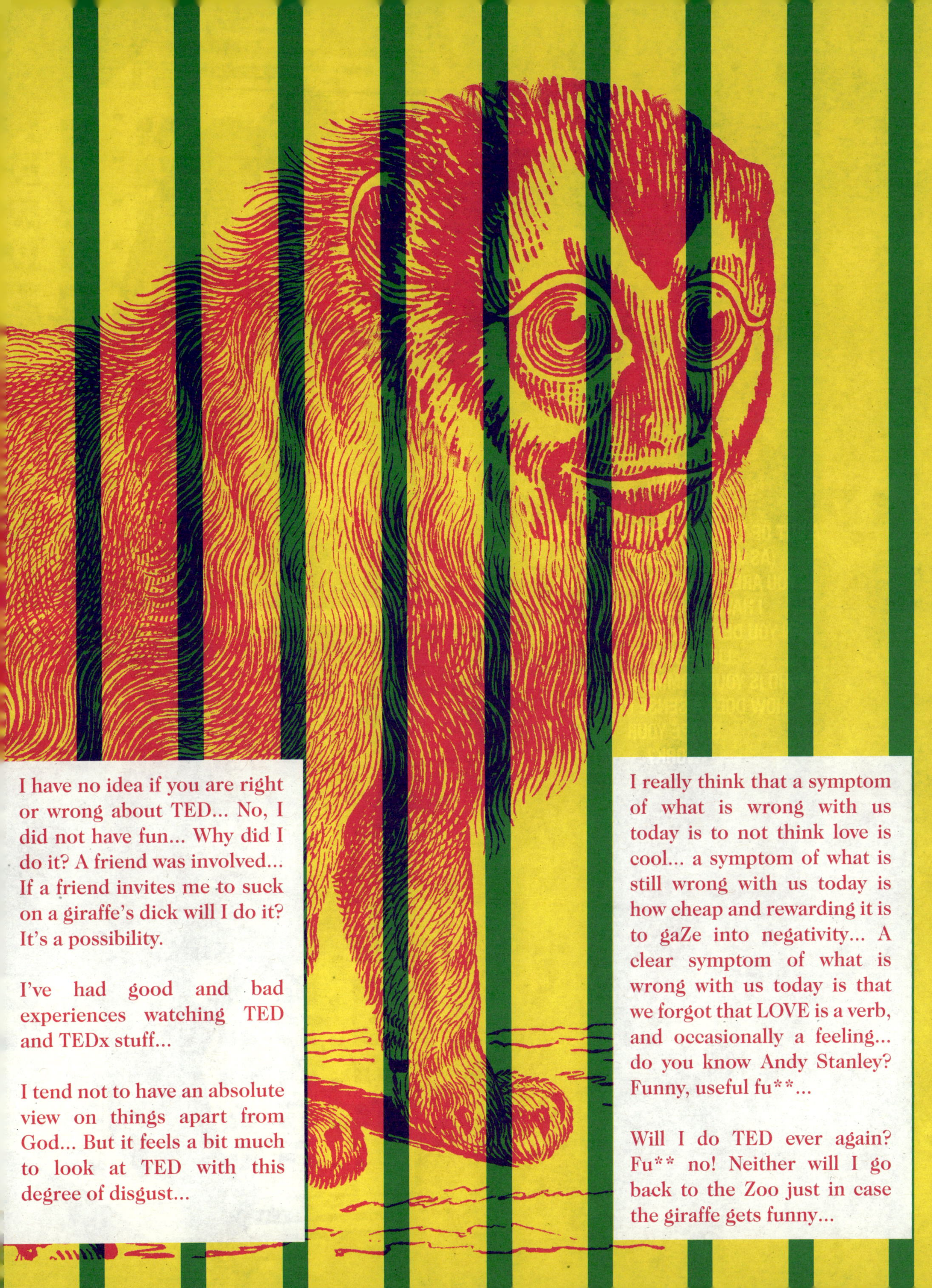

I have no idea if you are right or wrong about TED... No, I did not have fun... Why did I do it? A friend was involved... If a friend invites me to suck on a giraffe's dick will I do it? It's a possibility.

I've had good and bad experiences watching TED and TEDx stuff...

I tend not to have an absolute view on things apart from God... But it feels a bit much to look at TED with this degree of disgust...

I really think that a symptom of what is wrong with us today is to not think love is cool... a symptom of what is still wrong with us today is how cheap and rewarding it is to gaZe into negativity... A clear symptom of what is wrong with us today is that we forgot that LOVE is a verb, and occasionally a feeling... do you know Andy Stanley? Funny, useful fu**...

Will I do TED ever again? Fu** no! Neither will I go back to the Zoo just in case the giraffe gets funny...

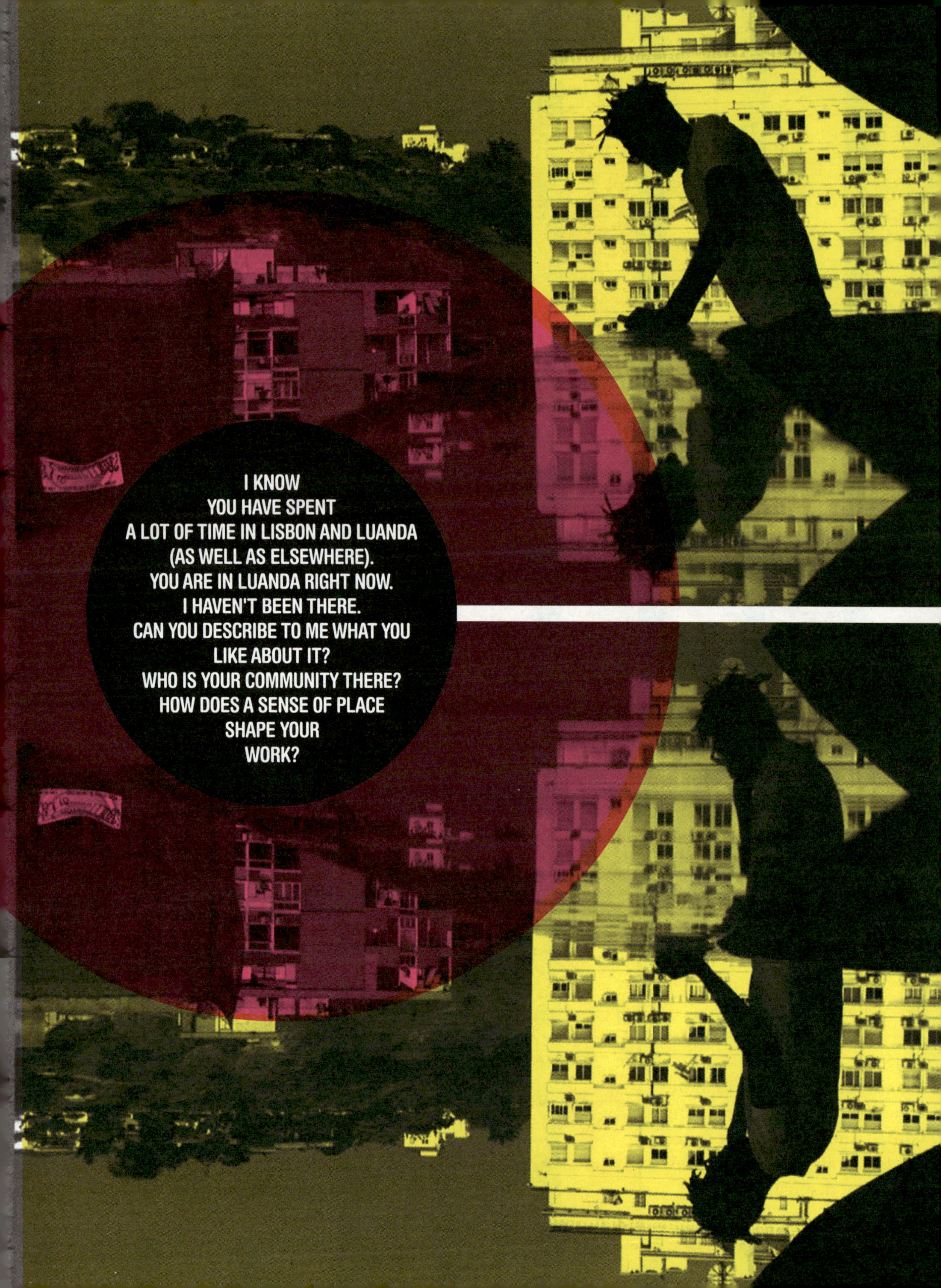

I KNOW
YOU HAVE SPENT
A LOT OF TIME IN LISBON AND LUANDA
(AS WELL AS ELSEWHERE).
YOU ARE IN LUANDA RIGHT NOW.
I HAVEN'T BEEN THERE.
CAN YOU DESCRIBE TO ME WHAT YOU
LIKE ABOUT IT?
WHO IS YOUR COMMUNITY THERE?
HOW DOES A SENSE OF PLACE
SHAPE YOUR
WORK?

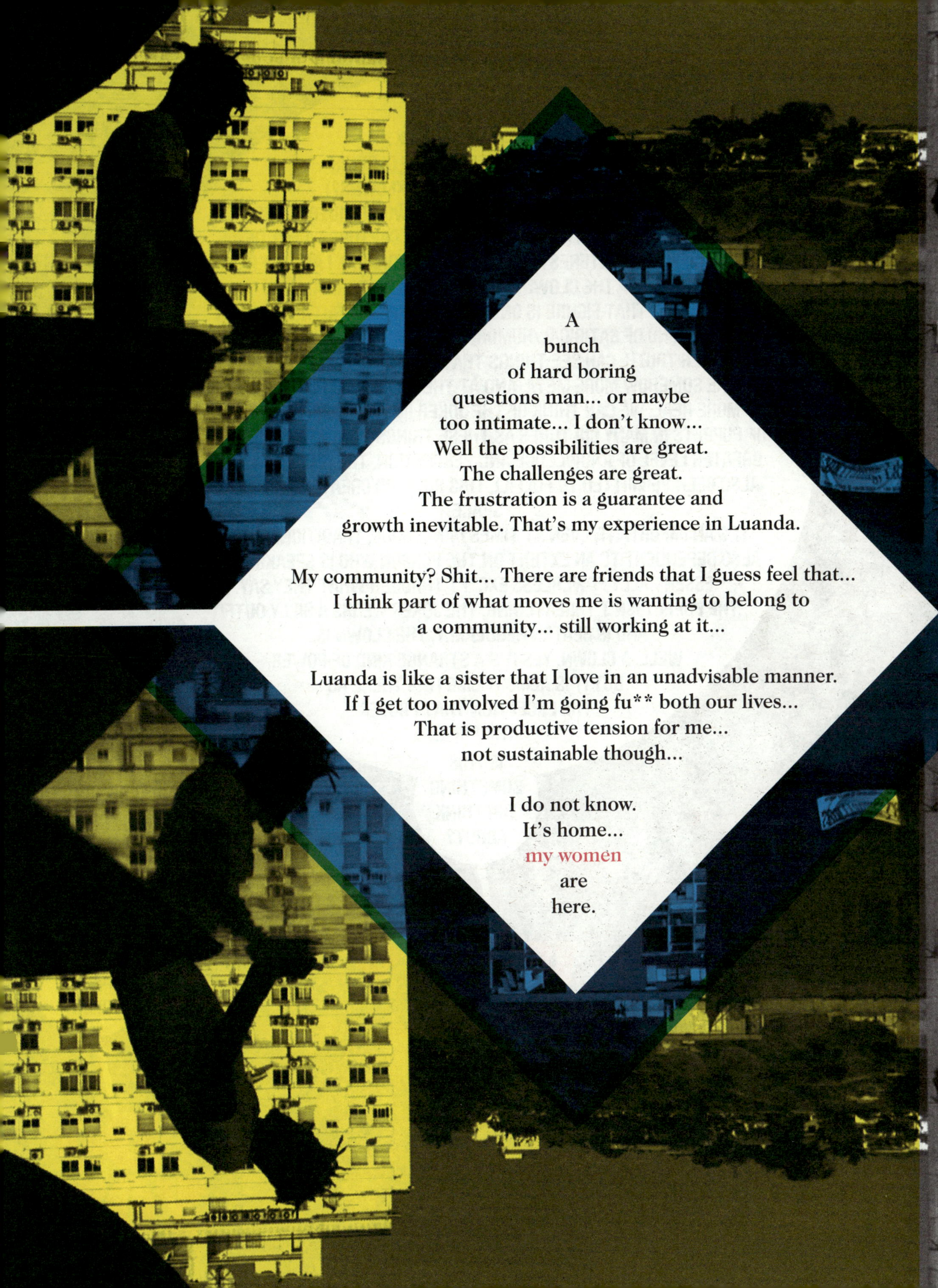
A
bunch
of hard boring
questions man... or maybe
too intimate... I don't know...
Well the possibilities are great.
The challenges are great.
The frustration is a guarantee and
growth inevitable. That's my experience in Luanda.

My community? Shit... There are friends that I guess feel that...
I think part of what moves me is wanting to belong to
a community... still working at it...

Luanda is like a sister that I love in an unadvisable manner.
If I get too involved I'm going fu** both our lives...
That is productive tension for me...
not sustainable though...

I do not know.
It's home...
my women
are
here.

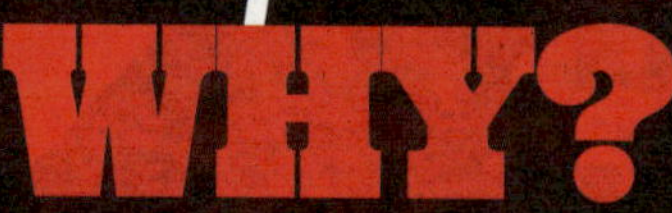
I KNOW
YOU STARTED WORK
ON A PIECE CALLED KING OF CLOWNS
(WAS IT WITH A K? KING OF KLOWNS?)
WHERE YOU WOULD PRESENT SPOKEN WORD, VIDEOS, MUSIC
IN A PERFORMATIVE STRUCTURE THAT CAPTURES A LOT OF
YOUR DIFFERENT INTERESTS AND WAYS OF WORKING. I AM INTERESTED
IN THE IDEA OF THE CLOWN, OR THE JOKER. HISTORICALLY IN MANY
CULTURES THAT FIGURE IS ONE WHO CAN SPEAK TRUTH TO POWER
THROUGH A KIND OF SATIRICAL/HUMOROUS SIDESTEPPING. THEY HAVE ACCESS
TO A DEEPER TRUTH, CAN SEE THINGS THAT OTHERS CAN'T SEE, BECAUSE THEY
ARE SOMEHOW MORE META, AND AT THE SAME TIME MORE HONEST,
MORE REAL. WE CAN THINK OF THE JOKER IN SHAKESPEARE, THE USE
OF PUPPETS IN MANY CULTURES AS THESE THINGS THAT HAVE ACCESS TO A
GREATER LEVEL OF KNOWLEDGE AND PERCEPTION. THE ARTIST HAS OFTEN
ALSO BEEN PERMITTED TO FULFILL THIS ROLE, OR CREATED THAT KIND OF
SPACE.
IT'S AN IMPORTANT, EVEN AT TIMES DANGEROUS, TRADITION. BUT IT IS
ALSO DEPENDENT TO AN EXTENT ON THE PERSON WHO IS SPEAKING BEING
ESSENTIALLY POWERLESS EXCEPT THROUGH WHAT THEY SAY.
THE PUPPET ISN'T THREATENING, THE JOKER WEARS A SILLY OUTFIT
AND IS BEATEN REGULARLY, THE CLOWN IS...
WELL, A CLOWN. YES IT'S A STRANGE KIND OF POWER,
BUT IT IS ALMOST LIKE IT IS THERE AS
THE EXCEPTION THAT PROVES
THE RULE.
IS THIS
SOMETHING
YOU THINK
ABOUT?
WHY?
DO YOU
REALLY WANT
TO BE THE
KING OF
CLOWNS?
YES!
ARE
YOU THE
ARCH
JOKER?
DO
YOU?

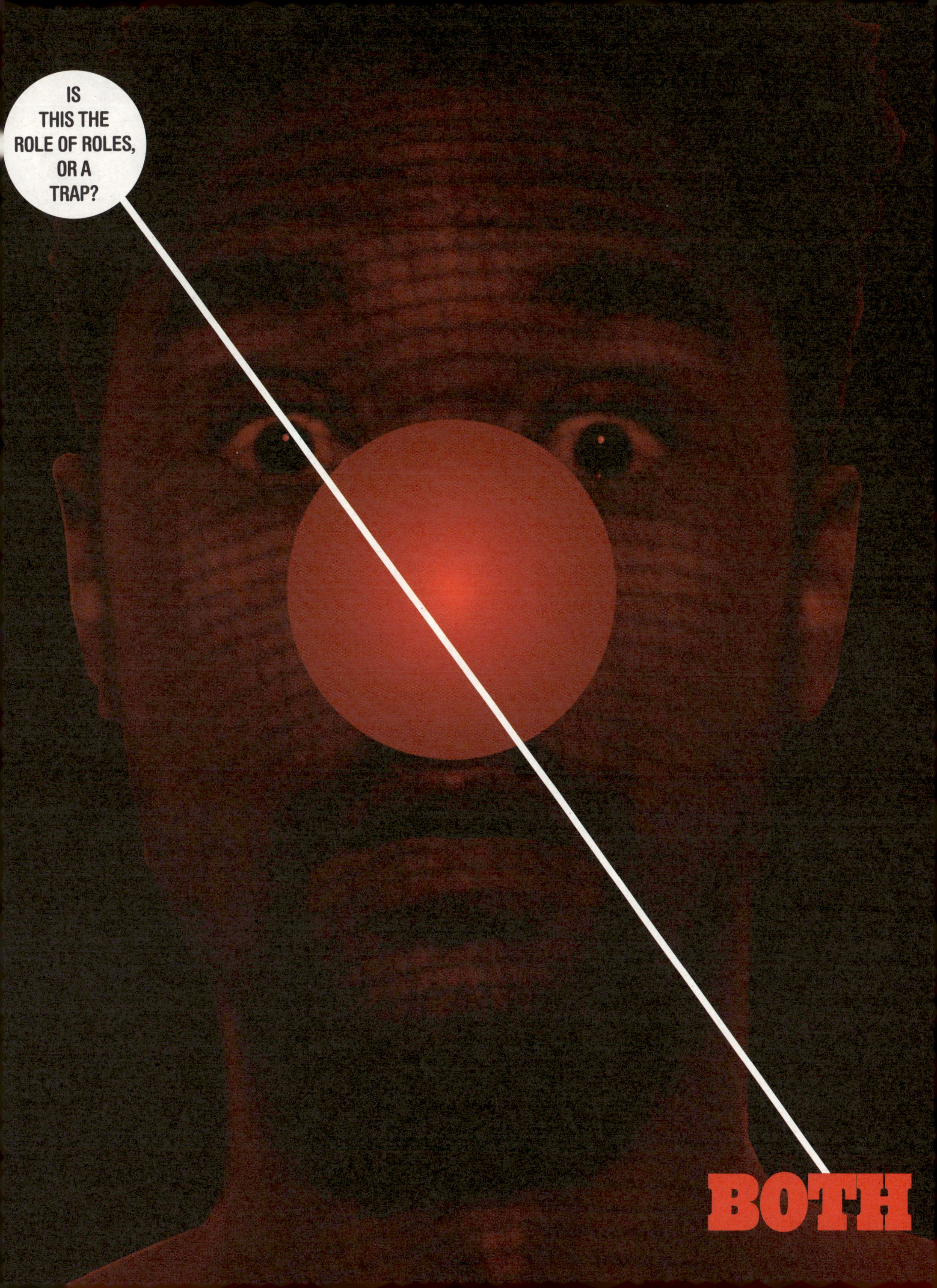

IS
THIS THE
ROLE OF ROLES,
OR A
TRAP?

BOTH

FUCK

Fuck that bitch... Nástia does not give a fu**... not even available to be part of the
Army Of The Individual... I wrote and said that on a poem and/or song called Tropa Do Indivíduo...

LOVE

If you and me, you in Ireland and I in Huambo,
are both driven by LOVE. We belong to the same individual army!
The same thing works for hatred unfortunately...

WEAPONS

It's a daily training and all weapons are real sharp and deadly. There's always one, and just one, take of all exercises and you move to the next one... your biggest asset is what you believe. Your biggest challenge is what you believe. Your biggest clue is whom you honor, and your biggest consolation is that your body will eventually die, guaranteed.
They call the training camp CORPOREALITY.

DRONES

You bet... And it is a bloody, unmerciful, disgusting fight.

IF SO WHERE?

There is a saying that says... if you want to avoid carrying dilemmas, make sure that wherever you go, don't take yourself along... they are fighting right there.

DOES IT HAVE DRONES?

If you do not pay attention you'll believe that that is all it has...

HAPPINESS

How happy (another verb, Happiness!) are you prepared to be? Answer that and you can decide for yourself anytime... no age limit to join in.

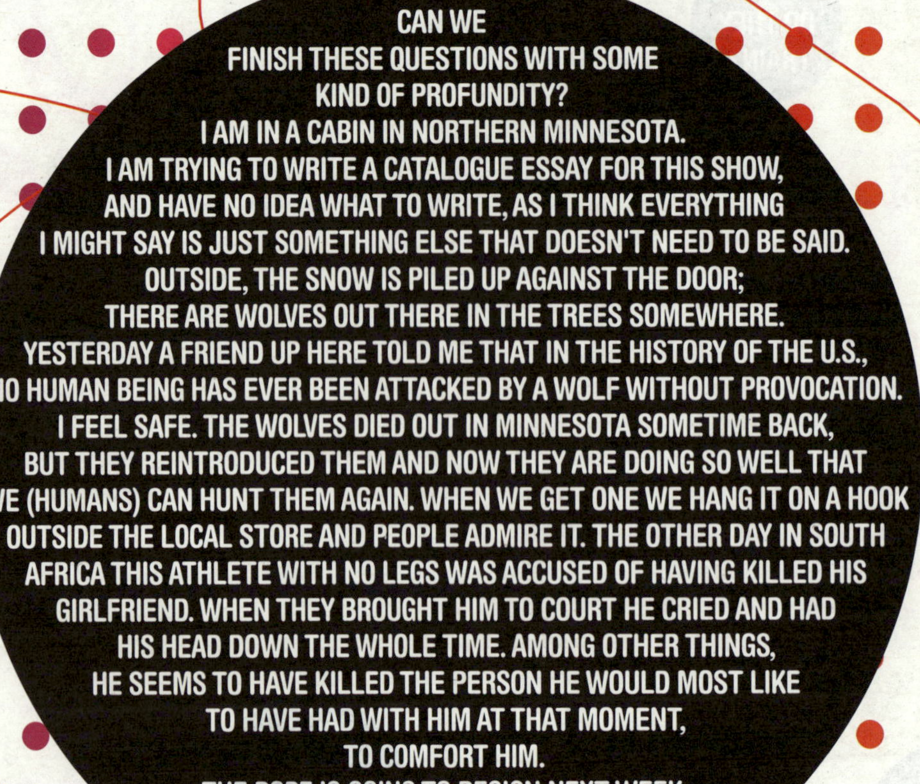

I'm in my apartment in Luanda. The electricity has been pretty stable, so I think a heavy group of cockroaches decided to move in. It's hot and the air conditioning is working. God had nothing to do with it, even though He is ALL. I think he is probably amused with the pope's move, God I mean... My girlfriend does not really care about me, well it's more complicated than that, and I suspect God has something to do with it! Thank You. I've been taking the longest time deciding if I will or will not go to Japan. I really do not like to make people unhappy, this always reminds me, making people unhappy, of when I ejaculate before a female reaches orgasm point during sexual interaction... I think very fewthings make me sadder. Been trying to figure out where that guilt built itself up on... Anyway it was a dream to be invited to Japan, happy it is real... are there wolves in Japan? In the zoo maybe? The Japanese zoo must be the most organized in the world, no? Maybe even a human cage out there... would that contradict zoology's reason to exist? When the subject of the debate about hunting, or not, foxes in the UK came out on newspaper's front pages it was time for me to leave... The guy with no legs is in deep trouble... I do not like success gone bitter; the guy with no legs was an amazing runner, how great is that? What force transforms that into murder? Dead Can Dance are going to perform in Lisbon and I will not be able to see them; I've been a fan for years... On a deeper note, yesterday I made a dream come true... not my dream... nothing is deeper... well a friend told me about a porn star and a horse... that is quite deep shit... this was about 10 years ago, as you can tell I'm still intrigued...

Liam Gillick

Berlin Statement

Hamburger Bahnhof–February 12, 2009

By the time a generation born in the early '60s had become activated recipients of a postwar social dynamic, they were simultaneously told that the physical manifestations of it—in varied forms of applied modernism—were failing. They were told that they were within something that should be succeeding and functioning in theory, but certain markers of progressive modern existence were dysfunctional, would never work, and no one ever really wanted them in the first place. Reconfiguring the recent past may start to account for the tension between this attack on progressive structure and the desire for individual expression. Such a rethinking of structure is a crucial component of a need to be involved in a discursive cultural framework that is often marked by these architectural and structural legacies of the recent past—from public housing projects to communal experiments—which were viewed as potential and failure by both right and left.

At the heart of the discursive is a reexamination of the "day before" as a model for understanding how to behave, activate, and present. It tries to get to the point *just before* the only option was for activists to role-play in front of the workers or cities to speculate rather than plan. In the past I have used this quite frequently as a device: the day before the Brass Band became the only option; the day before the mob became the workers; the day before the factory closed; the day before "Hotel California" was released—the idea of a French bar in the middle of nowhere, with nothing to listen to and everyone waiting for the arrival of the "soft" future.

We are currently in a situation in which suspension and repression are the dominant models. There is anxiety about who controls the reshaping of the stories of the recent past and attempts to capitalize on the near future. As a result, the discursive framework is predicated upon the rejection of the idea of a dominant authored voice. Clear-cut, authored content is considered to be politically, socially, and ideologically suspicious as it denies the potential of difference and collectivity. However, there is still the feeling that stories get told, that the past is being reconfigured, and that the near future gets shaped. There is a constant anxiety within the discursive frame about who is doing this, who is marking time. The discursive is the only structure that allows an artist to project a problem just out of reach and to work with that permanent displacement, but the problem is that it does so without a dominant

critical voice. Every other mode of practice merely reflects a problem, generates a problem, denies a problem, and so on. The discursive framework projects a problem just out of reach, and this is why it can also confront a socioeconomic system that bases its growth and collapse upon "projections." In the discursive art process we are constantly projecting. We are projecting that something will lead to something else "at some point." True work, true activity, true significance will happen in a constant, perpetual displacement.

Maybe it's possible to explain the discursive cultural framework within a context of difference and collectivity—"difference" being the key word that defines our time, and "collectivity" being the thing that is so hard to achieve while so longed for. We have to negotiate and recognize difference and collectivity simultaneously. It is an aspect of social consciousness that is exemplified in the art context. Difference and collectivity as social definitions and processes of recognition feed to and from the critical presence of modern and contemporary cultural work. But art is nurtured and encouraged via cultural permission to be the space for what cannot be tolerated but can be accommodated under the conditions of neoliberal globalization. This is its strength and its weakness.

Difference and collectivity are semi-autonomous concepts in an art context. The logic of their pursuit leads us to the conclusion that we should destroy all traditional relations of production in order to encourage a constant recognition of disagreement and profoundly different aims within a context of desire. The focus of the discursive is more on the aims and structural efficacy of the cultural exercise than what is produced. In turn, what is produced operates in parallel—unfettered by the requirement to be the total story.

All of this is problematized by the idea of nostalgia for the group. Art provides a reflection of values yet within the discursive this is inextricably related to role-playing as part of an educational legacy of cooperation. We are sometimes in thrall to structures from the recent past that were not supposed to be a model for anything. Some of the structures that we use, as cultural producers, echo a past that was part of a contingent set of accommodations and dynamic stresses within the postwar social project—producing a socially flexible group of people who could accommodate their own redundancy. Yet around this there remain old relationships of production that still exist outside complex theories of the postindustrial that are at the heart postwar "developed" societies. The discursive thrives when we are increasingly alienated from sites of traditional production owing to the displacing effects of globalization and the increasing tendency toward infinite subcontracting. Struggles over ideas at the site of production still exist, but they are constantly displaced and projected—the struggles are reported but are resistant to identification across borders within a context that offers an excessive assertion of specificities and tense arguments on the left about how to accept difference and protect the local at the same time.

If you try to use art as a fragmented mirror of the complexity of contemporary society, you might try to develop a system of art production that is equally multifaceted and misleading and that functions as a series of parallels rather than reflections of the dominant culture. If you emerged during a period of difference—of revised forms of identity and new understandings about relativism in relation to cultural meaning and social structure—then you must also dissolve a little as an author. The sense of responsibility for authorship, or the level of authorship, should be questionable. The location of the art moment will not reside with a consistent presence. It will intentionally exist at different moments within the work, in different forms and at varied intensities.

In early modernism you can see a quite urgent exchange between the process of modernity and the critical reflection of modernism but, as time goes on, these things get further and further apart. And it's that gap that is interesting to me: the space between the trajectory of modernity and the critical potential of modernism and postmodernism. I always used to say that I was more interested in Anni Albers than Josef Albers. I am interested in applied forms of modernism, the attempt to have a more functional role in relation to daily life, yet I want to do this while primarily operating in an art context —an undermining of exquisite values rather than a Habermasian attempt to provide a horizontal terrain of responsibility. People describe me as critic, writer, designer, artist. My artistic practice includes different activities. Together these things are the work. Together they are the only way to occupy the gap. There is no differentiation.

Yet art is a place where you can develop modes of refusal that are qualitatively and ideologically different from the production and negotiation of other objects and ideas in the world—in terms of intentions and results. As such art is a place to

heighten contemporary discussions of the way we reconfigure relations between each other and the places that we occupy and/or are forced to operate within. However, many artists take a cultural form of the Fifth Amendment or a refusal to engage. By doing this they attempt to allow the work to sit as the location of complexity, contradiction, and even beauty that might be necessary in order to create alternative visions of the world without conditions or explanations but never free of them. In my work there is a constant rechecking across from the ideas to the realizations and back again, but no resolution of these parallels. There are moments when the conceptual discourse at the heart of the work overwhelms the lightness of the objects and vice versa. But there are also times when you could argue that the multiple entry points into the work overwhelm any singular reading. Art is a problematic territory once people assume that it might carry more inherent significance than any other complex structure in the world. When you are primarily operating as an artist, there tends to be an assumption of potential and particularity. There is a sense of being "artisted" at all times. In common with most artists, I am interested in areas other than art. Art is a convenient term for a mind-space location where you need new forms of cultural permission to carry out certain corrective tasks in relation to the society in general.

In the work there is a critique of the centre ground, both socially and politically, so there must also be a critique of liberalism as much as there is an echo of liberal ideologies. At some level I am negotiating the idealism of others, which of course is an activity with its own specific history. We are surrounded by dynamic reworkings of language; generally these changes and shifts are absorbed by the dominant management culture. So you could argue that I am working against a verbalisation of neoliberalism via challenging relativism and trying to avoid getting caught up within the same language games, for these are my subjects. Of course to do this I must reclaim and play with some of those modes of language and behaviour. As such I remain interested in literary and scripted modes of complexity and idea development. You could argue that one of the great ideological battles of the twentieth century was between speculation and planning. It looks as if speculation has won and lost in equal measure. My idealism is rooted in discussion, negotiation, and examination of these devastating compromise states via a play with discussion, negotiation, and recuperation.

Art has a pragmatic function. What takes place is connected to a flickering sense of function, ideology, aesthetics, and critique. So when the work operates best, it is in a constant state of flux between these perception states. Titles exist for many different reasons—many of them operate as rhetorical tools, to reclaim certain territories and try and find a way to address middle-ground ideas. If you try to do this while avoiding didactic information as material, you end up with some notional space where ideas are set in motion, rather than over-determined and described back to the culture in general. There are clearly designed moments within the work that are not completely incorporated into the language of the built world. The work stands as a series of markers that offers a temporary series of specific non-places that function because the viewer or user of the work brings applied ideas to bear on what they are passing by or considering. As long as you remember that the work might be addressing how the near future is controlled in a postutopian situation or how to function in a culture that is supposed to have been resistant to crisis, then you can see both the problem inherent in its construction and the potential when it works. We are not seeing a picture or a description. The question of whether the work is fiction or documentary might be a better one. The focus is on production, not consumption.

I am interested in the idea of continuing the legacy of the late modern project where you occupy small spaces within the society and open them up. Exposing moments where there is an inability to know how to proceed within the terms of classic neoliberal capitalism or didactic self-consciousness alone. Since the battle between planning and speculation was won by speculation, we have seen the rise of the consultant and advisor with catastrophic consequences. I was never really interested in this idea of the consultant as a subject, but I am quite interested in the ongoing question that was very central to the book Discussion Island/Big Conference Centre—"How is the near future controlled in a postutopian environment?" How do we function in a managed and infinitely analysed culture? The work has therefore also been scenario-based. What happens when there is no collective vision of how to proceed within an architectural, design, or art community beyond the contingencies of reconstruction, development, and pastiche? How do things still get decided? Not what will they look like next week, month, or year. My interest is in creating and occupying an aesthet-

ic that can engulf these complications. Speculation as planning and planning as speculation. What traces does that leave—within a context where fiction and documentary constantly pull in and out of focus?

My work concerns the construction of ideologies in relation to the built world. I am interested in a populated environment, but not overly defining the relationships we are expected to play in relation to those environments. I present a generalised and specific perspective that is corrected by moments of scepticism and enthusiasm in equal measure. I come from a distracted background where there is also an element of delusion toward what you feel you can address. I am interested in whether it is possible to play with this middle ground. I want to see if there is something within this central zone where you can activate without escaping to the reassurance of the subcultural on one hand or hyper-referentiality on the other. I decided the way to avoid role-playing or picturing was to look structurally at preproduction and postproduction. To use a cinematic analogy, I am more interested in developing a scenario, editing, and distribution than directing the movie myself. The key to the work is the fact that you end up with some work, you end up with some stuff but the thinking behind it is based on preproduction and postproduction rather than on the articulation of some fundamental values or reflection of the way it is. These are very important structural games that I use to ensure that the implications of authorship are no more over-defined than they need to be. There is a lot of "becomingness" and "artisting" that takes place around visual culture, which means I don't have to get involved too heavily in the things that overly emphasize the authorship element of the work. So if I look at strategic planning and dissemination or car production and Georgian opium eaters, then the art in the middle and at the edge emerges as a set of functional tools around which you can sustain these other discussions, but only if you are prepared to try.

My work functions in parallel to the collapses at the centre of neoliberal, Anglo-Saxon social organisation in tension with the legacy of articulated mini-utopias. I am therefore obviously influenced by conceptual art as it emerged in the dominant culture and remain in a dialogue with many of those artists. However, I am not as involved as they were in a clear statement about the potential of art. Most conceptual art was involved in projecting a set of terms into the future under which the artist could function without having to alter the initial ideological base of their work. My work is a constant renegotiation of the nature of an ideological basis. This does not mean that I am against conceptual art, just that I am working within the influence of their legacy and making use of the options that they revealed for all of us. Their reinforcement of the potential of art as a semi-autonomous component within the broader cultural sphere is crucial, especially in the work of Lawrence Weiner. Especially if you view his work as an applied art that does not attempt to negate the potential of an art of critique even as it sits integrated into its various sites. My work is rooted in a negotiation of the way ideologies leak through into the built world. I am not interested in architecture alone, but in the revised practices of the most dynamic and potentially most dangerous people involved in changing the way our urban environment looks and feels. The problem with many people involved in contemporary art in relation to architecture is that they ignore the most dynamic setups that are possible in the discourse around contemporary urbanism. They focus on the products, not the production methodology.

So if we agree that we are in a postutopian situation, where consensus has exploded into the devastating logic of the neoliberal, then how are things still being planned and executed? I am interested in apparently secondary factors, like this twentieth-century battle between planning and speculation rather than detailed discussions around the ironic failure of modernism. I am also involved in researching and playing with the suppression of the left in a US context and looking for earlier pragmatic visions of how things could be. I am interested in the gap left behind by this twentieth-century battle between speculation and planning. Strategy, compromise, renovation, critique are the tools. These factors all affect the final look of any project. I am not trying to synchronise with a building or site, but attempting to overlay a set of concepts on top of the structure that functions as a structural alternative. Within this frame, some of Bourdieu's ideas remain relevant—the relation of the cultural sphere to the corporate sphere, and a play with all the tensions that result from a consciousness of social and cultural capital. Maybe this is the tragedy and potential of an artist born in the suburbs.

The contemporary exhibition is a place where the visitor is occupying a specific type of negotiable location, which is very different from the classic late-modern idea that the visitor completes an exhibition. However, the contemporary exhibition is still activated by people in the sense that the work does not necessarily function best as objects for consideration alone, but is sometimes good as a backdrop or as a décor rather than a pure content provider. Self-perception has changed in the one hundred years since the development of cinema and the subsequent arrival of television and the dispersal of focus that results from the Internet. Self-image has been heightened for long enough that we no longer sense the cataclysmic shift. This doesn't necessarily mean that self-awareness has improved; it has just been shared, atomised, and dispersed. We have a reflected sense of an image of ourselves in space while we carry out certain given tasks. Children, when they play sport, commentate on their actions. This stems from a sense that we can picture someone else watching an image of ourselves as we take part in something. This fundamentally altered the way we address art and our relationship with artlike structures.

Artists should therefore try to find gray areas, which are easier to expose and occupy through art than with most other activities, despite the rhetoric surrounding neoliberal business practice. Working by default without being purely aesthetic or purely formalist is one option, but it is the world of settings and even décor (as a partner of the scenario) that can be really productive. The creation of provisional structures carries the potential to provide temporary ideological shifts. We should be interested in reversal processes, where you are not necessarily using art to tell a story, but you are using it to play with certain conditions that might be toward or derived from narrative structures. Within the work it is possible to apply varied conditions to similar thinking and assess what happens each time. The introduction of an incomplete character is quite useful in this respect, as it replaces the artist with another personality who can operate in the space alongside the trace left by the artist and the distracted presence of the viewer operating simultaneously in the spaces of encounter.

These are the spaces in our socioeconomic and psychosociological space that are constantly reframed. This leaves enormous gaps that can only be described with difficulty, but they need some degree of analysis if their effects are to be understood. Many artists find productive territories within a search for fundamental moments and effects. Others remain within a purely analytical play with the products of complexity. I was interested to develop a sequence of parallel relations with the areas of our life that are most vulnerable to exploitation and control. The implicit freedoms implied in the notion of discussion are not value-free. They are hard-won and offer an alternative set of tools toward making dilemmas and disagreements less dangerous. In my case the work does not direct discussion but uses the notion of the discursive as a subject.

This central zone was traditionally seen as problematic in relation to creating functional art. Whereas in the past many artists flirted with the central zone of administrative activity, I was more interested to look at some of its environmental effects. The notion is elaborated in the work around my book <u>Discussion Island/Big Conference Centre</u>, just before and just after publication. The book was an attempt to address some of the structural social and political implications of my earlier texts and scenarios like <u>McNamara</u>, which concerned a series of meetings between Robert McNamara and Herman Kahn of the RAND Corporation in order to define a culture of management and speculation, and <u>Erasmus Is Late</u>, a text that focused on the potential of the "other" in framing the dominant discourse within the framework of pre-Marxist thought. In both cases I wanted to look at the notion of how the near future and recent past is controlled. I always wanted to escape the "eureka" moment, where art is based on a revelatory singularity, and found that the creation of a condensed core of ideas could lead to a more complex set of parallel starting points. Yet when I began <u>Discussion Island</u>, I found only collapsed narrative problems, for I wanted to push on to an examination of the results of those earlier social and perceptual manipulations. Initially, I attempted to create a series of backdrops and contingent structures that could shift around and create settings for the emerging narrative. At one point, I put the text away completely and concentrated on addressing some out-of-focus ideas. I began to make work around the idea of discussion, negotiation, compromise, and strategy. Not creating structures that might illustrate these ideas, but things that could designate a provisional space where it might be possible to consider and reassess such effects. This process of aesthetisisation of the abstract middle ground unlocked the text and allowed me to write a book without having to project the kind of space it might be taking place in. The book runs parallel to a sequence of structures but does not describe them. Equally, the

work itself spun free and became a productive series of visual markers in its own right.

I began to refer to art as prototypes and provisional structures in order to address certain ideas from the compromised centre of action and thinking—to denominate the art object. I began to create a series of overhead platforms and related work that could offer up a space where it might be possible to consider key issues before too many words had been written. The objects really work <u>toward</u> a text. They are not emptied out because no one is expected to fill up some notional sublime void with complex thinking. Instead, it might be possible for the work to act as a backdrop within which a series of scenarios may be thought out. We are no longer dealing with mute object meets profound thought—the relationship is more functional and brittle—a constant flickering of idea, intention, and potential toward an excess of access and a reclaiming of the middle ground. Playing out some scenarios within a visual context that mashes design and dogma. At all times elements spin off and affect the reading of the work in a corrective way. My interest in time and the middle ground ensures that hierarchies are corrupted but not suppressed into useless structural equivalence.

If you are a distracted and deluded person, you can become interested in complex social phenomena as a way to mirror your sense of multiple entry points. You might also develop an interest in the way art has historically worked as a locus of scepticism. This will inevitably include self-conscious ideas in terms of cultural refusal and sidestepping. I always found the idea of consolidating form and content difficult. Another big problem in the recent past has been the question, "What is the idea behind your work?" A lot of my work is derived from how to get around the singularity problem and instead find multiple sources, often self-created multiple starting points. Certainly, a lot of my structures and projects are not resolved in the sense that dealing with any specific thing doesn't necessarily lead you to a moment of consolidation or sublimation or any of these other things that art traditionally did. The point of entry into the ideas is multiple. Certain things work as lures or attractors while other things hold you away in a web of text. If you are interested in providing a critique of the middle ground, then you have to consider questions of contingency, strategy, negotiation, compromise, and refusal. These are the abstractions at the core of the work. And recently, I have realised that the key marker here is a reexamination of the notion of difference in relation to cultural production.

I tend to work on many things simultaneously. I am generally trying to sustain multiple entry points, multiple ways of thinking, and multiple ways of operating within the proviso that there is some conscious recognition of the potential of the art object as a "critical exception" that exemplifies "difference." This crosscutting allows you to retain a degree of criticality without creating didactic or overdetermined structures that merely reinforce what the dominant culture already knows.

I am looking for a new methodology rather than a new form. My ongoing project, <u>Construcción de Uno</u>, has been connected to the idea of trying to get a grip on some slippery elements concerning how shifts in European culture have had an effect on recent modes of cultural production. It has therefore emerged gradually, slowly revealing the ideas necessary to develop a potential text. The whole project and the related lectures are rooted in an examination of the notion of production and the social in primarily northern European social democracies. A lot of the source material is derived from Brazilian academic papers on industrial production methods in Sweden, but the scope of the lectures reaches into many assumptions about how things accumulate value within European social democracies.

I used to ask people, "Where's the local glitter factory?" and no one could ever tell me because, in fact, very few people knew where glitter comes from. Subsequently I found out it was invented in 1934 on a cattle farm in New Jersey, where you can still buy it today. At one point I found out that glitter, kilo for kilo, is a druglike commodity. You can go to Vienna and buy two kilos of glitter for the same price as a tiny vial in Stockholm. It has a very under-exploited commodity status. Part of this is to do with the fact that very few people could ever tell me if glitter was made by Chinese children or was a by-product of the arms trade. Maybe it was an innocent material made by well-paid artisans. To this day, I've still never been to a glitter factory. I can't tell you if people are happy in glitter factories, whether glitter factories are organised collectively, or if a "Glitter Board" regulates them. I have used it in my work as a constant. My use of glitter exposes certain production complications along with an acknowledgment of modernist art history and a fairly pragmatic task: cleaning the floor with whisky or vodka mixed with glitter. Once you have done this, you can see where the floor has been cleaned

and labour is exposed. The works are a cumulative negative: so if cleaning is a reductive act, then cleaning with glitter is an additive reduction. At the Palais de Tokyo in 2005, I just spread vast quantities of red glitter with no cleaning, but of course, red glitter is red snow and red snow is what you get in times of revolution. My work is often about defining the softer, unclear spaces within the social context that were intended to ameliorate conditions. It is diagnostic rather than viral. But there are times when you need a picture that has been transposed.

I am increasingly interested in the question of the "postwar" as a completed historical period in Europe. This is concomitant with an examination of the history of the postwar as an era of realignment within European culture and subsequent neoliberal attacks on the progressive legacies of postwar social structure within a context of the suppression of the productive aspects of extreme resistance to that system. I became very interested in the way the neoliberals first went after industries that were at the interface with the people. How do we proceed and what aesthetic traces are left in the culture from this process of strategic privatisation embedded in populist strategy? What I am trying to do through the work is look at some of these processes: see how they function, how they collapse, and how they leak into the forms that surround us. But it is not a consistently stable mode of practice. There are such allusions in the work but very few didactic or transparent references.

I'm a European Socialist. I believe that people need to get together, organize, and make things work better without rationalising their own redundancy. The 1970s were a moment of failure and confusion on the left and the emergence of a significant new pragmatic radicalism as the neoliberal agenda was forced into place. It was also a disturbing time. We were told that the postwar experiments toward the creation of a better living and working environment had already failed. This was generally an attempt by right-wing politicians to use the urban fabric as a site of "otherness" that could be demonised and used as a scare tactic toward gaining political support from the suburbs and countryside. The developing narratives of "difference" and "progress" were turned into an accusation. My work is often related to attempts to recuperate the progressive moments of applied modernism in the context of "difference." Not to picture or illustrate, but to produce a parallel narrative of potential. The idea that the postwar is complete and the claim that the edge of Europe is being reached are important points of departure when trying to imagine the potential of the discursive.

Loss is a term that is beloved of people who are not interested in addressing what is actually taking place. It is a part of a melancholic tradition and extremely important for retaining a critical position in relation to the culture. I am more interested in locating moments in the culture where there is a sense of possibility. Where people come together and attempt to image productive environments. The notion of loss is political, it can only occur to people who have sensed or experienced the potential of something. It is understandable that people are drawn to discuss loss when faced by the collapse of ideologies and progressive social models. However, loss can easily become a default notion for people who don't want to address the actual conditions under which we operate. We know that there is an acceptable form of art that revels in loss as an indicator of its seriousness. I am more interested in constructed critical structures than in any broad singularity. Loss may be an element, but my work is not about an ironic response to the failures of the twentieth century. It is an attempt to examine how ideas are expressed within the built world. It is stranded, beached, and terminally parallel. I have written a number of small books over the years. Each one has a conceptual base, which attempts to expose key elements that determine contemporary Western conditions: the incompleteness of the eighteenth- and nineteenth-century revolutions in Europe; how things are still decided in a postconsensus environment; the legacy of communal practices in societies that rejected communism; the legacy of applied utopianism in modernist architecture and how we can resuscitate the progressive practices of the last quarter of the twentieth century in order to understand how to proceed. These are precise interests, but can only be expressed in partial episodic form if I am to avoid the reassuring lure of the didactic and the documentary and retain a mutable role.

I address decision-making and the role of the scenario within the social. Within an art context it is an attempt to bypass singularity, and to delaminate the "work" itself from a moment of completion. The work becomes "provisional," "prototypical," and "potential" rather than a direct statement in relation to other art. Of course this may not be immediately apparent by looking at any specific work alone. The "what if" is a tool of modern projection within the postindustrial period. It is connected to cinema and television and the rise of consultancy and strategic play. When other people remain interested in sex and death or refusal and subjectivity, I find it more interesting to examine the activities that are determining the way our society develops. The "what if" has now merged with the "here you are, in this rendering, having a café latte." Or more lately, here is where you were going to be until we ran out of steam. We have to rethink the "what if" in an age where old superstitions have returned, where the dominant culture and the resistant culture both pray to their gods for guidance. The "what if" has turned into an episodic eternal. The first scene of the book <u>Discussion Island/Big Conference Centre</u>, in which a character is thrown through the window of a newly developed Conference Centre and lands on top of a Toyota, positions my work at the centre of a collective critique of the speculative terrain that has predictably collapsed.

This is about wanting to be separate, but not marginal: a legacy of my Irish heritage. In the book <u>Literally No Place: Communes, Bars and Greenrooms</u>, I told the true story of a bar in Derry in the north of Ireland situated in close proximity to a functioning British army checkpoint. This story had little to do with going out onto the street and banging dustbin lids or trying to shoot a soldier or making art about things we already know. It was about the setting up of a social checkpoint opposite an army checkpoint—a place of discourse within confrontation. Sitting in a bar in a bunker right underneath an army post. A normal bar on a Friday night with chintzy things hanging on the walls, nice red wallpaper, old ladies, children, and Guinness settling up on the bar. From the outside it's a concrete bunker and an incredible site of resistance and on the inside it's a place of the familiar and of difference. A site that refuses to reflect back to the dominant system that which it already knows but muddies the message within the chatter of the everyday. Separate but not marginal, an articulation of difference rather than contradiction. A site of exclusion within the context of a desire for autonomy. The picture of a series of relationships where the question is not "Am I included in this structure?" "Does it represent me?" "Does it fulfill a fantasy of social work within the cultural terrain?" or "But what about 'them?' " but an implicated space of pleasure and resistance.

©2009 Liam Gillick

Deny the problem.
Growth.
Collapse.
Projection.

She reaches out warmly and takes his hand and the cat's paw in hers. She explains that this room they are in is the Poiesis, the generator chamber of rhetoric and poetics:

We are like a blood cell that transforms and continues the world. We used to send out texts and generate knowledge on a regular basis, but now a new ideology, a new organizational mode and system of production has replaced the work of the Poiesis with a more efficient system of e-mails and information technologies, sweeping away the Poiesers who used to take care of linguistic constructions, messages, meanings. They have forced us to convert to this system, but something has gone wrong and now the place is a total mess: letters and words stick to the windows, the e-mail system is engulfed with information that flies randomly through high-speed cables. Meaning is not making any sense and you can't even see the horizon through the windows anymore. There is a delay in the process of transformation, there is a delay in radical criticism.

Language represents the medium in which objects meet and enter into relationships with each other, in their essences, in their most volatile and delicate substances, even in their aromata.

The cat sneezes, looks around, and without hesitation:

Meow.

have to believe in some kind of trajectory. We do our best to open lines of flight, like the bridges that will facilitate the process of transformation. We speculate, dream, and sometimes also we act.

The ceiling stops vibrating. The colors are plain and silent again. The cat has been listening carefully; she stares at the subcontractor again, waiting for him to take some kind of initiative. He says and does nothing, but his body fluids are flowing fast and heating his body. He feels full of energy and incredibly weak. His face and ears are red like chili peppers, his legs are trembling, his pupils dilate, his eyes are lost in space as if he is coming up on ecstasy. He is staring at the horizon. *It looks different from here.* The cat joins him. She rubs against the subcontractor's shins as if to rescue him and then sits upright, staring at the multicolored horizon with pride. *Things look different from here.*

Scenario 4.1.3 Of Bridges and Borders (of Relations)

How do you get there?
There where?
On the other side.
You are on the other side.

The subcontractor and the cat are staring at the horizon. They have a silent conversation. Telepathy. Rare quality in these days of sensual and emotional confusion. They turn their eyes up. The ceiling is silent. They can see the sky through it. There is a roll of colored film leaning on one corner next to one of the windows. Unconsciously, the subcontractor reaches and takes it with him. They can go now. They take the lift again. *Dling.* Doors close. They have no choice this time. The lift takes them to the 166th floor. *Dling.* Doors open. A sign reads POIESIS. An old Belgian office desk, the size of a kinderdesk, and behind it sits a young, elegant-

ly dressed woman with a fur collar. She has a nice smile and with a gentle gesture invites them to find a seat and take an orange juice and a glass of water. The subcontractor apologizes, for they might have taken the wrong way. They were supposed to go back to the ground floor. The place looks like a guest lounge for a big company; it is cosy and somehow familiar. Have they been here before? The cat walks up and down and around as if looking for something. What exactly?

The elegantly dressed woman with a fur collar insists that they have something to drink and reassures the two that they are in the right place. *There is no other place in which you can be. Haven't you ordered an orange juice and water?* she asks. Colored letters and words cover the windows, there is a couch that looks like a big L, seats in the shape of a U, and there are also ornamental plants in the shape of a T. The subcontractor and the cat sit on the couch, while the mannered woman takes out some papers from one of the side drawers of the desk. She looks at the subcontractor and hands him what looks like a script for a movie. The first line reads: *The speculator. A discursive structure. A precarious job. A highly creative environment. Projections into the near future.* The cat lifts up her black, noble tail. The subcontractor reads and rereads the long list carefully. From time to time he lifts his head and tries to look out the windows. But words cover up the view. He concentrates on the list again, reading some words aloud:

Dysfunctional.
Structure.
Individual expression.
Just before.
Speculate.
Plan.
In the middle of nowhere.
Suspension.
Anxiety.
Repression.
Generate a problem.

The yellow yells: *Can we talk about light? I am too high. I can't see the sun. I feel repressed, and I am getting depressed over here.*

The orange whispers: *What about difference? Can we address the subject? I feel it's a good time to discuss the variety and multiplicity of positions and attitudes and viewpoints and perspectives. Without difference there is no equality.*

The blue joins the party: *Why don't we talk about trajectories!? At this point, it seems necessary to think about trajectories. There are many of them that have remained unexplored. They are open, waiting to be discovered. Trajectories, not ends, not means. Trajectories like lines of flight.*

The red observes: *Sorry, we haven't been introduced. We are the Gamble Theory Collective (GTC). We are a discursive platform. We are a model for nothing. We are a parallel structure. We are connectors. We are mediators and also a little bit of thought-radiators. What's your profession? Oh, my apologies. You are creatives, right?*

We are not creatives, the subcontractor answers. The cat looks disappointed.

The red: *So, who are you? You really look like two creatives, you know. Why would you be here otherwise?*

The subcontractor: *I just followed the cat and we ended up here. But this is crazy. Who is behind this, behind the curtains, hidden in some control room, making fun of us?*

Annoyed by such an assumption, the blue attacks: *I don't mean to be impolite, but you talk like a gray, churlish, ordinary apparatchik. You speak like a bureaucrat. Do you represent an institution? We have been working together for a while to get rid of institutions*

and their language. To imagine a place and a time in which everybody can experience the pleasure of "Theatre" or "Sun" or "Eye" or "Philosophy" beyond canons and norms. The Gamble Theory disdains the discursive that is instrumental to the rhetoric of power.

The colors chant together: *There is a delay in the process of transformation. There is a delay in radical criticism.*

The subcontractor bursts out: *I am not an institution. I am a subcontractor. I try my best to meet the expectations of my commissioners. I get paid for that. And if I don't meet their desires, I have wasted my time and don't get paid. What delay, what transformation?*

The red intervenes: *What does it mean to "meet desires"? Does it give you pleasure? The Gamble Theory Collective has been working to rethink infrastructure for people like you. To give you real pleasure. We need your help.*

Meow. The cat is ready to join, to participate. She likes collective actions.

The subcontractor: *I am an incomplete character. I am not autonomous. And I don't know how to help you if you don't articulate your desires and expectations properly, in a comprehensible manner.*

The orange: *I don't know what a subcontractor is. Perhaps it's better than a "creative"? You don't need to be autonomous. The Gamble Theory Collective believes in the displacement of the normative. And everybody can displace a norm as everybody can refuse to answer a question. You don't need to be a subversive. And we don't need to articulate anything. We speculate, dream, and act. Help with that if you like.*

The yellow: *Yeah Yeah. You don't need to be a subversive. You need to find a collective, perhaps subcontractors like you, and then you had it. There is a delay in the process of transformation. There is a delay in radical criticism.*

He peeps through the cat paws, reads the text twice. He is thirsty. Two fat, oversize cheeseburgers with bacon arrive. *What? We haven't ordered meat. Cheated twice: by a stupid digital waiter and by a smart cat.* And he isn't a Bohemian at all. Gamblers! Nothing good could come from a Bohemian, only trouble. And the message? It is nonsense language, like everything you see on TV. Information pollution. Why would anybody trust language anyway? In the Speculator bar there are no waiters, after all. No need to talk to anybody to order your meal. People are isolated or in small groups, many don't even look up. Only the screens are obsessively sending messages, talking to each other, talking to people. Monologues more than dialogues. Fingers typing on little keyboards. The screen-table enquires insistently:

Would you mind inserting more information? What's your trajectory, your next destination?

4.1.2 Maybe It Would Be Better if We Worked in Groups of Three

They leave the place. They are on the carpeted floor again. And "the delay in the process of transformation and radical criticism," like an unsolvable dilemma, is haunting the thirsty brain of the subcontractor. He ruminates on the words of the screen.

The cat follows a long cable running along one of those tremendous skyways, while the subcontractor mindlessly follows. The cable gets thinner and thinner. It magically disappears in front of an elevator. She stops. *Dling.* Doors open. The cat gets in and looks back at the subcontractor as if waiting for him to get in as well. He does. *Dling.* Doors close. The cat waits. He presses 133. They rise. *Dling.* They step into a big room. It looks like a conference hall or

a secret society's meeting place. There is a red triangular table in the middle, six black leather chairs, and a rectangular patterned carpet. There is a bottle of spring water on the table. The windows are covered by colored film that makes the horizon look brighter. A psychedelic experience. A similar film covers the glass ceiling in four long strips of yellow, orange, blue, red. The cat is confused, the subcontractor fascinated by the many colors and materials. This must be the office of some creative agency. *Why did the cat take me here; why is she so obsessed with creativity?* It's sunny outside. The shining light touches the colored plexi surface, creating multiple rainbows. Hypnotic. Something moves. They both scan the space attentively looking for someone to appear. Nobody.

Blup. Blup. Blup.

They look up. The ceiling is vibrating, changing patterns. The yellow, orange, blue, and red strips on the ceiling produce sounds. *Are the aliens arriving? Is this their Earth station? Are they trying to communicate with us?* The subcontractor is incredulous, speechless.

Pling. Brrrrraaaa. Titititii. Bobobo. Dlingdlong. Zeeeez. Paparara.

The sounds are becoming more intense. The light is getting brighter and the surface of the ceiling looks like a dance floor, only upside down. The subcontractor would like to run away. He is not interested in exploring unknown territories. He is a subcontractor, after all. Why take this risk? He doesn't have any option but to be patient and wait for things to calm down again.

The red strip speaks: *Would you like to submit your abstract? There are many subjects we can talk about, but only if you want to join the conversation. Sorry. I am red. Who are you? [laughter] You are two creatives, I suppose.*

makes a move. The subcontractor is relieved. She has made a decision. Now, it is the subcontractor following the cat. They walk unnoticed through corridors along a dusty gray carpet decorated with flower patterns, through a seventies futuristic bar with orange leather seats and metal coffee tables, through a hyper-colored, Memphis-style conference hall, and then through a Zen-modernism restaurant with a long, minimalist counter, reflecting walls, big black leather couches, and terrible chill-out music. If the cat could speak, she would be infuriated by the pretentiousness of human beings, their ordinary design, cheap food, and fake breasts. She moves with elegance, jumping up to a marble front desk and then leaping down to the glittery black floor of a lingerie shop. They move through another shop and another one. He thinks:

This place looks like a factory. A factory that has stopped producing. A factory of consumption.

4.1 The Horizon Produced by a Factory Once It Had Stopped Producing Views

Going in a circle. In the factory of consumption. From point A to B, C, D, and back to A. This is what the subcontractor and the cat have been doing. They are exhausted. They have to stop. There is a bar. A big yellow sign at the entrance reads: The Speculator. There are many people inside: office workers with their thin black ties and ordinary suits, students with headphones staring at their laptops, boys and girls compulsively texting on their smartphones, an old couple sipping tea, and a group of gossiping ladies slurping diet drinks. The space looks like a revised version of a seventies science-fiction movie set, including a spaceship, strange animals hanging from the ceiling, and exotic plants. The subcontractor and the cat find a table. He sits while the cat leaps to the surface, which immediately lights up a plas-

ma screen. A menu appears. They can order their drinks and food via Internet. They have to fill out a form and send it. He orders an orange juice and a glass of water for the cat. The server is slow, but after a few attempts they get a reply: *Your order has been successfully registered.* The cat seems to be attracted by the colorful, interactive screen. She plays with it a little to familiarize herself. She paws the surface; the screen reacts by changing colors. It looks like they are having some sort of conversation, the cat and the screen. The subcontractor observes the scene, amused. The cat, however, doesn't enjoy it. She is struggling, fighting the flat surface. A page pops up on the screen. She must have clicked something:

Do you believe in the future? We predict your future and provide you with the right answers. Please insert your profession.

Almost half an hour has passed, but their order hasn't arrived. It must be lost somewhere between their table and the main server connected to the kitchen. While waiting for the drinks, the bored subcontractor types in his profession. The response:

We are sorry. You have no future. Please try again. Change your profession type.

A total waste of time. Where are the drinks? The subcontractor is getting angry. But the cat, who is now seriously engaged, types the letters C-R-E-A-T-I-V-E with her big paws. A new page opens with new questions: *Are you a knowledge-based worker or a Bohemian?* No, he is a subcontractor for a condom corporation. And even though he is working in the Research and Innovation Department, his job is as boring as any other job on the planet. The cat taps her paw against the text that reads "Bohemian." A new text appears:

You better find a job or invent one. You have lost control of your environment, if you ever forgets about her. He is many mental spans ahead exploring new professional horizons when the terrible cold brings him back to his senses. It's not a good idea to be outside in a Minnesota winter. He takes one of the Medical Arts building's entrances, climbs the stairs two at time. It's late. He walks rapidly through a cosmetic shop, which looks like a candy store full of colors and delicious smells of peaches, strawberries, roasted chestnuts. He is looking for one of those skyways, which will take him to a new building and through another building and another one to the place of the interview.

The subcontractor keeps walking, passing swiftly through piles of toys, underwear, children's books, handbags, pajamas, bras, high-speed electronic toothbrushes, second-hand eyeglasses, hiking shoes, plasma TVs. He can't find the right way. Overwhelmed by all these items, he misses the exit and finds himself facing a wall. It is there that he realizes the cat is following him. The cat has an elegant black tail and a funny spot on the left paw, which looks like the first letter of the alphabet. She looks straight at him, lifts the left paw up. But, the subcontractor doesn't have time for pleasantries. He makes his way back to the closest skywalk hoping to find the right direction. The cat follows him. Just a few step behind. *Left, right, then left, then left again, and right*. Lost, sweaty, desperate as he has never been before, he doesn't want to give up. But it is too late anyway. He feels trapped in a labyrinth of corridors, all similarly alienating: an intricate web of streets, passages, and items that could only be navigated with the help of a sat nav. The cat comes closer and with a skillful gesture rubs against the subcontractor's shins. She stretches her furry head. Rubs against him again.

Meow.

A phone call: *Hi. We regret to inform you that the position has been assigned. We haven't seen you and assume you are not interested anymore. By the way, we wish you all the best with the future of your professional career.* Gone. His only chance is gone.

Now, they are staring at each other, the cat and the subcontractor, while people travel past in all directions. The cat likes to cross the paths of others. Not everybody. Only when she likes their shoes or appreciates their pace. It is like a game: counting the people passing by; observing their movements; second-guessing their mood, their job, their life. *Why is the cat following me? What can be so entertaining in following a desperate subcontractor, a loser with no autonomy, who only executes the tasks assigned by someone else, who can't even make his way to a job interview?*

The architecture of the place doesn't help. The space is stuffy, chaotic, and inhospitable. Things are accumulated without criteria. It is like a city in which there is no urban planning, but a building appears (or disappears) whenever a spot of land is available. Commercials. Information. Lights. Noises. He stops. He feels a bit shaky. His legs are weak; his body feels like it is floating in the absence of gravity. The cat is waiting for the next move.

Meow.

The subcontractor scratches his head as if rubbing the magic lamp to get Aladdin out. He would like someone to tell him where to go. Unfortunately, nobody can tell him which direction to take or what to do with his life. The cat moves impatiently up and down. Her small nose imperceptibly vibrates, stimulated by the smell of something. Perhaps it's the smell of good food, or the fragrance of Christina Aguilera's perfume. The subcontractor would like to run away from the cat. He is not the kind of guy who can make decisions for others. He can barely take care of himself. He hates the situation. The cat

His head is bent, heavy thoughts are pressing against his strong neck so that he can't look up. He observes his big feet. He is carrying the weight of his body, as if carrying the pain and the sins of the world. He is worried about something, but it is difficult to guess exactly what. The sky is like a blank piece of paper when a track's wheel has swamped and flattened it to the ground. The snow has rendered everything strangely shapeless: the difference between things, between a car and bench, is a matter of intuition and some knowledge of geometry. The cold has frozen the majestic chestnut trees, whose numbed branches are bending down sympathizing with him. He is a subcontractor. Technically, he is hired by a general contractor to perform a specific task. The incentive to hire subcontractors is either to reduce costs or to mitigate project risks. In this way the general contractor receives the same or better service than could otherwise have been provided, at lower overall risk. He has many friends, all subcontractors and all hard workers. They used to go out for drinks and make jokes about their jobs. They call themselves Zombies with Agency as they don't really have a choice but to appropriately perform their assigned tasks. As in many professions, they also have their subcontractors' self-improvement rules that ensure they will be engaged and fairly paid: be educated, diligent, systematic, competitive. At the same time be creative, flexible, and multitasking. Know how and when to speak. He has followed these basic rules to the letter. Yet, he doesn't know what has changed in his life or what is really happening around him, as he doesn't have time to look up, out the window, into the street, into the lives of others, while the city is moving, changing at fast pace.

The thing he knows best is the flat surface of the screen in front of which he spends most of his time. He skims through the web in search of companies that produce low-cost Polyisoprene, a synthetic version of la-

tex used to produce "softer and stretchier condoms for a more natural feeling." He is a subcontractor for the Research and Innovation Department. A prestigious position, although his job is boring, mainly consisting in contacting small companies that produce the fiber at a very competitive price, negotiating costs and conditions for production. Recently, due to the crisis, he also had to cover another position, Supervisor of Design Process. He has got to know many people and learnt about modern slavery. Yet, the latter doesn't really bother him, but what is really troubling is the design part, for he is expected to be extremely innovative. *How many different variants of condom can one really develop?* he asks himself. *You can play with attributes (fruity, salty, sensitive, smart, high-performance, green, yellow, blue, red, super thin, ultra thin, et al.), but not with its basic grammar, its form. I mean a peanut is a peanut, after all.*

Now he is walking absentmindedly, his face beaten by the harsh cold wind blowing in from the north. He is going from his office to another building situated on the west side of downtown for a job interview. An empty office building has been converted into a storage space and the company is looking for someone to hire as storage manager. He wants to end his career as condom-hunter. *I am sick of this job! Even if the salary is excellent, I can always find something part-time. A morning job in a café. And in my free time, I can get an online business started. Everything will be easy. I can manage it from home or while I am at the warehouse. When was the last time I had sex?* He is speculating about possibilities. Planning a new life. At least less frustrating than the one he has.

A cat crosses his way, furtive and unexpected. She disappears behind the trees, running along the fences that protect corporate buildings from the curious eyes of potential competitors. *Where is the cat running so fast?* He

Federica Bueti

A delay in the process of trans-formation

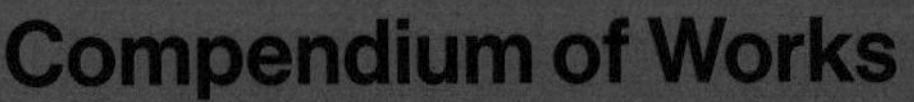

Compendium of Works

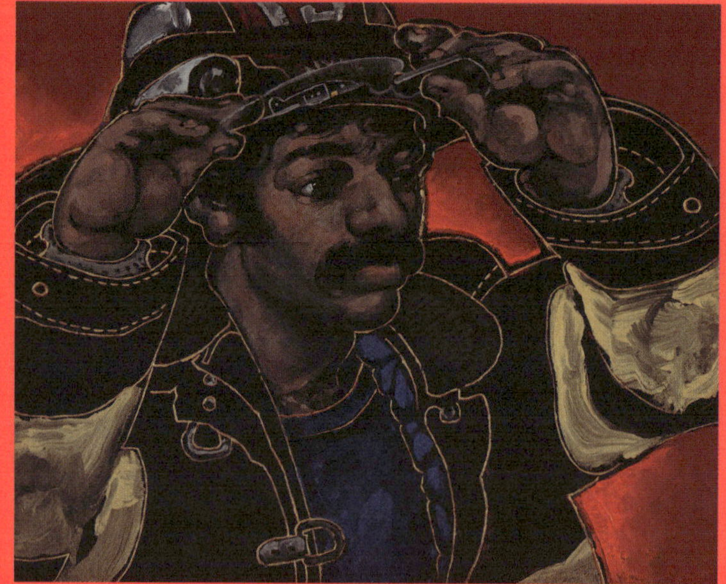

1

2

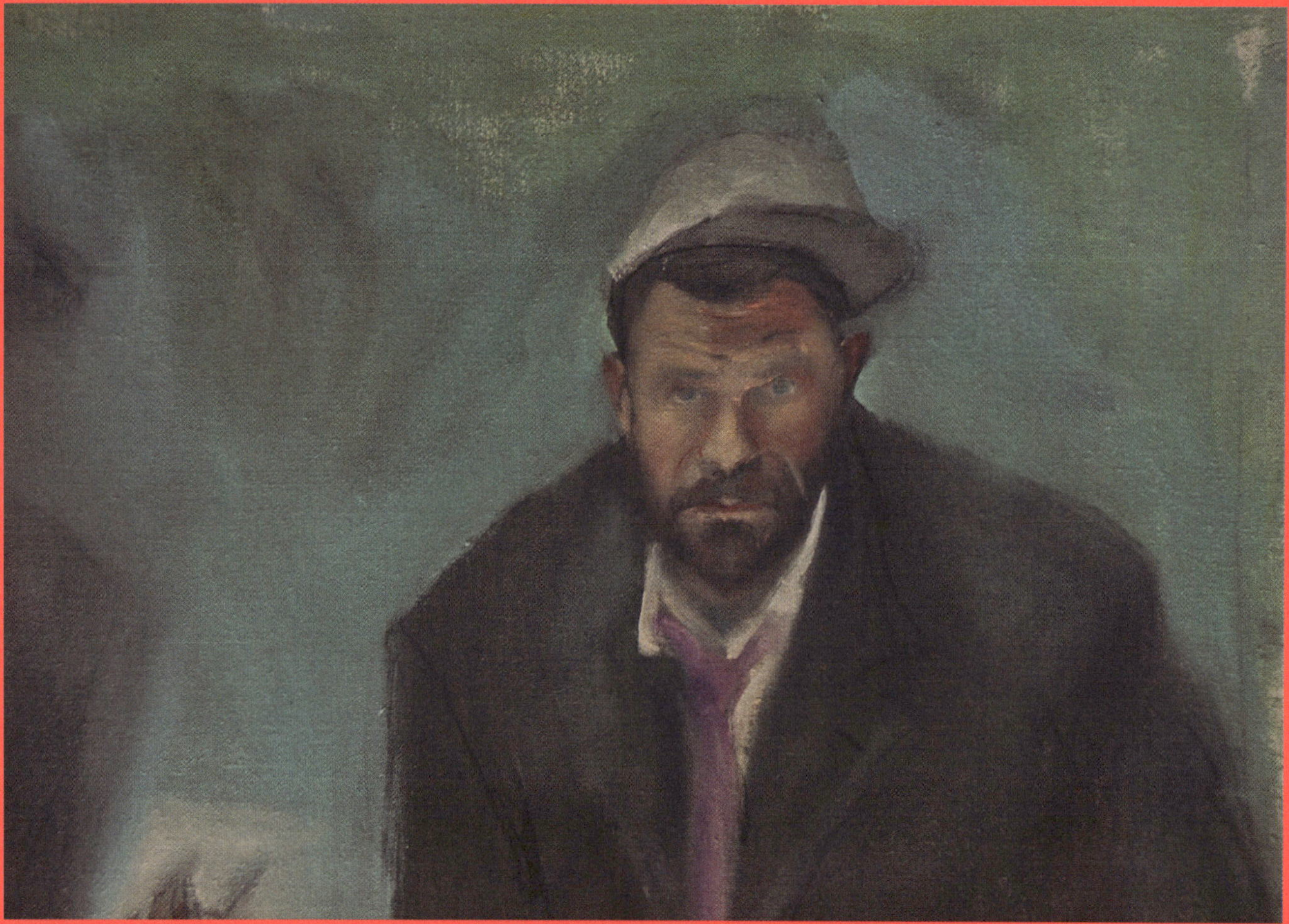

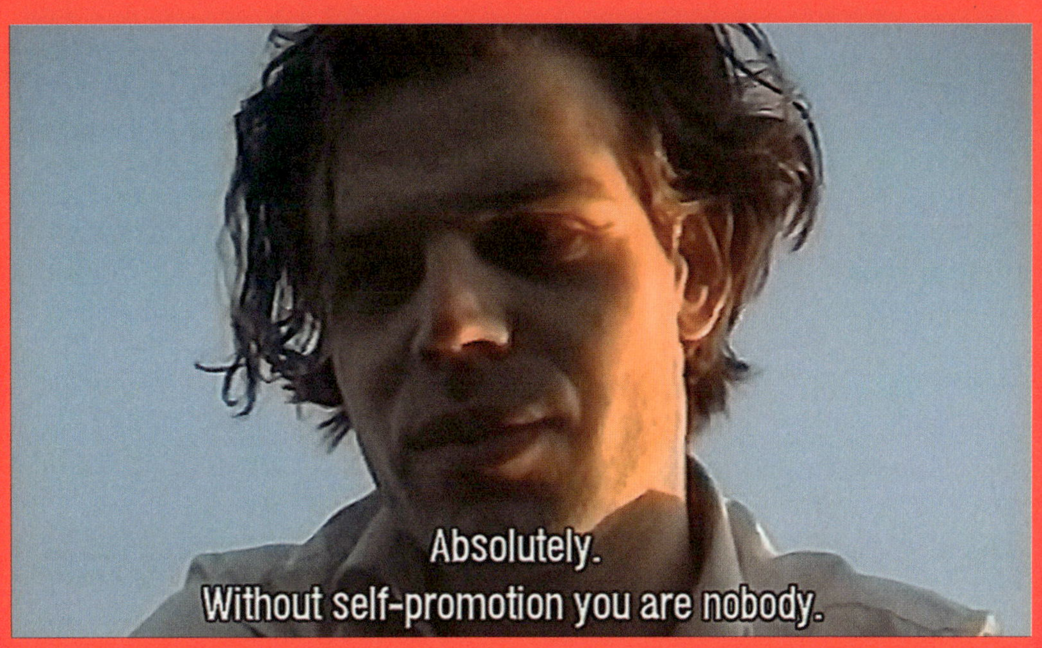

3

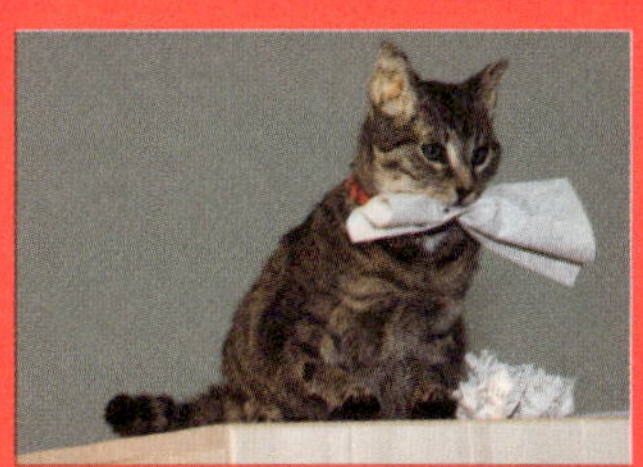

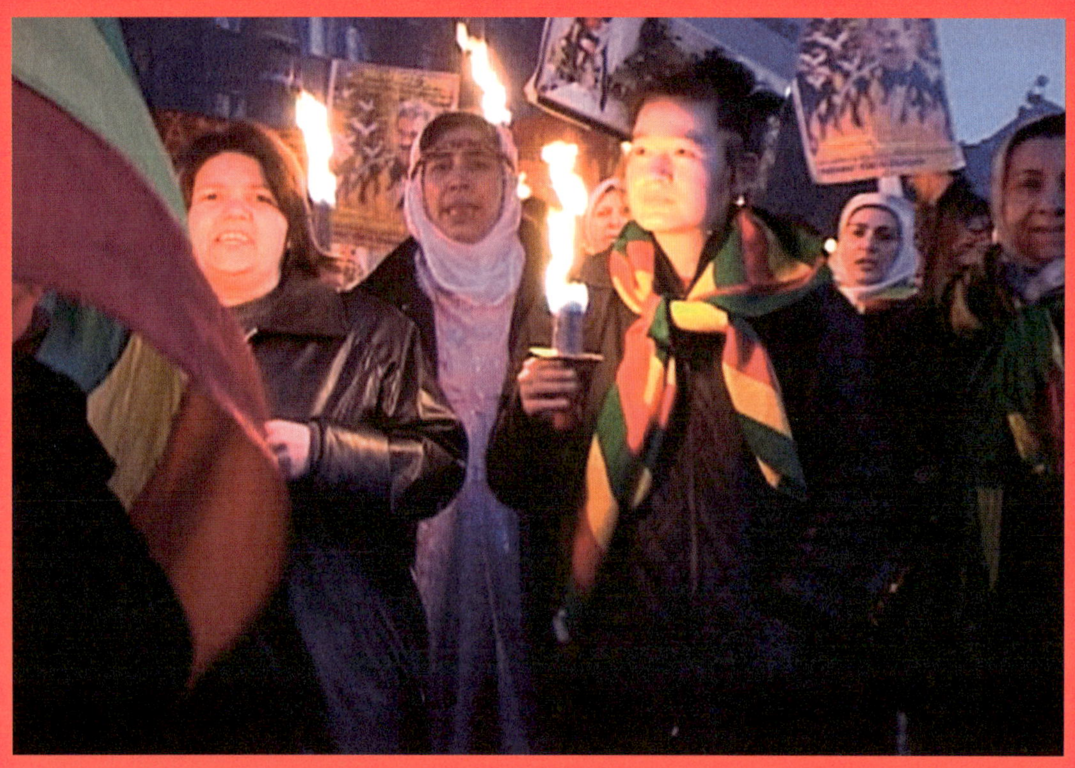

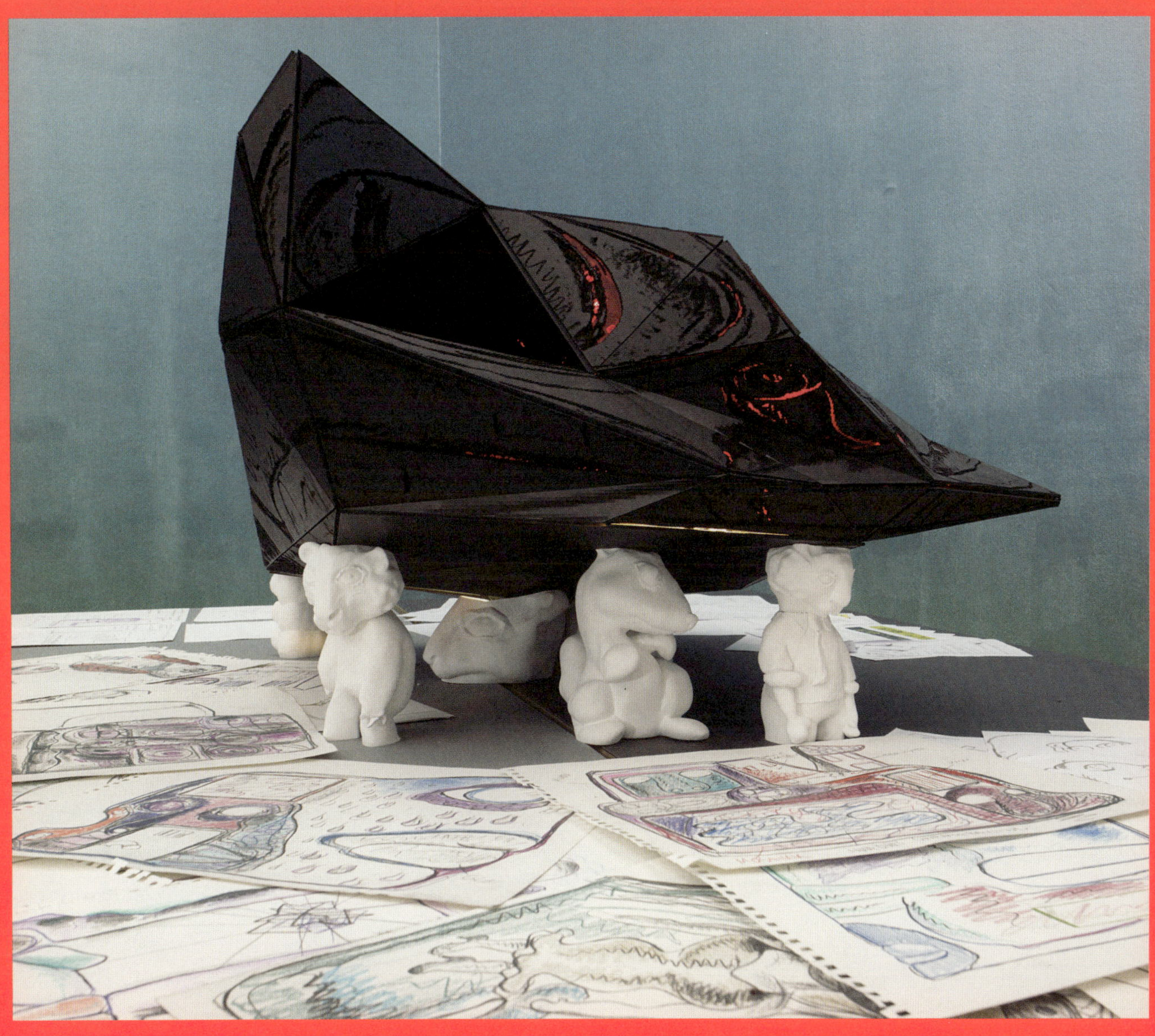

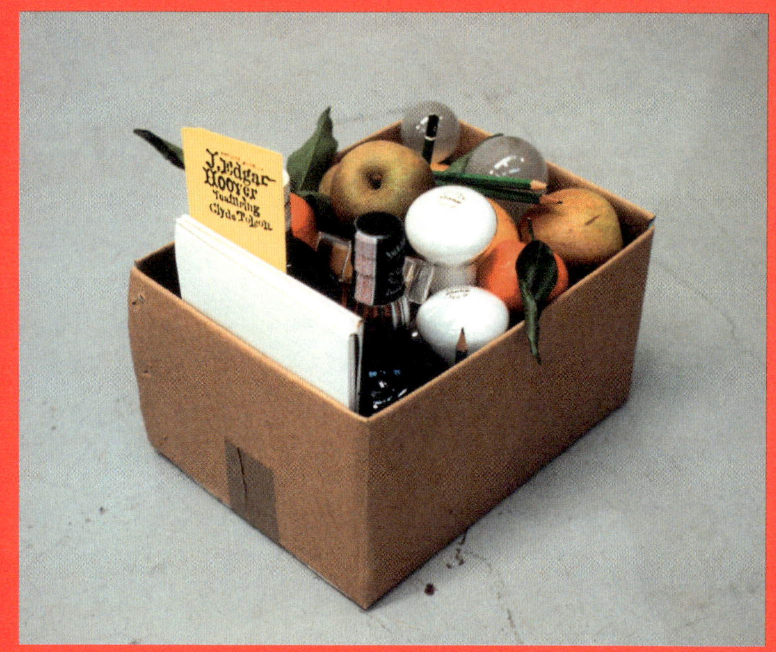

7

8

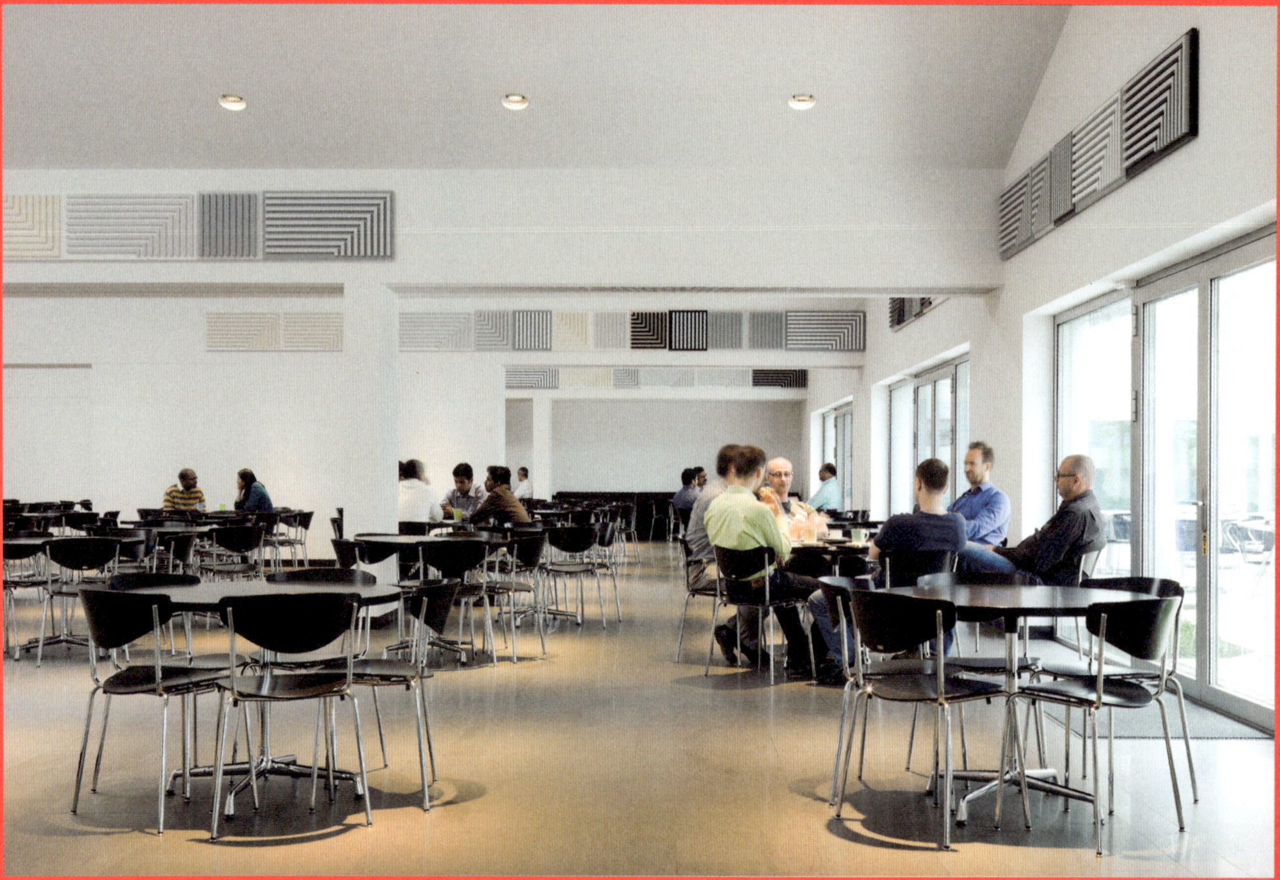

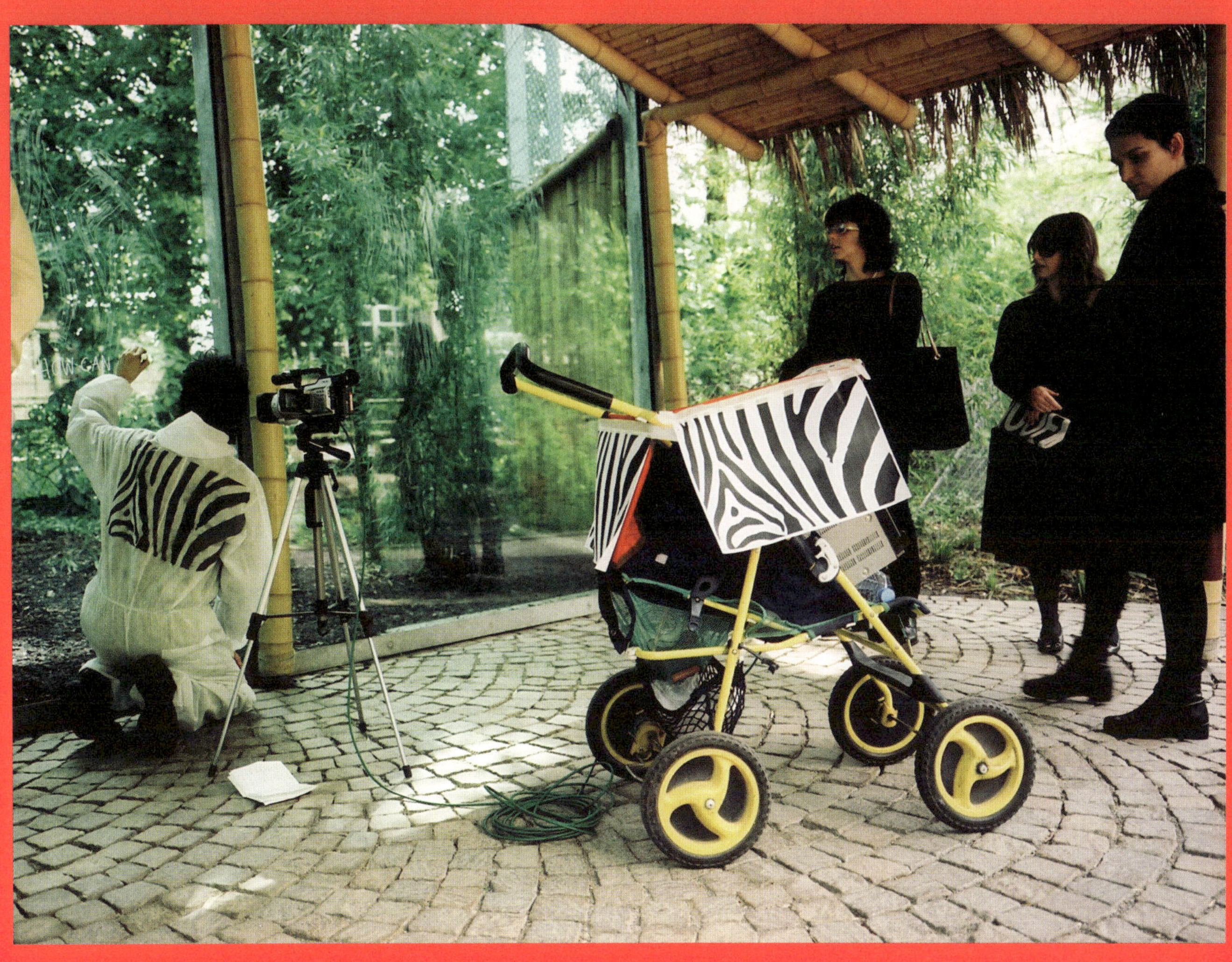

9

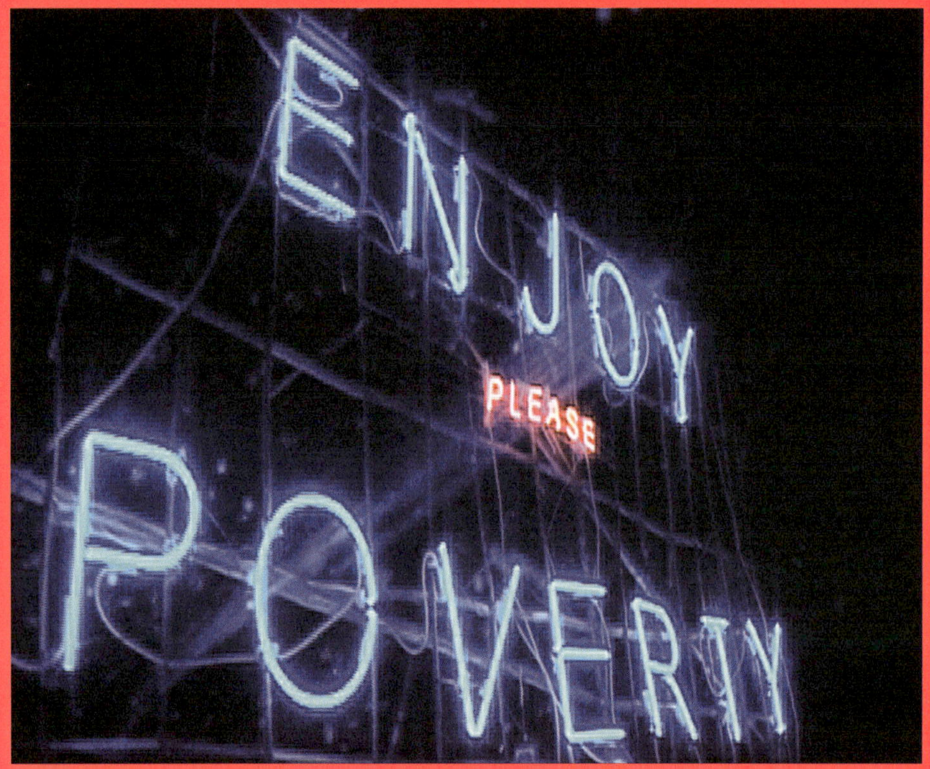

ENJOY
PLEASE
POVERTY

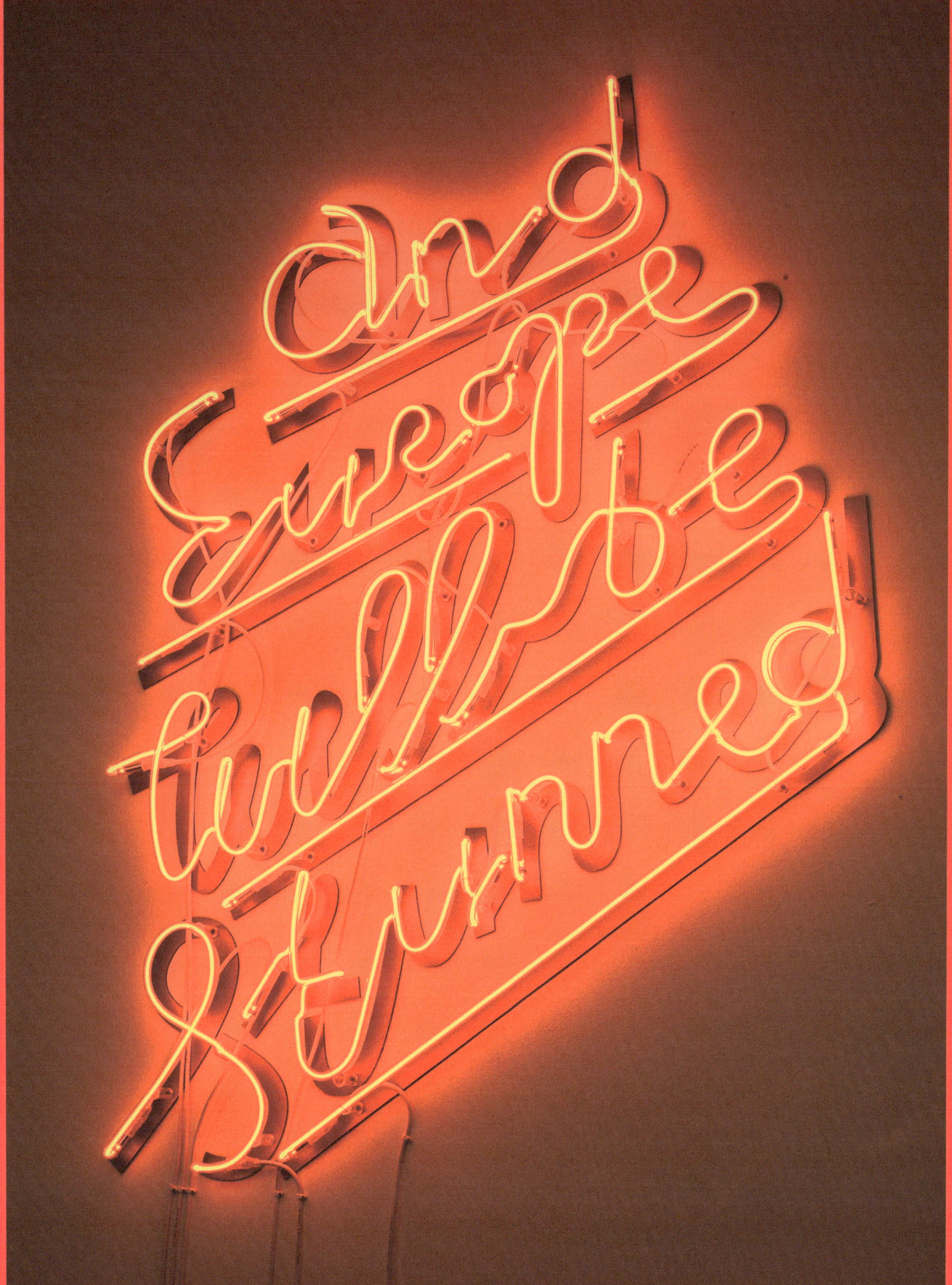
And
europe
will be
stunned

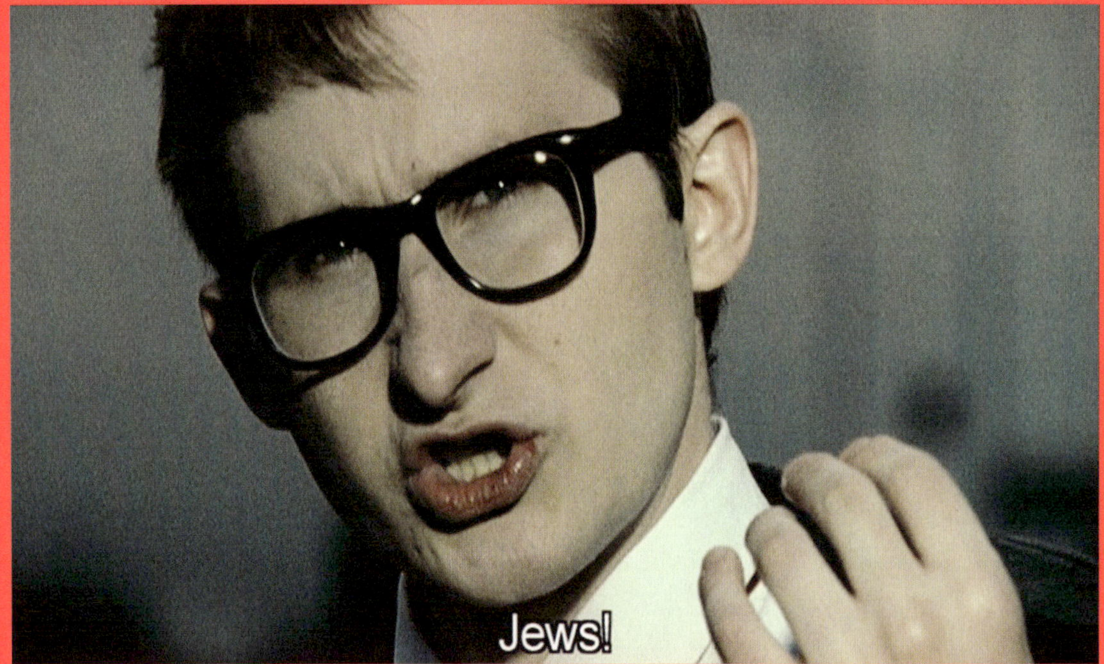

12

13
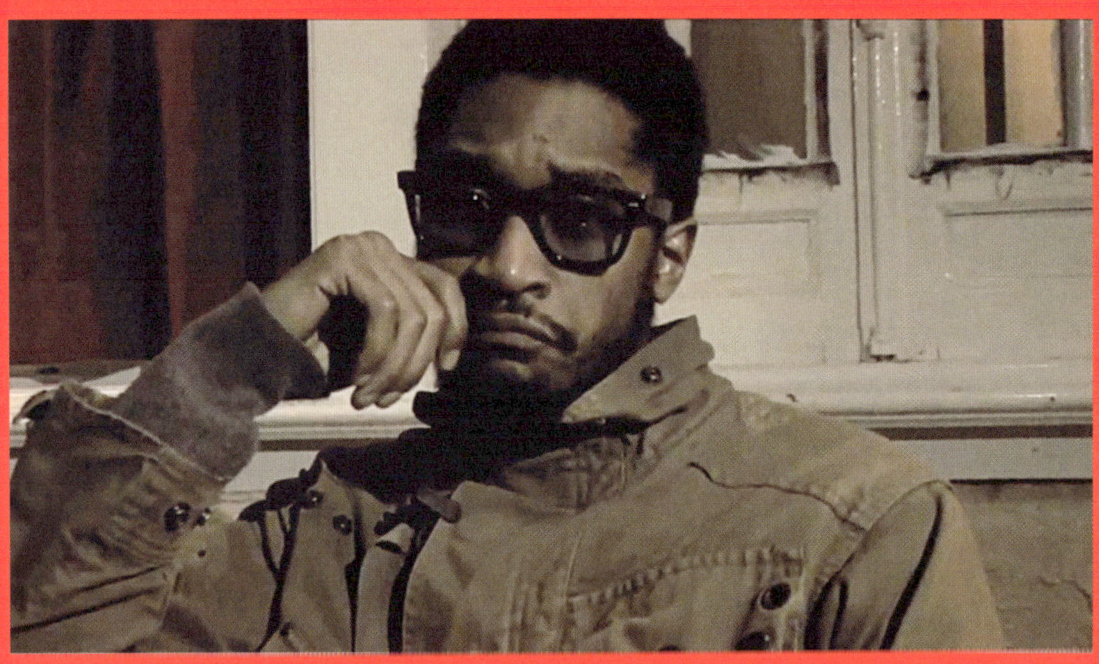

the
whatnot
itself
becomes
a super state

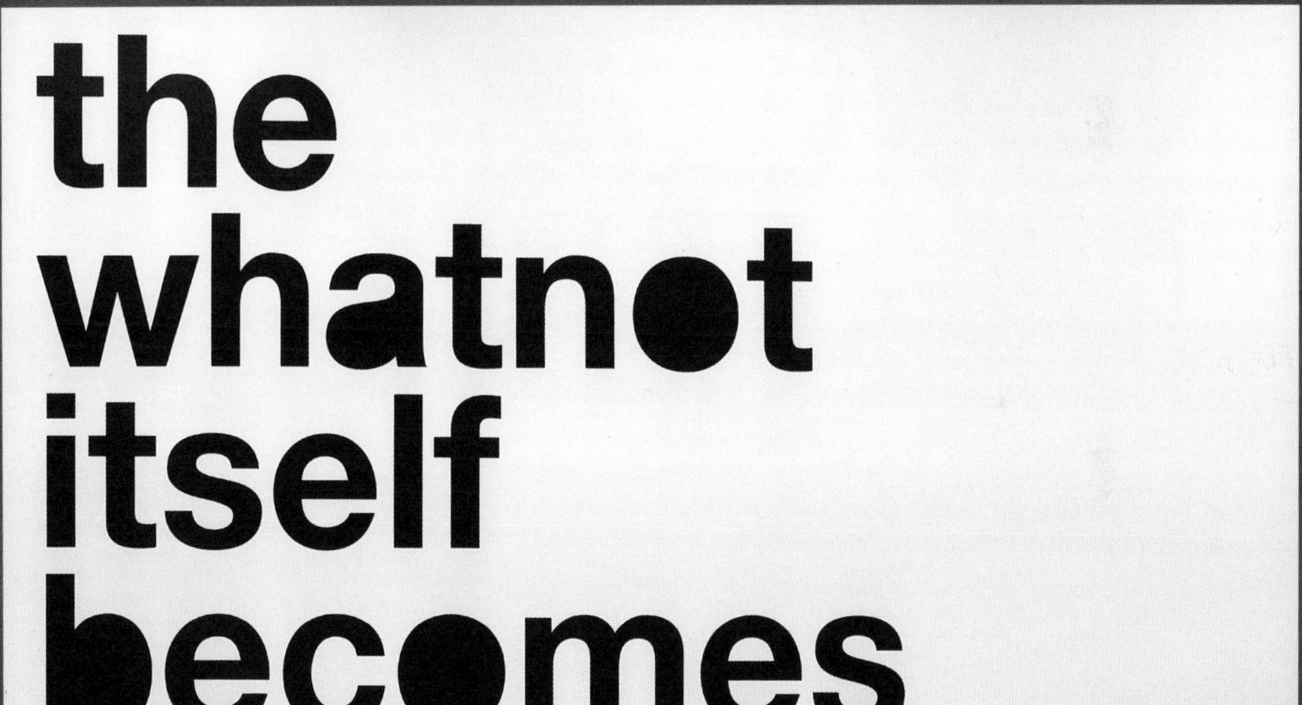

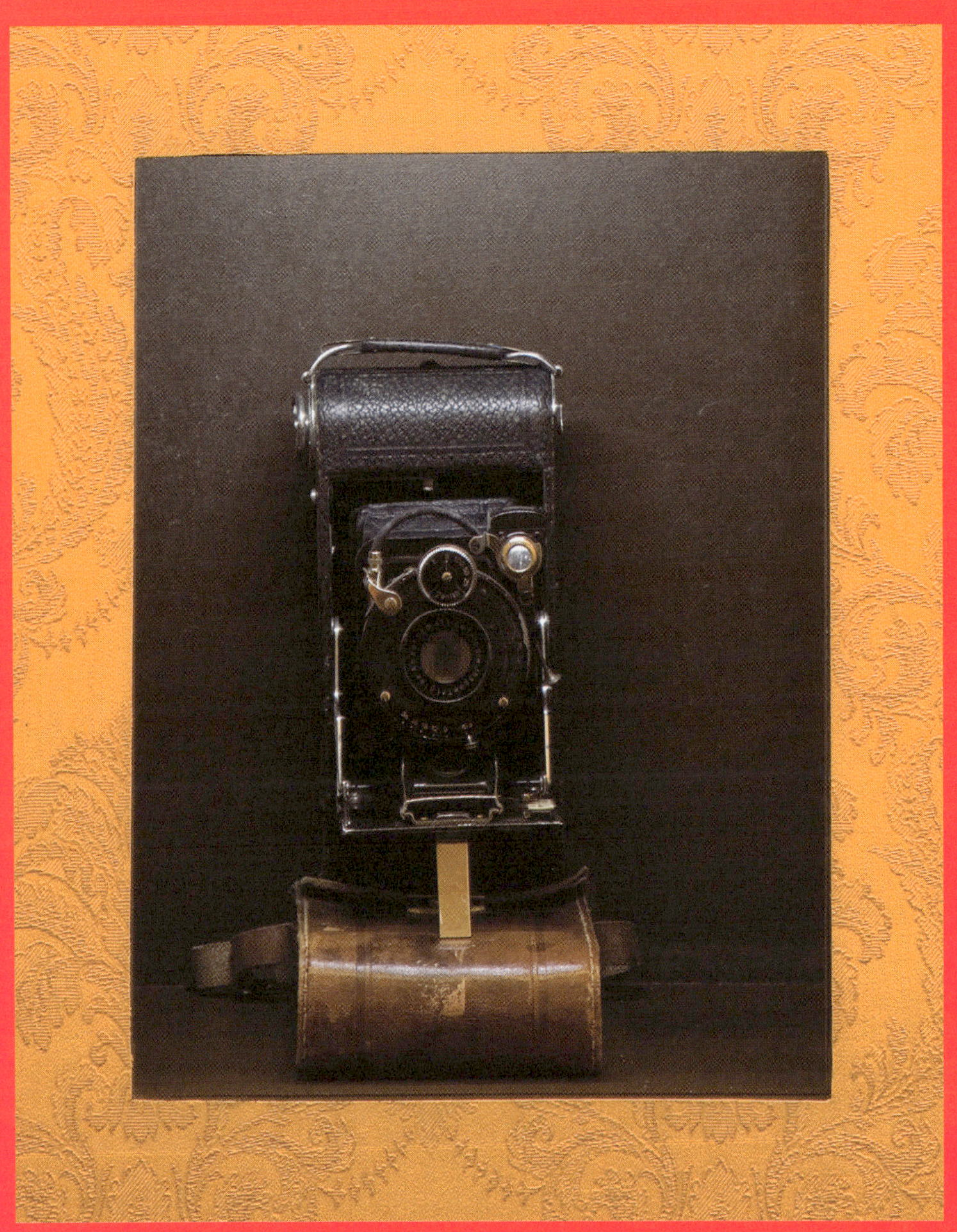

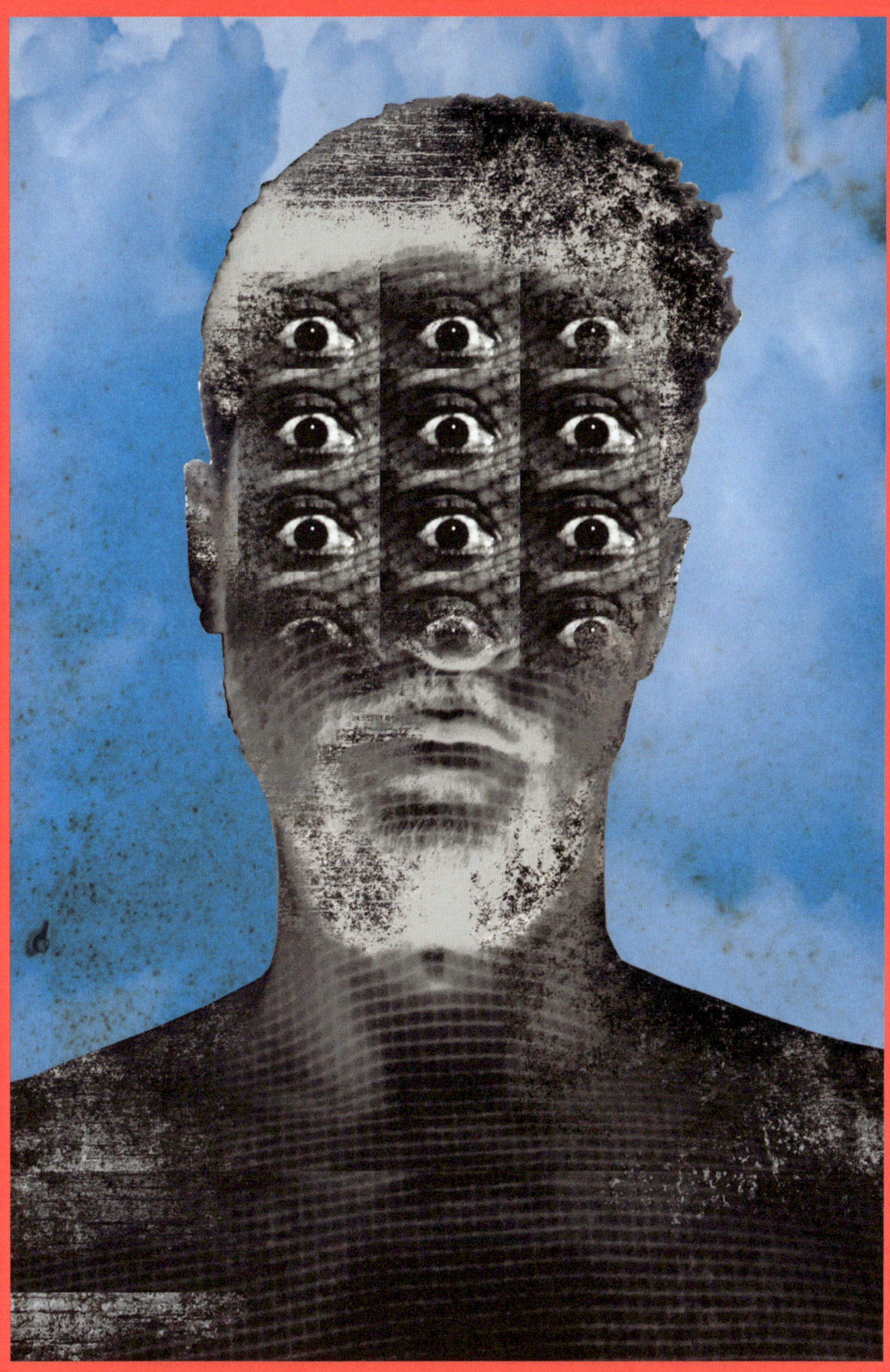

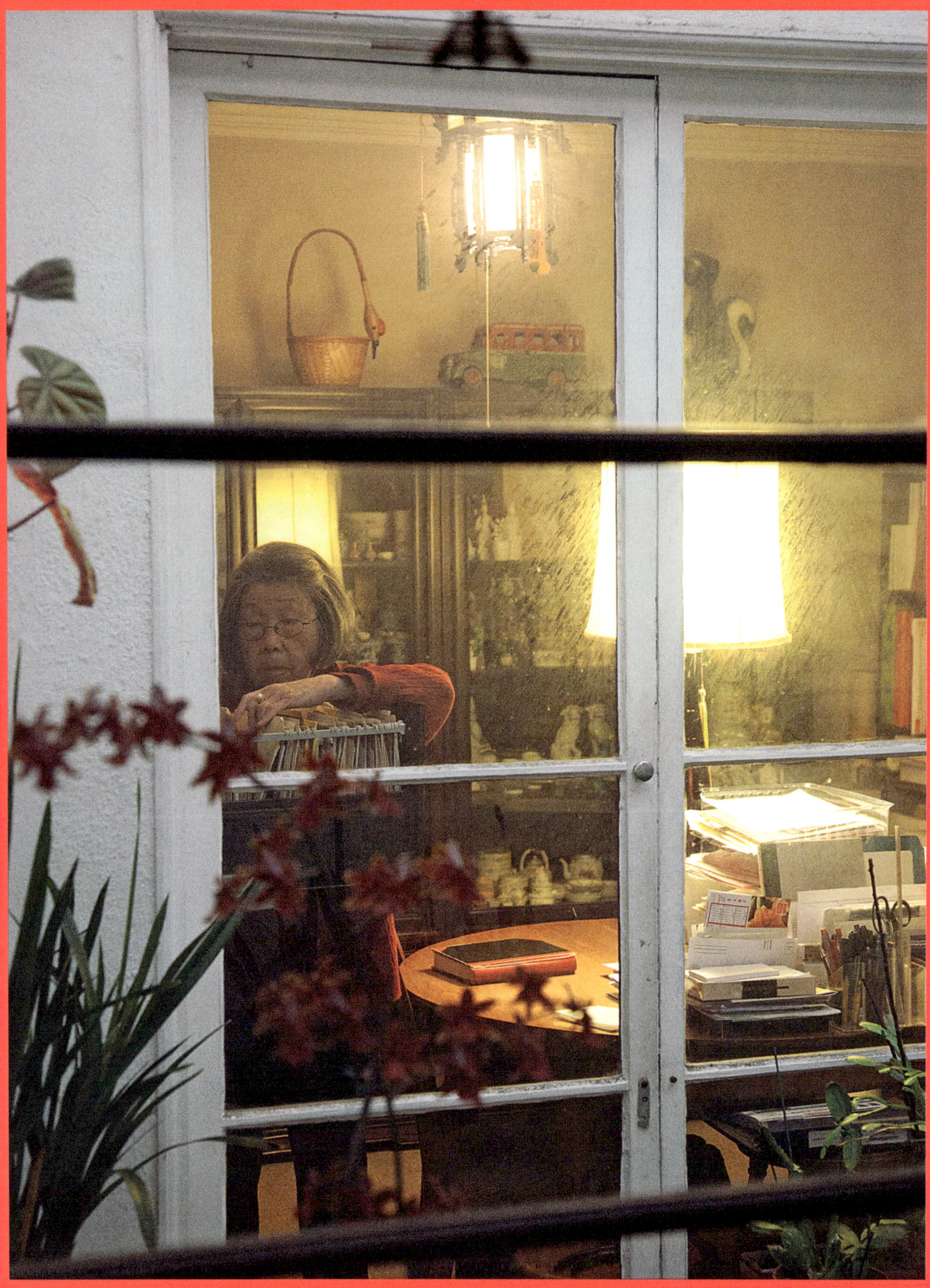

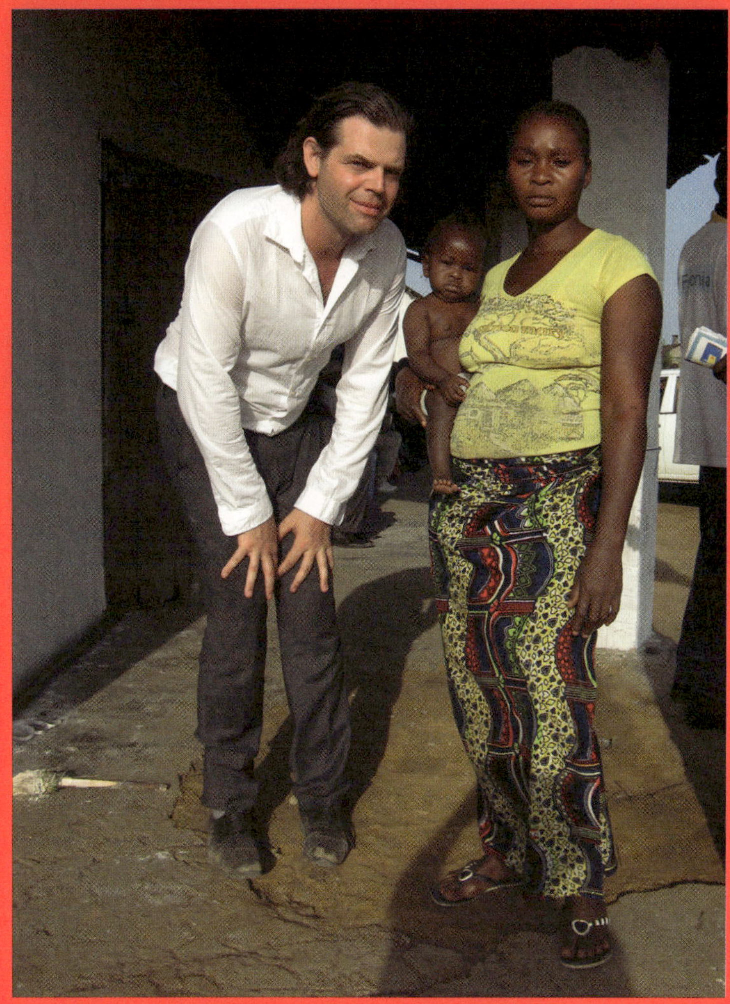

19

18

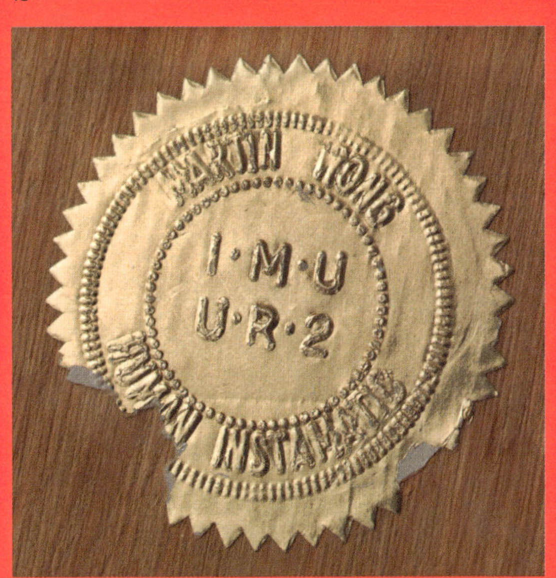

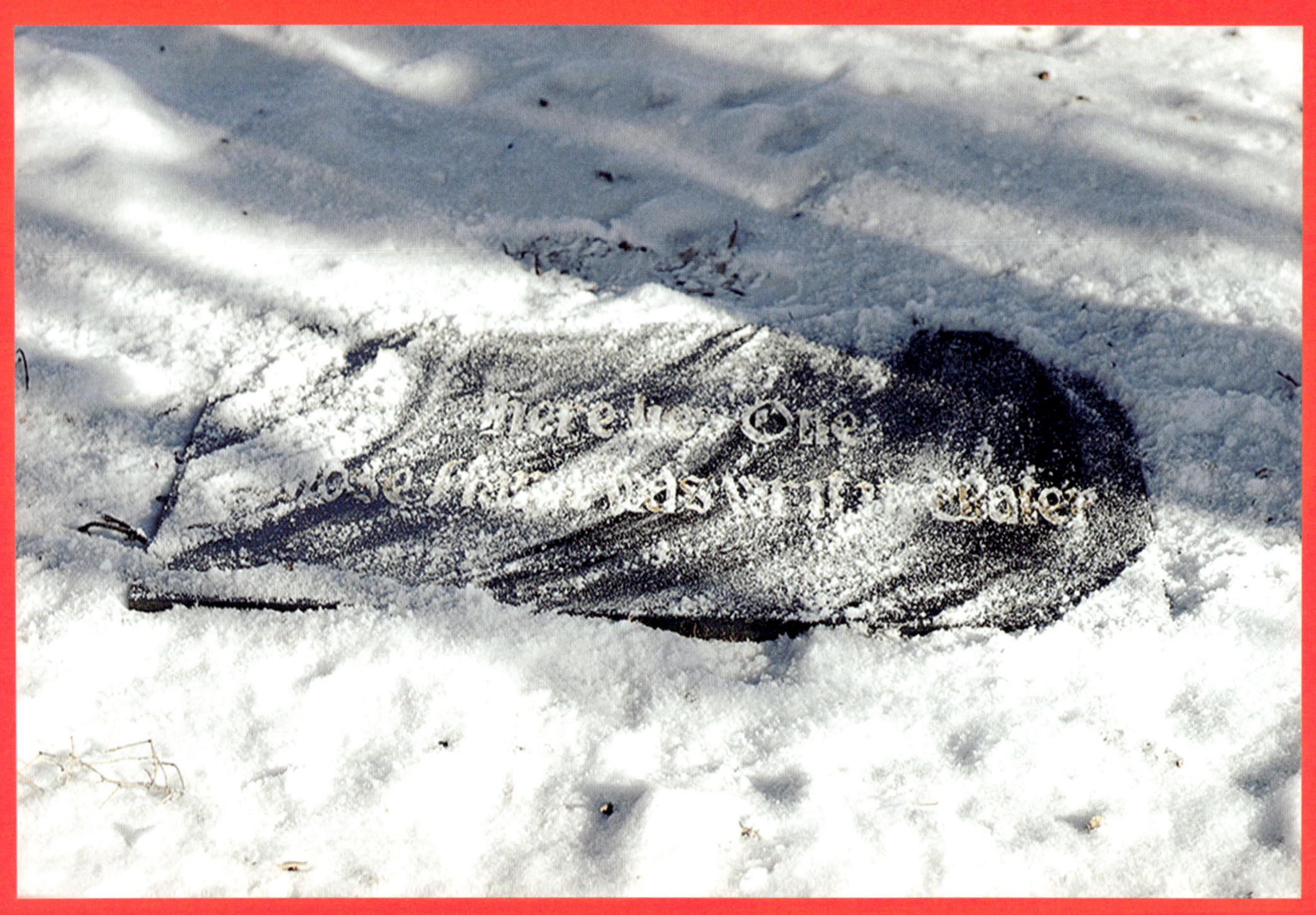

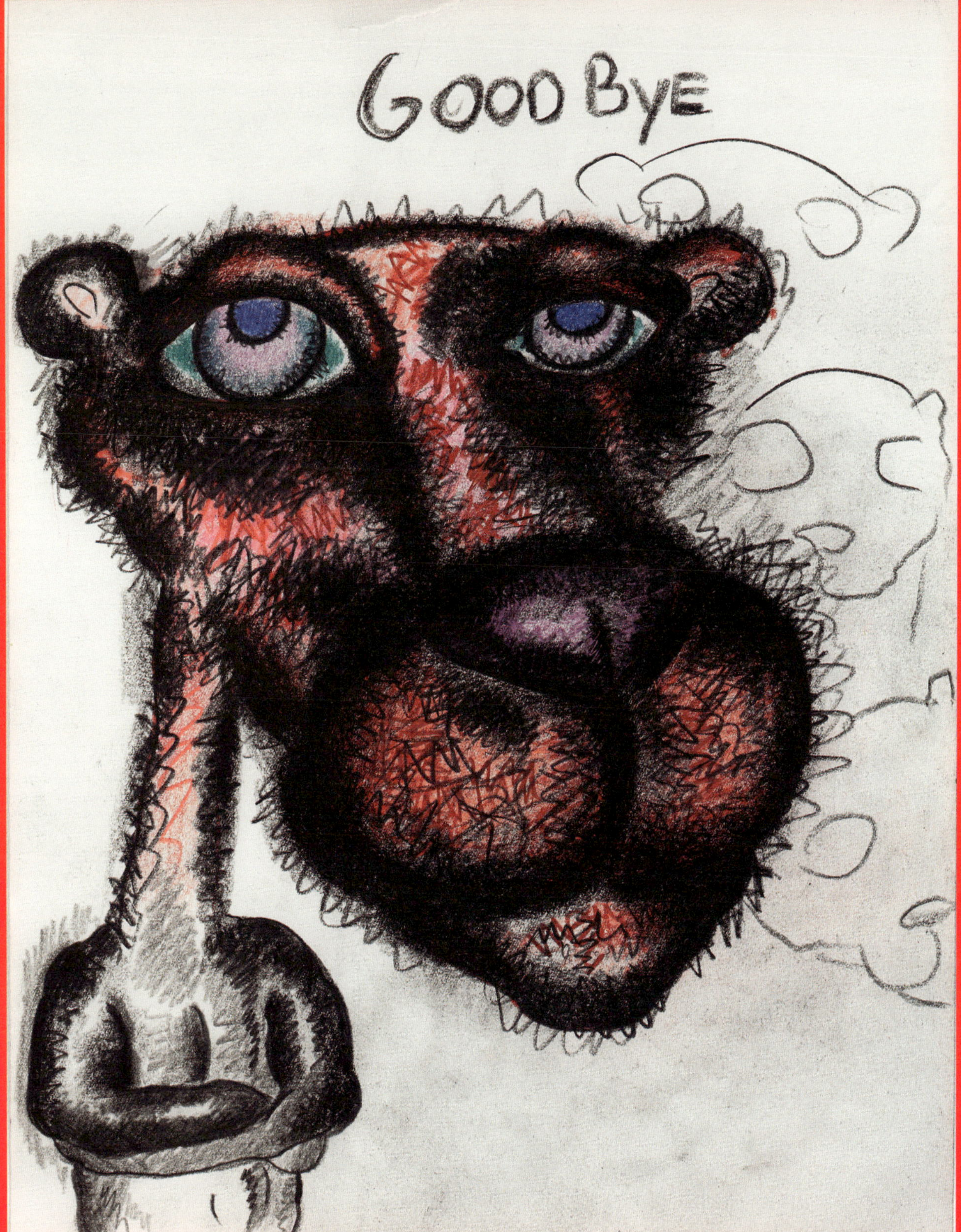
GOOD BYE

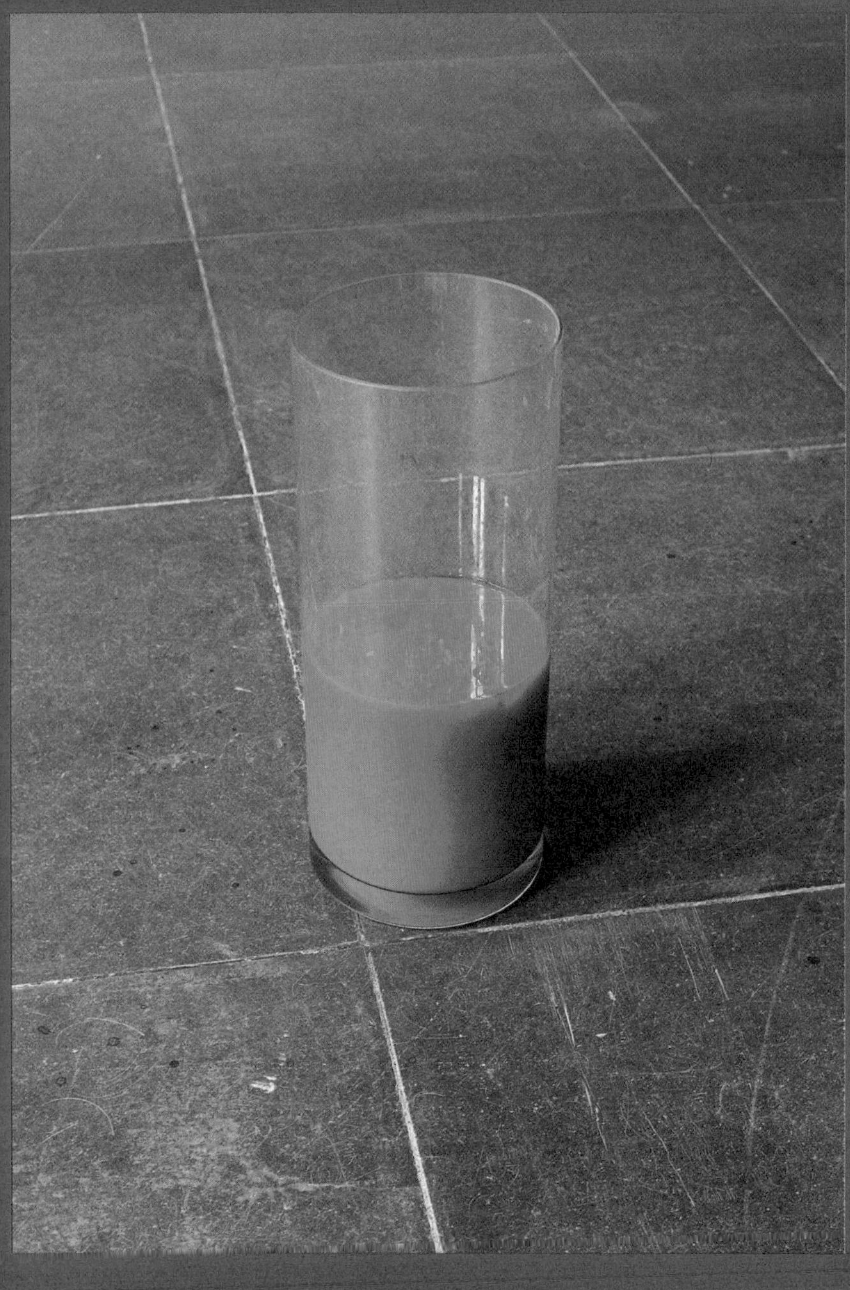

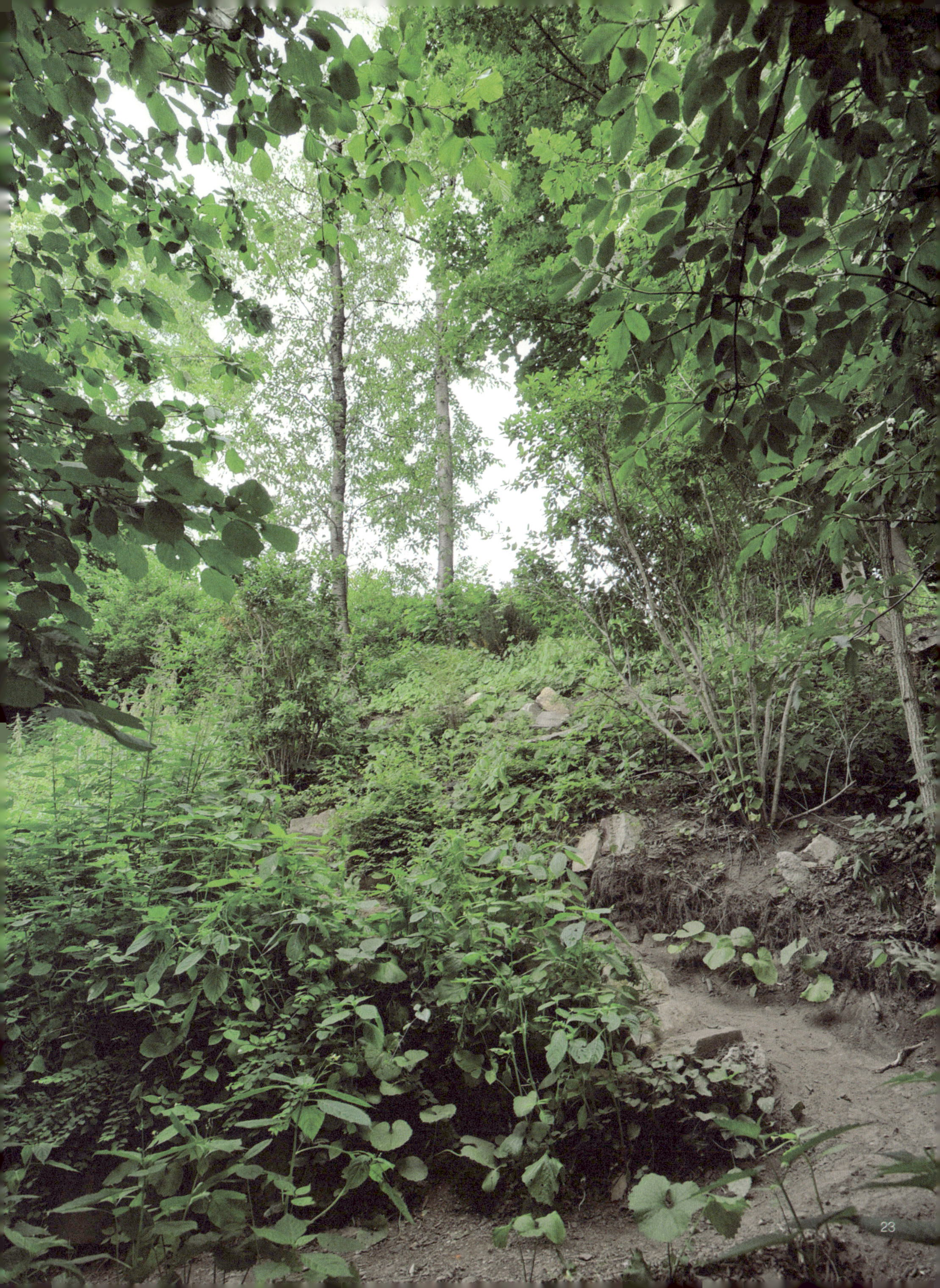

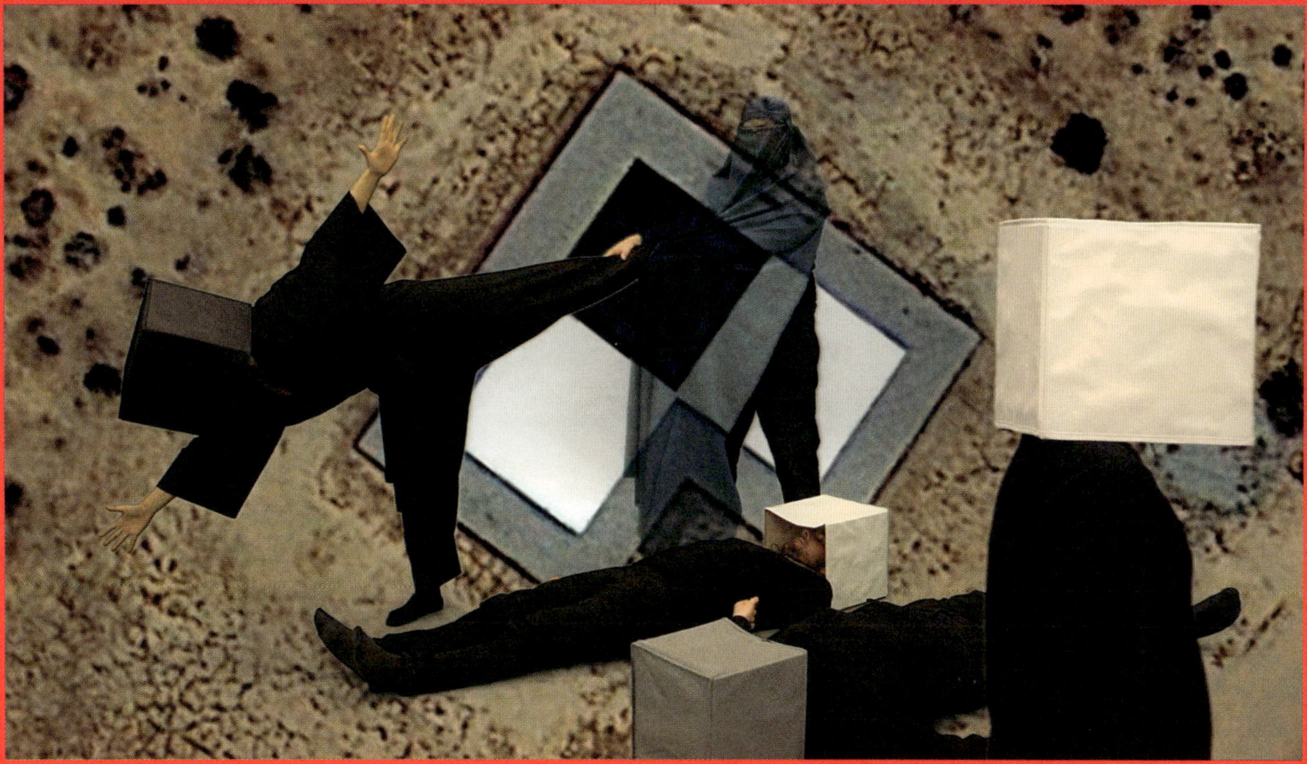

25

26

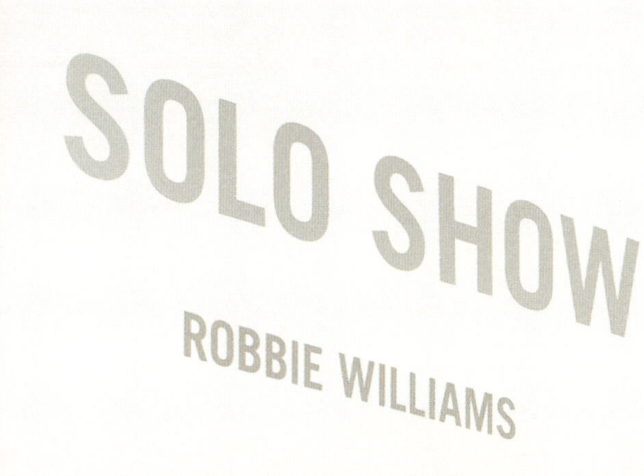

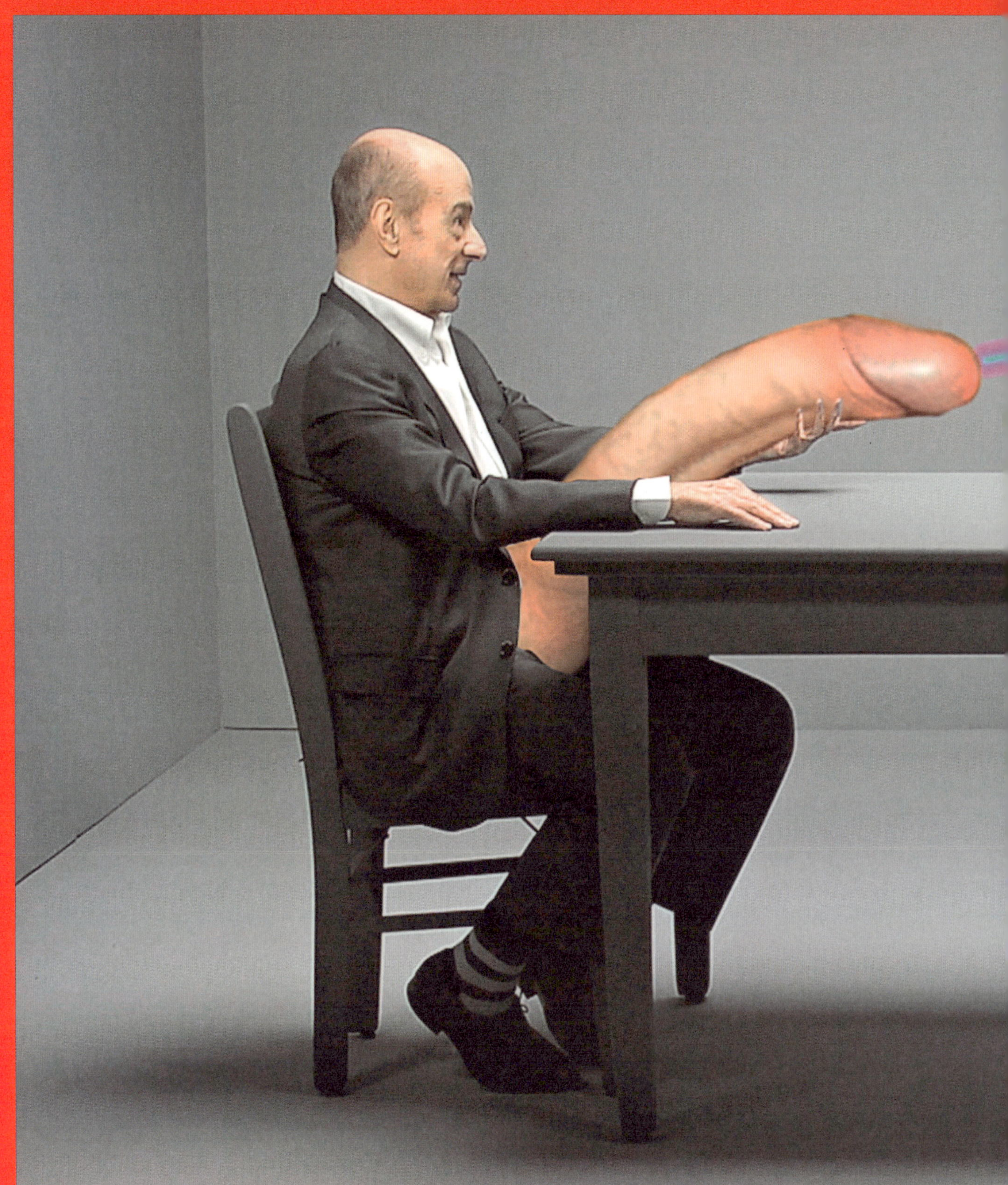

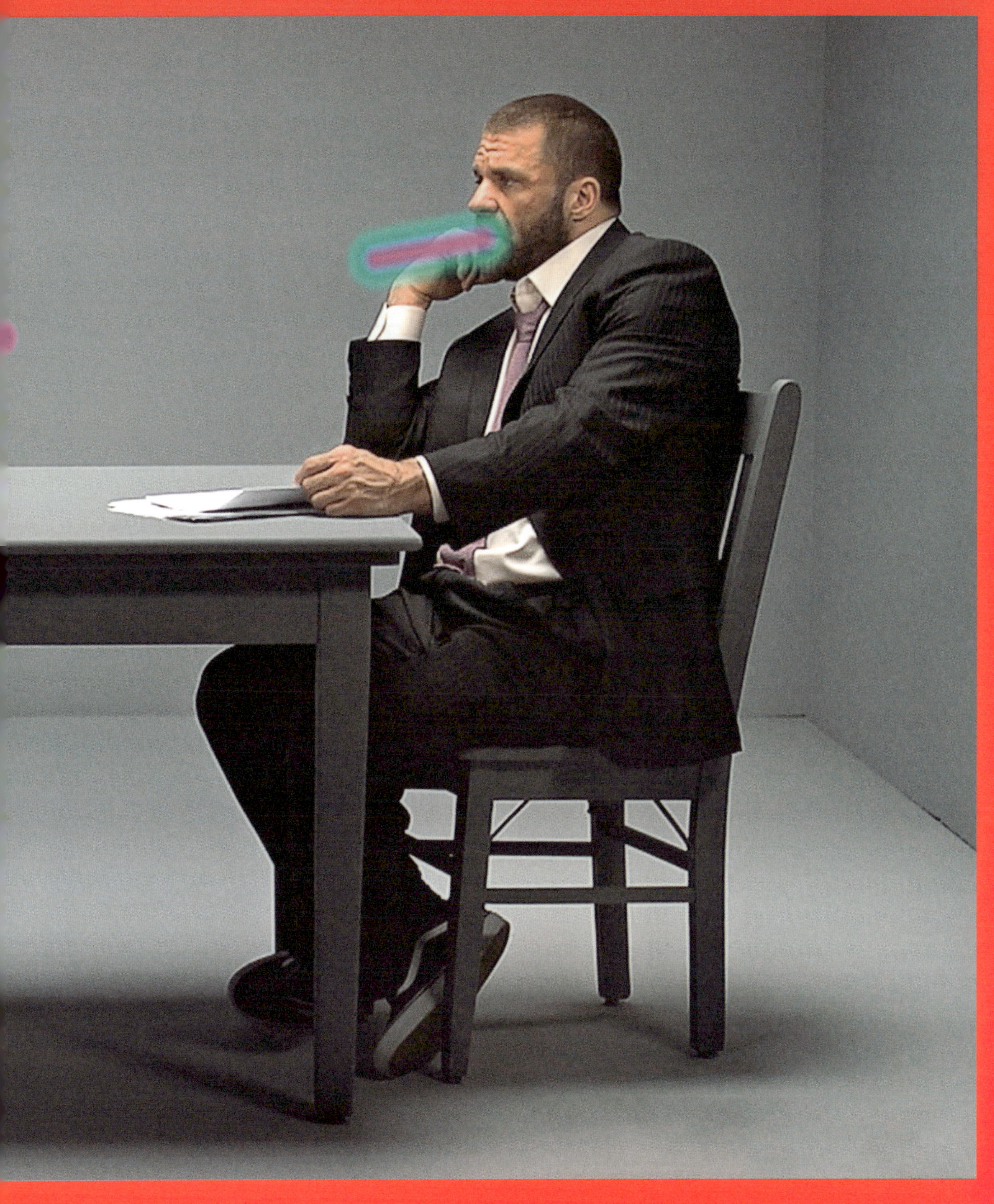

Toxic aid, turn on war, turn off war
Feed me, feed mine
Collective perpetuation just begun…
WELCOME
LADIES AND GENTLEMEN
WELCOME
TO THE WONDERS OF POP CIVILIZATION
YESTERDAY, TODAY, YOU… PLANET YOU

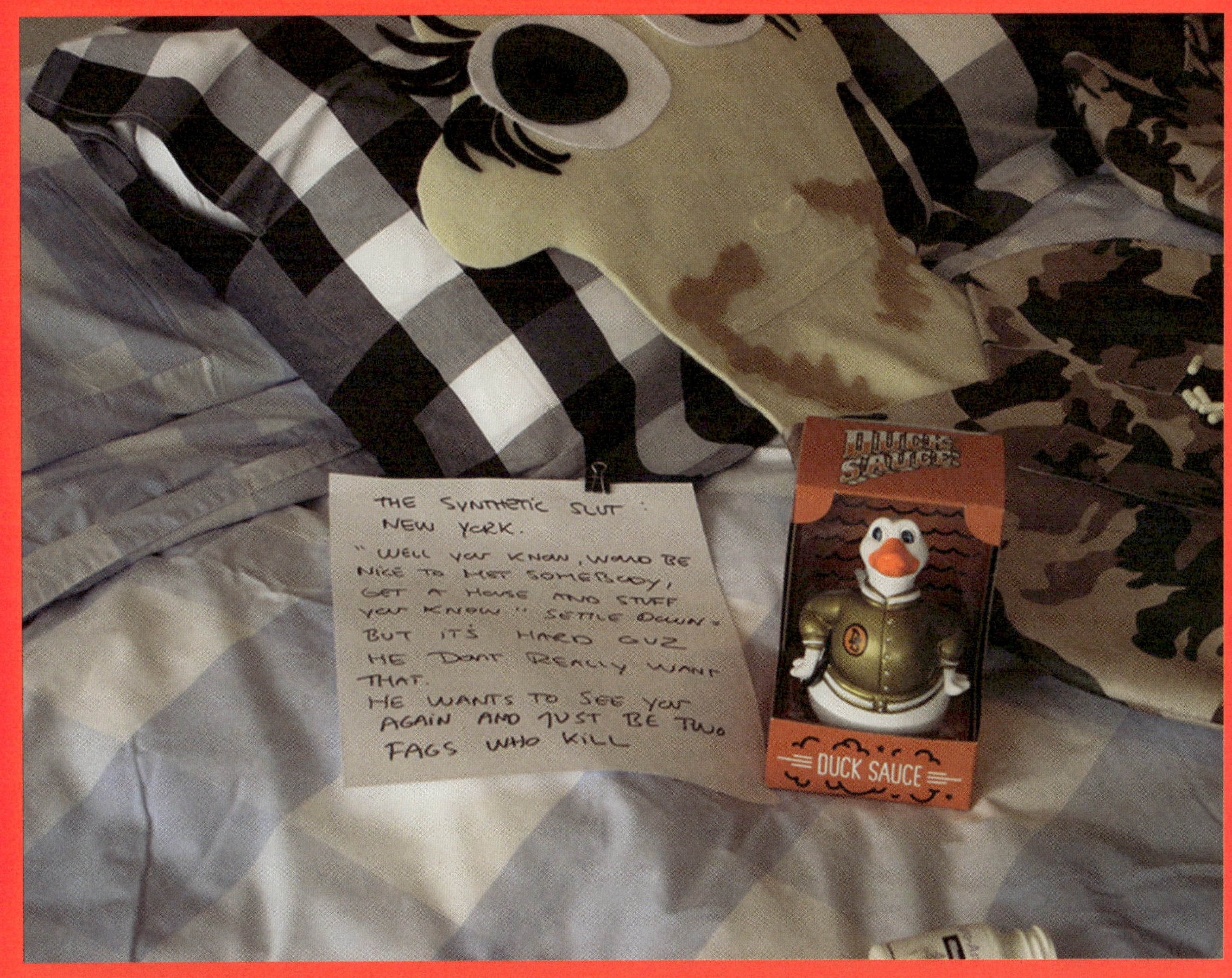
THE SYNTHETIC SLUT :
NEW YORK.
" WELL YOU KNOW, WOULD BE
NICE TO MET SOMEBODY,
GET A HOUSE AND STUFF
YOU KNOW " SETTLE DOWN "
BUT IT'S HARD CUZ
HE DONT REALLY WANT
THAT.
HE WANTS TO SEE YOU
AGAIN AND JUST BE TWO
FAGS WHO KILL
DUCK SAUCE

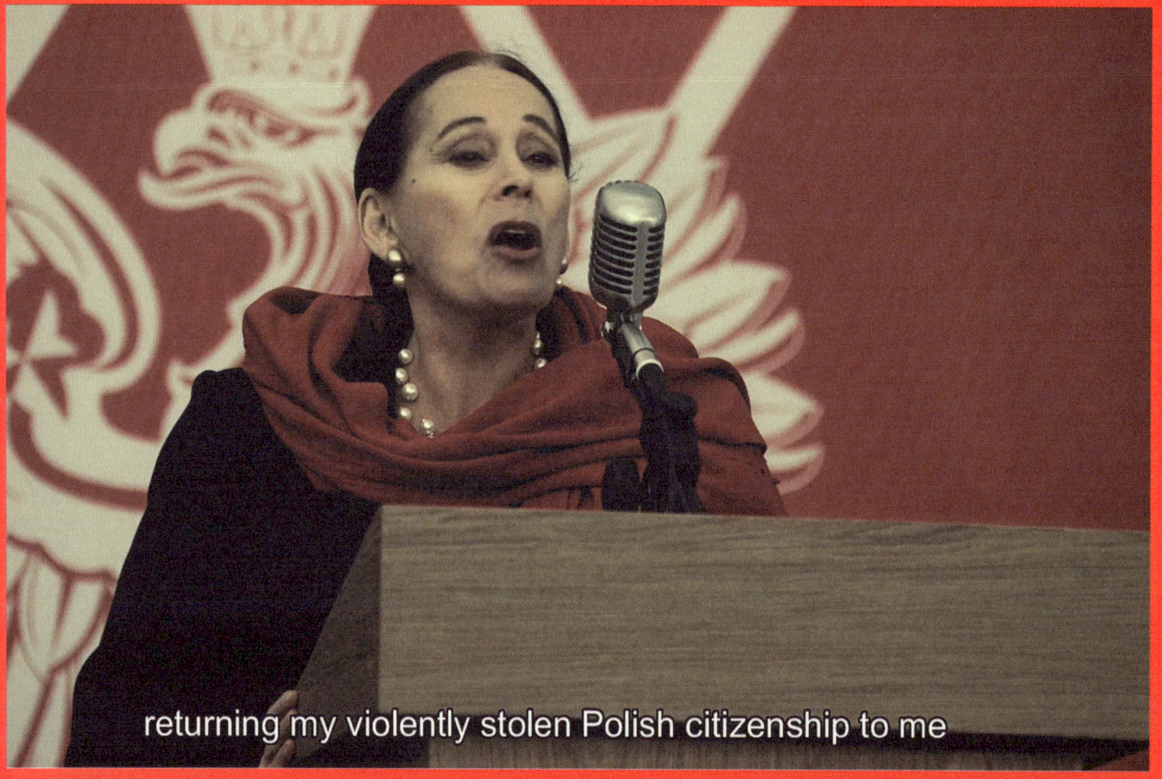
returning my violently stolen Polish citizenship to me

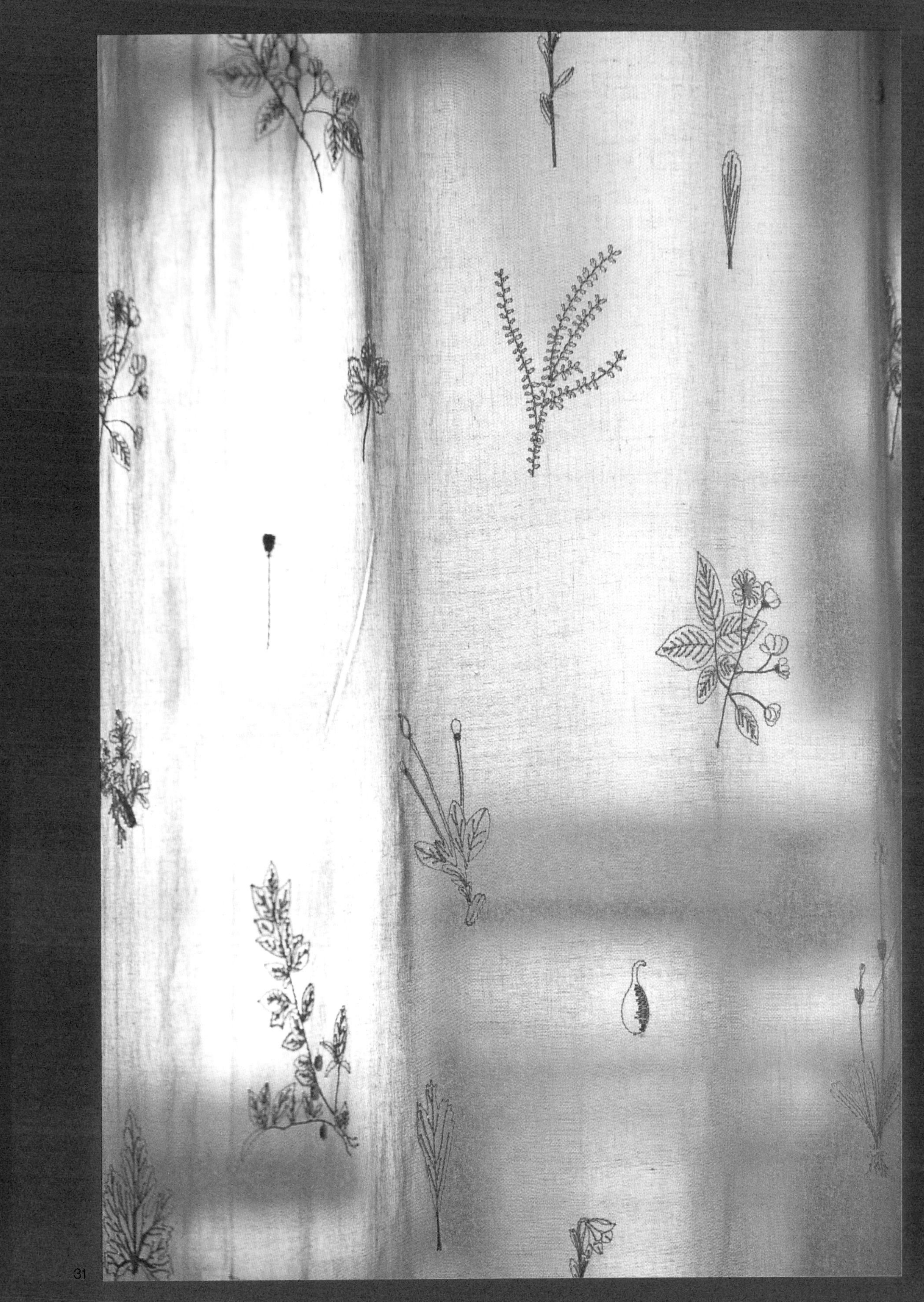

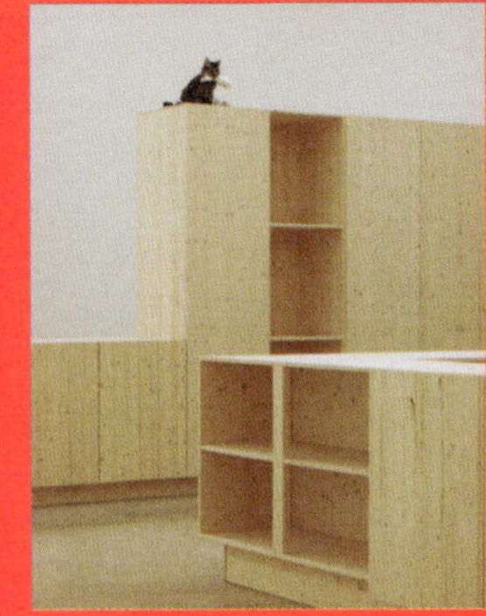

Repeat
yourself
Repeat
yourself

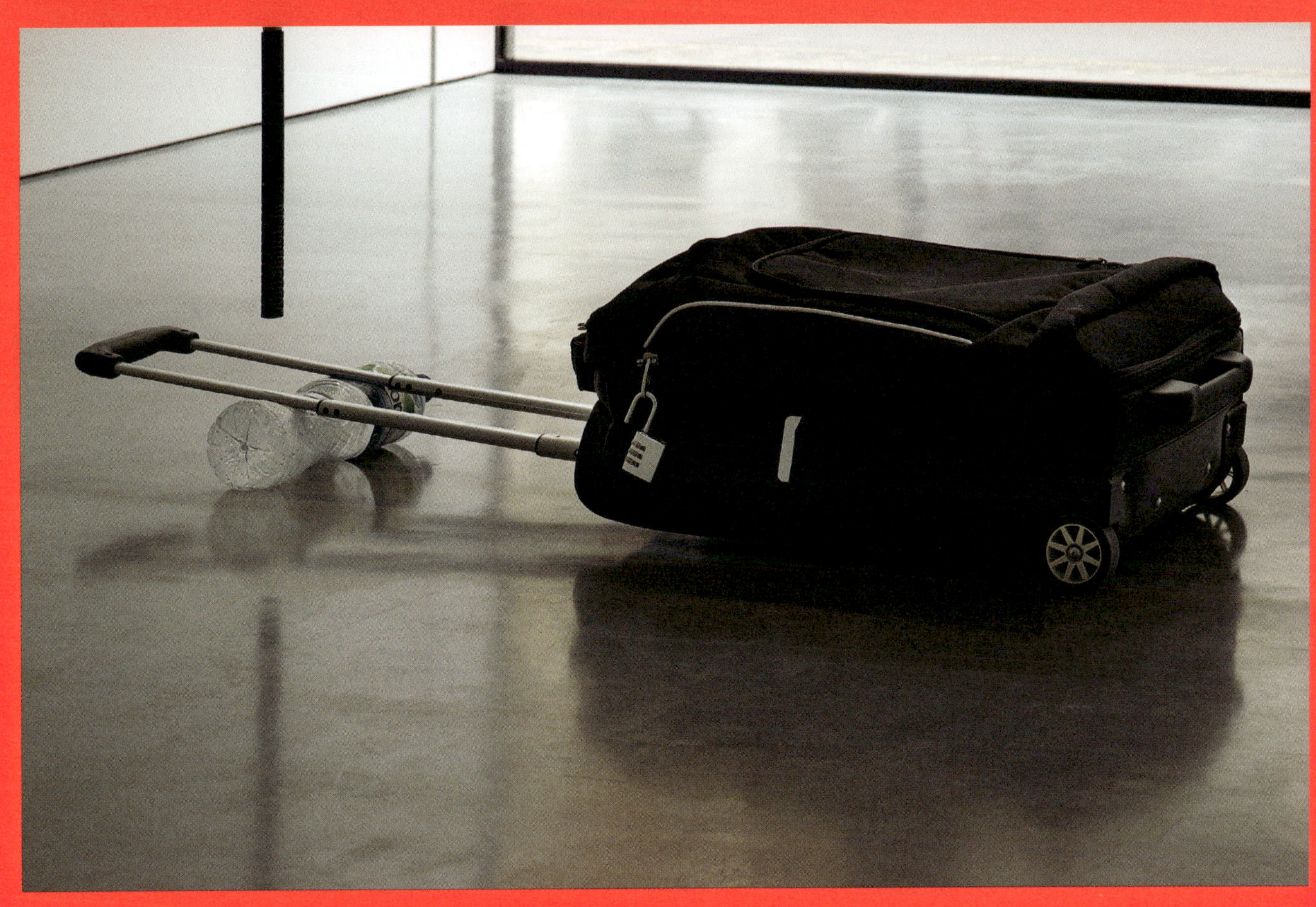

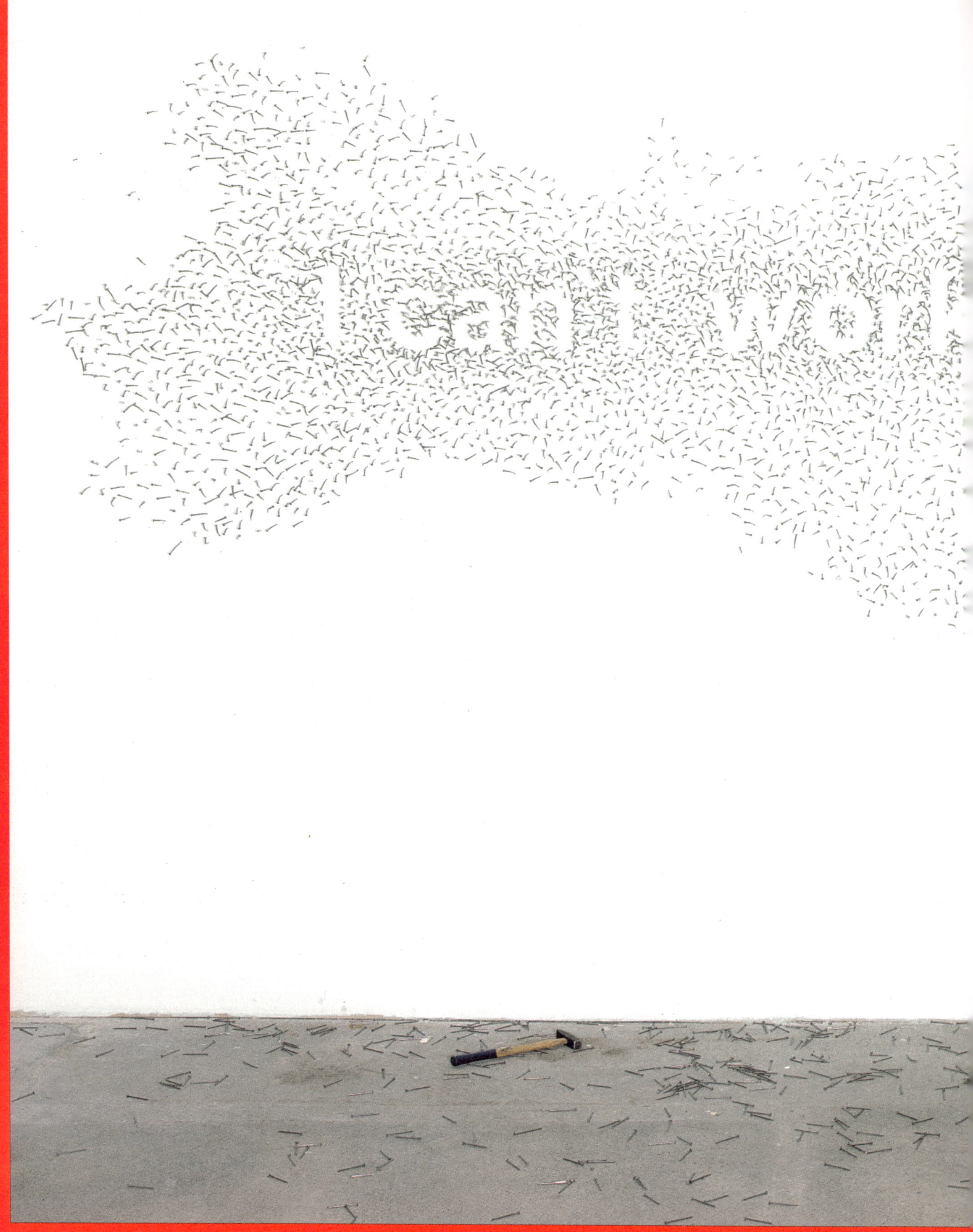

teamwork

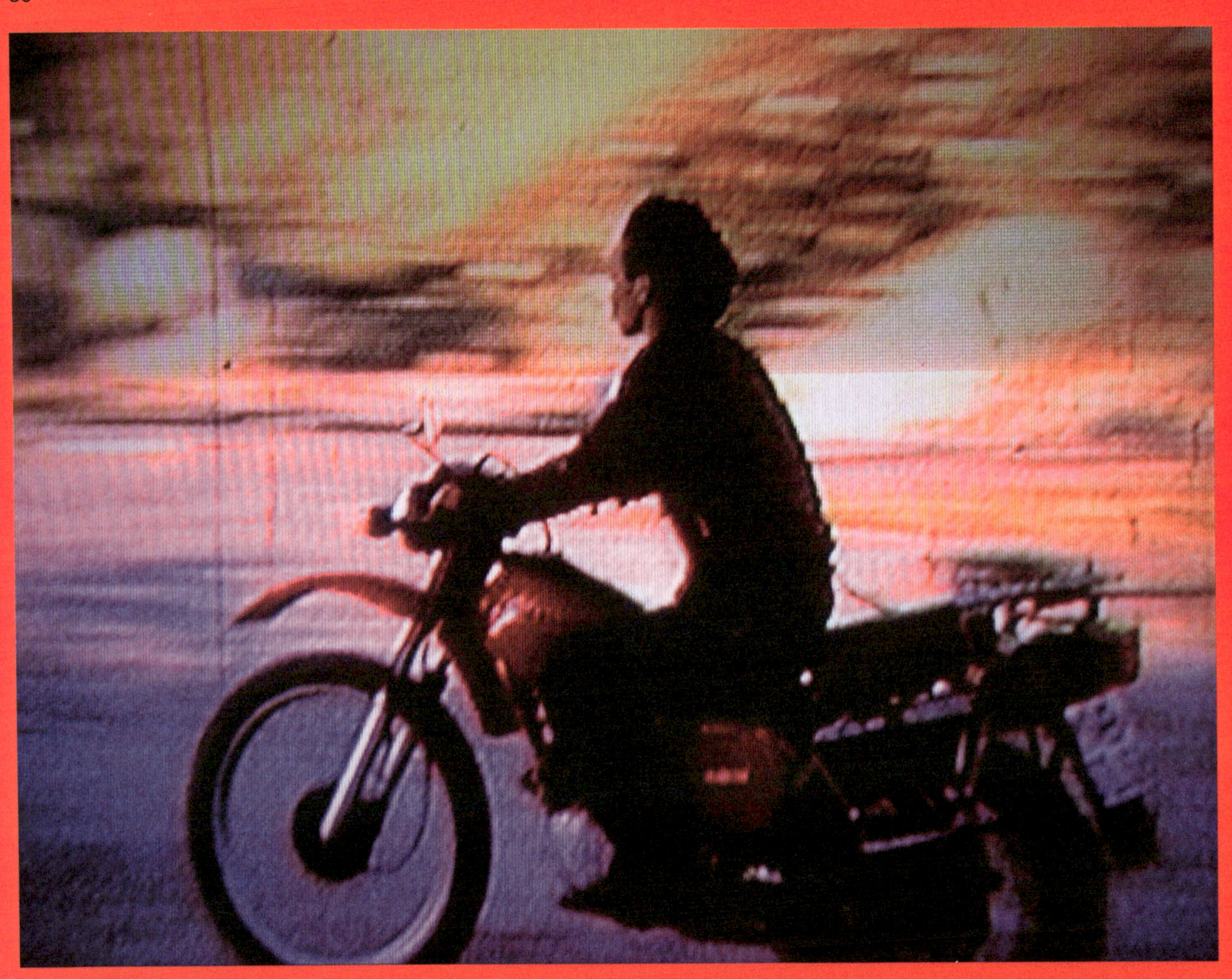

If You Are Willing:
The Army
of the Individuals

Bartholomew Ryan

Many of today's contemporary artists have nomadic, dematerialized, and adaptable practices—traveling from biennial to residency to gallery exhibition. Often based in cities far from their place of birth, they inhabit hyphenated geographies that speak to their embeddedness in the contemporary global spirit. Leveraging funding from the public and private sectors, they build consensual transnational networks of colleagues, collaborators, and supporters. They could be said to be ideal representatives of one of the blandest discourses of globalization: the cosmopolitan agent who is well traveled, urbane, tolerant, and a sophisticated interpreter of cultural difference.

While the eight artists in this exhibition share many motifs from the above sketch, they also proceed with a deep understanding that in spite of increased proximity and the smoothing narratives of neoliberalism, material forces continue to determine access and marginalization. They witness firsthand the entrenched nationalisms, the unequal distribution of wealth, the myriad exploitations, exclusions, and stereotypes that continue to condition our world. They see defined identities as a means of freedom and organization, but also as a mode of containment and control. Rather than function as new masters of the universe (the aforementioned global citizen), they are implicated, compromised, and self-aware. Some are adept manipulators, entrepreneurial spirits who cohabit with the market while attempting to maintain critical and ambivalent positions in relation to the worst excesses of the free-market culture.

It goes without saying that they might be parents, divorcées, lovers, alcoholics, difficult, brilliant, witty, selfish, driven, or whatever you are having yourself. At the Frieze Art Fair they deliver talks on "refusal"; for e-flux journal they pen essays on "occupation." Endlessly caught up in the necessity for contemporary self-positioning, they nevertheless pursue political-aesthetic approaches that are dedicated to exploring this complexity. Using their own backgrounds and identities as material, frequently in antagonistic or subversive ways, they operate with an understanding of their own complicity within geopolitical dynamics, seeking to use that awareness as a means to arrive at a more realistic representation of the foundations of the present.

The exhibition's title refers to a time when new artistic movements emerged with seeming inevitability (the 1966 Minimalist exhibition *10* at the Dwan Gallery in New York, for instance), when art could still be discussed as a chain of progress from one breakthrough to another.[1] Today no such sense of progress exists, and many lament its passing. *9 Artists*, however, celebrates this confusion, and represents the disjunction between now and then by adopting a title that conjures the ghosts of a time when a handful of centers, curators, and critics defined the art discourse. The deliberate lack of a named ninth artist signals a rupture with the past that the exhibition is meant to convey. Is the ninth artist the curator, a figure increasingly criticized for co-opting artistic authorship? Is it an undeclared work by an undisclosed participant? Is it the public invited in true contemporary museum style to participate in the making and interpretation of the work? The neutrality and literalness of the title presents the artists as if their presence in the show were inevitable. It is a proposition that sets up an unruly group of artists as if they are the best representatives of the expansive ambitions and capabilities of contemporary art today, which of course they are not, because nobody makes those claims anymore.

1 The exhibition *10*—which included artists Dan Flavin, Donald Judd, Sol LeWitt, Agnes Martin, and Robert Morris—is perceived by many to be the definitive moment of the emergence of Minimalism. While my argument does not rest on this exhibition—and I admit that the clarity we perceive in relation to its relevance in hindsight was much less obvious in the present—it is certainly the case that the artists understood themselves as moving from one form of art-making to the next, something that is virtually impossible for contemporary artists to articulate with the same cogency, even if they wished to, and many don't.

Recognizing that the art-historical movements that shaped the postwar period are becoming less and less germane to the current epoch, the artists exist within a world that is more expansive, networked, and horizontal than ever before. Within this sphere, it has become harder to identify key trends, and many artists are resistant to this kind of traditional classification. What characterizes the work of the individuals in *9 Artists* is an ability to access, name, refabricate, and catalyze a whole range of contexts—material and immaterial, art-historical and social, geopolitical and personal. They have the capacity to mine these variegated tendencies, and to hold within their hands many possibilities at once.

If there are two words that have followed me throughout this process, they are "complicity" and "contradiction." Each of these artists proceeds with an awareness that there is no *space* outside of the sociopolitical contexts we all navigate, and they acknowledge the fact that we are inevitably locked into behaviors, systems, and structures that can cause harm to others and to ourselves. That power wields itself with increasing visibility/invisibility, albeit asymmetrically, depending on who you are and the choices you make in life, if you even have a choice. This is not necessarily a new awareness, but what makes it special is that it is attended by a "What next?" Yes, we are all socially constructed, and yes, we are conditioned and shaped by forces outside our control, but we still have to live within that reality, and where possible, we should take some responsibility for questioning that.

At a basic first level, that means avoiding the pitfalls of prefigured theoretical tracts and guilt-associated binaries, and at the very least, trying to afford a vision of reality that militates against the various simplifications. In Bjarne Melgaard's recent novel, his narrator writes, "Contemporary art is there to make people feel inadequate."[2] I know what he means: the whole terrain is certainly set up as if for exclusion—the specialized language, the ivory towers, the wealth displayed at art fairs and elsewhere, the assumption of an exceptional status, the opinion factory, the ideologies all know are present but that barely articulate themselves—because we all operate within a culture of social networking in which people need to get on so they might be invited to write that piece, participate in that panel, be in that show. So yes, contemporary art is certainly elitist, but it is also, from my perspective, one of the few spaces that actually allows some oxygen for complex and uneasy ideas and thinking to develop. This happens in spite of all the money swirling around, not necessarily because of it.

In the text that follows, I try to give a sense of the artists and their work. Naturally it is subjective and partial, and despite its length, I feel I have left too much out. Be warned, not all the works I reference are in the exhibition, and a number that are in the exhibition are not referenced. I also abstain from drawing endless overt connections between the artists with this kind of sentence: "Where Danh Vo's biography has risen to the status of a foundation myth, Natascha Sadr Haghighian avoids biography altogether." I feel confident that what connects and differentiates the artists will be evident, and while that might seem a cop-out, it is not born out of casualness but is a genuine ethic that requests an engagement on the part of the reader. I would rather look at this essay as a collage of perspectives that readers can mine for what they will; where possible, I bring in the artist's voice directly, and I don't always then proceed to decode what has just been quoted. Yes, the text is long, but please feel no pressure to read it all. I am happy enough for you to bounce around, perusing paragraphs here and there, which is not to say that that is what you should do. I am just saying that such an approach is fine with me, and I might even prefer it, depending on your disposition.

2 Bjarne Melgaard, *A New Novel by Bjarne Melgaard* (Oslo: Aschehoug, 2012).

When I first started researching one of the artists in this show, Nástio Mosquito, I came across a short text by curator Marjolijn van Heemstra about a performance and exhibition in Germany. She quotes a sentence with which Mosquito closed a work, "I do represent, if you are willing, the army of the individuals."[3] This line struck me then in relation to *9 Artists*; despite its militaristic undertones, the firmness of its intent, coupled with its entreaty to participate in the possibility of it being true, seemed like an invitation. The army of the individuals conjures images of both collectivity and singularity. In an age of seemingly rudderless but mushrooming mass movements—often ridiculed for their lack of clear message or defined leadership, yet capable of provoking enormous change—the statement seems suitably prescient. It has a quality that I would like to hold onto for the duration of this text. The artists in this exhibition variously discard, problematize, and upturn passive identifications based on biography, nationality, or other convention. Their loyalty is to the individual—not one who exists in splendid isolation, but one who acts within a community, even if this community has yet to be invented.

I. Happy Pixels Hop Off into Low-Resolution, Gif Loop!

Hito Steyerl (born 1966 in Germany; lives and works in Berlin)

One of the fascinating things about the work of Hito Steyerl is its restlessness. Since the 1990s she has become one of the leading voices among artists who play with the conventional formats of the documentary genre, borrowing from its reputation for objectivity while acknowledging its ongoing history as a means of propaganda and indoctrination. Yet her mode of engagement with these questions has evolved as rapidly as the dematerialized digital world itself, ebbing and flowing with new breakthroughs in pixelated resolution, escalating social media engagements, the ever-shifting and evolving world of Internet memes, YouTube virility, 3-D animation, and digital printing capabilities. Not so much an early adopter as an eager adapter, her work has an eerie sense of timeliness, of being able to read the tea leaves of historical materialism within the present.

Steyerl is known equally for her somewhat performative theoretical essays and her moving-image work. A key text from 2007, "Documentary Uncertainty," reveals some of the themes she was then exploring, and paves the way for subsequent developments.[4] In the essay, she relates how the global image bank is shaped by a networked corporate media culture that largely controls its dissemination. Within this regime of the image, politics have not just been aestheticized, but have become aesthetical as such, working on an affective level through the senses. The idea of "truth" has become synonymous with the supposed objectivity of the document, which is by no means a neutral artifact, but something that is already a carrier of bias and ideology. Therefore, to draw one's legitimacy from the supposed legitimacy of the document is to start off from already shaky foundations. The critical "documentary" artist must therefore acknowledge from the outset the uncertainty inherent to the form itself. Critic T.J. Demos sums up Steyerl's conclusions in the essay:

> What we need to do, according to her analyses, is replace the current economy of affect—one based on fear and anxiety—with another one; but the problem is that, as Steyerl confesses, such a new affective and political constellation does not yet exist—or at least let us add, not in the way it should.[5]

3 Marjolijn van Heemstra, "Nástio Mosquito's collage of perspectives," *The Power of Culture* (December 2008), accessed June 10, 2013, http://www.powerofculture.nl/en/current/2008/december/mosquito.

4 Hito Steyerl, "Documentary Uncertainty," *A Prior Magazine* 15 (2007).

5 T. J. Demos, "Traveling Images: Hito Steyerl," in *Hito Steyerl* (Cologne: Verlag der Buchhandlung Walther König, 2010), 40. This volume is part of the book series edited by Marius Babias for Neuer Berliner Kunstverein (n.b.k.).

The 2000s for Steyerl are a key period in which she contends most directly with the documentary as a form, seeking to explore what she terms its "outer limits." These works in fact did clear the way for the artist to move *beyond* documentary, to begin to model the very "affective constellation" that she refers to in her essay. Nowhere is this more apparent than in her film *November* (2004), which tells the story of Andrea Wolf, a German revolutionary who joined the PKK (Kurdistan Workers' Party) and was killed by Turkish forces in 1998 in the mountains of Kurdistan. As teenagers Wolf and Steyerl were close, and she became the dynamic star of Steyerl's first film. Shot on Super 8, it presents an idealized world in which women fight gangs of chauvinistic men and beat them up. As such, it depicts a morally clear universe in which bad men with weapons are defeated by good women without. Wolf is so charismatic that she is virtually a rock star, and the men are so nice that when they are hit, they obligingly fall to the ground and feign death. At its conclusion, Wolf in leather jacket climbs onto a Suzuki and rides off into the sunset, ready to fight another day (plate 36).[6] On a thematic level within *November*, the Super 8 is inserted as the "fiction" against which the "real" world of subsequent events must be juxtaposed. Wolf leaves the symbolic heroic world of the film to enter the "real" world of revolutionary action. Steyerl meanwhile remains as an artist in the realm of the production of representation. The skill and problem of *November* is to demonstrate in form and content how contingent and amorphous these separations are.

The majority of the video is composed of found footage from television programs, early porn reels, Eisenstein's *October* (1928), and Bruce Lee's *Game of Death* (1978). It also incorporates documentary segments created or found by the artist: Kurdish activists marching in a crowd in Berlin holding aloft posters of Wolf, who has become an icon of Kurdish liberation; or a clip of Wolf in military fatigues on the mountains of Kurdistan declaring that she will soon return to the German revolutionary movement with the new skills she is learning amongst the PKK.

Within the logic of the work, Steyerl pits the innocence and idealism of *October*, an era of revolution, against the reality of its aftermath. Or, more accurately, she pits the "idealized" representation of *October* against a world that cannot be idealized. "November" becomes shorthand for complexity, and a self-reflexive one at that. At one point in the film, Steyerl is shooting a march in Germany against the Iraq war by Turks and Kurds; she joins for a period and is recorded by other media, which make her the face of the march on the news (plate 5). Here a German artist is translated into a Kurdish demonstrator for mass consumption, and the fact that she is not a Kurdish demonstrator has little importance, as she has functions within a narrative frame in which she herself is essentially irrelevant.

Held in the world of *October* by complex forces, Wolf becomes an endlessly refracting cipher: the Kurds lionize her as an "Immortal Hero"; the Turks as a terrorist aggressor who fakes her own death; the early Super 8 as a confidant heroine. Pulled from *October*, the symbolic sphere into which Steyerl first inserted her, Wolf enters a space beyond fiction, a depressing but potentially promising space because it is in *November* that the martyr becomes a person. According to artist Ursula Biemann, "The essayist does not seek to document realities, but to organize complexities."[7] Hito Steyerl says in *November*, "anything without contradiction is false." *November*'s is a world of contradictions, away from the inspiring landscape of the Super 8 where the teenagers beat up their male friends, but also away from the frightening rigidity of ideology.

In 2007, Steyerl followed *November* with two related works that debuted at Documenta 12 in Kassel: *Lovely Andrea* and *Red Alert*.[8] *Lovely Andrea* is another work born from Steyerl's own biography. In the late eighties, the artist attended film school in Tokyo, where on one occasion she posed nude in the style of Japanese rope bondage—*nawa shibari*—to make some cash. In the video, Steyerl returns to search for the images from that shoot, partly to reclaim some sense of ownership over what was for her a traumatic experience. Without any contextual memories of who took the photographs and where, she enlists as a translator the female bondage artist Asagi Ageha,

6 Plate references throughout the text refer to images in the Compendium of Works (pages 132–163).

7 Carles Guerra paraphrasing artist and theorist Ursula Bieman. See Carles Guerra, "Negatives of Europe: Video Essays and Collective Pedagogies," in *The Greenroom: Reconsidering the Documentary and Contemporary Art 1*, ed. Maria Lind and Hito Steyerl (Berlin: Sternberg Press, 2008), 150.

and together they meet with industry insiders in a sometimes humorous but ultimately disturbing search. The video combines a dynamic soundtrack with a range of visual materials, including pixelated images of Abu Ghraib, clips of Spiderman spinning webs, and takes of Ageha hanging from ropes—an activity that she paradoxically says makes her feel free. Ultimately, Steyerl finds the images in a sex museum, and discovers that she had taken on the pseudonym Andrea. She meditates on our increasingly networked lives, on images as an extension of subjectivity, juxtaposing freedom and force, independence and dependence (words that flash across the screen in bold letters), and how, as one of the protagonists states, "In a wider sense, bondage is all over the place."

Red Alert features three identical computer monitors hung vertically, side by side (plate 24). To look at the work is to see three static glowing fields of red color monochromes emanating from the wall. In "Documentary Uncertainty," Steyerl pointed out that cable news and other media have begun to equate low-res, fragmentary images with the truth. And so the highly pixelated cell-phone image of a foiled bomber on a plane or the virtually abstract live-video feeds broadcast by embedded journalists during Operation Iraqi Freedom are perceived to be the most authentic documents of real, lived experience: the less you can see, the more is being revealed. The work also takes a cue from Constructivist artist Aleksander Rodchenko, who believed in 1921 that he had reached the logical conclusion of easel painting by applying paint monochromatically to three canvases in red, yellow, and blue.

Steyerl's triptych similarly imagines a logical end to the documentary medium in abstraction. Rather than replicate Rodchenko's colors, Steyerl chose the color of the highest level within the US terror alert system. In the 2000s, red had been ingrained in the psyche of those of us who live in this country as a symbol of ongoing dangerous potential. At any moment, the color reminded us, we may be attacked. The documentary form ends then not in pure abstraction so much as pure affect: reality summarized as raw political manipulation. In addition to intimating the threat of violence, the red lights of the piece (think red-light district) also allude to another key pillar in the contemporary production and dissemination of images: the manufacturing and manipulation of desire as a product, which is a key aspect of pornography. In fact, the work was made, according to Steyerl, as "a necessary consequence" of having just completed *Lovely Andrea*.[9]

In more recent works, Steyerl seems to have moved away from any pretension toward documentary per se. And why not? After all, as *Red Alert* declares, documentary is dead. Steyerl killed it. First she established the conditions under which it had always existed: precarious, shifting, contextual, and subjective. Then she made the triptych that was its logical conclusion: the abstract monochromes taking documentary to pop civilization's ecstatic apex of totalized violence and pornography. Documentary, as such, is *so* 2007.

Having dispensed with documentary, Steyerl is now moving into pedagogy, with her fifteen-minute video *How Not to Be Seen: A Fucking Didactic Educational.Mov File* (2013). In this piece, which recently debuted at the Venice Biennale, truth and fiction have collapsed as concepts into irrelevancy. The film is a toolbox for how to be invisible in a world where "Resolution determines visibility. Whatever is not captured by resolution is invisible." In contrast to *Red Alert*, where the most pixelated images are closest to the real, Steyerl is contending with the world circa 2013 with ever greater capacities to see. The trick then becomes how to be invisible within such a regime. For Steyerl, invisibility is conceived to be desirable as a mode of evasion from control, identification, and most explicitly, death by drone. However, it is also something undesirable, a consequence of various forms of voluntary or forced retreats from society, such as living in a gated community, being a woman over fifty, or spending one's time in the dark corners of the Internet.

Composed of a variety of lessons, for the most part incanted by two cyborgian-mildly-English-accented-Mac-computerized readers, one male and one female, the video obviously riffs off really fucking didactic educational videos, but it quickly dispenses

8 Befitting Steyerl's democratic approach to distribution, the videos *November* and *Lovely Andrea* are available for viewing online. See http://ubu.com/film/steyerl.html.

9 Hito Steyerl, conversation with the author, September 2011.

with any pretension toward the flat-footed nature of such productions. This isn't some laborious project shot in some lame New Jersey studio in the 1990s for the edification of people learning how to drive, or whatever (probably employing, I admit, several people at least for the period of a week to ensure the quality of the analog educational brick). This is a .Mov file, goddammit, and as such it can do what it wants; it's digital, baby, it's fluid, unencumbered, individualistic, silly, and potentially, yes, meaningful.[10]

There are about seven lessons, the earlier of which feature Steyerl as a model/protagonist dressed in a black kimono.[11] Standing in front of a green screen, she demonstrates the actions that the voices dictate. For example, for "Lesson III: How to Become Invisible by Becoming a Picture," Steyerl applies green-screen-hued makeup or has it applied to her in a variety of responses to the seven instructions that the lesson entails (to camouflage, to conceal, to cloak, to disguise, etc.). As there are mesmeric digital patterns projected on the green screen, the parts of her face with makeup literally become a projected surface dissolving into the digital whirlygigs of the background. As the lessons progress, the instructional answers become more and more abstracted and absurd. For example, in "Lesson V: How to Become Invisible by Merging into a World Made of Pictures," we learn that there are fifty-four ways, but the cyborgs probably get through about three. Given that they are digital in nature, it is unsurprising that the cyborgs suffer from congenital ADD, and the video's progression therefore is broken by tangents that create a whole other meta-level to the proceedings.

To sum up these segments, which roll out episodically over the course of the video: the green screen is actually set up on a cracked tarmac giant resolution target "that measures the resolution of the world as a picture." The target, located somewhere in the Californian desert, was set up by the US military sometime in the 1950s or '60s to measure the resolution abilities of analog cameras from the sky. The planes would fly over it at a given height, take photographs, and measure the resolution by controlling for the visibility of the large white stripes that covered the tarmac. With the advent of digitalization, the target was decommissioned in 2006 in favor of a pixel-based resolution chart that works explicitly for digital cameras. In 1996 we learned that digital cameras could achieve accuracy from the sky of twelve meters per pixel—in other words, one pixel equaled a twelve-meter squared space on the surface of the Earth. Today we learn that one pixel equals a foot. Therefore, as a cyborg states, while the piece cuts to dancers with one-foot cubes on their heads, "to become invisible, one has to become smaller or equal to one pixel" (plate 25). The video is friendly, colorful, and appealing, but also sinister; the dancing cubes are easily applicable to Muslim families and friends on the borders of Pakistan and Afghanistan or in Southern Yemen, targeted by extra-judicial US drone attacks. They really need to be invisible to survive.

As it progresses, the controlled world of the green screen gives way to a long promotional, three-dimensional rendering of a luxurious, large-scale gated community, with lush greens, a mall, cinemas, lounges, and happy white-silhouetted human forms haunting the space as stand-ins for prospective owners and their kids. Much of the action takes place within this immersive dystopia, which Steyerl has clearly appropriated from somewhere. She inserts her own figures, who don't behave as they should. The .Mov file introduces more and more of these, an army of pixels refusing to behave, becoming brasher and more confidant as the work progresses. In one section, a chorus of women in green burkas swirls in the cracks of the decommissioned target as the cyborg states, "Rogue pixels hide in the cracks of old standards of resolution. They throw off the cloak of representation." These pixelated pixies are surely "the lumpen proletarian in the class society of appearances, ranked and valued according to its resolution" that Steyerl refers to in another of her important essays, "In Defense of the Poor Image."[12] They are the low-resolution, low-value JPEGs, ripped AVI files, and otherwise downtrodden denizens of the global digital bonanza:

10 The "didactic" in the title is possibly also a play on that most asinine of criticisms generally laid at the feet of politically engaged art by people who love the word "didactic," because yes, this art is supremely political, but yeah it's a .Mov file, so anything goes, and it doesn't feel didactic in that way.

11 Steyerl is part Japanese, and clearly she is paying homage to this important aspect of her identity in the videos *Lovely Andrea* (2007) and *Abstract* (2012) by wearing a Ramones T-shirt.

12 Hito Steyerl, "In Defense of the Poor Image," *e-flux journal* 10 (November 2009), accessed July 10, 2013, http://www.e-flux.com/journal/in-defense-of-the-poor-image/.

They testify to the violent dislocation, transferrals, and displacement of images—their acceleration and circulation within the vicious cycles of audiovisual capitalism. Poor images are dragged around the globe as commodities or their effigies, as gifts or as bounty. They spread pleasure or death threats, conspiracy theories or bootlegs, resistance or stultification.[13]

In the video, the pixels have figured out how not to be seen, or realized that even if they are seen, they are too fluid, too independent, too unimportant to do what they are told. In the closing minutes everything comes undone: the cyborgs have run out of Ritalin and disappear altogether; we return to the cracked tarmac, green screen, and desert landscape; the pixies literally throw off their cloaks. Covered in green-screen-colored Lycra body suits, they run rampant over the video, dancing, sashaying, and otherwise causing mischief to the upbeat soundtrack and background green-screen projection of the Three Degrees' 1973 live video recording of "When Will I See You Again."[14] There are shots of Steyerl's crew grinning beside a camera crane and the three singers dancing their routine as soulful silhouettes in various prime sites of the manicured, gated community while other silhouetted figures escape the enclosed mediocrity and stroll happily across the desert. The whole pedagogical, neoliberal order is blown open by a disorientating upbeat dissolution of the sensical.

The video closes with the emancipated army of pixels creating a new affective world, in which they do whatever they damn well please; unburdened by the coil of representation that anyone but them can see, they are willing to represent *themselves*. Action lines flash in titles over the last several shots—actions that no one needs to actually produce: they are having too much fun, and we get it … why bother? As she proposed to try at the close of "Documentary Uncertainty," Steyerl here models new kinds of effects, for real!:

> Camera crew disappears after invisible energy rays
> emanate from iPhone.
> Make 3-D animation!
> Pixels hijack camera crane.
> Camera crew gets tied up by invisible people seen from above.
> Three Degrees dance on resolution scale for real.
> US Air Force drops glitter from stealth helicopter.
> Happy and excited pixels filming from crane
> Shoot this for real
> And fly away with drone!
> Happy pixels hop off into low-resolution, gif loop!

II. Our Interdependency Is Not about Love, It's about Function

Nástio Mosquito (born 1981 in Angola; lives and works in Luanda)

The core of artist Nástio Mosquito's work is an intense commitment to the open-ended potential of language, arrived at through deliberate strategies of reinvention. At stake is a rejection of transparency, of the linear way in which meaning is conferred through politely digestible approaches. Mosquito makes music, performances, objects, and videos, often under a range of monikers such as Saco, Nasty-O, Cucumber

13 Ibid.

14 Three Degrees, "When Will I See You Again," YouTube video of a 1973 performance, posted by "fritz5134" on August 21, 2009, https://www.youtube.com/watch?v=v2xPwMevgE0.

14 See Nástio Mosquito & We Are Here! Films, *Nástia's Manifesto: Hypocritical, Ironic & Do Not Give a Fuck*, Vimeo video, posted by "Vic Pereiró" in 2011, http://vimeo.com/21977569. See also plate 33 in this catalogue.

Slice, and Zura, Zurara. He has performed and exhibited at various places in Angola, Europe, and elsewhere. Several years ago I came across the artist's manifesto online (well, the manifesto of Nástia, an alter ego and the feminine form of Nástio in Portuguese). Titled *Hypocritical, ironic and do not give a fuck*, it features seventeen instructions for the good life, delivered in rhythmical succession by the artist in a rich, put-on Russian accent. His face is framed in close-up with a projected screen behind him showing dissociated outtakes, past performances, etc. His pearls of wisdom are also delivered visually, Karaoke-style, line by line in loud, graphic tabloid headlines. The instructions are counterintuitive, crude, and elucidatory, mining various clichés and stolen pastiches. They are a mix of clownish nonchalance, perception, and arrogance. Some advice at random:

> 3
> Outcome
> Enjoy the process, but
> You better deliver
>
> 14:
> Stand on every
> one's shoulder
> Look
> Listen
> Learn
> Filter
> Imitate
>
> 15:
> Stop living your dream through other people's lives.
> Fuck you *American Idol* viewer; good luck for all the contestants,
> I hope your dream materializes.[14]

Running through most of Mosquito's work is a demand for self-questioning and an imperative for personal growth, though not one that is found through the notions of productivity and success as defined by the oh-so-narrow metrics of capitalist models of the same, but a critical and self-aware engagement with the processes by which we are made, and can make. Mosquito seems to embrace the artist-as-outsider role, a contemporary jester tantalizing with lucidity, deploying simultaneously banal pop-culture tropes and self-important intellectualizations that he rejects even as he is making them. It's a tricky territory to occupy, and one that he has developed and further problematized in subsequent works.

While it's fair enough to say that an aspect of his practice can best be described as spoken word, it should be distinguished from the mainstream US tradition of same that emanates from a desire to articulate distinct subject positions along lines of class, race, gender, and sexuality. The US version develops out of a faith in the power of positive self-representation, and is attended by self-essentializing positions as a mode of making visible/giving access to/pushing into the public sphere hitherto marginalized identities. Often, and perhaps obviously, this genre cleaves to normative conventions of language, rhyming couplets, narrative progressions, a range of emotions developing over the arc of the performance. Mosquito's work has little relation to this tradition. In fact, it self-consciously resists, sidesteps, and overturns any idea of a stable subject, not as some point of nihilism (there's no such thing!) but as a mode of engagement that allows him to be a proactive shaper of identity rather than passive respondent. Like many of the eight artists, all of whom will hate this sentence, he is (within reason) his own institution and plays a part in constructing the vision of what that might mean.

Mosquito occupies a multiplicity of spaces within culture: in Angola he has produced and distributed LPs; he makes music videos with his collaborator, Madrid-based

15 See plate 28 in this catalogue.

16 Gabi Ngcobo, a curator and artist based in Cape Town, South Africa, first showed me Mosquito's manifesto some years ago. See the video *Nástia Answers Gabi*, http://www.dzzzz.info/gabi.swf, accessed June 10, 2013.

Vic Pereiró; he has an iPhone app on which you can download his latest tracks in Portuguese or English. In 2010 he worked with Barcelona collective Bofa da Cara to produce *My African Mind*, a stunning video about Western constructions of Africa, with a voiceover by the artist that floats along with a dramatic 1940s Hollywood-style soundtrack. It also contains a flowing chronological montage of cutout representations of Africa ranging from early slave trade depictions, Tarzan and *Tintin in the Congo* comics, and movie ephemera from *The African Queen*, etc. through the period of decolonization and after. His language is enigmatic, ironic, bitter even:

> Healthy black monster
> Five finger, with thumb
> Useful animal, so minimal

It touches on the ideological construction of race as a justification for colonialist expansion as well as the complications of modernity and the feedback loop between Western aid, the NGO industry, and the continued exploitation of resources:

> Toxic Aid, turn on war, turn off war
> Feed me, feed mine
> Collective perpetuation just begun…
> Welcome ladies and gentlemen
> Welcome
> To the wonders of pop civilization
> Yesterday, today, you…Planet you[15]

Mosquito's "Planet you" conjures some pan-global audience of viewers, each capable of engagement, albeit on radically different terms. Yet we are all united by the spectacle of Pop civilization, which is impossible to divorce from a history intimately connected to the implicated relationship between representation and power: of representation as an illustration of how power inscribes itself on the world. For better or worse, Mosquito implies, we are all caught up in this mess—yesterday, today—where it is becoming increasingly difficult to trace the tendrils of history back to some definitive moment of "Oh yes! That is it. That is where it all began."

Mosquito sometimes inhabits the role of postcolonial respondent, while mocking the stasis of such an imposed position. In conceiving his participation in this book, for example, he insisted that I send him questions to which he could respond. Now, he knows that I know that he knows that any questions I send him will be turned on their head, reversed to show the inherent ideological workings, the call and response of the US-based-curator mounting an exhibition with at least some smatterings of a global mission. He's played this game before. In his video *Nástia Answers Gabi* (2009), the artist answers a series of text-based questions from curator and friend Gabi Ngcobo.[16] She also proceeds with wariness, engaging the dance, at times using a specialized art language, at times turning the questions in on themselves, aware of their inherent contradictions. The most profound of which is that she, like me, is seeking some moment of insight from someone who has already stated that he does not give a fuck.

She addresses them to Nástia of the manifesto. She gets him, but here there is a profound displacement from the previous work. Gone are the digital screens, the rapid succession of mediated images, the verbal efficiency and rapid-fire editing. Instead we get a slow panning shot of a vast, empty, dilapidated warehouse, and the sound of Mosquito's (Russian-accented) voice, slowly singing a Rolling Stones classic, a cappella, "Time is on our side, yes it is." Pop civilization has given way to entropy. Asked a question about justice that appears in white text on a screen, the video cuts to an exterior wasteland beside a highway; Nástia is taking a shit in the tall grass, saying, "Now what would be very just is if someone would give me some toilet paper."

In the final scene, Nástia sits on a chair inside a small room (plate 13). His expression introspective, in voiceover he addresses the viewer, asking, "What are you going to do with your education? Become part of a structure or build a structure?" Here Nástia is more telling in his engagement; he has established within the video an energy that can't be mistaken for entrepreneurial exuberance. This is not consultancy-speak, or even life advice from a manifestly plugged-in digital warrior/performer as in the initial manifesto. Nástia's is a body occupying space that is manifestly nonproductive. His warehouse is not poised for urban renewal, the docks he walks down are deserted, the room he sits in is bare, and paint peels from the wall. Throughout the video he privileges *knowledge* over *information*. At one point he says, "I don't give a fuck about you out there, I only give a fuck about all of you out there." He clarifies this in the final scene. For Nástia, at least, the question is not one of a cosmopolitan global interconnectivity that can be routed through love of the other: "I don't love you personally. Accepting our interdependency is not about love, it's about function." In other words, like it or not, we need each other, and that acknowledgment might not be a happy one, with all of its implications for compromise and self-sacrifice.

In the video, Nástia has stepped out of a condition of time associated with the endless present tense of digital information flows into a temporality that allows for reflection (history) and projection (the future): knowledge versus information. In dismissing the singular "you" out there, he is refusing your identification with him; unlike the singer, politician, or preacher, he is not speaking to "you," touching "you" with his words. Yet he obviously validates individuality, the ability and desire to build one's own structures. And here is the conundrum: in addressing a collective "you" rather than the singular, he is actually emphasizing the importance of individuality, of decoupling the conventional chain of identifications, and creating some autonomy around who *you* are.

III. He Wants to See You Again, and Just Be Two Fags Who Kill

Bjarne Melgaard (Norwegian, born 1967 in Australia; lives and works in New York)

Since his emergence in the mid-1990s, Bjarne Melgaard has situated his entire career as a mode of subjective excess, a dedication to an expressionistic self-realization through art, a belief that art presents a total freedom unbounded from imperatives to "correct" expression. He attempts to represent reality as it *is* rather than as we pretend it to be, de-sublimating the netherworld of human experience. Citing influences ranging from Edward Munch to New York–based writer Kathy Acker, Melgaard also performs a kind of fictional self-biography. His life experiences, desires, and thoughts permeate his work in such a way that the viewer walking through one of his installations or reading his writing experiences a state akin to an aghast voyeurism: where does this person end and the fiction and projection begin? I first encountered an installation of his work in 2010 at Greene Naftali Gallery in New York, where the artist had recently moved after a peripatetic journey through Europe over the previous decade, culminating in some mythic bust-up in Barcelona. Titled *The Synthetic Slut: A New Novel*, the exhibition was designed by Melgaard as one mutating narrative: opening with typographic vinyl sentences on the floor, extending to large, graffitied texts—everywhere language excessive and shifting from floor to sculpture to painting to wall. Luxury readymades—from Maison Martin Margiela suits to couches—were cast around the space, torn, wrecked, and splattered.[17] Paintings on view displayed a host of styles—scatological and gloopy impastoed near-abstract works beside over-painted photorealist portraits of the hulking and muscular bearded artist opposite the buttocks of naked boys captured from vintage NAMBLA (North American Boy Love Association) photographs.

Much of the text-related exchanges were of an explicit and aggressive sexual nature, men fucking and getting fucked, caught in a highly racialized power-play of abuser and abused, aggressive top and submissive bottom, generally with the black male embracing an enslaved subjugation to the figure of the powerful and frequently explicitly infected white cock. Neoclassical busts, elaborate aquariums with exotic fish, marble pillars, tacky and tawdry kitsch interior design memorabilia, nature photos of a duck-billed platypus—all were conditioned and made somehow palatable by the hypnotic and sensual soundtrack *aNYway*, the disco dance mix by American-Canadian DJs Duck Sauce.[18]

The music came from a video playing on a large flat-screen television propped on a king-size bed with lush duvet and pillows. About three minutes long, it showed homemade footage of soldiers in the countryside somewhere, pulling masked and bound men from the back of a truck, lining them up on the side of a road facing into the brush, and slaughtering them one by one in a hail of bullets—allowing the fear to sink in before moving to the next shaking figure. It cut to the soldiers laughing and drinking, gathered around a roasting pig on a spit. The video was overlaid with primitive vision-mixed graphic squares in primary colors, throbbing rhythmically to the beat of the music, offering up the material as so much affect: as a coolly distant transformation of content into style. The video depicted Serbian militia slaughtering Bosniaks, but within the context of the power plays thematized throughout the exhibition, it was hard to divorce it from the specters of Abu Ghraib, the sexualized humiliation of another group of Muslim men—here Iraqi—by grinning and titillated American soldiers. Indeed, two hyper-masculine mustached figures made of cut felt—one black, one white—lay on the bed wearing Serbian soldier uniforms and looking faintly comical. Around them were strewn materials from some kind of crystal-meth pig party: bottles of poppers, syringes, and a notepaper in hand-drawn cursive that read, "He wants to see you again, and just be two fags who kill."[19]

Melgaard likes to ridicule any overt political read to his work, insisting on the artwork's freedom from ethical responsibility. And while of course he is free to express these views, his insistence on the artwork's autonomy tempts me to claim the autonomy of the critic from the intentions of the artist. Melgaard's work displays a keen politics that deliberately opposes itself to that of consensus, propriety, and representation that simplifies, essentializes, purifies, or sublimates the messy factitude of human experience. He is obsessed with identification in a bizarre feedback loop between reality and fiction that maps onto the well-worn debates arising from postmodern discourse by way of queer, feminist, and postcolonialist theory. The perennial realization is that the subject is a figure constructed in language, by society, conditioned to certain behaviors and experiences, some dominant, others marginalized. And the retort that while all this is true, that we *are* constructed as human beings, it does not mean we can escape that construction in our lived lives: we are inevitably embedded in the material conditions of race, class, gender, and sexuality into which we are born, though of course we can somehow shape, distort, upset, and transform aspects of these inheritances. So, if the subject is somehow a fiction, while also being a tangible concrete reality, where does that leave the fictionalism of Melgaard?

It seems to me that he profoundly identifies with the power dynamics within certain roles, but only if they are self-consciously acknowledged as that, as constructions. And so the highly racialized sexual play apparent in many of the paintings is derived from a consensual interchange of sexual fantasy, much of the language drawn from that actually exchanged between Melgaard and his online hookups from Manhunt and similar sites.[20] Yes, it's true that these fantasies are derived from real-life taboos that emerge out of, for example, the historical subjugation of African Americans, or for that matter the manner with which homosexuals (of every race) historically came to view their own body: something aberrant and always already

17 The exhibition titled *The Synthetic Slut: A Novel by Bjarne Melgaard* was presented at Greene Naftali Gallery, New York, May 14 to June 19, 2010. The press release, in the form of a long stream of consciousness list, conditioned the viewer to the type of material and tenor they could expect from the installation: "YOU WANNA BE A WHITE MANS BLACK BITCH? TWO MINUTES LATER A REPLY COMES: YES; tote bags; duct tape; flat-screen TV; white, pink, and black marble sculptures; Men Without Love; Old Holland oil paint tubes; Krink inks; black Chanel Ballerines; The Synthetic Slut: New York; Smith & Wesson bear claw knives; Winchester Bowie knives; Manhunt portraits; mounted photographs ..." For the press release and images of the installation, see the Green Naftali Gallery's website, accessed June 10, 2013, http://www .greenenaftaligallery.com/exhibition .php?id=3774&jumpTo=images.

18 Duck Sauce (Armand Van Helden and A-Trak), "*aNYway*" (official video released 2009 by Fool's Gold Records), YouTube video, posted by "datarecord-suk" on October 9, 2009, http://www .youtube.com/watch?v=vWM5D3MwSgA.

19 See plate 29 for a detail of this work.

20 One of Melgaard's personal ads read something like, "You want to be a white man's black bitch." The artist in conversation with the author, 2012.

diseased. Theorist Tim Dean has described the exchange of cum in barebacking (often attended by a desire to infect others or exchange the HIV virus) as motivated by a form of "radical intimacy."[21] Still others have sought to redeem it as a profound will to self-harm experienced by gay men holding up a mirror to a society that will accept them only if they conform to its normalizations: either an emancipatory rejection of mainstream culture's sense of correctly assimilationist behavior, using the body as an ultimate instrument of reclamation and power; or a nihilistic—albeit pleasurable for some—surrender to self-abnegation and obliteration. Whatever the case, Melgaard's strong thematic identification with a barebacking subculture relates acts that are entered into with consent, in profound distinction, say, to the fate of the children in the NAMBLA images, the Bosniaks in the video, or the prisoners at Abu Ghraib.

It's where identifications occur without a sense of their essential and essentializing problematics that Melgaard is at his most belligerent. Take, as a shallow poll, the following series of his quotes taken from interviews in 2006 and 2010:

On Bears:
> And anyone who wants to call himself a "bear" from my point of view is a complete idiot! I think it's just a gay excuse for being fat! They could also call themselves reindeer or ponies or whatever, but I just don't like the fact that they refuse the more general feminine traits of homosexuality. I like guys when they are really "homo" and not just "whatever." I like men who are not just into ANY men, but into GAY men.[22]

On Class:
> The notion of class is something I never thought about before I entered art school. I'm absolutely not interested in any kind of sentimentality or belief that the working class has a more pure take on art. In the art world you have a lot of upper middle-class kids, especially in Europe. I think it's really weird, these ideas of Marxism that you learn that are filtered through art theory. I don't understand how people can believe in that today.[23]

On the Art World:
> If you look at the art world, you find so many art works about the "power structures" but very few works about the REAL power structures in the art world itself, which would be the most natural starting point for most artists! But, nobody seems to have problems with that! Still, galleries take 50% of an artist's income for doing nothing except for hanging a picture on a wall! Or how curators really corrupt the art and the artist. I mean, when Wolfgang Tillmans ends up taking pictures of Tony Blair it's just something really constitutionally wrong. All respect to Tillmans, but maybe we need to see also where stuff develops and not just where it started? What does it mean when gay men so easily portray figures of power and end up giving interviews about how "nice" they are?[24]

Sentimentality and hypocritical assertions of purity based on the authenticity of the other (class); the identification with tropes of hyper-masculinity offered by a homophobic mainstream culture (bears); or the bland assumption of "criticality" in artists even as they assert conditions of power (Tillmans): all of these positions steadfastly refuse to float Melgaard's boat. As can be seen from the above quote on bears, however, he is not opposed to identification per se, so long as it is entered into consciously with an understanding of its implications. He likes gay guys who reject men who are not gay, who are into gay men—in other words, men who take a political position toward non-assimilation. That quote comes from eight years ago, and no doubt his position has evolved, especially given that his work is characterized by a radically shifting contextual and relational set of values opposed to any new manifestation of a self-satisfied inhabitation of a position. Yet as I say, it is an example of a self-motivated identification entered into with eyes wide open. In contrast, take the two soldiers on the bed: first, they are soldiers, the ultimate symbol

21 Tim Dean, *Unlimited Intimacy: Reflections on the Subculture of Barebacking* (Chicago: University of Chicago Press, 2009). In this book on the subculture of barebacking, in which gay men, often HIV positive, deliberately have sex without condoms (a process referred to by some as "pozzing"), Dean examines ways that the conscious sharing of the HIV virus creates "a new network of kinship among the infected."

22 Bjarne Melgaard quoted in Slava Mogutin, "Anabolic Warrior: Interview with Bjarne Melgaard," *Butt Magazine* 16 (2006), accessed June 10, 2013, http://slavamogutin.com/bjarne-melgaard/.

23 Bjarne Melgaard quoted in Kayla Guthrie, "Painter as Pig, Painting as Prostitute," *Art in America* (June 16, 2010), accessed June 10, 2013, http://www.art inamericamagazine.com/news-opinion/conversations/2010-06-16/bjarne-melgaard-the-synthetic-slut/.

24 Bjarne Melgaard quoted in Mogutin, "Anabolic Warrior."

of the erosion of individual autonomy in the cause of a "greater good," most likely the nation state (the "army of the individuals," after all, is deliberately oxymoronic). Next, they are gay men, or men who have sex with men, and do so within a rigidly adhered-to version of masculinity (the soldier). They are the embodiments of how society structures and naturalizes violence within conformity to given ideals. The "soldier who kills" can be the hyper-masculinized gay warrior pozzing his comrade; the Appalachian soldier leading her prisoner around on a leash; or the militiaman chewing on pork. Sexual expression and violence can be seen as a byproduct of a sublimation of the self in the service of idealizations and forms of purity.

The focus of mainstream gay politics in the United States over the last two decades has been on the question of rights, the ability of gays and lesbians to participate in the institutions of the state, to openly serve their country as soldiers, to enter into the marriage contract just like their straight neighbors. To achieve these goals, there has been an increasing tendency toward assimilation. The narrative goes something like this: gay soldiers can be just as ruthless as straight soldiers and can refrain from trying to suck their comrades off in the shower; that lesbian couple who has just been denied a marriage license has been in a monogamous relationship for forty years, they have *proven* themselves. Derivations from an aping of the values of hetero-normative society, from the conventional modes of intimacy declared as paramount by that world, are condemned, ignored, or ridiculed. Homosexuality as a political position that demands at least an antagonistic relationship to mainstream values has been transformed as gays and lesbians scramble to be accepted and tolerated. So rather than actually reinvent society, gay liberation has become subsumed by the norms of that society, or is dependent for its continued "freedom" on its conformity to those norms. It is probably fairly obvious at this stage that Melgaard holds such a position in contempt, something he elaborated further in his 2010 exhibition at the Venice Biennale, *Baton Sinister*, in which he worked with students at a local university to imagine the palazzo in which they were exhibiting as the headquarters of a gay terrorist separatist group dedicated to overthrowing all sedimented and assimilationist tendencies within gay rights discourse.[25]

It should be said that Melgaard's presence as a body and person with a real biography and history is an undeniable aspect of the work and its mediation, as I've mentioned. It's always impossible to decide where the fiction ends and the subject begins (as if such a determination is ever possible), but he has explored a diverse range of sexual activities, has struggled with addiction to methamphetamines, steroids, and sex. It's easy enough to burlesque him, to turn him into a figure so excessive that he can be both lionized and ridiculed, but his work rewards strong concentration and has evolved with a rigor and sensitivity that is deserving of more careful attention. His most recent novel is a complex, disturbing, and transformative work that continues the difficult play between modes of sexual freedom, biography, and fictional asides so traumatic and visceral that it is difficult to not assume Melgaard lives life in a very difficult personal terrain, albeit with some generosity in his insistence on laying himself bare.[26] He has been condemned for his work and exhibitions have been censored, and meanwhile his activities have been spun into a web of half myths and conjectures, some of which he certainly contributes to in his own statements, writings, and work. His production is voracious, ranging from group shows that he curates to solo exhibitions at galleries or institutions, writing books, conducting classes, industrial design, or managing his website (stabterrorfrenzy.com).

After my first visit with the artist, we got a car from his studio in Bushwick across the Brooklyn Bridge. En route, he showed me a laminated printout from the Internet with step-by-step instructions for how to fuck a dolphin. He was going to add it to some installation, fascinated more by the idea that someone out there would see fit to post these details than by the act itself. Melgaard was on his way to meet Norwegian bankers who wanted him to design the first actual *platinum* platinum card. I wondered if he was going to show the instructions to the bankers? Suits are different in Europe, I guess.

25 Melgaard's project was commissioned by the Office of Contemporary Art, Norway. In addition to the exhibition *Baton Sinister*, which took place in the Palazzo Contarini Corfù, the project was accompanied by a postgraduate seminar given by Melgaard at the University IUAV titled "Beyond Death: Viral Discontents and Contemporary Notions about AIDS," which explored militant potentiality of non-assimilationist behaviors, using the discourse of AIDS as a starting point. The exhibition involved the collaboration of the artist's students, and included as a centerpiece a video titled *Bjarne Melgaard interviews Leo Bersani*. Bersani, a noted queer theorist radically opposed to assimilationist tendencies in mainstream gay culture, was a guest lecturer at the University at the time. In the conversation titled "Illegitimate Gays: The Loss of Activism," Melgaard interviews Bersani, Charlie Rose–style, about the continued relevancy of Freud's theorization of the death drive, the misguided utopianist optimism of some contemporary queer theorists, and contemporary gay activism, among other things. While Bersani resists Melgaard's gestures toward violent militancy throughout the video, he does suggest that a radical restructuring of intimacy, and therefore society itself, is required. In postproduction, the artist introduced numerous animated disruptions that had the effect either of undermining the discourse, or of heightening it through an almost Brechtian displacement, depending on your point of view. For more on the exhibition and seminar, see John Kelsey, "The Ignorant Schoolmaster," *Artforum International* (September 2011): 295–297. See also plate 27 in this catalogue.

26 See Bjarne Melgaard, *A New Novel by Bjarne Melgaard* (Oslo: Aschehoug, 2012). Too involved to elaborate here, the book is an episodic diary of a character called B, documenting his personal life and journeys through the art world. Critic Ina Blom's Afterword to the book is a useful analysis of Melgaard's written oeuvre.

IV. On a Dark Day in a Dark Building

Liam Gillick (born 1964 in England; lives and works in New York and London)

At key moments in his 30-year career, Liam Gillick, an artist who is rarely talked about in relation to biography, has turned to his own identity as a person with Irish roots growing up in England during the 1970s to help explain his particular abstract approach to language and art-making. Intimately invested in the legacy of modernism, Gillick makes sculptures, text-based works, and publications that owe much to the programmatic failure of its Utopian promise to design a more egalitarian society. One of the preeminent representatives of a discursive turn in art, Gillick is often grouped with a number of artists associated with what has become known as Relational Aesthetics of the 1990s. In a famous defense of this moment in art, Gillick situated his mercurial approach and that of his immediate peers (Rirkrit Tiravanija, Dominique Gonzales-Foerster, Philippe Parreno) as being influenced by hybrid cultural backgrounds (Irish, Thai, Columbian, Algerian) that refused to take a didactic position in relation to society, adding, "This is a group whose complex and divided family histories have taught them to become skeptical shape-shifters in relation to the dominant culture in order to retain, rather than merely represent, the notion of a critical position." [27]

Gillick's whole career has been situated along lines that privilege a determined opacity against a universalizing transparency, a philosophy that takes place on the level of language, form, and content, and represents an ethics of practice that is deeply articulated across his many texts, projects, exhibitions, collaborations, and public lectures. It should be said at the outset that for Gillick the idea that form and content would unite into a cohesive unity of intentions (what he refers to as the "singularity problem") is deeply suspect, and one of the features that marks his art-making is a determination that these strands should exist as parallel tracks, informing each other, certainly, but never meant to cohere in a single work. [28] His practice is complex, and for many frustrating, in its refusal to decide upon a definitive site in which the "art" exists; rather, he insists on multiple points of engagement.

A graduate of Goldsmiths College London in the late 1980s, Gillick was grouped for a time with the artists who became synonymous with the Young British Artists (YBAs) of the 1990s, and indeed was featured in the Walker Art Center's celebrated 1995 exhibition *Brilliant! New Art from London*, which was the first international presentation of that now canonical group. [29] Yet from the beginning, Gillick felt uncomfortable with both the rhetoric of the "movement" and the conceptual premise of much of the art that arose from it. For this, he partially blamed the pedagogical structure of Goldsmiths, which encouraged an individualism that for Gillick was anathema to his way of working.

This disdain for what Gillick has related as a near-Thatcherite individualism among the YBAs was born from the artist having been deeply influenced by the labor movements of the 1970s, and the fact that he came of age in the 1980s under the systematic destruction of labor by the Thatcher government. For the artist, this failure and ideological defeat played itself out most tragically in the built world with the

27 Liam Gillick, "Contingent Factors: A Response to Claire Bishop's 'Antagonism and Relational Aesthetics,'" *October* 110 (Fall 2004): 106. In an interview with critic Saul Ostrow, referred to a number of times in this text, Gillick further qualified the relationship of biographical background to his working practice, "I don't think every artist has to deal with their biography, but I come from a background of strong identification with Irish Republican politics, which is full of subterfuge, misleading statements. It's not imbedded in my way of seeing things, but when I'm told that the correct way to be a politically conscious artist is to have transparency throughout everything you do, I'm not sure that I think that every politically conscious activity is surrounded and best served by transparency. So while I have moments of clear positions, they're often muddled by this distrust of transparency, distrust that the good artist and the good political artist is always a transparent artist, who will always reveal sources, desires and needs." "Venice Preview: Liam Gillick Practical Considerations: An Interview by Saul Ostrow," Art in America (June/July 2009): 130–136.

28 Liam Gillick conversation notes, Center for Curatorial Studies, Bard College, New York (March 2009).

29 *"Brilliant!" New Art from London*, a 1995 touring exhibition curated by Richard Flood and organized by the Walker Art Center, featured twenty-two young British artists and was the first major institutional show to cover the emerging tendencies of British art of the time.

political determination that a planned society was no longer sustainable or practical—that all that was left was speculation: a neoliberal embrace of the forces of the market and privatization rather than an ambition to work communally toward a more equal society. For those familiar with Gillick's sculptural objects, design aesthetic, and graphic sensibility this may be hard to fathom, in part because of the obvious sleekness of production, high design values, and structural abstraction, all characteristics that many have come to associate with a corporate design culture. But Gillick stresses the roots of his aesthetic in an applied modernism that actually sought to give everyone access to this level of infrastructure: where architects, engineers, city planners, and politicians believed in an egalitarian public sphere.[30] He has often stated that he is more interested in the work of Anni Albers than Joseph Albers; in other words, he is more invested in the applications of modernism in the lived world as a compromised applied negotiation of contexts than in any notion of purity in relation to the creation of form.

In 2008 it was announced that Gillick had been selected to represent Germany at the 53rd Venice Biennale to take place the following year. Nominated by German curator Nicolaus Schafhausen, then director of Witte de With Center for Contemporary Art in Rotterdam, the selection was met with some surprise and controversy, particularly from conservative elements in the German national media.[31] His selection also received a positive reception and was seen as an example of Germany's mature and receptive cosmopolitanism. Gillick had exhibited regularly in that country since the 1990s, and had a strong reception and context there, at least among an influential cadre of critics, collectors, and institutions. Meanwhile, Berlin had developed into a celebrated international art center, home to a range of contemporary artists who flocked there for low rents and an international and diverse milieu.

While many see the national pavilion structure of Venice as outmoded in an era of globalization, the tradition has been (un)surprisingly resilient. The core of national representation in Venice is found in the Giardini, inhabited by some 30 national pavilions, most built at a time when Europe's colonial nations were competing for prestige. The German Pavilion, originally erected in 1909, was "refurbished" in 1938 by German architect Ernst Haiger to better represent Nazi aesthetics, becoming an icon of Fascist architecture with the addition of monumental and austere pillars and the word GERMANIA engraved on its facade. Naturally, in the postwar years artists have felt compelled to contend with this troubled legacy. Perhaps the most famous response was by German born, American-based artist Hans Haacke, who in 1993 simply tore up the marble flooring in the central room of the pavilion, leaving the fragments for viewers to navigate.

This episode in Gillick's prolific career is a useful point of concentration for this text, because the artist undoubtedly faced a moment of reckoning, what he himself has referred to as "a test," where the limits of his contextual, shifting, and adaptable practice came up against that resolutely over-determined slab that is National Socialism.[32] In a key interview with critic Saul Ostrow in the lead-up to the biennale, one gets a sense of Gillick's working method. His is a process of interrogation of context and mediation, a field of expectations that he is both responding to and creating for himself. The essential problem as he sees it is that the context here can't be ignored; to do so would be too irresponsible. And yet, if he as an artist needs to intercede in the fabric of the building as a historically burdened site, then surely he also needs to interrupt his own comfort zone, to shift his practice in some way as a necessary consequence? Furthermore, is the very choice of Gillick as a non-German national—the first artist to represent a full national pavilion without having a passport from that country—meant as a symbol of Germany's progress? Is he in a sense the figure who renders symbolically the maturity of German culture in relationship to its history of identitarianism? If he proceeds as normal, does he sanction this reading and become his own form of amnesia? And so he explores a range of possibilities, some of which move toward a "grand gesture" that normally would be anathema to him. For example, on a visit to the site he realizes that

33 Ibid.

34 Ibid., 136.

35 Liam Gillick, *One Long Walk… Two Short Piers…*, Kunst- und Ausstellungshalle der Bundesrepublik Deutschland (Bonn) (Cologne: Snoeck, 2010), 32.

36 Ibid., 33.

37 Adrian Searle, "Bodies, babble and blood," *The Guardian*, Monday 8 June 2009, last accessed, July 30, 2013: http://www.theguardian.com/artand-design/2009/jun/09/venice-biennale-elmgreen-dragset.

38 McDonough, "Liam's (not) Home," 147.

39 It is interesting, a few years after the fact, to go back and read an interview with Gillick in which he discusses the aftermath of the exhibition: "I wanted to do something new; I wanted to push something that's quite hard. You suffer a little bit when you do that, even if you know in the back of your mind it's the right thing to do. I left the pavilion on the day of the opening with the clearheadedness that you get sometimes after a breakup or after something's gone wrong, or after you've just witnessed an accident: It's not elation or satisfaction, it's the feeling that you know that this is the only thing you could do, but it's not going to achieve a certain satisfaction." Louisa Buck, "There's a Perversity in My Method," *The Art Newspaper* 229 (November 2011): 54.

Haacke's famous destruction of the pavilion floor encompassed the center of the building, not the anterior spaces. He debates calling Haacke and inviting him to finish the job. In another idea, he considers "turning off the building" by showing video, literally making the walls disappear into a black box. Still another approach—riffing off a joke Gillick would often tell about there being no toilets in Fascist buildings—was to install some basic amenities in the pavilion.[33]

The text by Gillick reprinted in this publication is a key component of the artist's effort to contend with the challenge of the invitation (page 116). Asked by Schafhausen in typical contemporary art style to build a discursive armature around the exhibition, his response was to compose what has become perhaps his most concrete statement about his own work. Titled "Berlin Statement," it was delivered at the Hamburger Bahnhof in Berlin in March 2009, some months in advance of the biennale. For Gillick, there was obviously a sense of responsibility, a desire to buttress his selection with a certain kind of contextualizing gesture. And yet that gesture also became a way for the artist to protect his process, in a sense to liberate himself from the burden of the symbolic move, the big idea that the pavilion seemed to call for. A deeply thought-out exposition of artistic principals, it marked an important milestone in Gillick's distinctive, discursive approach to art practice. One of the more nuanced defenses of the poststructuralist stance of endlessly deferred subjectivity and meaning, the piece brushed the glitter off Gillick's dandified lapels, and focused retroactively on a practice whose deeply articulated ethics were often suspected, but rarely so carefully confirmed.

Having itemized a fascinating mise en abyme of potential responses to the problem of exhibiting in the German pavilion, Gillick closes his interview with Ostrow (made a few months before the exhibition), relating how the composition of the text allowed him to finally divest himself of the search for the grand gesture; to once again privilege production over consumption, an ethos that he has always placed at the heart of his art-making:

> But the question really is how do you find a working method or a working, productive context within which ideas can be produced? And that's really the key. It doesn't help you to know whether you'll arrive and there'll be no building, or there are great toilets, or a large number of rather mute, corrupted formalist artworks. I became truly free—in fact I'm not stressed at all—when I realized the problem wasn't what to do, because if I'd asked myself over the years, what should I do, I probably wouldn't have done half the things I've done. I would have done a different kind of art.[34]

Gillick traveled to Venice with a team of fabricators from Berlin, and worked on-site for a number of months. A viewer visiting the pavilion on the opening day of the biennial would have entered through a colorful plastic strip curtain at the entrance into a large, white-walled pavilion structure. Running through the main space and passing into the anterior galleries was a long row of modular kitchen cabinetry, surfaces, shelving, closets, all cut from an unvarnished pine. On top of one of the cabinets sat an animatronic cat, a roll of paper in its jaw, who tells a story (with Gillick's voice) about a talking cat who is visited by two children (plate 32). The story is told in the future anterior (which will have been the best tense ever, by the way), framed as something that "will have happened," someday. The children, we learn, are nervous and shy, the cat "will have been mildly depressed, suffering from ennui and even bored by its role as the only talking cat in the whole world."[35] The mood of the story is not unlike one of Oscar Wilde's children's fables, which pack both a romantic punch and a great deal of tragedy, yet Gillick's recorded story doesn't resolve itself, but loops back to begin again:

> The cat will know that school starts in five minutes and the children will definitely be late. But today of all days, it won't care. It won't mind if the children miss out on their lessons or their playtime. It won't care if they miss lunch or free time in

the library. All it will care about is that someone is here on a dark day in a dark building. It will sniff. The breath of the children will be close. It will have learnt that humans know that cat's steal their breath. The cat will know that this is nonsense. It is buildings like this that steal people's breath. Anyway. What's wrong with borrowing some child's breath for a while? All cats know that it smells sweet and is full of intelligence and goodness and fun.

It will take a deep surreptitious suck of the children's breath and as they reel and swoon, glide and dream, it will begin to tell them a true story about the wisdom of a kitchen cat....[36]

Titled *How are you going to behave? A kitchen cat speaks*, the exhibition was covered widely in the press. For many foes of Gillick's way of working, both old and new, the profile of the event afforded them a perfectly scaled target with which to finally pin that Scarlet Pimpernel. For example, Adrian Searle in *The Guardian* called it a "strained performance," saying that Gillick's work was always, "a heavy-handed mix of the decorative, the intellectually arch and the overdetermined."[37] Writing in *Texte zur Kunst*, on the other hand, Tom McDonough celebrated Gillick's surprise decision to move away from his more "familiar forms and colors" and also to avoid addressing the building through some grandiose move, finding a critical dimension for the project within the critical context of the talking cat.[38]

Gillick's kitchen was inspired by the 1926 Frankfurt Kitchen of Austrian designer and anti-Nazi activist Margarete Schütte-Lihotzky, a major work of applied modernism that democratized access to a kitchen designed as an efficient and ergonomically aware environment. It also riffed off of Gillick's own post-studio practice—the artist spent many hours in the run-up to the exhibition sitting in his kitchen in New York smoking, being bothered by his son's cat. He remembers asking himself, "Who gets to speak? And who has the authority to do so?" Ultimately, of course, it is him in this context, but he can only bring himself to do so through the filter of the cat. In a sense, what Gillick did was bring together the domestic, the subjective, and the social: elements that militate against the building's grandiose ideological structure. With the kitchen, Gillick enters the mid-space location typical of his work: an interstitial conduit through different moments of the day—at once the most vital part of a home while also being the least formal. Germany in the 1920s saw a battle between two visions of the utility of standardization within design, one (associated with the Marxist-leaning Bauhaus) dedicated to social inclusion and equality through making good design universally accessible, the other dedicated to militarism and a nostalgic re-creation of past tropes of German aesthetics (Fascism). In a sense, Gillick was using German history itself as a model to contend with the legacy of the building, resurfacing a contestatory vision within the culture that had opposed Fascism at the very point of its rise.

Virtually libertarian in its worldview, meanwhile, the cat does not do well with training, and has a scant opinion of anyone who would have it step in line. Less interested in charismatic speeches than some chow and a good nap, the cat has an integrity all its own and is surely less than susceptible to Fascist indoctrination (certainly less so than the dog). In the story the cat steals the children's breath, but only enough to make them woozy, to make them receptive to his tale and open to the mesmeric task of representation. The building, meanwhile, has the real power: it can rip the oxygen from their lungs. In Gillick's oeuvre, there is a constant quest to test the limits of a deluded and distracted engagement with the world, using art as a device to skirt the obvious, to privilege the gaps that in themselves are the elusive foundations of all determined structures. It's a complicated position, and one that continues to resonate in the work of an artist who is surely one of the more influential, and strangely complicit, of our time.[39]

V. I Can't Work Like This

Natascha Sadr Haghighian (bioswop.net)

In 2004 Natascha Sadr Haghighian created bioswop.net, a website for the free exchange of résumés and biographies. She described the project as arising from a gut reaction the first time she was asked to send a CV for inclusion in a catalogue. The CV acts as a legitimizing filter, conferring status within an art-world economy. For Haghighian, it simplifies, distorts, and excludes the complexity of contemporary practice, the means with which artists make their decisions, the range of collaborations, and the networks they develop. It also has a tendency to situate artists in terms of points of origin, nationality, ethnicity, etc., which is all very well if you can play a part in what that might mean, but in an art world and institutional culture obsessed with proving its global credentials, artists can often be instrumentalized for their points of difference along lines of geography and ethnicity, rather than mediated for their work in which these factors may or may not play a strong role. In a 2007 interview with curator Max Andrews, Haghighian describes the origins of bioswop.net. It's worth quoting at length:

> The idea for exchanging artist's biographies which bioswop is based on originated from my multiple attempts to play with the conventional formats of art catalogues. If you want to study the mechanisms of representation, catalogues are a good thing to start with. Actually there is almost nothing about an art catalogue that I don't find funny. More than anything else it shows that there is a great doubt about the value and necessity of art in general but also about every single artwork. So its foremost purpose seems to be validation and valuation. First it usually starts with a text by a specialist who is appointed by the art world to validate meaning and quality. Then it continues with presenting the artwork mostly in an iconic, fetishist, absolute fashion in order to make it impassible. Lastly it ends with the artist's biography which localizes the imagery that one just saw in places of appointed significance. It proves the artist's acknowledgement by the art world and helps evaluating his or her importance and relevance. In my eyes this format is the result of sheer paranoia and lack of confidence. But more importantly it is mostly just not interesting.... So starting the website bioswop.net first of all had practical motivations. As it is tiresome and time consuming to come up with new bios all the time I wanted to have a place where I could just go and click on something. But secondly I thought that it might be an interesting practice to share with more people. Maybe it would become a new movement. People exchanging, borrowing bios just like anything else that you get tired of.[40]

Haghighian's desire to study the "mechanisms of representation" is also a desire to evade them, or at least to disjoint the easy flow of prescribed information, the ready formats with which the institution of art ascribes and maintains value, and the ideological currents, albeit shifting, that underpin this. At this point the artist is still generally introduced by way of bios constructed or shared from bioswop.net. However, in an art world conditioned by strategic placement and positioning, the gesture itself can become shorthand leading to and identifying the particular strategies of the

40 Max Andrews, *Uovo Magazine* 12 (2007): 156–173. See also Johann König Gallery website, http://www.johannkoenig .de/6/natascha_sadr_haghighian/texts .html#.

artist. Her calling card as it were: something that situates her within the discourse, a gesture absorbed like most others into the ongoing building of cultural capital.

Yet, as Haghighian points out in her contribution to this publication (page 4), even in the years since 2004, the artist CV has become an increasingly archaic tool, with less and less utility in light of the expansion of the World Wide Web and its associated social networking and search capabilities. Now an artist, dealer, critic, curator, or the rare art historian who might attempt such a thing is much more likely to simply Google an artist's name than to request or even search for an online résumé. There they will find a much more satisfyingly colorful portrait of their object of study by way of Facebook pictures, artist statements, interviews, YouTube records of lectures, scrappy reviews, or in-depth features.

In her text, Haghighian describes her surprise when a friend e-mails her a link to the website ArtFacts.Net, which collects data on artists and posts it online, creating a basic metric of success based on institutional affiliations, and ranking the artists accordingly for the elucidation of bottom-line cautious collectors. Despite the fact that the algorithms and data-collecting bots deployed by the website have miscategorized her biography based on data that she herself inserted into circulation, she is disturbed by the website's assumption that it has the right to undermine her own artistic project, and also to present her within such a narrow metric. Yet, despite an initial attempt to have the information removed, Haghighian comes to the conclusion that to fight the cloud is as futile as Don Quixote tilting at the windmill. Instead, she embarks on a meditation about the shifting sands of identification within a world where the body and the subject are becoming ever more imbricated within that cloud. She takes up the call of Hito Steyerl and others to identify with the object, rather than the subject, exploring the possibilities for a renewed form of agency within this approach, one that acknowledges the power of market forces to manipulate how we are formed and subjugated as subjects, by way of commodities that act as portals to this or that lifestyle and construction of one's sense of self.[41]

She thus identifies with the object of the graph, which on ArtFacts indicates her rising and falling fortunes as an artist since 2006. She converses with it, animating it through her address, so that ultimately it is decoupled from its narrow function and can be seen, at least provisionally, as an entity participating in a conversation. In a sense, what happens with this approach is that she subjectivizes the object (an interesting reversal on the objectification of the subject). The reader becomes aware of the curve as something with agency, and then can meditate on its enslavement by ArtFacts, see the structures that contain it, and embargo its freedom. After all, perhaps it is just as unhappy with the situation as Haghighian? Perhaps it would rather redefine the metrics of its own rise and fall along more intuitive lines in dialogue with the artist. Rather than go down in the months where the artist does not exhibit, why not go down when she has a cold? Or conversely, rather than go up because of an exhibition at the Walker, why not go up when she is reading a pleasant romance novel on a breezy afternoon in Berlin? She and the curve enter into a complicity that, even if only provisionally, sidesteps the narrow intentions of its owners and consumers, emancipating it through a kind of perspectival displacement.

Haghighian further problematizes and explores these questions in her text, so I will dispense with my summary here. What's important to hold onto is the contextual and shifting means with which the artist engages the world and her place within it, whether through videos, online projects, texts, installations, or designed events. Haghighian is known for her site-specific projects, or investigations of the format with which she is invited to participate, often highly collaborative engagements with other writers, makers, and thinkers whose ideas influence her and whom she in turn influences. It's a shifting practice, certainly associated with the history of Institutional Critique for the way in which it can subvert, upturn, and point out the workings and inherent ideologies of institutional processes. In my first conversation with the artist, she mentioned that her New Year's resolution might be to stop being reactive in relation to a prospective project, to be able to accept the terms and then proactively pursue her

41 Hito Steyerl, "A Thing Like You and Me," *e-flux journal* 15 (April 2010), http://www.e-flux.com/journal/a-thing-like-you-and-me/.

own interests within it (as many artists do). Yet often she feels like that very pursuit is inevitably closed down by the way in which the invitation demands her participation with it: that the structures of inclusion or exclusion are such that she has no choice but to deal with them first. Nevertheless, rather than adopt arch positions that situate her in the role of heroic and enlightened outsider, she, like every artist in this show to greater or lesser degrees, navigates her involvement with a sense of the complicity with power dynamics that is inevitably associated with participation within an art industry, or any industry for that matter.

For example, when invited by her gallerist in Berlin, Johann König, to contribute a work for an art fair, she ultimately agreed (it remains the only work she has produced for this purpose), and after a month of being in a bad mood submitted the piece, an installation constructed out of nails hammered to a wall in such a way that the negative space spelled out the declaration "I can't work like this…" (plate 35).[42] The piece had a conceptual richness, deploying the same material of construction that is used to mount art fair displays, an economy of means that also draws attention to the most proletarian signals of labor itself (hammer and nails). It is perhaps unsurprising, given the universality of the sentiment and the clarity of the final piece as an "object" (i.e., collectible item), that this work might be termed Haghighian's most successful to date (following the metrics of success that ArtFacts would enjoy). That is: it is featured on the gallery website as the introductory work to her oeuvre, and was snapped up by collections, including that of the Guggenheim Museum.

To give another example of Haghighian's way of working, she was on her way to the Sharjah Biennial and met Uwe Schwarzer of mixedmedia Berlin, a company that helps with the manufacturing and development of artworks.[43] She befriended Schwarzer and visited his Berlin factory, scene to the production of countless artists' works in different styles bound for various art fairs, biennials, and gallery exhibitions. While Haghighian rarely works with assistants, she doesn't dismiss anything that fails to arise from the artist's hand. Nevertheless, she was curious about Schwarzer's disavowal of his own contribution (or that of his staffs) to the authorship of the works, his claims to be following the personal style of a given artist to the letter, despite the obvious occasions where he would need to intuit or interpret what such a personal style might mean. She wished to look into these questions further, but Schwarzer was understandably reluctant to have her document the inner workings of the company, given the discretion with which he must often proceed. Haghighian and Schwarzer devised a foil with which they could continue their investigations, namely the fictitious artist Robbie Williams, whose debut exhibition would be composed of works produced by mixedmedia Berlin. They settled on the name because, as Haghighian relates, people would generally be satisfied not to ask too many questions so long as she clarified "the artist, not the singer." She expanded:

> The name also carries the connotations of the glamour and tragedy of a solo career. And that is an important aspect of the Solo Show project. It is about the construction of the "solo" artist, whose name floats above the Tate Modern in big bold letters. But actually he relies on a huge team of people, specialists, technicians, architects, assistants, engineers, management staff, etc. At best, their names will be listed in the imprint of the catalogue. But the public is fed the intact image of a singular individual whose extraordinary talents or whatever have enabled his works to float so boldly above the Tate Modern. There is a discrepancy, a distortion of the actual relationships in the art scene that is increasingly veering towards a mega-event culture. So we needed an icon to engage in iconoclasm. And "Robbie" took the job.[44]

Robbie did a really good job; his exhibition *Solo Show* opened at MAMbo in Bologna in 2008.[45] The white cube exhibition had two entrances; in one was a series of five sculptures that took show-jumping fences as their inspiration—they were made in a number of styles with a host of materials that acted virtually as quotations of

42 For more on this work and the artist's oeuvre in general, see the excellent artist talk she gave, "when night falls in the forest of static choices," at the Guggenheim, organized by associate curator Katherine Brinson: "Natascha Sadr Haghighian: Conversations with Contemporary Artists at the Guggenheim," YouTube video, artist talk presented as part of the Conversations with Contemporary Artists series at the Solomon R. Guggenheim Museum, New York, on January 21, 2012, posted by "Guggenheim Museum," March 12, 2012, accessed June 10, 2013, http://www.youtube.com/watch?v=IPc-kMMjBZ4.

43 The artist discussed the project in some depth in Raimer Stange, "Natascha Sadr Haghighian: Nobody Does Anything on Their Own," *Mousse Magazine* 15 (October/November 2008): 72. See also Johann König Gallery website, http://www.johannkoenig.de/6/natascha_sadr_haghighian/texts.html#.

44 Ibid.

45 The exhibition *Solo Show*, curated by Andrea Viliani, was on view at Museo d'Arte Moderna di Bologna (MAMbo) from September 7 to November 2, 2008.

46 "Natascha Sadr Haghighian: Institutional critique and collective authorship; money, fruit and Robbie Williams," *Frieze* 119 (November–December 2008), accessed June 10, 2013, http://www.frieze.com/issue/article/natascha_sadr_haghighian/.

contemporary sculpture. For example, one was composed entirely of televisions, another of fabric folds, and a third of a birdhouse platform with ensconced drag-style wigs. A *Frieze* review at the time described it as "looking like weird hybrid mockups for artists such as John Armleder, Monica Bonivinvi, and Liam Gillick."[46] The mixed-media installation certainly mined the history of postmodern sculpture, from contemporary pop culture–inspired assemblage works to media-based installations and feminist craft-based reclamations. The gallery included the title of the show and Robbie's name. In the next gallery, a series of elegant speakers were hung in the round with a looped surround sound of a horse galloping and jumping. Here a vinyl text listed the names, without hierarchy, of some fifty individuals who had contributed to the project, including Haghighian and Schwarzer.

It's perhaps unsurprising that the reviews of the exhibition concentrated on the structural conceit of its instantiation rather than the material and conceptual properties of the exhibition itself. What would it have meant to review it on face value, to tease out the relationship between the horse and the sculptures, the delicate and perceptive play of the materials, the deliberate vulnerability displayed by the artist(s) in making such an over-determined relationship between the objects and the jumping horse? Is the horse the figure of the artist, on show for the pleasure of its owners who move from vernissage to vernissage following the upward and downward curve of its motion, waiting for the next horse to take its place? Is the horse a stand-in for the career of Robbie Williams? (The singer, not the artist.)

Perhaps it is obvious that we are not trained to consider the decisions of a collective as deserving of such consideration (the group of individuals who authored this collaborative work). At the same time, there is a sensibility to the project that belies any idea of a one-liner. Why not collectivize under a name and produce for a market? Is it because you are doomed to simply imitate the production of a more singular voice? Or isn't it true that without the parameters of imitation of this particular structure, the collective might be capable of something far more radical?

VI. Here Lies One Whose Name Was Writ in Water

Danh Vo (Danish, born 1975 in Vietnam; lives and works in Basel, Switzerland)

Any of the recent copious articles or features on the work of artist Danh Vo generally begin with a story: Danh Vo (pronounced "yon voh" according to a helpful recent *New York Times* article) was born in 1975 in Vietnam; in 1979 he escaped on a boat built by his father.[47] The boat was picked up by a Danish vessel and because of this Vo and his family ended up in Denmark, where they eventually became naturalized citizens. That's it. After that things diverge. There are different stories to tell, different moments in his industriously productive career to explore. The narrative has taken on the status of a foundation myth (albeit empirically provable), one that the artist has variously resisted or manipulated, which has paved the way for work that engages, among other things, questions of identity and biography, though not as one might expect. In an interview in Dutch magazine *Metropolis M* in 2010, the artist talked about his emergence: "I just started to do things but my work was quickly categorized as 'working with identities.' But I thought: if I am working with identity, then it should be a bit more fucked up, because identities aren't stable nowadays, they are complex and schizophrenic."[48]

Vo's work can be seen as a philosophy of practice that runs through his many projects, exhibitions, and relationships—a keen attention to art-historical precedence as well

47 Roberta Smith, "Awash in a Cultural Deluge: 'The Hugo Boss Prize 2012,' Danh Vo Works at the Guggenheim," *New York Times* (March 14, 2013), accessed June 13, 2013, http://www.nytimes.com/2013/03/15/arts/design/the-hugo-boss-prize-2012-danh-vo-works-at-the-guggenheim.html?page-wanted=all&_r=0.

48 Danh Vo, interview about his then current Stedelijk Museum exhibition *Package Tour*, in Erik van Tuijn, "Danh Vo: Identities are complex and schizophrenic," *Metropolis M* (July 30, 2008), accessed June 10, 2013, http://metropolism.com/previews/interview-with-danh-vo/english.

49 See curator Luigi Fassi's fascinating text on the artist in Luigi Fassi, "Terra Incognita," *Artforum International* (February 2010): 152–159.

50 The artist in conversation with the author, 2011.

as geopolitics and the implications of living in a world that is more imbricated than ever before. People, objects, history, and various identity formations all become material in his expanding and accumulating oeuvre, producing a profound portrait, not necessarily of himself, but of the complicities and complexities of life today. In this sense, Vo can often use the personal as a bridge to wider considerations, or fold contexts into his work less as a form of appropriation than as a meditation on context and relation that spans time and geography. What happens if I bring this into my lexicon? And now this? And now this? It's a shifting, rich, and provocative world of references and strategies that also sidesteps a binary approach to, say, the history of colonization or questions of sexual identity. Biography is mutable and contextual, history fluid and unsettled, always inhabiting the present as an evolving open work capable of producing new revelations. Friendship and intimacy are key and often reflected in unexpected quarters; the artist has turned the incidents of history into so many collaborators as eclectic and vital as his roving and expanding entourage (friends, family, artists, writers, and supporters), many of whom have become key agents around and within the work.

To give an example, in 2002 Denmark became the first country to legalize gay marriage, but the rights afforded to LGBT couples did not include several afforded to straight, such as the right to adopt children. Meanwhile, in Copenhagen, city authorities began clearing trees in a park that was traditionally associated with gay cruising. Vo felt that the institution of marriage being offered to gays and others was about the exertion of a certain form of control. And yet life is full of institutions with which we can engage that are meant to serve specific functions. Vo wanted to make the institution meaningful for himself, so he decided to use the marriage system as a way to project personal memories within his name (I think of it almost as marriage-as-tattoo). He married people with whom he felt some personal affinity, and then divorced them while retaining their legal names. So far he has married two individuals, a Rosasco and a Rasmussen, but conceptually the project is still ongoing, and theoretically he could (as one critic pointed out) marry people until ultimately there are too many words to fit on the marriage certificate.[49]

There is something fascinating about this project and how it relates to a story Vo once told me about coming out to his parents. Catholic and socially conservative southern Vietnamese, they seemed fine with it, and began trying to get him to marry acquaintances in Vietnam so that they too could escape to Denmark. His point was that with their Vietnamese make-do attitude, they could always find the use in something even if they couldn't find the meaning. The Rosasco Rasmussen project is interesting when aligned with that sensibility. Vo finds the use in marriage, even if he can't find the meaning. But then again, the opposite could equally be true, and perhaps that's the point—it depends upon your position in relation to the something being discussed.[50]

It's worth noting that when Vo arrived in Denmark as a child, the authorities mixed up the family's names. Many Asian countries put the family names first and the given names second. Vo's name in Vietnam was Vo trung ky-Danh ("trung" means "middle" and "ky" means "special"). On his arrival in Denmark, the authorities simply shuffled the "Vo" to the end so his middle name became his first, Trung Ky Danh Vo. When you add in the names from the marriages, and then the different combinations with which the artist uses them, you have someone who has embedded within his legal nomenclature a shifting range of potential identities. This is something with which the artist plays in his own movements, as his existence is fairly nomadic—constantly on the go from one project, exhibition, residency, or opening to another—requiring him to have at least some structure in various cities where he lays his head. The names become tools in the process of navigating through the various legal, immigration, and financial bureaucracies he encounters. Vo often sends his acquaintances JPEGs of images he has shot on his travels. A few years back, I received one of a debit card from Bank of America. He had chosen to have a themed card, and his template featured the words "Military Banking" in large black type and a Blackhawk helicopter hovering in sinister silhouette against a sunset. The name on the card reads "Trung Rasmussen." Somehow this simple gesture, one that is likely never intended to be viewed in an "art" context, captures so much about the ways in which Vo both utilizes

51 Francesca Pagliuca, "No Way Out: An Interview with Danh Vo," *Mousse Magazine* 17 (February 2009), accessed June 10, 2013, http://www.moussemag azine.it/articolo.mm?id=8.

52 The contract that governs the acquisition was negotiated over the course of a year with the assistance of Mary Polta, the Walker's chief financial officer, Walker registrar Joe King, and lawyer J. Hazen Graves of Faegre Baker Daniels LLC. It also required the collaboration of Marta Lusena and Isabella Bortolozzi of Isabella Bortolozzi Galerie, Berlin, in addition to, of course, the artist, his father, and family. The negotiations included a provision whereby Phùng Vo drew up a will establishing his assent to the terms of the agreement, and the Vo family was obliged to buy a family plot in the graveyard in anticipation of the exchange.

53 The incidents of this event are elaborated in Edmund White, *Genet: A Biography* (New York: Alfred A. Knopf, 1993).

54 The artist in conversation with the author, July 2010.

55 This work was first shown in the exhibition *All your deeds in water are writ, but this in marble* were presented at the Isabella Bortolozzi Galerie, Berlin, October 2 to November 7, 2010. See also the Isabella Bortolozzi Galerie website, accessed June 10, 2013, http://bortolozzi .com/exhibitions/danh-vo-all-your-deeds -shall-in-water-be-writ-but-this-in-marble -isabella-bortolozzi-galerie-berlin/.

and points to the bureaucratic absurdities that condition our world. The gay Danish artist of Vietnamese descent with a militaristic banking card that features a US air force helicopter and names that are as apt to describe the owner as any other: the army of the individuals indeed.

"Here lies one whose name was writ in water." So reads the inscription on a black stone with gold-leaf engraving that was installed in the Minneapolis Sculpture Garden in the spring of 2012. Titled *Tombstone for Phùng Vo* (2010), it's one of several works by Vo recently acquired by the Walker Art Center (plate 20). On the death of the artist's father, Phùng Vo, the stone will be shipped to Denmark and placed over his grave in Vestre Kirkegård, a large cemetery in Copenhagen. It is in part Vo's history that has given him a profound understanding of the importance of documents, which the artist has described as "equivalent to a performance, since through paper and institutions our society has already determined our movements and actions."[51] Just as immigration documents have controlled his family's movements in life, the Walker's acquisition of Vo's work has led to contractual obligations that will impact various activities after his father's death: among them, Phùng Vo has created a will for the Walker that confirms arrangements for his funeral.[52] In addition to other details, the will bequeaths to the institution four artifacts of personal significance, including a gold crucifix with a chain and three objects he purchased soon after he arrived in Denmark. These items—a Dupont lighter, an American military class ring, and a Rolex watch—have since been "upgraded" to newer models. Phùng Vo bought them originally because to him, as a recent immigrant from communist Vietnam, they symbolized a particularly Western brand of success and masculinity.

Whereas the tombstone will rest within the protective enclave of the Walker until it is sent to the cemetery in Copenhagen, these four objects will be part of Phùng Vo's daily life until he dies. After the tombstone arrives in Copenhagen, the artifacts will be delivered to Minneapolis, where they can be installed in a vitrine designed by the artist. In this regard, the work can be seen as a performance scripted by a series of documents—the contract, the will, export papers, etc.—that enacts itself over many years and involves many players, from Vo family and Walker staff members to the lawyer whose expertise was needed to ensure the purchase and anyone else who finds out about the work and becomes engaged with it over time. The tombstone is not just the sum of its parts, but also the stories that coalesce around it in its journey from the institution of the museum to the institution of the cemetery.

One of the remarkable things about the tombstone is the way in which it manifests relationships and lines of thought that move across geography and history: relationships, for instance, between two individuals who were buried in exile and one individual who will be, someday. Near the end of his life, French playwright and activist Jean Genet taught his lover and his lover's son to mimic his handwriting so they could help him forge the old manuscripts he sold to stay afloat. After his death in 1986, Genet was buried in the Spanish cemetery in Larache, Morocco. When the plaque on his gravestone was stolen, his lover's son carved Genet's signature into the rock. Because he was trained to write in Genet's hand, it was as if the playwright had signed his own grave.[53] This story was a key strand in Vo's thinking about the tombstone work, as was a visit to the Protestant Cemetery in Rome in 2009, where the artist came across the grave of Romantic poet John Keats, who died in the city in 1821 at the age of 25 after traveling there to seek a cure for tuberculosis. Largely unknown at the time of his death, Keats asked that the words "Here lies one whose name was writ in water" be carved on his grave. Vo later wrote, "When I first encountered Keats's tombstone, I believed everybody deserves such a beautiful inscription."[54]

The artist asked his father, a skilled calligrapher, to make sketches of the inscription. Phùng Vo experimented with a number of treatments before settling on a Gothic type style (prevalent in Rome) because he found it "exotic." Using his father's design, Vo had the inscription carved onto a slab of black absolute granite and inset with gold leaf. At some point in the process, he asked his father if the work could serve as his tombstone. Phùng Vo assented.[55]

In the future, people wandering through the Minneapolis Sculpture Garden will come across the rock sunk into the earth amid a line of trees on the fringes of a pathway just feet from the traffic of Hennepin Avenue. Then someday on a return visit, they will perhaps notice that the stone is gone. If they care to dig further, they will realize that it has made the trip across the water to Copenhagen. The stone will remain a part of the collection, though the Walker will have no legal obligation to maintain it over time. Rather, it will act as any gravestone would, kept in good care by the Vo family until the reasons for doing so are forgotten.

VII. Enjoy Please Poverty

Renzo Martens (born 1973 in the Netherlands; lives and works in Brussels and Kinshasa)

Renzo Martens has become known over the last decade for two documentary works in which he plays a central role. In *Episode I* (2003) he travels to Chechnya, ostensibly to document the fallout of the war between Russian soldiers and Chechen militants. To make the feature-length *Episode III*, he spent two years in the Congo, one of the world's most ravaged and impoverished countries, and set out to prove that poverty is in fact the region's greatest resource. The films each function as Western meditations on Western narcissism, with Martens uncomfortably intervening in the action, making the subject of the film as much himself as any of the material conditions he is investigating.

The press release accompanying Martens's forty-five-minute film *Episode I* began as follows:

> Renzo Martens pushes his way into Chechnya—alone, illegal, and carrying an Hi8 camera. He takes the role of the ubiquitous, yet forever undefined, television viewer whose attention everyone is fighting for. Against a background of ruins and bombings, he does not ask refugees, UN employees, and rebels how they feel. Those stories are already known. They already play a role. Instead he asks them how they think he feels.[56]

Martens spends time with NGO workers, wanders the refugee camps interacting with people, visits the city of Grozny, and surveys the ruins. At a checkpoint a Russian soldier laughs at the impertinence of Martens's question, "What do you think of me," responding, "You're just an idiot looking for adventure." Clearly an outsider in the situation, the artist exploits his own position as a documentarian to gain access to people, homes, and situations, with the subjects of the film assuming that he is there with a "theme" in mind, an approach that will at the very least raise awareness, create images to join the countless others that reveal the trauma to viewers elsewhere. Used to being hailed as victims, the refugees are both understanding of the mechanisms of aid and the need to be viewed within a regime of humanitarianism, and also tired of it all, suspicious ultimately of the intentions of those who capture them within their pixelated prison and depart satiated.

As indicated in the release, Martens is not presenting a fly-on-the-wall documentary, with its implicit call and response to the subject to narrativize their exploitation and misery for a sympathetic audience in lands far away. His is more personality driven, bordering on the fly-in-the-ointment characteristics of a Michael Moore, Louis Theroux, or even Werner Herzog. Yet, unlike these directors who seek ultimately to use their personali-

56 Renzo Martens in conversation with Niels Van Tomme, "Enjoy Poverty: Disclosing the Political Impasse of Contemporary Art," *Art Papers* (September 2010): 22–27. See also plate 3 in this catalogue.

57 Ibid.

58 Ibid.

ties to drive forward a theme that will prove elucidatory in some way, either revealing a deep universal truth about humankind (Herzog) or raising awareness around a tangible issue (Moore), Martens makes the subject of his films himself. By extension, he is the consumer, because his distracted, narcissistic behavior becomes a correlative for persons who engage with television or film as just one of many incidents throughout their day, for whom the documentation of trauma is conceived as both an address meant to raise awareness but also a form of entertainment, a mode of communication that always constructs the viewer as somehow outside looking in, rather than implicated and somehow always also responsible for that which is being viewed.

One strand of Martens's writing and speaking about his own work is to insist on its lack of ability to promote social change, to emphasize the work's status as an artwork that self-referentially points out the structure of its own making. It's virtually a modernist assertion, which cleaves to some notion of autonomy—the medium pointing out its own construction, self-reflexively reaching for the nadir of a documentary that reveals its own structures. Never mind, it seems to suggest, the content or the subjects who fill it are just paint and canvas; it's what you do with them that counts. But of course what he means by the film being about the conditions of its own existence is simply that it points out the social, political, and economic function of reportage. Or more pointedly, it reveals the ethics of looking and recording rather than assuming that these things arise from a transparent intention to show. For him, autonomy is not predicated on lack of reference to the outside world, but rather:

> I think something can also become autonomous if it somehow folds back onto itself, if the piece somehow becomes accountable for its own existence in the world. And that's something that is often missing in contemporary art's documentary practices. The position of the piece vis à vis what it's depicting is often not included into the equation. I've somehow tried to make a work of art that shows something in the world by virtue of dealing with its own mode of production and representation. The piece investigates itself and in a way it's precisely this self-referential quality that makes the world visible.[57]

And here is some of the complexity of Martens's project, the insistence in various interviews on its lack of social effectiveness, while also constructing an ethics of self-reflexivity that is after all a pedagogical tool of laying bare the hierarchies that govern and direct representation and notions of the visible.

In *Episode III*, the artist goes to the Congo, and over two years documents a series of encounters. The essential through line is his thesis that poverty is the greatest resource of the Congo; it leads to the huge influx of NGOs, the mass media's infatuation with images of conflict. Co-opting the language of neoliberalism, Martens insists that all that is needed is for the locals to take control of the means of production of this poverty, to become entrepreneurial spirits in the mediation of their own oppression, an exercise that he attempts to direct. He tries to persuade young Congolese photographers that they can make more money through images of suffering than by photographing happy weddings in between the inevitable conflicts that sweep through their village. In one of the film's many vignettes, the artist stands in a suit before a blackboard, like countless colonialists before him (or for that matter, the father of social sculpture, Joseph Beuys himself), seemingly educating the natives on the nature of their oppression: pointing out the basic economics that privilege images of rape, malnourishment, or trauma. It's a self-aggrandizing role, painful to watch, steeped in irony: "I just try to teach them some of the basic laws of capitalism: create the most added value possible, using the natural resources you have at your disposal."[58]

At a hospital, they photograph malnourished children while Martens points out the special features that will improve the digestibility of their images for an international audience. As a conclusion to this strand of the film, Martens accompanies the photographers to a Médecins Sans Frontières encampment in an effort to secure press passes. A man goes through the prints and rejects them based on the lack of aesthetic virtue in their inability to capture the essence of trauma but merely to represent it, and what good is that? After all, the international trade in such images, unless amateur shots of, say, a bomber on an airplane, is predicated on a certain regulatory premise, the standards of professionalism of a well-taken image. There is something very uncomfortable about Martens's process that militates against one's understanding of right and wrong. And indeed there is a utilitarian sensibility to his work, an approach in which the ends justify the means. The exploitation of the individual is necessary to approach a much more structural analysis of ways that media and representation function within a global image world wherein the means of production are largely held by vested interests ranging from the corporate media to the NGO industry.

The various incidents of the film have been well documented elsewhere; just Google it and you'll receive multiple vantage points and perspectives.[59] The artist travels to a remote village, accompanied by porters who, it turns out, are carrying a giant neon sign, which he debuts at a gathering. It reads "Enjoy Please Poverty," with the "please" flashing, politely insistent (plate 10). A French-speaking villager asks the artists if "poverty" is misspelled, to which Martens responds that English is the language in which the film will be consumed, as the international lingua franca of the art world, the economy of distribution for which the film is destined. Earlier, the artist trails international press photographers who themselves follow in the wake of NGOs who can offer greater levels of security. They document bodies of militants lying decaying in the long grass. Martens befriends a European photographer and the following conversation ensues:

> Renzo Martens: Who is the owner of these pictures?
> Press photographer: I am the owner. I can use them if I want to make a vernissage, or a book. Not with any money… how do you say?
> RM: You don't have to pay for that. Yes. And the people that are on the pictures. The people you have photographed… are they the owners of the pictures, too, or not?
> PP: No
> RM: You are the owner. And the people on the pictures own nothing?
> PP: No, because I took the pictures…
> RM: You took the pictures…
> PP: So I'm the photographer, the author of the picture.
> RM: But they organized everything that is on the picture. You just came and made the picture.
> PP: What do you mean "organized?"
> RM: Well the situation that you made the picture of, they made the situation.
> PP: But not due to me…
> RM: No, not because of you…
> PP: No, yeah, sure. But, it's me that made of that situation a picture…
> RM: Right
> PP: There are thousands of situations. But it's me. I choose the one that I think will make a good picture. And that makes that picture *mine*.
> RM: OK

What Martens has done is perhaps a demonstration of the politics of representation that every media studies student understands de facto, but there is something devastating in this sequence. People are the resource that the photographer exploits, even as the international corporations exploit those people's natural resources. It's true that the film's relentless concentration on exploitation makes little room for hope or individual agency, and there are few moments here where the subjects of the film display some aspect of personal autonomy or differentiation. Everyone, from a plantation owner to NGO workers to the young photographers,

59 See, for example: Els Roelandt, "Renzo Martens' Episode 3: Analyses of a Film Process in Three Conversations," *A Prior Magazine* 16 (February 2008), accessed June 10, 2013, http://aprior.org/article-detail/renzo_martens_episode_3.

60 Irish writer Jonathan Swift's *A Modest Proposal for Preventing the Children of Poor People from Being a Burden to Their Parents or Country, and for Making Them Beneficial to the Publick* was first published anonymously in pamphlet form in 1729.

61 All quotes are from Dieter Roelstraete, "On Leaving the Building: Thoughts of the Outside," *e-flux journal* 24 (April 2011), http://www.e-flux.com/journal/on-leaving-the-building-thoughts-of-the-outside/.

62 It should be said that Roelstraete makes this point in a footnote to his essay, but it proceeds with his usual (and very enjoyable) aplomb, so it might as well be in the main text.

is depicted through Martens's relentless world view. Even the artist himself is given short shrift, or at any rate the Renzo Martens of the film, who may or may not be the Renzo Martens who fed me baguette and Camembert during my first visit with him (one gets the sense when meeting Martens that the cameras are still rolling, which perhaps is the point).

What is perhaps difficult about Martens's work is that he crosses a basic line from satire to real-life instrumentalization. He has cited as an influence Jonathan Swift's "A Modest Proposal," in which the man of letters proposed that Irish children be served up as food on English aristocratic dinner tables as a means to deal with the problem of poverty in that country.[60] Martens goes one step further than this foundational text of political satire, and seemingly nibbles on the children to prove his point, in that he implicates real people to drive home his message.

To Martens's credit, he rarely retreats from an opportunity to discuss the work, defend its motives, and discuss the themes that arise from it. Screenings of the films are frequently accompanied by conversations with the artist. Indeed, in his essay "On Leaving the Building: Thoughts on the Outside," curator and critic Dieter Roelstraete has noted, with frustration, that in such talks the artist seems to accept all criticisms and inure himself to them. Referring to *Episode III*, he writes, "For if one of the film's core themes is guilt (and, correspondingly, responsibility), the problem encountered by anyone seeking to challenge some of the project's critical assumptions with regards to the cultural exploitation of guilt, is that Martens gladly and emphatically assumes all responsibility for it." Martens has, from Roelstraete's point of view, created the ultimate cynical artwork: "If ever the postcritical era in art (which most people seem to agree we inhabit) would need an inaugural, manifesto-like artwork, this could well be it." This, because "it" conjures a totalizing world of late capitalist globalization, a world of complicity and implication to which there is no outside, no possibility of escape. In the context of *Episode III*, Martens's world implicates all. To continue Roelstraete's critique:

> We all have blood on our hands—in the Central-African context of *Enjoy Poverty* that means, among other things: we all eat chocolate, we all use Coltan-enhanced electronics, we all shrug our shoulders at the sight of yet another crying malnourished baby—and all (i.e., not just the least) we can do is hold those bloody hands up in front of the camera for all (but first and foremost ourselves) to see.[61]

Roelstraete's essay is a cri de coeur for what he calls "theology"—not the belief in God necessarily, but the belief in an alternative here arrived at through a conviction in the notion of distance, of an ability to move beyond implication into a space that, although not quite pure, at least has the capacity for action, response, and agency. He finds this ultimately in the act of making, the creative action of writing, for example, as a means to construct hitherto unheralded readings/realities. Against Margaret Thatcher's declaration that there is no alternative outside the new world order of global capitalism with its inevitable privatization and therefore fencing in of all modes of interaction, Roelstraete adamantly insists that the commodification of thought itself can be resisted. He likens Martens's work, in which his presence is such a naturalized inevitability, to the contemporary vogue for immersive artworks (replicating the interiority that is itself a construction of capitalism, wishing to perpetuate the notion that there is no alternative to itself). Or to the cult of the artist's presence as found most cogently in Marina Abramović's *The Artist Is Present* performance at MoMA in 2011, "one of last year's biggest box office hits in the Western world's postwar art capital—a powerful sign of the general audience's thirst for the artist's 'presence' in these personality-starved, yet celebrity-obsessed, times."[62]

Perhaps it is with Abramović that it is useful to part ways with Roelstraete and his insistence that Martens proceeds through cynicism to immobility, that the acknowledgment of implication and complicity is in itself a form of self-inoculation to the possibility of action, rather than a necessary first step toward it. Complicity is an important word for this exhibition because its acknowledgment is not an end game, a surrender, but a necessary process of recognizing reality in all its complexity, not purifying it or proposing some magical thinking alternative. Contrast Martens's project with Abramović's.[63] She becomes a mythic being, a queen in a gown relentlessly engaging the viewer, hour after hour, day after day in a durational performance that is documented and then edited for HBO and other outlets in order to show the sentimental highlights: her confrontation with Ulay (surely anyone who watches this cannot help but be moved to tears, especially when the violin soundtrack commences); her resilience and ability to reset the gaze for each new encounter, each new deeply personal trade-off with a viewer who has lined up for hours for this privilege of making eye contact with her.

She is, in effect, some kind of "theology," elevated above the status of mere mortal, institutionally set on a pedestal, constructing her own outside, which is in truth more deeply implicated and complicit than anything that might arise through Martens's work. Sitting opposite her, making eye contact with her, is its own form of collaboration, with no observation of the structural components of that transaction. A purified affect elevated to the beyond, totally consistent with the relentless drumbeat of self-empowerment, individual transformation, the personal "you" addressed by pop civilization that Mosquito has also identified. Yes, it's true that in Martens's projects the artist is present, but what an artist is and the function of art is key to his investigation, and his conclusions might well be cynical, but it is a cynicism born of anger, and that anger proceeds from one project to the next, honing its message and means, laying the artist bare, certainly, but so much else besides.

In the endless cycle of press, interviews, accusation, defense, and self-justification that followed the debut of *Episode III*, it was assailed for various reasons, most of which I've outlined already, and even among its defenders led to much soul-searching and interrogation. Martens himself could be variously sensitive and obnoxious; rarely more of the latter than when explaining the significance of *Episode II*, the unfinished film in this trilogy, which he describes as the middle of a triptych, the prime central panel on a medieval altarpiece. Apparently, the "outer panels" (Chechnya and the Congo) show "earthly narratives," and lead to the production and consumption of images that contribute to "confusion," rather than "truth or beauty." Whereas, with the as-yet-unrealized middle panel, Martens hopes to "somehow create a fountain that sprinkles its love and clarity over the two outer panels, and thus change them on a cellular level." This prospective third panel, then, will function as the theology that renders the outer panels palatable by way of a romantic love that spreads its fairy glitter on the other panels, revealing an "outside" that envelops them in its sense of wondrous possibility.

His project, as articulated, is of course a form of institutional critique, driving home the narcissism of the art world and the artist through the arrogance and audacity of his wishing to shape this material into the wings of a drama at the center of which is his own personal love story. Yet the realization of this Gesamtkunstwerk dedicated to demonstrating, whatever the cost, the essential narcissism of contemporary production and consumption seems to have been sidetracked by Martens's experiences in the Congo, and his journey with the film's reception. Life gets in the way.

Currently the artist has taken a rather monumental detour, departing on a five-year gentrification project on a plantation on the Congo River some eight hundred miles north of Kinshasa. He has spent the last few years establishing the Institute for Human Activities (IHA), building funding and corporate sponsorship for an exercise that strikes at the heart both of art's claims for its own criticality and broader questions to do with the dematerialization of labor and accumulation of capital. The IHA's newsletter, present in this publication (page 68), does a decent job of outlining its mission and raison d'etre, so I won't go into much detail here. Taking on art's claims for its own criticality, the IHA's activities take place on a former Unilever plantation, where workers were paid subsistance wages for the production of

63 Marina Abramović's *The Artist Is Present* was a performance accompanying her retrospective of the same title at the Museum of Modern Art, New York, from March 14 to May 31, 2010, which was curated by Klaus Biesenbach. The artist sat in the atrium of the museum for a celebrated durational performance in which members of the public would line up and one by one sit in a chair at a table across from the artist. There were many dramatic moments, none more so than when Abramović's early collaborator Ulay showed up and they had a transcendent moment with a large portion of the New York art world coincidentally in attendance. This was a highlight in the recent HBO documentary about the project. See a clip at EDW Lynch, "The Dramatic Reunion of Performance Artists Marina Abramović & Ulay," YouTube video, http://laughingsquid.com/the-dramatic-reunion-of-performance-artists-marina-abramovic-ulay/. In the HBO version, the moment they make eye contact a violin soundtrack starts and then they reach across the table.

palm oil that went into Unilever soap. This British-based multinational has been until recently the primary sponsor of the Tate Modern's Turbine Hall projects, which often feature artists renowned for their critical or conceptual edge, such as Ai Weiwei or Tino Sehgal. Martens has become interested in asking the simple question, "Why does critical art always perform itself at the site of art's critical reception rather than at the location that serves as the subject for its criticality?" Obviously the distribution and reception of *Episode III* is one such example, exhibited as it was in galleries in Europe for the most part. This reality is one for which Martens hopes to make amends, albeit with something of an edge.

The proliferation of art fairs and biennials throughout the globe has been attended by an invigorated understanding among city planners, politicians, sheiks, and mayors of the positive benefits that attend the arrival of cultural capital for the image of a city or state: attracting tourists, skilled workers, companies, and other forms of investment. This benefit has been well documented, most notably by the neoliberal urban theorist Richard Florida, author of the seminal book *The Rise of the Creative Class*.[64] In this publication, he extolls the virtues of cities, towns, and villages that attract a class composed of artists, designers, gay people, musicians, technology workers, etc. According to Florida, these people form the backbone of productive, appealing communities, helping to shape the places where other people, who actually make money, might want to live. This is because they encounter a proliferation of cool institutions; pleasantly kooky coffee shops; and nice creative atmospheres where happily civil-partnershipped and cuddly-looking gay-daddybears and delightfully tattooed graphic designers pass them cheerfully on the neighborhood crosswalk as they stroll the pedigreed pooch they picked up at the local, flower-muraled, lesbian-owned dog-rescue center. (Well, something like that.) On the slightly sinister side, it is the places that fail to make a comfortable environment for such "high bohemians" (as Florida terms them) that will become the wastelands of the future, populated by people who are just not *that* wealthy and just not *that* interesting.

In essence, what Florida advocates is essentially using the creative class as an advance guard for urban regeneration, aka gentrification. A negative value if you are your average discursive art-world denizen (critic, philosopher, artist, or what have you). And here is the perplexing thing: the success of a contemporary art fair or biennial is largely dependent on it being perceived as having a certain degree of critical chops; its hosting panels, conversations, and symposia by people who are critical of gentrification itself because it is a means by which poor people, artists, and others are driven from their communities, forced out by rent hikes, and other such indignities. Martens's idea, and the mission of the IHA, is to reverse this rather odd affair. Why not bring critical art to the site of its intervention, not its reception, and turn the possibilities of gentrification into a positive value: the creative classes coming as the vanguard of regeneration in the Congo? Why not indeed? To launch the IHA's activities, an opening seminar was held at the site last summer, and highly respected critics and philosophers were in attendance. While Florida could not make it, he did have a keynote conversation with Martens via Skype, he in his office, Martens sitting outside in the bracing humidity. To facilitate the conversation, the IHA cleared several trees and put a satellite dish with generator on top of a shed. The edited transcript is available in this publication. As an expert on these issues, Florida provides some real words of encouragement. While he knows it won't be easy, he really feels it best not to just complain, and to get things done with gusto.

64 Richard Florida, *The Rise of the Creative Class: And How It's Transforming Work, Leisure, Community and Everyday Life* (New York: Basic Books, 2002).

VIII. We Will Be Strong in Our Weakness

Yael Bartana (born 1970 in Israel; lives and works in Berlin)

In 2008 I was assisting on an exhibition in New York City that debuted at Parsons The New School for Design a few weeks before the presidential election. Titled *OURS: Democracy in the Age of Branding*, it featured a fairly global array of artists, many with activist leanings, and was an attempt to look at the political sphere from the point of view of the manufacturing and manipulation of desire.[65] One participant was Israeli artist Yael Bartana, with whom I helped organize a performance in Union Square on a sunny fall afternoon. The piece was based on her video *Wild Seeds* (2005),[66] in which a group of teenagers roll around on a hill overlooking a green scenic valley. They are playing some kind of rough and tumble game—it's difficult to determine the rules, but they are clumped tightly together, some screaming, some gripping each other while others try to pull them apart. It's a two-channel video; the second is a black screen with white subtitles that translate the Hebrew cries: "Desert the army, traitors," "A Jew does not deport another Jew," "Shift up a bit (girl grunts)." There's tenderness to the piece; despite the violence, the kids seem involved in a shared secret, an intimacy that transfers itself to the viewer. In a recent publication, the artist describes the origins of the work:

> [...] created by a group of young Israeli activists, some of them just before their IDF [Israeli Defense Forces] recruitment, others future objectors. I met the group through my niece, who is now nineteen. She was among the few young people who refused to be recruited by the Israeli army. The video was taken in the Occupied Territories, in the beautiful landscape of the Prat settlement, but the game may be played any place and at any time the group chooses. Named "Evacuation of Gilad's Colony," the game was the youngsters' response to the forced withdrawal of Jewish settlers from the Occupied Territories and the resultant violent confrontation between the soldiers and settlers at Gilad's Farms in 2002.[67]

If anyone remembers that confrontation, whatever your political position in relation to the Occupied Territories, the withdrawal from Gaza initiated by then prime minister Ariel Sharon was fairly unprecedented. Video footage showed rows of seated settlers with arms entwined challenging the IDF, who pulled them one by one from their ranks to cries of "traitor." The historical violence accompanying the vision of Jew against Jew was moderated (or perhaps accentuated) in a fascinating way by the obvious respect and tact with which the forces of the state went about their business. Here then were some kids, who in reenacting the whole affair were perhaps mocking it, puncturing the national mythology of unity of intentions and asking new questions about identification. But they were also duplicating by default the conditions of the event—the lines between oppressor and the oppressed became blurred; the ultimate sense being that of people locked within a structure, the rules for which have been ordained, which must play itself out whatever their personal feelings on the matter.

A constructed scenario then, found by the artist, was documented and translated into an artwork and then transferred to a performance on the concrete landing of an idyllic New York urban park, itself associated through the years with various activist movements. Titled *Wild Seeds in America*, the game commenced at Union Square, about fifteen of us clumped on some dusty blanket. We had been instructed to occasionally

---

65 The exhibition *OURS: Democracy in the Age of Branding* was hosted and organized by Parsons The New School for Design and curated by Carin Kuoni, director of the Vera List Center for Art and Politics. It launched the center's 2008–2009 program cycle titled *Branding Democracy*. Along with Jakob Schillinger, I served as a curatorial assistant for the exhibition. See also http://www.branding-democracy.org, accessed June 10, 2013.

66 Bartana's performance *Wild Seeds in America* (2008) took place in New York's Union Square on October 19, 2008. It was commissioned for the exhibition by Parsons The New School for Design.

67 Yael Bartana, *och Europa kommer att häpna = and Europe will be stunned*, Moderna Museet Malmö Utställningskatalog Series no. 357 (Malmö and Berlin: Moderna Museet Malmö and Revolver Publishing, 2010), 24.

68 In a conversation convened with Bartana and several others in *Frieze* art journal in 2004 to discuss the relationship between art and documentary, it emerged that they had little in common: some intervened within the fabric of reality to construct their scenarios, others such as Bartana *apparently* did not. Yet, when artist Anri Sala asked, "Why are we all around this table? Our practices are all very different," Bartana responded, "But we have one thing in common. We are not documentary filmmakers." What precisely the artist meant by that was not perhaps so clear at the time, though it certainly seems prophetic now. See Jörg Heiser and Jan Verwoert, "'What's the Difference?': Discussing the relationship between art and documentary filmmaking with artists Yael Bartana, Annika Eriksson, Anri Sala and Gitte Villesen," *Frieze* 84 (June–August 2004), accessed June 10, 2013, http://www. frieze.com/issue/article /whats_the_difference/.

69 Yael Bartana, "A Conversation Between Yael Bartana, Galit Eilat & Charles Esche," in *och Europa kommer att häpna = and Europe will be stunned*, 47.

throw out sentences such as "No, we won't move" or "You can't force us." I remember starting it fairly nonchalantly, surrounded by a gathering random audience, and thinking that I should be careful not to hit my head (the game was potentially lethal, by the way; I had helped secure the permit, so that was another concern). Two big guys began patiently pulling us out, looking for the weak link, starting on the edges, like friendly wolves.

About fifteen minutes in, it became obvious that this was not a game but an unfurling tragedy: each time someone left the group you could feel the gasp of the crowd, feel a heaviness and loss. The stakes became higher, the imperative to remain together stronger. As the wolves tired, a member of the crowd joined them, gleefully participating in the dismantling. At some point I was extracted, fingers ringing as they were unclasped from someone's leg. I stood with the crowd, watching as it came down to two women holding each other tightly. They were being pried apart when one of them screamed, "You're hurting me." The wolf unclasped her, and she quickly grabbed her comrade again, clamping in tight, laughing. But yeah, it was a pyrrhic victory.

Bartana had a solo exhibition opening at PS1 MoMA that day. Later, a number of us sat in the museum in Queens watching *Wild Seeds* (the real one) and understanding that there was something epic about these human relations. What, I wondered, had Bartana achieved by her decontextualization? The original piece involved an abstraction of a real event, but this transferral to Union Square was completely displaced from the original sociopolitical context. Why was the structure she set up so enervating? In earlier videos, Bartana made selective documentations of real world events, choosing often-ritualized aspects of Israeli society, and observing them. What perhaps was not so evident then, but what became more obvious from *Wild Seeds* on, is a key theme in the artist's work: an investigation and then intervention in the processes by which communities convene, subjects are formed, national mythologies maintained, gendered behaviors enforced.[68] All that good stuff that goes into the making of who we are or believe we are as people in distinct places at distinct times. With *Wild Seeds in America*, the artist had created a very simple social experiment; each participant in the event in the park naturally identified with their role, and despite the looseness of the ideological underpinnings of various positions, felt a desire to unify, to protect, to be part of and to defend a group.

Perhaps this interest in how groups form themselves is partly influenced by the fact that Bartana has spent much of the last decade outside of Israel, first in the Netherlands, then Poland, and now Berlin. In a recent conversation, she spoke of the condition of being an immigrant: "The writer Eva Hoffman said that every immigrant is an amateur anthropologist. You're always an outsider as an immigrant: you look at society in a different way. The same thing can partially happen when you step outside of your own nation and look back at it."[69] Bartana became increasingly interested in the inherent conflicts of Israeli society and identity, the Utopian promise of socialized collectivity and unity offered by the state's formation and Zionist rhetoric, together with the inherent blind spot: the problem of displacement that necessarily attended the formation and maintenance of a state formed around Jewish identity. Where initially these investigations were focused specifically on Israeli identity, they became abstracted to a more general interest in how individuals and groups are socialized.

Bartana has taken up this impulse to create scenarios that border on social engineering in subsequent works, but always with an eye toward creating a self-awareness in participants that mitigates any sense of pure (i.e., fascist) manipulation. Such works take on a feeling of reality through the artist's clever casting of real political and social figures and keen attention to, and reuse of, past documentary conventions. The most celebrated project within this body of work is *and Europe will be stunned* (2007–2011), which recently entered the Walker's collection. It is significant in and of itself that the work debuted in a dramatic installation at the 54th Venice Biennale, where the artist represented the Polish Pavilion, the first non-Pole to do so.

At the time of the project's conception, Bartana had spent time in Warsaw, and noted a nostalgia among the intelligentsia there for the Jewish culture absent since WWII

70 See Yael Bartana, *Mary Koszmary* (*Nightmares*), YouTube video, posted by "Yael Bartana" on March 5, 2012, http://www.youtube.com/watch ?v=S1ILSaTCbGI. See also plate 12 in this catalogue.

71 See Yael Bartana, *Zamach* (*Assassination*), YouTube video, posted by "Yael Bartana" on March 5, 2012, http://www.youtube.com/watch?v =LL8I0578pX0.

72 The speech, which lasts about five minutes, closes with the following state-ment: "Voices are heard today saying the Zionist Movement was conceived in sin, that it is outdated and has no future, that it is on its deathbed. The Holocaust, it has been said, indeed took place in Europe, but the reparations for it are at the expense of the Palestinians. Dear members of the movement, for all your good will, you fail to understand the sim-ple, incontestable fact that the state of Israel and its army are the only guarantee against another Holocaust. The Jewish Diaspora, Ladies and Gentlemen, ended in Auschwitz. May you rest in peace, dear innocent Pole."

and subsequent pogroms. The works document the rise of the Jewish Renaissance Movement in Poland (JRMiP), a real group founded by the artist, but with a fictional history that the videos relate. In *Mary Koszmary* (*Nightmares*) (2007), a charismatic young man played by Polish activist Sławomir Sierakowski, founder and chief editor of *Krytyka Polityczna* magazine and a co-author of the speech, stands in the empty and overgrown Olympic Stadium in Warsaw, surrounded by a handful of children dressed up as scouts (or proto-Fascists, depending on your point of view). Standing on a small dais, with a 1940s-style microphone, white shirt, red tie, and a leather coat cast about his shoulders, the speaker makes an impassioned speech that echoes around the stadium. He calls out to "Jews" and declares that Poland is haunted by their absence. He describes an old woman who wakes at night experiencing nightmares provoked by the repressed memory of how the Polish people betrayed their Jewish neighbors. He declaims, "Let the three million Jews that Poland has missed stand by her bed and finally chase away the demons. Return to Poland. To your country....This is a call, not to the dead, but to the living." Meanwhile the children use stencils to spell out large chalk letters on the grass, and the camera pulls back to give a sweeping view: "3,300, 000 Jews can change the life of 40, 000, 000 Poles."[70] The speech is a cry for diversity, a statement that challenges both the Polish history of anti-Semitism and its current ris-ing tide of nationalism and raises provocative questions about two key and at times competing visions of Jewish identity: the diasporic versus the Zionist. The aesthetics of the film borrow from Leni Riefenstahl's legendary Nazi propaganda documentaries of the Nuremberg Rallies, such as *Triumph of the Will* (1935), full of pulsing crowds, im-passioned Aryan youth, and rhetorically savvy Nazis. Yet, rather than duplicate Hitler's anti-Semitism, the speaker embraces the Jews as crucial to a healthy Polish culture. And rather than address a throng of supporters, here the man receives the attention of a few children. The film ends with the leader and the children marching a motley and disorganized crew around the stadium.

In the second film, *Mur i wieża* (*Wall and Tower*) (2009), the JRMiP has become an emerg-ing force within Polish society. Inspired by the words of its founder, a group of Jewish immigrants labor to build a kibbutz in downtown Warsaw on the site of the former Jewish ghetto. The film is highly idealized, featuring visual stylizations (close-ups of workers staring optimistically into the distance) and an upbeat soundtrack borrowed from Zionist propaganda films of the 1930s. The effect is of a people determined to build a new life, steadfast in their faith in the possibilities of the future. The enthusiastic laborers design a flag that combines the Star of David with the Polish eagle; they learn Polish, and seemingly embrace their new life. Yet all is not quite as it seems; the kibbutz is surrounded by barbed wire, and it becomes a symbol of communitarian liberty, while also conjuring concentration camps (keeping people in) or defense (keeping people out). At the film's close, elderly Polish citizens stare at the kibbutz warily. Perhaps they are not as ready for the return as one might hope: there are ghosts, after all.

With the final film, *Zamach* (*Assassination*) (2011), the movement reaches full maturity and self-awareness. The leader has been assassinated and the film features his fu-neral and memorial. Here the JRMiP has reached out beyond its Jewish beginnings and mushroomed into a diverse, multicultural, and hopeful community. They demand that identification move beyond ethnic, nationalist, and other forces, making the val-ues of displacement, otherness, and independence the key rules for a revised notion of citizenship. Walking through Warsaw in a mourning parade, they dress in uniforms reminiscent of Fascism, yet the group is too diverse and too individualized to be identified with that movement. Young and old, people with tattoos, nose rings, and yes, even blond hair and blue eyes convene to mourn the loss of their leader. But for the uniforms, it could be a march by Occupy Wall Street; there is a distinct queering of the properties of Fascism, and an almost flatfooted optimism in the possibilities for change. This army of individuals is unified around the manifesto of the JRMiP, which seeks to "revivify the early Zionist Phantasmagoria" by creating a new home in Poland. It insists, "We direct our appeal not only to Jews. We accept into our ranks all those for whom there is no place in their homelands—the expelled and the persecuted. There will be no discrimination in our movement. We shall not ask about your life stories, check your residence cards, or question your refugee status. We shall be strong in our weakness."[71]

The formation of the JRMiP becomes allegorical for the formation of a state, attendant with many of the same foundational myths (a call to arms around a specific goal, an early enthusiasm tempered by tragedy and martyrdom, a new unity born from maturity and suffering), yet Bartana injects a strong sense of pragmatism into the work that militates against the utopian rhetoric. Or, to put it another way, she makes clear her own acknowledgment of the proposal's utopianism, offering space for voices that reject it on its merits. The artist invites three speakers to address the crowd, and gives them carte blanche to make of the JRMiP's proposals what they will. Two are Israeli nationals who temper the JRMiP's utopian call with the historical weight of the Holocaust. Alona Frankel, an Israeli writer and illustrator of some note, relates her biography as a Jewish Pole who departed in 1949 during a renewed spate of anti-Semitism. She eloquently demands the return of her Polish citizenship that was violently stolen from her, while making clear she has zero desire to return (plate 30). Frankel is followed by Israeli journalist Yaron London, who steadfastly mocks the idea of a Jewish return to Europe, calling it a "brainless task." He continues, "For us, the Jews, this isn't a hopeful promise, it is a nightmare." He celebrates the strength of the Israeli army, declares that the Jew will never be defenseless again, and mocks the naiveté of the JRMiP. He concludes, "The Jewish diaspora, ladies and gentlemen, ended in Auschwitz."[72]

His speech is compelling, and one can certainly see his point, yet as he talks a woman emerges from the crowd, suitcase in hand, and approaches the stage, standing below him, looking steadfastly into the camera. She is the Polish Rivka, a fictional character that has haunted the films through their three iterations; she is the "ghost of return" that refuses to go away, the embodiment of the Holocaust but also a spirit of renewal. Trapped in the loop of history, she says in an earlier monologue, "I am here to weave the torture of identity from the threads of forgetfulness." In the context of Bartana's film, Rivka is the enigmatic ghost who reaches beyond language, who bypasses the rational rhetoric of London. She might represent equally the right of return of the Palestinians, of the Jews, of citizenship, of memory, of a certain kind of hope or justice. Perhaps it is with Rivka that we find Roelstraete's theology? I hope so. Whatever the case, Bartana has woven from the tortured strands of identity a trilogy that ultimately opposes itself to nationalist posturing, that seeks to suture *and* expose the wounds of history, that takes language out of the mouths of the eloquent and passes it into a cavernous realm of complexity and possibility.

Epilogue

In putting together this exhibition, I started with a title and a number of artists whose work I was interested in, and whose approach to art in general I felt was challenging and provocative within the field and more broadly. One of the methodologies has been to present these different approaches in proximity and then see what emerges. Throughout the essay, I rarely make pronouncements about the artists as a group, but I am prepared to do that a little now. When I write of complicity, I understand that I am in a sense talking about power, and how artists relate themselves to it. There is a politics to acknowledging that one is positioned in a world of implication, and this acknowledgment can produce surprising intimacies and routes to understanding.

When Yael Bartana folds into her project the proud voice of a man whose defense of Israeli militarism and exceptionalism is manifestly opposed to the positions she has developed in her work, she is creating a kind of threshold. We can listen to him, and understand his positions; even as he has taken a step into her structure, one has a sense of possibility. Some years ago, at an opening in LA, Danh Vo was approached by an old white American man who invited him to visit his home. Vo gladly did so. There he found a trove of materials from the man's time working for the Rand Corporation in Vietnam in the late 1960s, including many voyeuristic and eroticized photographs of young Vietnamese men. I think there is something significant about this moment in time, where rather than decry the colonial and sexual politics of the man, Vo befriended him. He exhibited the photographs almost as if they were portraits of the youth in Vietnam that he never actually had. He became the subject of this erotic gaze, and also *duplicated* it, creating a call and response with the author and the subjects of the images, one that acknowledged the implicit power dynamics but also sidestepped the dead-end binaries that attended them.[73]

I am often surprised within the art world—which is, after all, such an open space—by the degree to which people simplify complex ideas based on ideological assumptions that they do not question. I don't want to relitigate battles that have been fought over the past thirty to forty years in art, but I do think it significant that there is such a resurgence of interest in art from the 1980s and 1990s in the United States, particularly work associated with identity politics. There was a sense toward the end of that period, which many people associate with the aftermath of the 1993 Whitney Biennial, that people got tired of the subject position battles. There was a backlash as artists, critics, and institutions grew weary of defending their privilege and more or less decided that the whole identity politics thing was over.[74]

Attendant with that has been a simplification of the art of the time, as if somehow it was lacking in formal or material complexity, and was merely artists stating self-essentializing positions as a way to make space for marginalized positions within an art world that had hitherto excluded them. And yet, of course, much of the art of that era continues to inform and enrich the present. While I am not suggesting that the artists in this exhibition represent Identity Politics 2.0 (as if identity politics ever ended, for that matter; it is everywhere, all the time, de facto, and we are all participants), they do represent artists who are unafraid to engage the world in broad and ambitious ways, and who deploy their identity, or at least a conscious acknowledgment of its existence, within the work. What feels different to me is that they all reconsider notions of loyalty to a group away from identification based on class, race, ethnicity, gender, and sexuality and toward some less codified organization of alliances. This happens most overtly in Bartana's JRMiP that welcomes, in effect, anyone who in theorist Julia Kristeva's famous formulation feels like "strangers to ourselves." But it's also there in Steyerl, who pits the organized oasis of the gated community, with its silhouettes aimlessly enjoying a purgatory of leisure time, against the dancing pixels of the wide-open desert who disarm US helicopters and fly away with drones. It's there with Haghighian, who uses a productive animism to commune with the object of the graph, decoupling it from its utilitarian function in the service of the narrow profit-based metrics of ArtFacts, and setting up a subjective model for engagement with the world through selective and strategic over-identifications with the object of one's oppression. Mosquito's "army of the individuals" is about a shifting contextual range of allegiances, a receptivity and openness to alliance, and—dare I say it—a relativistic embrace of community formed around elusive but contagious moments of participation and intimacy. Even Melgaard's gay separatist terrorist group is less about a trenchant ideological position than it is about presenting, through excess, the redundancy of mainstream notions of intimacy, collectivity, and behavior. When Liam Gillick asks the visitor to his exhibition at Venice, "How are you going to behave?" it's as if he is throwing down the gauntlet, saying, "It's not about me, it's about you ... if you are willing." He has in that moment, to my mind at least, laid himself bare, and what you make of it

73 The photographs by anthropologist Joseph M. Carrier were first exhibited in Vo's exhibition *Good Life* at Isabella Bortolozzi Galerie, Berlin, in 2007. They were accompanied by other items from Carrier's archive, including a letter, a business card, and a camera (see plate 15 in this catalogue). The photographs and camera were displayed in elegant spot-lit vitrines surrounded by gold flock wallpaper. The press release accompanying the exhibition was written by Carrier and told how he had come to meet Vo in LA: "I immediately felt attracted to him and knew that I wanted to have some kind of close relationship." And indeed, Vo and Carrier developed a friendship in subsequent years. See Kirsty Bell, "Danh Vo," *Frieze Journal* (September 2007), accessed August 1, 2013, http://www.frieze.com/issue/review/danh_vo/.

74 In recent years, there has been a resurgence of interest in the historical context of identity politics, as executive director Olga Viso points out in the Afterword. See page 208.

is partially dependent on your capacity for empathy or generosity. The you that he addresses personalizes the interaction, turns the visitor from an identification with a group—here possibly the art world cognoscenti drifting in an opinion-fueled haze from one pavilion to another—to an engagement with their own individual subjectivity and agency. Gillick's question could be echoed by Mosquito's "What are you going to do with your education, become part of a structure or build a structure?"

An acknowledgment of one's complicity and ability to display a self-awareness in relation to the structures one navigates, of course, is not in itself a panacea for forging an optimistic path into the future. But it also can't be ignored as a position. It certainly proceeds with a greater integrity and sense of possibility than work that assumes that language and culture and the artist, for that matter, are transparent carriers of meaning—imagine, for example, an exhibition that is titled *9 Artists* because there are nine artists in it. I like to think that everything is more complicated and then simpler than it initially appears. From the point of view of subjectivity and representation, we are entering an age of ever-increasing surveillance—with chilling effects on individual expression and the nurturing of difference, but also of access to multiple competing and elucidatory sources of information. It's a moment of opportunity, of increasingly distributed and enigmatically enacted democratic impulses. It feels like a pivot point in global history, where everything is both possible and impossible.

Entries are listed in order of appearance on pages 132–163.

Exhibition Checklist

The works listed represent the working checklist for the Walker Art Center presentation of the exhibition; the checklist may vary with each tour venue. Dimensions are listed height × length × width.

Yael Bartana

and Europe will be stunned 2007–2011
three-channel video and sound installation;
edition 3/3 + 2 AP
61 minutes
Collection Walker Art Center, Minneapolis
T. B. Walker Acquisition Fund, 2013

and Europe will be stunned 2010
neon
49 3/16 × 43 5/16 in. (125 × 110 cm); edition 1 AP
Collection Judy and Ken Robins, Denver

Manifesto of the Jewish Renaissance Movement in Poland 2010
offset print
39 3/8 × 27 9/16 in. (100 × 70 cm)
Courtesy of Annet Gelink Gallery, Amsterdam, and Sommer Contemporary Art, Tel Aviv

Liam Gillick

Del Charro 1994
lightbulbs, writing paper, pencils, fruit, bottle of Jim Beam, bottle of Ballentine's Whiskey, tape, card box, printed text, storage boxes
dimensions variable
Courtesy the artist and Casey Kaplan, New York; Private Collection, Italy

(The What If? Scenario) Communication Area 1996
rug, earth device, glitter
dimensions variable
Courtesy the artist; Casey Kaplan, New York; and Maureen Paley, London

David (He doesn't turn to see her) 1999
big glass, Bloody Mary
dimensions variable
Collection Andy and Karen Stillpass, Cincinnati

The State / Commune Itself as a State / Commune 2006
vinyl on wall
dimensions variable
Courtesy the artist and Galerie Micheline Szwajcer, Antwerp, Belgium

The State Itself Becomes a Super Commune 2006
vinyl on wall
dimensions variable
Courtesy the artist; Alistair Cookson; and Esther Schipper, Berlin

The Commune Itself Becomes a Super State 2007
vinyl on wall
dimensions variable
Courtesy the artist and Maureen Paley, London

The State Itself Becomes a Super Whatnot 2008
vinyl on wall
dimensions variable
Collection The Museum of Modern Art, New York
Scott Burton Fund, 2008

The Whatnot Itself Becomes a Super State 2008
vinyl on wall
dimensions variable
Courtesy the artist and Casey Kaplan, New York

Natascha Sadr Haghighian

present but not yet active 2002
video; edition of 3 + 2 AP
12 minutes
Courtesy the artist and Johann König Gallery, Berlin

I can't work like this 2007
wall installation, nails, two hammers; edition of 3 + 2 AP
86 5/8 × 177 3/16 in. (220 × 450 cm)
Courtesy the artist and Johann König Gallery, Berlin

de paso 2011
multimedia installation, carry-on suitcase, plastic bottle, microphone, loudspeakers, computer, various documents
dimensions variable
Courtesy the artist and Johann König Gallery, Berlin

performer/audience/file 2013
Performance at the Walker Art Center, Minneapolis, on October 26, 2013
Elements of the performance include: sketchbook, paper, marker pen, cyclone vacuum cleaner, smartphones in the audience, and headphone singing by the artist
dimensions variable
Courtesy the artist

Renzo Martens/Institute for Human Activities

On Gentrification 2013
Installation featuring lecture on the Institute for Human Activities delivered at the Walker Art Center, Minneapolis, October 17, 2013
vinyl, photographs
dimensions variable
Courtesy the Institute for Human Activities

Bjarne Melgaard

Untitled (Bjarne Melgaard Interviews Leo Bersani) 2011
digital video; edition of 6
98:19 minutes
Produced by Bjarne Melgaard, directed by Sebastian Mlynarski
Courtesy the artist and Gavin Brown's enterprise, New York

Untitled 2012
colored pencil on paper
17 ¾ × 14 in. (45.1 × 35.6 cm)
Courtesy the artist and Gavin Brown's
enterprise, New York

Untitled 2012
colored pencil on paper
14 ¾ × 11 in. (37.5 × 27.9 cm)
Courtesy the artist and Gavin Brown's
enterprise, New York

Untitled (Britt Ekland) 2012
colored pencil on paper
11 × 14 ¾ in. (27.9 × 37.5 cm)
Courtesy the artist and Gavin Brown's
enterprise, New York

Untitled (Britt Ekland and Peter Sellers) 2012
colored pencil on paper
14 ¾ × 11 in. (37.5 × 27.9 cm)
Courtesy the artist and Gavin Brown's
enterprise, New York

Untitled (Dear Britt) 2012
colored pencil on paper
14 ¾ × 11 in. (37.5 × 27.9 cm)
Courtesy the artist and Gavin Brown's
enterprise, New York

Untitled (Good Bye) 2012
colored pencil on paper
14 ¾ × 11 in. (37.5 × 27.9 cm)
Courtesy the artist and Gavin Brown's
enterprise, New York

Untitled (I am nobody's fucking sugardaddy anymore) 2012
colored pencil on paper
14 ¾ × 11 in. (37.5 × 27.9 cm)
Courtesy the artist and Gavin Brown's
enterprise, New York

Untitled (My self respect) 2012
colored pencil on paper
14 ¾ × 11 in. (37.5 × 27.9 cm)
Courtesy the artist and Gavin Brown's
enterprise, New York

Untitled (Pink Panther Making Britt Ekland) 2012
colored pencil on paper
17 ¾ × 14 in. (45.1 × 35.6 cm)
Courtesy the artist and Gavin Brown's
enterprise, New York

Untitled (Pink Panther with Bleeding Heart) 2012
colored pencil on paper
17 ¾ × 14 in. (45.1 × 35.6 cm)
Courtesy the artist and Gavin Brown's
enterprise, New York

Untitled (Prima Donna) 2012
colored pencil on paper
14 ¾ × 11 in. (37.5 × 27.9 cm)
Courtesy the artist and Gavin Brown's
enterprise, New York

Untitled (Study for Depressed Pink Panther) 2012
colored pencil on paper
17 ¾ × 14 in. (45.1 × 35.6 cm)
Courtesy the artist and Gavin Brown's
enterprise, New York

The awakening and consumption of Heidi Fleiss as she talks to a brioche named Austin 2013
archival pigment prints on aluminum
8 ½ × 12 ¾ in. (21.6 × 32.4 cm) each of 212
Photography by Johannes Worsøe Berg
Courtesy the artist and Gavin Brown's
enterprise, New York

Bjarne Melgaard and Marie Karlberg

untitled 2013
video
Courtesy the artists

Nástio Mosquito

Nástia's Manifesto 2008
video (color, sound)
4:10 minutes
A collaboration with Vic Pereiró
Courtesy DZZZZ ArtWork

Nástia Answers Gabi 2010
video (color, sound)
19:44 minutes
Courtesy DZZZZ ArtWork

Nástia Answers Ryan 2013
video (color, sound)
A collaboration with Vic Pereiró
Courtesy DZZZZ ArtWork

Hito Steyerl

Red Alert 2007
digital video (color, silent), flat screen monitors,
Mac Minis; edition 3/3 + 2 AP
30 seconds each of three, looped
Collection Walker Art Center, Minneapolis
T. B. Walker Acquisition Fund, 2012

How Not to Be Seen. A Fucking Didactic Educational .Mov File 2013
HD video file, single screen; edition 2/10 + 2 AP
14 minutes
Commissioned by the 55th Venice Biennale,
2013
Courtesy the artist and Wilfried Lentz,
Rotterdam

Danh Vo

Selections from *All your deeds shall in water be writ, but this in marble* 2009–
Collection Walker Art Center, Minneapolis
T. B. Walker Acquisition Fund, 2011

2.2.1861 2009–
ink on paper
Last letter of Saint Théophane Vénard
to his father before he was decapitated,
copied by Phùng Vo. Title and number of
existing copies remains undefined until
the death of Phùng Vo. Each handwritten
text will arrive in an envelope and be
post-mailed by Phùng Vo directly to the
buyer, whose address as recipient will be
archived by Phùng Vo.
11 ⅝ × 8 ¼ in. (29.5 × 21 cm)

All your deeds shall in water be writ, but this in marble 2010–
empty glass vitrine
On the death of Danh Vo's father, Phùng
Vo, property left in his will and testament:
a Rolex watch, Dupont lighter, American
military class ring, and golden crucifix with
necklace, will be displayed in the vitrine.
26 ¾ × 20 1/16 × 20 ⅞ in. (67.9 × 51 × 53 cm)

Tombstone for Phùng Vo 2010–
black absolute granite, gold
23 ⅝ × 35 ⅜ × 3 ⅛ in. (60 × 89.9 × 7.9 cm)

Untitled 2010–
offset lithograph on paper, sewn binding
8 × 6 ½ in. (20.3 × 16.5 cm)

Untitled 2010–
engraved brass, paint
15 ¾ × 11 ⅞ × ⅛ in. (40 × 30.2 × .3 cm)

Will (Phùng Vo) 2011
ink on paper
11 ⅝ × 8 ¼ in. (29.5 × 21 cm)
Courtesy the artist

I M U U R 2 2013
Installation featuring more than 4,000
artifacts from the Martin Wong Collection,
as well as paintings and drawings by Martin
Wong and a sculpture by Danh Vo
dimensions variable
Courtesy the artist; Galerie Buchholz, Berlin/
Cologne; and Marian Goodman Gallery,
New York

Acknowledgments

9 Artists has been in genesis over a number of years, and during that time the artists in the exhibition have been generous, receptive, and engaged. I thank them variously for their commitment, and can only say that it is an immense privilege for me to be able to work with people who understand that there are stakes in the world, and who approach every day with that in mind.

I owe much to Minneapolis, my home of the past four years. It's a place that has room for many approaches to art, where healthy dialogue exists, and where people are invested in what you are trying to do, will engage it, and will demand much of it. I'd also like to thank the Walker for its support of this project. The Walker is an art center, not a museum, and perhaps that accounts for the odd freedom that one can feel here. Born out of a Depression-era, New Deal–supported alliance between the Walker family and the public, the Walker from its inception has been staffed by artists and approached the art of its time with an openness that has survived as a culture in the institution's DNA. I'd like to thank my colleagues past and present, my friends, and the broader Twin Cities community for creating an environment in which one must work with ambition, and a legacy with which one must contend.

I am particularly grateful for the major funding *9 Artists* received from the Andy Warhol Foundation for the Visual Arts. I want to express my deepest gratitude to the foundation's board of directors and president Joel Wachs for their generous support of this project, which follows a long history of ambitious Walker exhibitions supported by the Warhol Foundation. I especially want to thank the foundation's program director Rachel Bers and senior program officer James Bewley for taking the time to meet with me in person about this project. I am also truly grateful to several Walker trustees who provided significant support for *9 Artists*, including Pat Denzer and his wife, Lisa, and Audrey Wilf and her husband, Zygi. I also want to acknowledge the Andrew W. Mellon Foundation for helping to underwrite the exhibition's catalogue through a grant in support of Walker Art Center publications.

I am delighted that this exhibition will be traveling to MIT List Visual Arts Center for the summer of 2013, and would like to thank director Paul Ha for his support of this project and assistant curator Alise Upitis for her collaboration and for steering the exhibition there.

Thanks also to the lenders to the exhibition, the galleries, and other individuals associated with the artists who provided immense logistical and/or creative support:

For Yael Bartana: Judy and Ken Robbins, Denver; at Annet Gelink Gallery in Amsterdam, Annet Gelink, Floor Wullems, and Macarena Dupouy; Sommer Contemporary Art, Tel Aviv; Foksal Gallery Foundation, Warsaw; Hermès; and at Bartana Studio, Saskia Wendland.

For Liam Gillick: Karen and Andy Stillpass, Cincinnati; at Casey Kaplan Gallery in New York, Casey Kaplan and Loring Randolph; Museum of Modern Art, New York; Cori Morva and Maureen Paley, London; Esther Schipper, Berlin; and Alistair Cookson.

For Natascha Sadr Haghighian: Galerie Johann König, Berlin; Carroll/Fletcher, London; Lofoten International Art Festival (LIAF); and Bassam el Baroni.

For Renzo Martens: The boards of the Institute for Human Activities, and all participants in the IHA's opening seminar, the outreach program, and the residency program; Wilkinson Gallery, London.

For Bjarne Melgaard: Timothy Hartley Smith, Artist Resources Management; at Gavin Brown's enterprise, Gavin Brown and Eleonore Hugendubel; Marie Karlberg.

For Nástio Mosquito: Vic Pereiró; Alice da Cruz; and DZZZZ Enterprises.

For Hito Steyerl: Wilfried Lentz Gallery, Rotterdam; at Steyerl's studio, Alwin Franke and of course, Esme Steyerl.

For Danh Vo: At Isabella Bortolozzi Galerie, Isabella Bortolozzi and Marta Lusena; at Galerie Buchholz Berlin and Cologne, Daniel Buchholz, Christopher Müller, Filippo Weck, and Katharina Forero; at Marian Goodman Gallery in New York, Marian Goodman and Rose Lord; at Vo Studio, Amy Zion and Stefan Pederson; Peter Broda; and Jamie Stewart.

The works appearing in the exhibition came to us with the help of many collaborators and institutions that have supported their production and existence in the world. Though there are too many to mention here, I would like to offer my profound thanks to the Solomon R. Guggenheim museum for doing so much work to realize the initial installation of Danh Vo's *I M U U R 2* for their Hugo Boss Prize 2012 exhibition of the same. Most particularly, I would like to thank Guggenheim associate curator Katherine Brinson for her fantastic work on that project, and for her encouragement and facilitation of its coming to the Walker. As befits the transition, the installation here will be different, but would be totally impossible without that previous engagement and also the work of Guggenheim registrar Maggie Honold and the entire team there. I am also grateful with regard to this project to Julie Ault, Amy Zion, Heinz Peter Knes, Florence Wong, Martin Wong, Peter Broda, Daniel Buchholz, and Christopher Müller.

Meanwhile, Yael Bartana's *and Europe will be stunned*, which recently came into the Walker's collection, was the result of an army of collaborators who joined Bartana in its initial realization for the Polish Pavilion in the 54th Venice Biennale in 2011. I'd like to thank especially James Lingwood and Artangel; Charles Esche and the Van Abbemuseum, Eindhoven; Galit Eilat; Annet Gelink and Floor Wullems of Annet Gelink Gallery; and also Slawomir Sierakowski. Other works that have recently entered the Walker's collection are Hito Steyerl's *Red Alert*, for which my thanks go to gallerist Wilfried Lentz for his passion and patience; and Danh Vo's *Tombstone for Phùng Vo*, a complex acquisition for which I thank especially Marta Lusena of Isabella Bortolozzi Gallery, together with Mary Polta and Joe King at the Walker and Hazen F. Graves of Faegre Baker Daniels law firm. Artist Marie Karlberg is making a new video with Bjarne Melgaard as this publication goes to print; I'm delighted she is on board.

While it is common practice to invite several distinguished thinkers to elaborate on an exhibition's themes in a catalogue, I felt that the artists in the show were this publication's best resource and their own best mediators, and I am immensely grateful to the many collaborators who joined them in developing their contributions. I'd like to acknowledge Eindhoven-based Israeli curator Galit Eilat for her ghost-written letters between Yael Bartana and the notorious philosopher Otto Weininger; writer Federica Bueti for her story about the subcontractor and the cat that forms an elusive counterpoint to our reprint of Liam Gillick's important "Berlin Statement"; Alex Scrimgeour for working with Renzo Martens to develop the Institute for Human Activities text, and the various participants whose transcripts from the IHA seminar are reprinted in that section (T. J. Demos among them, whose writing on a number of these artists has been influential to me). This contribution went to press as the IHA was experiencing some surprise developments that are not reflected in the text. I'd also like to thank Brendan Dugan of An Art Service for his design of the Melgaard section of this catalogue (one of many collaborations between them, all memorable). The images in the section that conjure a kind of cinematic travelogue of Melgaard's movements in the world were all taken by Norwegian photographer Johannes Worsøe Berg, and I thank him for allowing us to use them.

Vic Pereiró's design for the Nástio Mosquito contribution is something that could only be born out of two people whose distinct visual language has developed symbiotically. Danh Vo's section at one stage was going to be in the calligraphic style of deceased Lower East Side painter Martin Wong. Vo's father, Phùng, who did the calligraphy, chose a different script, but we kept Wong's name because it felt right to do so, as he is certainly an influence in the piece. I'd like to thank Phùng Vo for his work on the text. We have never met but I feel we are inevitably tied for the rest of our days. Vo's assistants, Amy Zion and Stefan Pederson, were also valued collaborators in this contribution. I'd like to thank gifted artist Karl Holmquist for allowing us to reprint and play with the formatting of his *Curriculum Vitae* text, and also Vo's nephew, Gustav, who is represented in that section.

At the Walker, the realization of this exhibition would have been impossible without the strong support of Walker executive director Olga Viso and Walker chief curator Darsie Alexander. I am very grateful to both for their support of me during my time here, and for encouraging me to be ambitious and providing an environment in which that is possible. The exhibition also benefited from the strong financial guidance of chief financial officer Mary Polta and her colleagues in the accounting department. Likewise, the development team led by Christopher Stevens brought acuity and dedication to fund-raising while never forgetting the Walker's mission, and I am immensely grateful to him and his talented staff. I'd like to particularly thank Marla Stack, who brings clarity and intelligence to complex grant proposals, and Dan Riehle-Merrill and Rosemary Price. I also extend my thanks to former chief of operations and administration Philip Bahar, and Walker deputy director and chief operating officer David Galligan for various contributions along the way.

I am grateful to my visual arts colleagues, past and present, who have approached their responsibilities with a creativity and diligence that I can only hope to emulate. These include senior curator Clara Kim, an influential colleague who brings a perspective that I have valued enormously in this process, as well as Siri Engberg and Eric Crosby. Former colleagues of note include Doryun Chong, Peter Eleey, Elizabeth Carpenter, Andria Hickey, and Dan Byers.

The organization of this exhibition would not have been possible without the attention to rights and reproductions of former curatorial fellow Yesomi Umolu, and the skillful work of current curatorial fellow Mia Lopez on this catalogue and the installation, mediation, and programming of this show. Lopez jumped on board at a late but crucial stage in this process, and I am very grateful to her for taking things in her stride.

Walker designer Andrea Hyde has done an outstanding job conceptualizing and shaping the book. I am very grateful for her commitment to making it work and her desire to make something special. Her cover concept was a complete surprise, but I think quite brilliant, and she and I have partnered to create a compendium of works section that is more of an associative sampling of the various practices than a plate section that illustrates works in the exhibition. Design director Emmet Byrne has been a conscientious presence throughout, and chief of communications Andrew Blauvelt has had his usual quiet influence on all things design-related. I'd like to thank them for their commitment to quality and creativity and also thank design studio coordinator Dylan Cole for keeping things on track through this complicated book's many twists and turns. I have been through many adventures with Walker editors Pamela Johnson and Kathleen McLean: they approach everything with a desire to make it succeed, and it's a privilege to work with them. I thank them for their keen attention to detail as well as their ability to ask and help answer questions about content and approach. Senior imaging specialist Greg Beckel, meanwhile, has used his magic to ensure the organization and quality of the numerous images in this publication; it's always a pleasure to encounter his specific form of diligence.

An exhibition like this brings myriad details in relation to contracts, opening, programs, touring, and so on. Exhibitions administrator Laurel Jensen has been a wonderful colleague throughout this process, and I thank her for her patience and good humor. I also appreciate the many contributions of departmental assistant Aimie Dukes. Cunningham fellow Abi Sebaly brings such a professional and committed approach to her work within the department that this project must have benefited through osmosis. Thanks to former visual arts intern Lydia O'Callaghan for collecting a voluminous archive on the artists and organizing it for me early in the process, which was an invaluable aid in the composition of my essay. Thanks also to current visual arts intern Vanessa Reubendale for helping with research to accompany the installation of Natascha Sadr Haghighian's work *de paso* and visual arts intern Alexandra Lovaas for many moments of assistance. University of Minnesota art history postgraduate student Lauren DeLand read through my research and offered notes on all of the artists in the exhibition. I wanted someone who would bring their own fresh analyses and response to the content, and that's what I got.

Many other people at the Walker contributed to this show's mediation, programming, and marketing. Director of education and community programs Sarah Schultz and her staff helped create myriad engagements for the Walker's diverse audiences. I am particularly grateful to colleague and friend Ashley Duffalo for her collaboration in developing and executing the programs accompanying this exhibition. I also thank Courtney Gerber and all of the tour guides for making the show accessible to people. I need to acknowledge outside program partners John Rasmussen and Megan McCready of Midway Contemporary Art; Christina Schmidt and Andrea Stanislav and the visiting artists' committee in the Fine Arts Department of the University of Minnesota; and Roderic Southall and Obsidian Arts for their collaboration.

Philip Bither, Doug Benidt, and their colleagues in the performing arts department have been valued partners in developing the Nástio Mosquito performance for the exhibition's opening weekend. Robin Dowden and other colleagues in the new media department as well as web editor Paul Schmelzer have ensured a strong online presence for this exhibition, and I also thank photographer Gene Pittman and videographer Andy Underwood-Bultmann for their many and continuing contributions. Ryan French, Meredith Kessler, Adrienne Weisman, Amy Fox, and Andrea Brown of the marketing and public relations department ensured the broad reach of the exhibition, and graciously made the best of an exhibition title that no marketing department could love.

Head registrar Joe King brings a fantastic flow to his department, which I know intimately, as my office is positioned in their midst. I am enormously grateful to exhibition registrar Pamela Caserta; this is the third show we have worked on together, and she brings great professionalism to all decisions around the show. Registration technicians David Bartley and Evan Reiter bring a spirit of camaraderie and effectiveness to the process. I am grateful to Cameron Zebrun, head of program services, for his great good humor and organizational diligence, and to lead technician Doc Czypinksi, who has somehow managed to realize this dizzyingly complicated exhibition exactly as I would wish.

I thank Peter Murphy and Jeffrey Sherman for accomplishing the myriad technical requirements of the media menagerie. Any installation at the Walker is a collaboration with those mentioned above, but also with crew members David Dick, Kirk McCall, and Scott Lewis, who bring many years of experience, the odd helpful raised eyebrow, and a commitment to quality that raises the bar on any installation here. They are joined by the Walker's talented temps, always attentive contributors to the installation process. Todd Gregory, John Lindell, and the Walker's dedicated gallery monitors ensured the well-being of the installation while also being open and receptive to Walker visitors.

To conclude these acknowledgments, which are exceeded in their long-windedness only by my gratitude, I would like to thank a number of people who have helped me along the way. They include Adam Pendleton, who taught me how to look; Tirdad Zolghadr, Maria Lind, Michael Brenson, Letitia Smith, Katerina Llanes, and Tom Eccles, all of whom contributed variously to my postgraduate education at CCS Bard; Gabi Ngcobo for introducing me to Nástio Mosquito's work some years ago; Aron Lorber for his intelligence; and variously Howard McCabe, Lawrence Alton, Mauricio Bustamante, Anna McMullan, and Brian Singleton for their educational chops. I would also like to thank my many friends in Minneapolis and elsewhere.

Finally, I come from a large and supportive family and community in Ireland, and I must acknowledge this immense privilege. I love and am grateful to all of them, but my biggest personal thank you goes to my parents for their warmth as people and their love and support: Nora Murphy Ryan and Phil Ryan.

There is no question that contemporary art—and society—is witnessing a period of unprecedented change and disruption as makers, presenters, and consumers respond to a world propelled by the trade, currency, and exchange of information. I am not alone in believing that art museums and other institutions must necessarily adapt to meet the challenges that come in the wake of such developments. How do we respond to the ever-increasing communication capabilities, the horizontal information flows, the global sense of interconnectivity, and the understanding that people want to play a role, participate, and be engaged—not just as passive recipients, but as participants in the making of knowledge and culture? As an institution, the Walker Art Center has some natural advantages in responding to these shifts. It has a long history of supporting cross-disciplinary artistic practices, of creating a fluid relationship between art, performance, writing, choreography, design, music, and film. In recent years, supporting artistic dialogue and exchange across disciplinary boundaries has been a passionate priority for an institution with a mission devoted to catalyzing creativity and fostering broad, open inquiry with our publics about the times in which we live.

Yet in this landscape in which we seek to support artistic experimentation in the face of exponential change, how do we responsibly react to a post-disciplinary world in which makers no longer feel allegiances to given fields, or to the expertise and constructs we fabricate as institutions, but proceed as if everything is open and available to them as spaces of possibility? How can we host, present, and responsibly *represent* the work of artists who themselves embrace the full range of these contingencies, who refuse to locate their work in a single moment of "Yes, that is it!" but demand an ongoing, diverse, and complex engagement in order to capture, or more accurately, intuit the qualities and ethics of what it is that they are about and what it means to live and respond to the urgencies and exigencies of our time?

The exhibition *9 Artists*, organized by the Walker and curated by Bartholomew Ryan, offers one possible response to and lens with which to examine these and other questions pertinent to the moment. And each of the artists represented takes on a broad and ambitious confrontation with some basic questions that have never lost their urgency: What are we doing? Why are we here? What is the role of the artist in all of this? What can I contribute to this conversation? Just who am *I*, anyway? Thankfully, there is no one answer that we—complex human beings from specific backgrounds, shaped in subjective and objective ways through personal experience, social construction, life!—can give to each of these questions. But, as Ryan eloquently asserts, we must engage the search.

As both author and interlocutor for the diverse artistic voices represented in the exhibition and herein, Ryan plays the role of chief navigator well in this earnest quest. Indeed, he enacts the role of curator with deft and courageous gentility. While he does not shy away from offering confident perspectives and curatorial "positions" in his engaged and thoughtful treatise, he acknowledges and continually checks his own complicity (as well as that of the artists) as a willing participant in the system. But more importantly, he ably calls into question the range of institutionalizing forces that frequently compel us, and society more broadly, to "fix," "name," historicize, and interpret our past and recent present. Although not explicitly stated, another guiding theme that the exhibition seeks to expound upon is the multivalent nature of contemporary identity. Throughout, Ryan—through his own voice and those of the artists— offers a refreshing post-post-identity response to the contemporary art world of the present moment. While the complex, often transcultural biographies of many of the participating artists are never obscured, their life stories also do not serve as an interweaving meta-narrative for the project. Indeed, for several artists, most notably Natascha Sadr Haghighian, Bjarne Melgaard, and Nástio Mosquito, their works manifest as outright abnegations and intentional obfuscations of the traditional modes of framing identity in the discourses of the contemporary art world today.

As a curator whose formation was defined by the identity debates of the 1990s and the expectations the art world put upon me as a "Latina" curator, I am keenly sensitive to and aware of this thematic in the show—both in its insistence and planful subversion. It is a timely exploration, as in recent years there has been a resurgence of interest in the historical context of identity politics, as seen in large-scale shows such as *This Will Have Been: Art, Love & Politics in the 1980s* (2012; the Museum of Contemporary Art, Chicago) and *1993: Experimental Jet Set, Trash and No Star* (2013; the New Museum, New York). Recent biennials have also mined the spirit of this time, such as the 12th Istanbul Biennial (2011), which situated itself explicitly in relation to the work of Felix Gonzalez-Torres, one of the preeminent artists of the 1990s. Concurrently, efforts to define a global paradigm have continued apace with exhibitions such as the Tate Modern's *Altermodern* (2009), ZKM's monumental *The Global Contemporary: Art Worlds After 1989* (2011), and the New Museum's *The Ungovernables* (2012). *9 Artists* is situated in relation to these various contexts, but also departs from them. It takes up the strands of identity politics as it has evolved within contemporary practice, shifting the discourse from essentialist frameworks to subject positions that are fractured, multivalent, and complex. The show also attempts to avoid being considered as a measurement of a global zeitgeist—an important approach to exhibition-making that nevertheless has a tendency to generalize and assign artists as markers of their geographical location.

9 Artists brings together a group of individuals with diverse backgrounds who are provocative, challenging, smart, and engaged. As Ryan states in his essay, they are in many ways their own "institutions," seeking to carve out space for their work to exist that allows it some sense of autonomy within our ever more imbricated lives. They build their own versions of reality (and what is "reality," after all, but a spectrum of perspectives?) through a conceptual interweaving of representation, aesthetics, and history. What Ryan has done is in many ways quite simple: he's brought together a group of artists in an exhibition space, produced a catalogue to which they are the main contributors, and ensured artist-focused programming and a strong online presence. Collectively, it is our hope that the various aspects that make up the totality of the show do justice to the artists' various ways of working and allow a broad public to process the work for themselves, while affording them some tools to do so. I see this exhibition as a fascinating and timely investigation of the role that art can play in contemporary society.

I would like to echo Ryan's thanks as conveyed in his acknowledgments and express my deep gratitude to all the supporters, lenders, staff, and of course the artists for going on the journey with him and allowing this project to take shape in the form it has. I am also grateful to the MIT List Center for Visual Arts in Cambridge, and to its director, Paul Ha, for participating on the exhibition tour and hosting the show following its opening here. The Walker is an international institution that likes to approach its work with both generosity and ambition. It has been allowed to do so by an extraordinary community here in the Twin Cities, and I offer my biggest thanks to them.

Olga Viso
Executive Director, Walker Art Center

Published on the occasion of the exhibition *9 Artists*, curated by Bartholomew Ryan and organized by the Walker Art Center, Minneapolis.

Major support for the exhibition is provided by the Andy Warhol Foundation for the Visual Arts. Additional support is generously provided by Lisa and Pat Denzer and Audrey and Zygi Wilf.

The exhibition catalogue is made possible, in part, with a grant from the Andrew W. Mellon Foundation in support of Walker Art Center publications. Additional support for the catalogue is provided by Isabella Bortolozzi Galerie, Gavin Brown's enterprise, Galerie Buchholz, and Marian Goodman Gallery.

Walker Art Center, Minneapolis
October 24, 2013–February 16, 2014

Massachusetts Institute of Technology, List Visual Arts Center, Cambridge
May 9–July 13, 2014

Library of Congress Cataloging-in-Publication Data
9 artists / Edited by Bartholomew Ryan ; Texts by Yael Bartana, Liam Gillick, Renzo Martens, Bjarne Melgaard, Nástio Mosquito, Natascha Sadr Haghighian, Hito Steyerl, Danh Vo. -- First Edition.
    pages cm
"Walker Art Center, Minneapolis, October 24, 2013-February 16, 2014, Massachusetts Institute of Technology (MIT), List Visual Arts Center, Cambridge May 9-July 13, 2014."
 Includes bibliographical references.
 ISBN 978-1-935963-06-6
1. Art, Modern--21st century--Exhibitions. I. Ryan, Bartholomew, 1976-
editor of compilation. II. Walker Art Center. III. MIT List Visual Arts Center. IV. Title: Nine artists.
 N6497.A14 2013
 700.9'04--dc23
                2013028065

Available through D.A.P./Distributed Art Publishers, 155 Sixth Avenue, New York, NY 10013.
www.artbook.com

ISBN 9781935963066

Design Director
    Emmet Byrne
Designer
    Andrea Hyde
Editors
    Kathleen McLean and
    Pamela Johnson
Senior Imaging Specialist
    Greg Beckel
Design Studio Manager
    Dylan Cole

Printed and bound in Italy by Gruppo Editoriale Zanardi